THE COLONEL AND THE PACIFIST

THE COLONEL AND THE PACIFIST

Karl Bendetsen — Perry Saito and the Incarceration of Japanese Americans during World War II

Klancy Clark de Nevers

Foreword by
Roger Daniels

THE UNIVERSITY OF UTAH PRESS
Salt Lake City

The Defiance House Man colophon is a registered trademark of The University of Utah Press. It is based upon a four-foot-tall Ancient Puebloan pictograph (late PIII) near Glen Canyon, Utah.

Printed on acid-free paper

20 19 18 17
5 4 3 2

LIBRARY OF CONGRESS CATALOGING-IN-PUBLICATION DATA

de Nevers, Klancy Clark.
The colonel and the pacifist : Karl Bendetsen, Perry Saito, and the incarceration of Japanese Americans during World War II / Klancy Clark de Nevers ; foreword by Roger Daniels.
p. cm.
Includes bibliographical references (p.) and index.
ISBN 0-87480-788-3 (hardcover : alk. paper) —
ISBN 0-87480-789-1 (pbk. : alk. paper)
1. Japanese Americans—Evacuation and relocation, 1942–1945. 2. Bendetsen, Karl R. 3. Saito, Perry Hitoshi, 1921–1985. 4. United States. Army—Officers—Biography. 5. Japanese Americans—Biography. I. Title.
D769.8.A6D44 2004
940.53'089'956073—dc22

2004000636

To the memory of my father,
Q. Kearny Clark

and his brother
John W. (Jack) Clark

CONTENTS

APPENDICES

FOREWORD

Roger Daniels

As one of my teachers at UCLA used to put it, even under the best of circumstances a book is a very poor instrument for capturing a human life. If this is true—and I believe that it is—Klancy de Nevers's task was more than doubly difficult. She is trying to capture not one but two human lives only metaphorically linked. The colonel not only deliberately concealed his origins but also lied repeatedly about his past and probably became delusional in his later years. Much of the life of the pacifist is obscured by the ignorance that surrounds the lives of most "ordinary" people after they have passed from the scene. Each man inherited potential or real hostility from most of his fellow Americans because of what he was. It is important never to forget that while the colonel is, quite properly, remembered as a persecutor, in his youth he also faced, if not persecution, at least a well-founded fear of persecution.

Karl R. Bendetsen and Perry H. Saito were both, in de Nevers's phrase, "sons of Aberdeen" in coastal Washington, born there fourteen years apart. We do not know that they ever met. One became a persecutor; the other was made a victim: de Nevers has linked their lives in an imaginative narrative. The ancient Greek writer Plutarch (46?–120) wrote a series of dual biographies he called *Parallel Lives*. Bendetsen and Saito lived lives that were tangential; that is, they touched at several points: in their common hometown; perhaps in the Finch or Becker Buildings where Perry was the "elevator boy" and Karl had his law offices; in the process begun in 1942 that was known euphemistically as the "Japanese relocation," which Karl helped to engineer and administer, and which Perry had to endure; and finally, during the 1981 hearings of the Commission on the Wartime Relocation and Internment of Civilians (CWRIC) when both testified, Perry in Chicago, Karl in Washington, D.C. In 1942 Karl, although a paperwork soldier, was a hero—a grateful government awarded him a Distinguished Service Medal for his role in incarcerating Japanese Americans —and Perry was a villain, a "Jap" who looked like the enemy, and perhaps was the enemy as far as many of his fellow citizens were concerned. In 1981 a different vision prevailed. Perry's testimony was applauded by its auditors and hailed in the press, Karl's was booed and hissed, and a former Supreme Court Justice all but called him a liar to his face.

I never met either man. Bendetsen and I were aware of each other—a student who had written to Bendetsen asking about the wartime incarceration also asked him if he had ever met me. Bendetsen replied in the negative but volunteered that I must be a very unpleasant person. When the student, whom I did not know, passed this information on to me, it made my day. I had never heard of Perry Saito until de Nevers brought him to my attention. Most of the Japanese American men of his generation that I know were warriors, but he may have been something like my Quaker friend, Gordon Hirabayashi. Both Perry and Gordon were sons of immigrants who had been members of the tiny Christian minority in Japan. I have great respect for Gordon and admire what Klancy has told us about Perry, but I will focus here on the man I know about, Bendetsen.

I had been aware of Bendetsen since my graduate school days, during which I was already preparing to write the book that became *Concentration Camps, USA*. I read Stetson Conn's brilliant first essay on the decision to evacuate the West Coast Japanese Americans some months after it was published in 1959. Conn's work made me aware of Bendetsen and his key role in the by then regretted decision. Most of my previous knowledge of the details had come from the army's mendacious *Final Report*, and when I went back to it I found that Bendetsen had just three index references, and that two of them, on the same page, were to his different titles, so that his name appears only once in the six-hundred-page text. (I later learned that he closely supervised its writing.) By contrast Bendetsen is a featured player in Conn's twenty-four-page essay: His name appears on more than half of its pages. Conn was the historian who demonstrated that Bendetsen was what I later called "an architect" of Japanese removal. This was a judgment that Bendetsen had put forth in his autobiographical sketch in the first postwar *Who's Who in America* (1944–45), accurately claiming that he "conceived method, formulated details and directed evacuation of 120,000 persons of Japanese ancestry from military areas." Later, when the tide of informed opinion about the evacuation had begun to shift, he insisted that he was just obeying orders.

As Klancy discovered and describes in detail, Bendetsen began lying about himself at least as early as his college days at Stanford when he concealed his Jewish identity. It is not clear if he was an apostate in terms of Jewish law, which requires formal conversion to another faith. Such an action was not a rarity: There were and are many forms of passing in America, as in any new country, and it was nowhere more prominent than in the American Far West: One of the traditional songs from Gold Rush times was "What Was Your Name in the States?" But for Bendetsen the initial dissimulation—it was impossible in Aberdeen where his family was well known—led to other misrepresentations.

While in uniform, he officially changed his name and, eventually, invented a fictional Danish great-grandfather. Sometime before 1967, he told journalist Allan Bosworth that he had gone to the Philippines in 1941 as an emissary to General Douglas MacArthur for Secretary of War Henry L. Stimson. Both principals were then safely dead. In a 1972 interview given to the Truman Presidential Library, he expanded the tale to include a stop-off in Hawaii to brief General Walter Short, the hapless Hawaiian commander at the time of Pearl Harbor. As de Nevers shows, this was a phantom trip.

In 1967 I consulted Stetson Conn, then the civilian chief of military history, about the army's role in the incarceration decision, and, in the course of two helpful interviews, he commented that Bendetsen had officially changed his name. I did not have the wit to follow it up, and I simply don't know if he knew the nature Bendetsen's subterfuge.

Neither I nor any of the numerous other scholars took a hard look at Bendetsen's past. That is just one of the things than de Nevers has done in this book. But she has done much more by rooting it in Aberdeen, which was her hometown too. A Stanford alumna, she knew that one-time WASP environment as well, and as a younger contemporary of her two protagonists, also knew some people who knew both men before she began what became a multiyear quest.

The result is a gripping and sometimes surprising story that links Saito and Bendetsen in what was a national tragedy. Much of the book's power comes from the fact that it focuses on a few American lives. It is particularly appropriate to reconsider this aspect of the Japanese American experience at a time when another group of American ethnics, the Muslim community with foreign roots, is under suspicion of disloyalty. The inspector general of the Department of Justice issued a devastating report on June 3, 2003, describing the arrest and confinement of 762 immigrants "in connection with the FBI terrorism investigation." While many were discovered to be in the country illegally—they were mostly visa overstayers—and were eventually deported, not one was charged with anything connected with the events of 9/11 or any other terrorist activity. Many were held for months, deprived of the right to counsel, verbally and physically abused, tried, and in some cases deported in secret. It was a shocking revelation of the Department of Justice's violations of its own rules. All of it was done in the name of national security after the shocking terrorist attacks of September 11, 2001.

The basic similarity of the responses of the government in these two instances, which occurred some sixty years apart, and each of which received the overwhelming support of the vast majority of Americans, indicates just how thin a shield our Bill of Rights can be in times of crisis. If they are fortunate, readers in the second half of the this century will have a text explicating our current national security crisis in the same kinds of human terms as Klancy has provided for the post–Pearl Harbor years and beyond. Some may think it inappropriate to link the two violations of human rights. Most of Bendetsen's victims were American citizens, while almost all of John Ashcroft's victims, so far, have been unnaturalized foreigners. But in each instance, the spirit if not the letter of the Constitution has been violated, and both the administration and its critics have used the Japanese American wartime experience as a debating point. The administration says, in effect, see, we're not that bad, while its critics fear that, as time goes by, the resemblances will become even more striking.

Cincinnati, Ohio
July 4, 2003

List of Works Cited in Chronological Order

United States Department of War. *Final Report: Japanese Evacuation from the West Coast 1942*. Washington, D.C.: GPO, 1943.

Stetson Conn. "The Decision to Relocate the Japanese from the Pacific Coast," in *Command Decisions*. Edited by Kent Roberts Greenfield. New York: Harcourt, Brace, 1959.

Allan R. Bosworth. *America's Concentration Camps*. New York: W. W. Norton, 1967.

Roger Daniels. *Concentration Camps, USA: Japanese Americans and World War II*. New York: Holt, Rinehart and Winston, 1972.

Jerry N. Hess, interviewer. *Oral History Interview with Karl R. Bendetsen*. October 24, 1972. Truman Presidential Library, Independence, Mo. http://www.trumanlibrary.org/oralhist/bendet1.htm

PREFACE

This book represents a project that got away. When I began to gather the stories of Karl Bendetsen and Perry Saito, I thought I would write a *New Yorker*-length article about the contrast between these two sons of Aberdeen, Washington, and about the town's reaction to the Japanese American evacuation. Aberdeen was my hometown, too, and I would be able to get people to talk about it. But the story grew larger with every interview, and grew away from Aberdeen. I used the Freedom of Information Act to obtain internment case files and FBI files for the story's principals. I was drawn into archives, libraries, old newspapers, census files, homes in Grays Harbor, and telephone conversations with old-timers all across the country and as far away as Japan. It will be hard to remember everyone who helped me investigate the Bendetsen story and understand the Saito family's view of the evacuation, but I will try.

I am indebted to Sandra C. Taylor for her knowledge of the Topaz, Utah, relocation camp, and for her putting me in touch with Professor Roger Daniels, whom she knew kept a remarkably comprehensive bibliography of Asian America. It is not possible to list the ways in which Roger inspired me and helped me avoid serious error; he also sent me invaluable further references. I thank him for all that and for his faith in me.

As the manuscript grew, I counted on patient readers—Sandra, Roger, Robert L. Bliss, Morse Saito, Wes Sasaki-Uemura, Brooke Hopkins, and my husband Noel—to keep me on course. My walking buddy and treasured friend Joan Coles listened to every twist in the tale and helped me find the deeper story. Sharyn Wallin accompanied me on numerous interview trips to Aberdeen. She is an observant, tireless, and delightful companion. Nancy Stauffer Cahoon, whose father knew Bendetsen professionally, followed the progress of the manuscript and encouraged me to pursue publication.

Dawn Marano has been a role model as a writer, as an extremely efficient organizer of the Writers@Work conference, and now as an editor. I've been delighted by her enthusiasm for this project, and her perceptive editing.

I thank Kai Bird for letting me listen to and quote from his interviews with Bendetsen. It was fascinating to hear Bendetsen's voice from the tape. ("He can really be charming," my husband observed.) I'm grateful that the Hoover Archive allowed me to access Bendetsen's un-catalogued papers.

Old Aberdeen friends Joel and Ruth Wolff have been my link to my past. I'm grateful for the pleasant hours and kind hospitality that they extended to Sharyn and me, and for their willingness, finally, to talk about Bendetsen. Ruth's sleuthing brought me Jackson Moyer's evacuation papers. Jim and June Moyer very kindly welcomed us to their home and shared the contents of the Moyer family scrapbook.

Perry Saito's widow Fumi is an inspiration. Morse Saito's love for Aberdeen is a match for my own; he shared his columns about the evacuation, and his memories of Aberdeen. Perry Saito's children, nieces, and nephews have been very helpful.

My cousin John W. Clark prodded me to go beyond the obvious story, to study the issues in Bendetsen's character. My Bay Area sister Kristine Hahn gave me bed, board, and love, enabling me to spend long days in the Hoover Institution archive. My sister Kathy Blomquist listened to my tales of discovery and offered encouragement.

My aunt Barbara N. de Luna started it all by sending me Morse Saito's letter to her high school class reunion. She is like an older sister to me whose accomplishments I admire but can never match.

Aberdeen *Daily World* editor John Hughes, who envied the airplane models Bendetsen gave his son, gave me encouragement and inspiration. Aberdeen librarian Sandy Lauritzen dug deep into the library's files. Lucy Hart, valued collaborator on *Cohassett Beach Chronicles*, penned beautiful maps of Washington and Grays Harbor. Countless old friends and acquaintances in Aberdeen and Hoquiam also helped.

Delta, Utah, schoolteacher Jane Beckwith brought the meager ruins of Topaz to life for me. I treasure the fragment of a teacup found among the weeds beside the edge of a vanished barrack. I can almost see a woman pouring tea into the cup with painted plum blossoms, wondering when she could go home.

I've dedicated this book to my father, who inspired in me the love of the apt word and of the beautifully composed page, and to my uncle, whose loss has kept alive my interest in World War II history.

I wish to acknowledge permission to use the following materials:

Excerpt from "Barracks Home" reprinted from "Camp memories" by Toyo Suyemoto Kawakami, in *Japanese American: From Relocation to Redress* by Roger Daniels, Sandra C. Taylor, and Harry H. L. Kitano, p. 28. © 1986 by the authors.

Map of assembly centers and internment camps reprinted from *Only What Thay Could Carry*, edited by Lawson Fusaso Inada, p. 418. © 2000 by Heyday Press.

INTRODUCTION

One Man Makes a Difference

Immediately after the Japanese attack on Pearl Harbor on December 7, 1941, public attention was drawn to two large Japanese populations in the United States: 157,000 persons of Japanese ancestry living in the Territory of Hawaii and another 125,000 persons of Japanese ancestry on the West Coast of the United States, living mostly in "Little Tokyos" and farming communities. Though there was public and official pressure to take action against them, the two groups received very different treatment, largely due to the efforts, in each case, of one man.

On the day of the attack, martial law was declared in Hawaii. General Walter C. Short was soon replaced, and authorities in Washington, D.C., urged the removal of Hawaii's Japanese American population. Yet only two thousand persons of Japanese ancestry in Hawaii were taken into custody or interned during the war. Although Hawaiian society was more ethnically diverse and racially tolerant than that of the West Coast, drastic actions against the ethnic Japanese were mostly blocked by the personal judgment of the new commander of the Hawaiian Department of the Army, Lieutenant General Delos C. Emmons. The president and the War Department repeatedly recommended an evacuation program. General Emmons did not see its military necessity and continually emphasized the practical problems such an evacuation would involve: loss of skilled labor in Hawaii, lack of building materials for internment camps, and lack of transport to the mainland. He chose to treat the ethnic Japanese as loyal to the United States unless proven otherwise, because "this is America and we must do things the American Way."[1] One man clearly made a difference.

On the West Coast, military commander Lieutenant General John L. DeWitt relied on then Major Karl R. Bendetsen, who altered the course of history for the West Coast Japanese Americans. In the first six weeks of the war, General DeWitt did not seem able to make up his mind about what action to take against the ethnic Japanese living in his command, though he believed that the Japanese Americans were spies for Japan who would go over to the side of their ancestral homeland if an invasion were to occur. He had no evidence of disloyalty or sabotage by Japanese Americans, and the army's general staff considered an invasion highly unlikely. Major Bendetsen was sent from the office of the provost marshal general in Washington, D.C., to clarify DeWitt's thinking. By mid-February 1942, Bendetsen had defined "military necessity" and had prepared for President Franklin D. Roosevelt's signature an order that permitted a military commander to forcibly remove "any and all persons" from certain "military areas." The order was almost exclusively applied on the West Coast to Japanese aliens, who were by law ineligible for citizenship, and to their American-born children, leading to the removal of more than 110,000 Americans of Japanese ancestry, two-thirds of them American citizens. Again, one man had made the difference.

Bendetsen, who had pushed hard to obtain the exclusion order, received a double promotion to colonel and was assigned to head the evacuation and detention.

Among the evacuees were former neighbors of Bendetsen from the small lumbering town of Aberdeen, Washington. Aberdeen's only alien Japanese resident, Mrs. Natsu Saito; her American-born children, Perry, Morse, and Dahlia; and Mrs. Towa Moyer and her children, a Caucasian-Asian family from neighboring Hoquiam, were soon ordered out of their homes and sent to one of the fourteen fenced and guarded camps (referred to by many as concentration camps) at Tule Lake, in the northeastern California desert.[2]

The Colonel and the Pacifist contrasts the stories of Karl Bendetsen and Perry Saito, both sons of Aberdeen. Like all the men of their generation, their lives were vastly changed by World War II, but in very different ways. Had they met, say in the elevator of Aberdeen's Finch Building, where Bendetsen had his law office and Saito ran the elevator after school, Bendetsen and Saito would have stood eye-to-eye at five feet eleven inches and been evenly paired for a middleweight boxing match at 160 pounds; they were both described as bright, personable, and self-confident.

In December 1941 Saito, the son of Japanese immigrants, was twenty and a confirmed pacifist pursuing a degree in music education. Bendetsen was thirty-four, a lawyer called up from the reserves and serving as a major (soon to be a full colonel) in the United States Army. As head of the Aliens Division of the provost marshal general's office, he was about to take charge of an operation that would totally disrupt the lives of the West

Coast Japanese and Japanese Americans, including Saito. A year later, while Perry Saito struggled to free himself from the incarceration that Bendetsen had organized, Bendetsen received a Distinguished Service Medal for a job well done. The forced removal and incarceration of the West Coast Japanese and Japanese Americans had repercussions for both men throughout their lives.

Perry Saito's story is that of a young Nisei whose country had turned against him.[3] Karl Bendetsen's story is that of an ambitious young man who hid and denied his Jewish roots (presumably to avoid discrimination) and used his education and talents to direct a program that trampled the rights and denied the humanity of another ethnic minority.

Both men came from families whose livelihoods depended, at least in part, on the logging industries in western Washington. In businesses that were only doors apart on Heron Street in Aberdeen, Bendetsen's father sold work clothes, blankets, and other dry goods to the logging camps, while Saito's parents ran an import shop and brokered sales of logs to Japanese ships docking in Aberdeen.

In 1942 the war interrupted the lives of all Americans, but it was disastrous for the West Coast's Japanese minority. Japanese immigrants and their citizen descendants were forced to leave behind, or sell at giveaway prices, the fruits of a lifetime of diligent labor and frugality—homes, crops, farm equipment, business inventories, furniture, and cars. At the war's end, few were able to recover their homes or gain recompense for lost possessions. After years of incarceration and relocation, scarcely half of the evacuees returned to former West Coast locations, and all struggled against lingering hostility to rebuild their lives.

In 1980 the United States Congress created a commission to find out why this executive order had been promulgated and to determine whether amends should be made to the affected Japanese Americans. Karl Bendetsen and Perry Saito each testified before the commission. Saito, by then a Methodist minister in Wisconsin, read statements from the General Conference of the Methodist Church "acknowledging the flagrant violations of human rights" and affirming the need for redress legislation. Bendetsen argued that it was impossible so many years later to understand the concerns of a country at war, and refused to admit that the evacuation had been a mistake. He also disclaimed responsibility for the evacuation program, even though he was the official who wrote the planning papers and the executive order. Working in an environment of invasion fears, racism, and press-inspired hysteria, Bendetsen, the only person among the decision makers to have come from the West Coast, contributed greatly to an event that is an embarrassing blot on our history and still reflects undeserved dishonor on America's ethnic Japanese. Although he went on to hold positions of leadership in the defense establishment and in industry, he found that his involvement in the forced removal and incarceration of America's Japanese minority would never be forgiven or forgotten.

AUTHOR'S NOTE

Karl R. Bendetsen was born Bendetson. He changed the spelling of his surname from Bendetson to Bendetsen on February 4, 1942, as he drafted the first detailed justification for the evacuation of all persons of Japanese ancestry from the West Coast. In subsequent paperwork under his control this spelling change stood, and eventually his military records reflected the new spelling.

At my request, the Hoover Institution opened Karl R. Bendetsen's extensive archive, which contained his personal army files from 1939 to 1945 and the files from his office as assistant chief of staff to Lieutenant General John L. DeWitt.

PART I

HOMETOWN

CHAPTER ONE

1981: Revisionism or Redress?

The evacuation case "was ever on my conscience."
—Supreme Court Justice William O. Douglas,
in CWRIC, *Personal Justice Denied*

Perhaps his mistake was living too long. As the youngest colonel in the United States Army in 1942, Karl R. Bendetsen had been a principal player in the evacuation of 110,000 Japanese and Japanese American citizens from what he and Lieutenant General John L. DeWitt called the Western Sea Frontier. A retired corporate executive in the 1980s, he had to endure the painful reevaluation of America's wartime incarceration of its Japanese minority in congressional hearings, public testimonials from evacuees, and pleadings in reopened court cases. The Japanese American community sought financial compensation for mistreatment and financial loss, and apologies from the United States government. To him the redress campaign was an abomination.

If there was one thing Karl Bendetsen hated, it was revisionism.[1] On first hearing in 1979 of the congressional plans to examine the justification for the executive order that enabled the exclusion, Bendetsen wrote to an old friend from Aberdeen: "It is hardly even a remote possibility than any significant number of people on Capitol Hill or elsewhere could recreate in their minds, or revivify in their memories, the circumstances as they developed out of the grim events of December 7, 1941, and the terrible months which followed."[2]

Bendetsen was accustomed to a laudatory press; he was welcomed at gatherings of business executives, and his opinions were still sought on defense issues. During his tenure as CEO and chairman of the board of forest products giant Champion International, he encountered respectful audiences. In almost ten years of retirement, he had delivered a foreign policy speech on détente, served as vice-chairman of the 1976 Defense

Manpower Commission, been cleared as a national security consultant for the Pentagon to work on a Strategic Defense Initiative project, cochaired a policy panel that advocated the concept of assured survival, and written monthly government affairs reports for Champion.[3]

From a sleek steel- and glass-furnished office on K Street in Washington, D.C., he maintained a large correspondence, dictating long, sometimes unsolicited letters giving advice and counsel and often receiving deferential letters from the prominent recipients.[4] In early 1981 Caspar W. Weinberger, President Reagan's nominee for secretary of defense, wrote thanking him for sending his opinions and a copy of the Defense Manpower Report whose development he had overseen.[5]

He began receiving critical letters as early as February 1980, as the movement for redress got under way. He had sent information about the 1942 evacuation and relocation project to Philip Tajitsu Nash, then active in the Asian American Law Students Association at Rutgers. Nash's return letter galled him. In thanking Bendetsen for the report, Nash mentioned that part of the Asian American Law Day program to be held in March would consider "the constitutional ramification of the forced removal of over 60,000 Nisei American citizens, using the 'military necessity' stratagem you devised." The planned panel of speakers was heavily weighted on the side of what Bendetsen later called "arrogant militants."

Referring to "your insulting response," Bendetsen wrote to Nash,

> I did not devise 'military necessity' and you have no basis for this irresponsible charge.
>
> While you are at it, I suggest that you look into the unspeakable brutalities visited upon the Filipinos, the people of Singapore, the rape of Nanking conducted by Japanese military personnel, the callous and wanton, bloodthirsty and deliberate violation of civilized convention and human behavioral standards toward prisoners of war and all civilians brought under heel by Japanese forces elsewhere. Your motivation is to disrupt free society by your satanic ruses. I challenge you and your cabal.
>
> If it is possible for you to have a constructive purpose in mind, you certainly cannot ignore the unprecedented cruelties which your people visited not only upon people of the same color, but on people of all colors during World War II. None of this is in the case books either.[6]

The Commission on Wartime Relocation and Internment of Civilians (CWRIC) was created by Congress in 1980 and chaired by Joan Z. Bernstein, former general counsel of the Department of Health and Human Services, and vice-chaired by Congressman Daniel E. Lungren (R-California). The commission's charter was to determine how and why political leaders, both in Washington and on the West Coast, decided to uproot the entire Japanese American community "when even the [U.S.] attorney general and the FBI director did not consider most internees a national security threat," as a *Washington Post* editorial reminded readers. The commission would have the difficult task of considering whether those who had suffered internment should be given financial compensation. Other "enemy" communities—German Americans and Italian Americans—had been largely untouched. The *Post* continued, "Japanese-Americans, clustered on the West Coast—bore the brunt of their fearful neighbors' post–Pearl Harbor mixture of racial antagonism, economic envy and genuine hysteria over a possible Japanese invasion."[7]

Bendetsen was invited to testify before the redress committee as one of the few surviving principals. He was not prepared for the hostility of witnesses from the Japanese American community, nor for what he considered the prejudice of the committee members, whom, he asserted, had their own agenda, namely, to force through a "raid on the Treasury."[8]

CWRIC hearings, conducted in cities across the nation, provided a forum for the aggrieved Japanese American community.[9] Bendetsen was offended that some of the persons who advocated redress hadn't even been alive during the war. He had noted in a 1979 letter, "The circumstances then prevailing bear no remote relationship to these times. . . . It is perhaps a truism that there are only two of us now living who have a complete active and accurate memory of everything that transpired. The other is the Honorable John J. McCloy, who was then the Assistant Secretary of War, with whom I worked so closely."[10] Because of their involvement in the evacuation, Bendetsen and McCloy were invited to testify at the last hearing, in Washington, D.C. Bendetsen put together eighteen pages of text.

When he appeared before the commission, Bendetsen "extemporized for more than an hour" over his prepared statement, rather than reading it.[11] He was kept in the witness chair for another three hours and "must have wondered whether he was a defendant in the eyes of a federal panel" investigating the internment.[12] Bendetsen was infuriated that parts of his testimony were greeted by boos and hisses from the audience in the caucus room of the Russell Senate Office Building. According to some observers, members of the commission seemed "amazed, frustrated and, at times, angered at testimony Bendetsen presented justifying the evacuation."[13]

Arthur J. Goldberg, a former justice of the United States Supreme Court, asked him three times about the necessity for the evacuation: "What restrains you from coming in and saying, in retrospect, 'it was unnecessary?'"[14]

Bendetsen replied: "Those who made the decision at the time were [acting] in good faith and could not predict the outcome of events. Therefore, I don't think we should sit here in judgement today and say, 'We made a mistake.'"[15]

In his written testimony, Bendetsen minimized his own responsibility in the decision, claiming he did not recommend evacuation of persons of Japanese ancestry and asserting that he had not had any opinion on the subject during the critical period before February 19, 1942, the day that President Roosevelt signed the exclusion order. The papers in his personal archive as well as the findings of the committee do not support these claims.

Records found in Bendetsen's recently opened archive show that it *was* Bendetsen who, on February 4, 1942, at the request of Assistant Secretary of War McCloy, wrote the analysis, "Alien Enemies on the West Coast (and other subversive persons)," that led to the promulgation of the executive order. In this paper he declared, without proof or even reasonable suspicion, that "a substantial majority of Nisei bear allegiance to Japan, are well controlled and disciplined by the enemy, and at the proper time will engage in organized sabotage, particularly should a raid along the Pacific Coast be attempted by the Japanese." The paper also presented the claim that their removal was justified by the argument of military necessity and by Bendetsen's recommendation that aliens and citizens be excluded from "certain military areas." He stated that "this will require an evacuation and internment problem of some considerable proportions."[16]

In an article in November 1942 reporting Bendetsen's receipt of the Distinguished Service Medal, *Time* noted that Bendetsen had "prepared Franklin Roosevelt's executive order."[17] The first *Who's Who* entry for Bendetsen in 1944–45 stated that he had "conceived [the] method, formulated details and directed evacuation of 120,000 persons of Japanese ancestry from military areas."[18] His son, looking at a later *Who's Who* entry for his father that barely mentioned the evacuation, said, "I always got the impression the person who was in there wrote their own [entry], basically."[19]

Such discrepancies between the written record and Bendetsen's statements were noted earlier by historians, by the commission, and in legal briefs prepared during the rehearing of the Hirabayashi and Korematsu cases in the 1980s.[20] It is not clear whether these inaccuracies were the result of sincere lapses of memory, a desire to avoid blame or criticism, wishful thinking, or the blotting of critical recollections by Bendetsen's incipient Alzheimer's.

Other events in his life suggest that Bendetsen was willing to shade the truth if it suited the moment. In 1929 he denied his Jewish religion to join a fraternity; years later he changed the spelling of his name, thus setting aside his Jewish grandparents; and later still, in another published biography, he claimed a fictitious Danish great-grandfather.[21] A pattern of denial continued in his calculated postwar transformation from important operative to dutiful soldier merely following orders. For example, Bendetsen attended a meeting in February 1942 at the home of Attorney General Francis Biddle, at which he claimed (in a 1942 letter) to have sold Biddle on the military necessity argument that sealed the fate of the West Coast Japanese Americans. In the 1970s Bendetsen contended that "of course, I wasn't in high-level meetings, I was just a Major."

Bendetsen once mentioned in an interview that "being from the West Coast," he had known "many, many Japanese." Though this statement seems doubtful, he would have known the family of Ransaku and Natsu Saito, who operated the Oriental Gift Shop and ship chandlery a few doors up the street from his father's store and his own law office in Aberdeen, Washington. Mrs. Saito, her two teenaged children, and her adult son Perry Saito were among the tens of thousands of Japanese Americans forced to leave their homes by the exclusion orders that he wrote.

> "If any American can be incarcerated without trial or even proper accusation, then it becomes a mockery for us to declare . . . 'All persons are created equal.'" —Perry H. Saito, September 23, 1981

In September 1981 Perry H. Saito, pastor of the largest United Methodist congregation in the greater Milwaukee area, traveled to Chicago to testify before the CWRIC. He presented resolutions from the General Conference of the United Methodist Church that represented the church's ten million members, and from the Wisconsin Annual Conference. These resolutions urged the commission to recognize the flagrant violation of human rights of "certain individuals of Japanese ancestry who were interned, detained or forcibly relocated by the United States during World War II." Both Methodist groups urged "appropriate remedies" such as "adequate financial restitution for losses suffered."[22]

Reverend Saito knew what he was talking about. He was one of those individuals.

He told his family's story first. "Two days after Pearl Harbor my widowed mother was imprisoned and held incommunicado for five months. Then she was released a few days before our evacuation in May 1942, to Tulelake [*sic*] Relocation Center. In order to make the trip we had to buy our one way bus ticket to Olympia, Washington, taking with us only what we could carry. Incidentally, my mother later taught [Japanese for] military intelligence at the University of Chicago."[23]

Perry Saito had to drop out of college to support his brother and sister after their mother was arrested. When he first heard about preparations for the evacuation of Japanese from the West Coast he felt sorry for the people who would have to leave. He assumed evacuation did not apply to him because he was a citizen, a resident of Aberdeen, Washington.[24] In his testimony he expressed his greatest fear, which was that such a thing could happen again.

"The hysteria whipped up by racists, the false rumors of sabotage and espionage by Japanese-Americans, the fear of things unknown, demonstrated 40 years ago how Presidents and politicians can be manipulated into strange behaviors, which we in the quiet of this assembly would judge to be *impossible now*, even as we thought *then*."[25]

Perry and his siblings were required by their Japanese immigrant father to recite the Declaration of Independence from memory. His father had been converted to Christianity by an Englishman and (according to family folklore) had learned English by memorizing the Gettysburg Address. Regardless of his efforts to be patriotic, he could not become a naturalized citizen in America, simply because of his ancestry. Perry recalled that his father decided that it would not matter, saying, "In Japan they called me a pagan and I knew I was a Christian and didn't care what they called me. . . . Being a Christian was simply believing in certain principles. . . . I am going to be an American because I am going to believe in certain fundamentals, certain principles." And his father had raised him to be proud of being American.[26] Social justice and respect for American law became important themes in Perry Saito's sermons to the mostly Caucasian congregations that he served in Illinois and, for most of his ministry, in Wisconsin.

He argued in his testimony that if the consequences of an unwise executive order were made severe enough, particularly in financial terms, it would "cause second thoughts to Presidents who might consider the abridgement of our Bill of Rights as a means of furthering our democratic ideals and American principles." The executive order itself had remained in force for thirty-four years, until it was revoked by President Gerald Ford in 1976. He quoted Ford, in part: "We know now what we should have known then; not only was the evacuation wrong, but Japanese Americans were and are loyal Americans."[27]

Growing up in Aberdeen, Perry had been well accepted—popular, in fact. His family spoke English most of the time, but he learned Finnish from the parents of his friend Rudy Kauhanen, and danced with the same girls Rudy danced with. Was it a shock to him to be lumped together with his country's enemy, "the Japs," and to be incarcerated among thousands of other Nikkei (persons of Japanese ancestry in the United States)? He must have wondered whether his pride in speaking almost no Japanese was misplaced. Though no charges of any kind were made against Perry Saito (or any other evacuee), it took ten and a half months for him to get the necessary clearance to leave the Tule Lake camp to attend college. Because of the delay he lost a chance to begin studying for the ministry and instead took a job with a pacifist group, the Fellowship of Reconciliation (FOR). While Karl Bendetsen was upholding General DeWitt's stringent policies and dealing with near-riot conditions in the relocation camps because of an ill-considered campaign to determine the loyalty of evacuees by requiring that they answer a questionnaire, Perry was sent by the FOR in early 1943 to speak before youth groups and service clubs in the Midwest and Northeast to seek people or groups to sponsor evacuees so that they could leave the detention camps. He also took part in some of the first nonviolent, direct actions (sit-ins) testing enforcement of state public-accommodation laws in the Midwest in 1944.[28] Throughout the last years of the war he endured aggressive surveillance by the FBI, which disapproved of his conscientious objector status and which demanded that he not say in his talks that he had been "cleared by the FBI," though FBI approval was an essential precondition of each evacuee's release.

Saito's testimony before the committee continued:

"Who's to blame? Who's guilty? Who should pay? President Roosevelt for his Executive Order? Congress which financed the discriminatory program? Perhaps the Courts which declared the whole program legal. Perhaps the Japanese-Americans, who by their docile acquiescence, supported an un-American, undemocratic and unjust action."[29]

During the era of the redress movement, Perry Saito and his wife Fumi joined the ranks of Japanese Americans across the country who prepared to speak out, many for the first time, about their experiences as evacuees during World War II. Though the shame of having been incarcerated as suspected traitors by the country of their birth could never be totally erased, many decided to talk about what had happened.

Altogether a hundred witnesses testified during two days of hearings at Northeastern Illinois University. The *Chicago Tribune* selected for excerpt Perry Saito's testimony, "perhaps the most eloquent of the day."[30] Two bills calling for redress and compensation to the Americans of Japanese ancestry who were interned were being considered in the United States Congress. Perry told a reporter in Wisconsin that what he liked about these bills was that they would acknowledge that incarceration had been a mistake. Though he did not want to make a "big deal" out of it, he said that the experience should not be forgotten.

"Democracy and justice," he said, "do require accountability."[31]

CHAPTER TWO

Birds of Passage

"America," they cried. "America is on the other side of the world! You will be in a strange country. . . . What will you do?"

– Toshio Mori, *Yokohama, California*, 1949

A well-dressed group of Japanese gathered on the deck of the SS *Chicago Maru* to pose for a picture with the captain and chief steward. It was May 1916, and everyone looked happy. It was cold as they steamed across the North Pacific; the women wore sturdy coats, mufflers, and hats; the men suits and ties.

One man, Ransaku Saito, also wore a life preserver bearing the boat's name and its home port, Osaka, Japan. A week or two later, Ransaku Saito and his Tokyo wife Natsu stepped off their ship in Seattle, planning to settle in one of the new West Coast lumber towns. William H. Moyer had ended his seafaring adventures four years earlier when he and his Japanese bride Towa sailed via the *Enaba Maru* to Seattle and then Hoquiam, Washington. Both couples hoped to find work and establish themselves as productive members of their adopted American communities.

The open door welcoming "your huddled masses yearning to breathe free" had already begun to swing closed for immigrants from Japan by the time Towa Moyer and the Saitos arrived on the West Coast. Anti-Asian sentiment in the western United States that had earlier banned further Chinese immigration was by then directed toward the Japanese. In 1906 the San Francisco school board ordered segregation of Japanese American schoolchildren from the rest of the school population. Shortly thereafter, inspired by further anti-Japanese agitation, the United States and Japan signed the Gentlemen's Agreement of 1907–08, which restricted the immigration of laborers. Other classes of Japanese were still allowed to migrate to the United States, and during this interval many wives of resident laborers arrived, as well as merchant class married couples. The immigrant flow from Japan was largest during the years of the European War (1914–1918). By 1920 approximately 111,000 Japanese lived in the continental United States.[1]

From the passage of the first naturalization act in 1790, the right of naturalization was limited to any alien who was a "free white person." After the Civil War the statute was interpreted "to prohibit any Chinese immigrant from becoming an American citizen."[2] It was assumed that this rule would also apply to Japanese immigrants. In 1868 the Fourteenth Amendment declared that "all persons born or naturalized in this country are citizens," thus assuring citizenship to freed slaves and their children. The inability of Asian immigrants to become citizens allowed legal discrimination. California enacted an Alien Land Act in 1913 forbidding ownership of land by Asian aliens, and most western states followed suit. In 1922 a United States Supreme Court decision held that Chinese, Japanese, and other Asian immigrants to the United States could be classified as "aliens ineligible for citizenship."

Immigration from Japan ceased with passage of the National Origins Act of 1924, which gave European nations a small annual quota of immigrants, but abrogated the Gentlemen's Agreement and forbade immigration by aliens "ineligible for citizenship."[3] It was Albert Johnson, a Republican Congressman from Hoquiam, Washington, who, as a coauthor of the National Origins Act, was largely responsible for the inclusion of the clause prohibiting Asian immigration. Johnson formerly published the *Grays Harbor Washingtonian* newspaper in Hoquiam; he became chair of the Committee on Immigration and Naturalization in 1919.[4] He defended the origins act as a defense "against a stream of alien blood" and asserted that "the myth of the melting pot has been discredited . . . the United States is our land [and] . . . we intend to maintain it so. The day of unalloyed welcome to all peoples, the day of indiscriminate acceptance of all races, has definitely ended."[5] Johnson probably did not develop his fear of Japanese aliens in his home district. In 1942 only 162 Japanese resided in the five counties surrounding and including Grays Harbor, and only a handful of these Japanese lived in Aberdeen or Hoquiam.[6]

The earliest emigrants from Japan to the United States had been students, student-workers, and merchants. After 1874 Hawaiian sugar plantation owners were able to import workers, and many of these later made their way to the mainland. Other laborers, farmers, and fishermen came directly to the mainland. Many of these arrivals, often called "birds of passage," came empty-handed but expected to become wealthy and return to Japan.

Japanese immigrants (the Issei) were tolerated because they were perceived as hard workers, but they were also greeted with fear and jealousy by Americans. Most of the Japanese immigrants arriving in the United States came from the working upper-middle class or from farm families; many had benefited from Japan's compulsory education program. Those from the working class were generally not destitute, but may have been individuals who had inadequate income to maintain their social positions in Japan. They were adventurous and ambitious; most were inspired by the "golden story," the belief that workers in the United States earned high salaries, that the streets were lined with gold, and that it was easy to get rich. The new Meiji government inspired belief in progress and the possibility of improving one's condition. Yamato Ichihashi, professor of history at Stanford University, and himself an immigrant, wrote that Japan was known to be "one of the most literate among modern civilized countries."[7] Many of its young men chose to emigrate rather than submit to the military conscription that affected men between the ages of twenty and thirty-one (the upper limit later was raised to thirty-seven).

The 1924 immigration act froze the demography of the Japanese immigrant population in the United States. Most of the earliest arrivals had been men; in the 1900 United States census, there were only 410 married Japanese women. The Gentlemen's Agreement had allowed the immigration of "wives of resident" Japanese farmers and businessmen (but not laborers). After an exchange of photographs by mail, many women, termed "picture brides," married by proxy and came to America to join husbands who they knew only by their photos. In 1910 there were 5,581 married Japanese women in the continental United States; the number had grown to 22,193 by 1920.[8] However, this left more than 40 percent of Japanese men in the United States unmarried and with little hope of finding spouses. Intermarriage was not desirable and was illegal under miscegenation laws in many states. Married Japanese were raising the next generation, which would not be old enough to marry until the 1930s. Since family formation is very important to a Japanese person, the plight of these unmarried men was a sad episode in American history.

The student-worker immigrants, often termed "schoolboys," were young men who worked in homes as domestics, but were free to attend school during the day. Many attended mission schools to learn English. Because they were ambitious, these workers changed occupations. Japanese immigrants were found among farmers, farmhands, merchants, unskilled laborers, clerks, domestic servants, railroad workers, gang hands, cannery workers, fishermen, dishwashers, cooks, and day workers. Most were located in the larger cities on the West Coast, and in mining and farming areas.

The formation of families and the birth of children changed the character of Japanese communities. Immigrants began to build permanent settlements. Much of the immigrant's life centered around Buddhist and Christian missions and churches. Groups such as the Patriotic League, a Japanese political club in San Francisco, and the Japanese YMCA established Japanese newspapers. Others formed civic organizations such as the Japanese Association, which exerted moral leadership in the community and sought to educate the American public about themselves to counter anti-Japanese sentiment. The Issei sent their children to the public schools and, like the Chinese, relegated private native language teaching to after-school hours.

Labor unions that had earlier excluded Chinese now feared Japanese workers. All the same arguments used against the Chinese were mobilized against the Japanese—that they were undesirable opportunists, would work for cheap wages, engaged in vices such as gambling and prostitution, failed to form families—or if they did, had too many children—or were treacherous, or not able to adapt to American society. The Japanese immigrants, who had a proud self-image and were largely diligent and self-supporting, found this comparison with what they considered ignorant Chinese laborers offensive. In any case, the good life in America and acceptance into American life was denied to the Japanese immigrant. That this was so became clear when the government decided to incarcerate all ethnic Japanese, even citizens, in the aftermath of Japan's attack on Pearl Harbor.

However, the years following the National Origins Act of 1924 were relatively peaceful. Most Issei gave up the get-rich-quick-and-go-home idea. Families grew, and people worked hard and lived frugally. By skimping and saving from meager wages, Japanese were able to equip businesses; buy fishing boats; lease land (if permitted); and raise their children, the Nisei, to be educated, hardworking, Americanized members of society. One of these frugal entrepreneurs was Ransaku Saito.

RANSAKU SAITŌ

This shopkeeper whose life ended in Aberdeen was born in 1883 in Onogami village in Gunma, a prefecture bordering Nagano.[9] Ransaku was the oldest son of rural landowner Kozaburo Saitō, himself the oldest son.[10] The Saitō farm sat in a mountainous area many days by horseback north of Tokyo.

Rural society had undergone changes in the years following the Meiji Restoration of 1868. Farm families experienced great economic pressure due to land reforms. Compulsory education and industrial modernization sparked the beginning of migration to the cities. The Saitō family preserved the strong traditions valued in Japan—the Buddhist shrine in the house contained the birth and death dates of eldest sons going back generations and centuries. In their small valley everyone was related, and clearly identified relationship lines among the people defined what was called "the wider family"; Ransaku's father was the head, and controlled things with more authority than a village mayor. When Ransaku left for America, his sister and only sibling married a man of lesser standing who was adopted; he changed his name to Saitō. The current landowner and son now bear his name, Shimpachi Saitō. Ransaku's father controlled a large area of land—in recent times, even after land reforms, it has required hiring fifty migrant workers to harvest its crops. The land, which in Ransaku's childhood was worked strictly with horses and manual labor, in the 1990s grew a nonirrigated crop called *konnyaku*, a root similar to sweet potato from which a threadlike substance used in sukiyaki is produced.[11]

As oldest son, Ransaku enjoyed many privileges. He attended local schools and continued beyond the compulsory levels to attend middle school where he studied morals, Japanese and Chinese, history, geography, mathematics, physics and chemistry, natural history, civics, industry (agriculture), drawing, singing, and gymnastics. Because of his status he was then sent on to a higher school that later became a college in the very structured Japanese educational system.

Ransaku was also the oldest son of the "wider family." When he later was called to fight the Russians, the wider family assigned a "cousin" to "take care of him." Ransaku Saitō and Kinai Saitō had the same surname though they were only distant cousins. The two men from nearby villages in Gunma Prefecture shared the same birthday and many childhood memories—Kinai forever bore a visible scar attesting to their relationship. Years later he explained the mark on his right hand to Ransaku's youngest son, Morse:

"See this scar? Your father cut me when we were playing."

The two nine-year-olds had taken the swords out of the *tokonoma*, or alcove. The swords had been handed down by a former samurai, and were sharp. Since Ransaku was the eldest son, he took the longer sword. They began to "play samurai." Within minutes, Kinai was seriously cut, and was rushed to the hospital.

Morse said that he then learned a lesson about Japanese customs from his "uncle" Kinai, who recalled, "I was severely reprimanded, but not a word was said to your father."[12]

At twenty-one, Ransaku joined the Japanese army and because of his education became an officer, as did many men from Gunma. His relative Kinai was saddened by the confiscation of his horses for the war effort. Then Kinai was told by the wider family to join the army also, to take care of Ransaku. However, according to legend, when they got to the train station, Ransaku sent his cousin home where he would be safer. Ransaku led a group of infantrymen during the Russo-Japanese War of 1904–05 and received several honors and decorations. His pride in this victory—the first time in modern history that an Asian power had defeated a European power—survived in his American descendants. He received another distinction, a small round red-and-white button ("slightly larger than my Rotary pin," his son Morse recalled) that he wore in the lapel of his tuxedo at his wedding, and that indicated that he had received an imperial decoration. (He also earned four medals, one for meritorious service in war in the thirty-seventh and thirty-eighth year of the reign of Emperor Meiji (1904–05), a medal of the Sixth Class Order of the Rising Sun for outstanding service to the Japanese nation, one reading "Military Virtue Society of Japan," and one that the FBI in 1942 could not identify.[13])

As Ransaku was growing up in Gunma, several writers and scholars published vivid accounts of travel outside Japan. Newspapers featured interviews with returning travelers. Writers argued that there was opportunity for young, educated men in America and that they could extend the influence and trading power of Japan by travel or emigration.

Between 1902 and 1904, a Christian organization, *Nihon Rikkokai*, sought to help indigent students wishing to emigrate, and published several guides to America. For example, *Tobei Annai* (*Guide to America*, 1901) and *Seiko no Hiketsu* (*The Secret of Success*, 1906), contained employment information and talked about the many small Japanese communities in the United States.[14] Having seen some of the world outside Gunma Prefecture during the Russo-Japanese War, Ransaku wanted more, he later told his son Morse.

After the war Ransaku left the army. He was unhappy with how the army treated the emperor "like a puppet." He found life on the farm limiting, possibly boring, and he had heard the stories of gold in the streets in

America. He may have been inspired by news of the Japanese "bridge-heads" in America. He persuaded his father to let him travel for a while. In about 1908 he came to the United States for what he later called a period of work-study, staying for three years. He traveled from New York to southern Oregon, a place to which he vowed to return. He wanted to become an American citizen, but first he returned to Japan to find a wife.[15]

In the early years of the century, while Ransaku Saitō searched for a place for himself, the young Natsuko Tsuzuki enjoyed a sheltered and privileged childhood as middle child of a banker, a wealthy man who may have been an official in the imperial court. She was the oldest daughter of his first concubine, whose children were included in his comfortable household located close to the palace in Tokyo. She was given the name for summer, Natsu, because of her August (1898) birthday. Though she recalled being sickly, she had had a happy childhood. All of her father's official families lived together; she had as playmates the many children of her father's wives, who had their own hierarchy. (If Japanese customs were followed, the concubines had no status in the household, and all the children would refer to the first, official wife as mother.) Because Natsuko was an acknowledged daughter she had a birth certificate (which is also a citizenship paper), with a copy of her family registry tracing her ancestors back for generations. Her father's ancestral home, as listed on this registry, was in Gunma Prefecture.

In a wealthy family such as that of the Honorable Rokuro Tsuzuki, even a daughter would receive a proper Japanese education. Natsuko attended what might be called finishing schools for girls, first *Yanaka* and then *Kaika Gakuen* (school). In addition to the usual study of morals, Japanese history, English, geography, mathematics, science, sewing, singing, and gymnastics, she studied the finer arts of literature, poetry, flower arranging, and the tea ceremony. For two years she attended Hitotsubashi Music College where she studied violin, mandolin, and the Japanese zither, called a *koto*.

One can see the effect of outside pressures on Japanese society of the Meiji period in the Tsuzuki family photograph albums. By 1905 the men had adopted Western business dress. Natsuko's favorite brother (whom she always referred to as Howard) wore Western styles, as did Natsuko near the time of her marriage. But, generally, in those years women and girls continued wearing the traditional dress, a kimono bound at the waist with an obi, and tabi and geta on their feet.

After his American sojourn early in the second decade of the twentieth century, Ransaku traveled from Gunma to Tokyo from time to time and may have had more schooling. Because he hoped to return to America, he may have found an apprenticeship with a business in Tokyo. It would have been difficult for Ransaku to meet an upper-class woman such as Natsuko. Perhaps the meeting was arranged; because of his former status as an army officer, his imperial decoration, or his clear ambition, Ransaku would no doubt have been considered by a matchmaker as a suitable candidate for Tsuzuki's daughter.

Ransaku became aware of Natsuko and wanted to marry her. But Natsuko's father, who had not approved of an earlier suitor, had other ideas. Perhaps because Ransaku could be said to be a "country bumpkin," perhaps because he seemed to be an adventurer with no obvious means to support Tsuzuki's pampered daughter, Tsuzuki turned down the good-looking young man's request.

Ransaku was insulted. In a fury, he put on his old uniform, complete with gloves, boots, and sword. He marched off to the Tsuzuki residence, swept aside the sliding front doors, strode into the house "boots-and-all," stomped onto the tatami mat where Natsuko's father sat, and vented his rage, calling Tsuzuki names. He then executed a military about-face, digging his heels into the tatami, turned his back on the startled man, and left.

The banker was impressed. As legend has it, he said, "Here's someone who can handle my spirited daughter, Natsuko."[16]

The men planned the marriage, but persuading the young woman, barely seventeen, was not easy. One day Ransaku arrived at the Tsuzuki home pushing a wooden cart full of dahlias— a recent import to Japan—a profusion of white, yellow, and red flowers. This gesture succeeded and was commemorated years later when the couple's third child and only daughter was named Dahlia.[17]

One wonders how Natsuko felt about marrying this man from Gunma. Tradition required that she conform to the expectations of the Confucian-based treatise, *Onna Daigaku* (*The Greater Learning for Women*), which dictated behavior for Japanese women based on obedience, chastity, mercy, and a quiet manner. Girls were expected to be well behaved, to honor and respect their parents, and to accept the marriage arranged for them. In marriage a wife was to submit to the will of her husband. In Japanese, *shujin* [husband] also means master. *Onna Daigaku* dictated: "The great life-long duty of a woman is obedience. . . . When the husband issues his instructions, the wife must never disobey them. . . . A woman should look on her husband as if he were heaven itself, and never weary of thinking how she may yield to her husband."[18]

Ransaku and Natsu were married in 1915. Two formal photographs taken at the time of the wedding are a study in contrasts. In one Ransaku wears a Western tuxedo, unsmiling Natsuko the traditional wedding kimono; in the second she wears a Western traveling suit with muff and cloche hat (in the style of silent-screen star Mary Pickford) and he is arrayed in his full military uniform, looking stern and determined. It was the last time that he wore that uniform.

During World War I, Japan allied with Great Britain in hopes of gaining control of German possessions in East Asia. Militarism was gaining the upper hand in Japanese politics. Though his former military comrades urged him not to, Ransaku Saitō and his new bride prepared to leave. Because tradition was strong, Kinai Saitō still maintained the relationship with Ransaku assigned to him by the wider family. He too had spent a few years in America; he also married a Tokyo woman, Kinko, and he decided to move to America with Ransaku. Another couple, Masuzo and Sada Maruyama, joined them.

The three friends and their wives booked passage on the *Chicago Maru*, which was a cargo ship rather than a passenger liner. An immigrant to Seattle wrote of his passage two years later on the same ship: "Passengers called our boat by the infamous name of the 'Crippled Maru' or the 'Shit Line.' Inside the boat the passengers lived together in a long straight line of [three-tiered] silkworm-type sections. Males and females were separated by a thin board, and even newly married couples were divided for the duration of the three-week voyage. There was no place to wash hands and faces, no place to bathe, and the crewman for this purpose put a long row of bowls on deck and filled them half full of water from a bucket. There we rinsed our mouths and washed our faces. Even though it was May, on the ocean it was chilly; moreover, the boat sailed into the offing of Alaska. . . . It was so cold then that we felt not like passengers who had paid for the trip but like criminals on a prison ship."[19]

The Saitos and their friends landed in Seattle in May 1916. They made their way to the area Ransaku had remembered and admired, the Rogue River valley in southern Oregon, a mountainous, forested place that looked like parts of Japan. They settled in Medford, Oregon, and became part of a tiny Japanese community in a town dominated by fruit growing, dairying, lumbering, and mining. Ransaku soon discovered that his ability to recite America's proud founding documents would not be enough to gain him citizenship.

A NEW WORLD

Many Japanese were attracted to Oregon during the first years of the twentieth century by stories of plentiful jobs. Though they may have dreamed of growing rich in American, most found that their "belief in the fruits of honest hard work" would be the mainstay in their new lives. One Japanese immigrant said, "Too hard work! Never in America have I picked up a penny from the ground."[20]

Mrs. Itsu Akiyama, who settled in Hood River, Oregon, in 1915, described the early immigrant years: "When we came over here, we had to work, work, work! No time off for anniversaries and celebrations. I had no friends, and I was always thinking of my parents—it was lonely. I wanted very much to go back to Japan, but Mother always said to *shinbo* [be patient] over here. It was difficult, but I did."[21]

The valleys of the Willamette and Hood Rivers attracted many Japanese farmers, and a number of Japanese settled in Portland. Southern Oregon was an unusual destination, and by 1920 only a few of the four thousand Oregon Japanese had found their way to its mountainous valleys and verdant forests.

Ransaku and Natsu liked southern Oregon, their son Morse recalled. "The climate was similar to Japan and the mountains and seacoast were ideal. Medford became home where two of their children were born."[22]

Within a year of their arrival in Medford, Oregon, Ransaku had established a small business, called the Japanese Art and Curio Store, on North Central Street. He helped his cousin get his start, and after a few years Kinai and his wife had their own cleaning and dyeing business. Mr. Maruyama got a job as steward and clerk at the Rogue River University Club. The latter two families continued in these situations until forced to evacuate in May 1942. Though barely settled in their new homes, the Saitos and several of their friends took part in the Fourth of July parade in 1918. Japan was an ally in this first world war. The men wore business suits and carried flags; Natsu Saito, in her best kimono, carried the Japanese battle flag and a parasol.

Mary and Charles Fujimoto joined Medford's Japanese community; for many years they operated the Diamond Cafe. Mary had come on a steamer from Yokohama to join her husband in Medford a year after the Saitos arrived. Kimi and Hyosabura Yokota came from Osaka to Medford in 1916, traveling in Western clothes that they had ordered from Paris. By 1937 they were raising flocks of turkeys on a farm near Medford. Because of the fine fishing on the Rogue River and the beauty of the nearby mountains, Medford was also a resort town that boasted several hotels. A man named Fujimoto ran the kitchen in the Medford Hotel, the town's finest. He and many of his staff of Japanese immigrants roomed at the home of Kinai Saito. Uncle Fuji, as he was known, remained a bachelor and quietly provided funds to help some of the Medford Nisei go to college in the years before the war.

Natsu Tsuzuki Saito had much to learn in her adopted country. The daughter of wealthy parents, she may never before have had to cook, wash clothes, or shop for food. In Medford she had to help her husband operate the curio shop, speak to customers in English, take care of all the housekeeping and cooking, and sew her clothing. Soon, she bore a son, whom they named Lincoln. Two years later, in 1921, Perry Hitoshi was born. In the same years, Kinko Saito gave birth to two daughters, Naoko and Akiko, who were called cousins to Lincoln and Perry.

The children of Medford's Japanese families grew up learning two cultures. There were enough Japanese families to allow the children to develop a sense of Japanese traditions, to hear Japanese spoken, and to learn respect for elders, hard work, and learning. But they also associated with the predominant Caucasian population in school and in the business world. They did not develop a strong sense of being discriminated against as did the California *Nikkei*. But the Saitos did not stay long in this community, and except for his year in the Tule Lake Relocation Center, Perry never again lived in a Japanese community.

Perry's cousin Naoko talked about the relationship between her father and Ransaku Saito. The family had assigned Kinai to accompany Ransaku. It wasn't exactly to "look after" Ransaku, she said. "My father was a stoic, calm person . . . a steady person—so maybe they thought this would be a good balance to Ransaku, who had, I heard, a rather impetuous temperament. Maybe they thought, like brother looking after brother. Because I do remember my father . . . saying, 'Oh, Ransaku should not have done this, should not have done that.'"[23]

Shortly after Perry's birth, Ransaku left his kinsmen and moved his small family to Marshfield (later renamed Coos Bay), Oregon. A small town located on a safe harbor in southern Oregon, Marshfield was surrounded by forests of tall evergreens. A spur of the Southern Pacific Railway ended at docks frequented by lumber freighters. He chose the port town because of the lumber trade. In Marshfield he and Natsu joined the Methodist church, and he set up an import-export bussiness, selling logs to

Japanese ships. It is thought that at this time he acquired some timberland with the intent of cutting and selling the logs. After their daughter Dahlia was born in 1925, Ransaku was again ready to move, and his wanderlust did not fade until he finally settled in Aberdeen in 1929.

The leap from Marshfield, Oregon, to the flourishing towns on Grays Harbor was quite natural. The two ports were connected both by lumber freighters such as those of the Hart-Wood Company that plied the Seattle-to-San Francisco trade routes, and by the railroad. Ransaku first brought his family to Hoquiam, Washington, where Morse was born in 1926. They joined the First Methodist Church in Aberdeen. Several years later they moved to Aberdeen, settling into quarters behind their Oriental Gift Shop on East Heron Street a few doors away from A. M. Bendetson's Red Front Store. They were the only Japanese family in Aberdeen in those years.

Aberdeen and its sister towns, Hoquiam and Cosmopolis, had taken root on a good harbor at the mouth of the largest river in southwestern Washington in the county of Grays Harbor. The towns sit in a wide valley surrounded by wooded hills. Flowing brown rivers with names like Chehalis, Wishkah, Hoquiam, and Humptulips create irregular peninsulas in the valley as each stream searches for an outlet. To the west the waters fan out inside a caliper of land that opens to the Pacific Ocean. And worthless land it can be, too—tide flats, salt grass marshes that can barely feed a cow, damp tidal plains that edge along raw dirt bluffs ravaged by logging and riven by gullies. Early settlers went miles up the Wishkah River to find suitable grave sites. Eventually the town sites were diked and filled. Sawmills populated the shoreline, and streets of bawdy houses, union halls, taverns, and flophouses sprang up at this place where the logs met blade and boat, and loggers looked for relief from backbreaking, dangerous labor in the woods.

A temperate rain forest gets more than a hundred inches of rainfall a year. Grays Harborites, who envy the duck its water-repellant feathers, have a hundred ways to describe precipitation. It comes in daily mists, brief showers, or steady drizzles, or is driven on 40 mph sou'westers that raise howls in many a weather-stripped door. The residents adopted rainslicks, galoshes, and umbrellas and made streets of sawdust and laid railroads; the land grew tall, straight trees.

The stores on Aberdeen's Heron Street were only a few blocks from the Wishkah River. There were cafes on each side of the Saitos' gift shop, then called Oriental Art Store, with small hotels above. In December 1932 "there was a high tide, it [had] rained for two weeks, and a 100 mph hurricane wind happened all at once. The river overflowed over the entire downtown." Bill Jones, a classmate of Perry's, recalled that during the flood he was told by his photographer father, "Take the car, drive onto the hill and park it." Though he was only eleven, Bill Jones managed to get the car up the hill and parked near the Methodist church.[24] The Saitos could move their car, but there was a foot of water in their shop and living quarters for days.

Mr. Saito's business was built around the Japanese ships that stopped at the mills in Aberdeen and Hoquiam to pick up lumber. These freighters might first have unloaded cargo in Puget Sound. The ships then came around to Grays Harbor, and Mr. Saito sold them "Jap Squares." The trimmed lumber fit better than round logs in the small ships that were hand-loaded in those days. Mr. Saito also operated as a ship chandler, a kind of agent, taking orders from the ship's steward, and making purchases from wholesalers for meat, food staples, and whatever else the ship needed. In addition the stewards ordered things that were not available or were impossibly priced in Japan; "things like MJB [canned] coffee were very popular," son Morse recalled.[25]

Sometimes Japanese crewmembers shopped at stores in town. Marvin Reiner (a classmate of Perry's in Aberdeen) recalled that some of the men who came into his father's jewelry store and pawnshop couldn't speak English. Usually they wanted a phonograph to take home. When he couldn't understand them, Ed Reiner would offer to go get Mr. "Sato" from next door to translate.[26] The seamen would say, "No, no Sato!" It is possible that they thought that the price would go up to give Mr. "Sato" a cut.

The Saito children attended schools in Hoquiam, and then Aberdeen. The children were well accepted by their classmates. While she was in grade school, Dahlia took a dance class from Mrs. Mary McEvoy along with daughters of other merchants and wealthy "hill people." In one elaborate dance production with an "oriental" theme, Dahlia was the dancer in the center, perhaps because she was authentically "oriental."

In 1928 Lincoln and Perry were sent on a Japanese ship to spend the summer with Ransaku's family in Japan. The boys were barely seven and nine, and must have spoken some Japanese to be allowed such a big trip without an adult companion. Snapshots of the two young Americanized boys have survived in the ancestral home in Gunma, as have stories of their unconventional (American) behavior in Japan.[27]

Perry and Lincoln played in the downtown alleys with Marvin Reiner, whose father's store was next door. Marvin once brought the two of them along on a Jewish picnic. At one point, in a scene that Lincoln reminded Marvin of years later, the men at the picnic gathered in a prayer circle. Marvin was included in order to make a minyan, or quorum. It was a memorial for someone, Marvin recalled. It was the feeling of being left out that Lincoln recalled, even after all the years of war and recovery.[28]

The Saitos lived in modest quarters behind their store, in rooms without windows. As soon as the boys were old enough, they got after-school jobs delivering the *Aberdeen Daily World.* In summer Morse washed windows for the store across the street. Perry ran the elevator at the Finch Building (where Karl Bendetson had his law office), then later moved when most of the professional people moved, to run the elevator at the newer Becker Building. Though their living style was humble ("That is, cheap," said son Morse), the Saito parents "felt nothing was to be spared when it came to education."[29]

According to Morse's memories, the gift shop made money only at Christmastime. "During some very slow times in the summer, my father would get out the sign 'JAPANESE NATIONAL HOLIDAY,' put it in the window and we would spend the day at one of the nineteen beaches near Aberdeen."[30] In early 1942 those "holiday" closings were described to the FBI by fearful neighbors who tried to turn them into something sinister.

In 1933, because he was the eldest son, Lincoln was sent back to Japan to get a Japanese education. His parents planned that he would renew ties with the family in Gunma to maintain family claims on the land, and perhaps become a trading agent for his father. There was a great deal of turbulence in Japanese life after the 1931 Japanese invasion of Manchuria. The parents did not realize the extent to which Japan was dominated by narrow-minded military leaders. Probably because he seemed too American and had little skill in speaking and reading Japanese, Lincoln was not comfortable in Japan and soon gave up the idea of a business career there.

Among immigrant groups on Grays Harbor in the early years of the twentieth century, the Finns were the largest. The Finnish community boasted several lodges and union halls, churches, a temperance society, brotherhoods, and a socialist association. Literacy was high among immigrants, and at one time Aberdeen was said to have the best Finnish library on the West Coast. Several areas of town became known as "Finn towns." Steam baths, or saunas, were built in backyards, and public steam baths followed.

Perry Saito found his closest friends in Aberdeen—Rudy Kauhanen and

Paavo Timo—among these Finnish young people. Rudy did not hear English spoken until he went to school, and that first day, having not understood the teacher, he went home for lunch and stayed there, thereby forever losing the chance for a perfect attendance award. Rudy recalled that Perry got along well in school—he was popular. "Perry was tall for a Japanese, and a wonderful dancer," Rudy said. "The girls loved to dance with him." Perry was in the Good Will Troop, band, orchestra, and chorus, and competed in a national music contest. He was often a class officer. In addition to high school clubs, he joined DeMolay, a Masonic organization for young men, and several Methodist youth groups.[31]

Rudy's parents ran the Crystal Steam Baths, located in a second-floor space on F Street, several blocks from the Saito gift shop. Given the Japanese love of bathing, it may have been natural that Perry would be friends with Rudy and his family. "Perry learned Finnish from my dad. Every time he came over, which was a lot, Dad would work on his speaking," recalled Rudy, retired manager of the family business.[32]

Perry learned enough Finnish to fool friends of Rudy's a few years later. Sometime in 1944 Perry visited Rudy's apartment in Minnesota where he and other Finnish men were attending the army language school, which was preparing troops for possible occupation of Finland. Rudy wasn't home, but Perry had a fine conversation in Finnish with the other men, who later asked Rudy, "What kind of town is Aberdeen that a Jap speaks Finnish?"

In return, Mr. Saito taught Perry's friends to shoot billiards. The billiard table was in the Saitos' rooms behind the store. The boys were young, not yet in junior high. Rudy recalled, "He taught us a three-cushion game—Mr. Saito was good."

"When the playing stopped, we thought he was mad at us. We didn't know he was going blind."[33]

It happened when they were in the ninth grade, Rudy recalled. Lincoln had already gone to Japan. "I was in class, Perry was sitting next to me. Perry was quiet that day. He was called to go to the office, it was about 11:30 A.M. That's when he heard that his father was dead. Suicide, "*hara-kiri*," he said."[34] It was March 10, 1936.

Perry recalled years later that his father had tried to warn him the day before he died, to prepare him for his death. Perry set the stage: "My father smoked a lot. . . . We were kind of poor. The Japanese were invading Manchuria and nobody was buying Japanese goods and my father wouldn't go to the doctors and his teeth were getting poisoned. Finally he passed out and they took him to the hospital and he could no longer see." That had been a week earlier.

His father said, "For the rest of my life I am going to be a burden to you and your mother and to your brother and sister and so I am going to leave you. . . . I don't want you to be ashamed. I want you to understand that it would be a dishonor for me to be a burden to your mother." Perry asked if he was going to kill himself, and started crying. His father, who had secretly bought a gun, lied, saying, "No, no, no, don't take it that way. I won't." The next day he did.[35]

Outsiders speculated about why Ransaku Saito took his life. There were rumors of financial problems or possibly a drinking problem, although he was known among Japanese ship captains as one who could hold his liquor. Stories were told that the Japanese ship captains had asked him to fill their ships with contraband and that he was in trouble because he sent them back empty. And after Pearl Harbor some would suggest that he had been a spy.

He may have been worried about his son Lincoln. The news of a failed uprising by a military faction in Japan, called the "February 26 Revolt," had just reached America and been published in the local papers. Prime Minister Keisuke Okada escaped death, but a former prime minister and lord privy seal, Admiral Makoto Saito had been assassinated, as had financial genius and finance minister Korekiyo Takahashi.[36] Though Saitō is a common name in Japan, Perry's friends speculated that Mr. Saito was somehow disgraced by the death of a possible relative and that his hopes for developing more trade with Japan were somehow shattered.

Mr. Saito had grown up in the Meiji era that began not long after feudalism ended. His family respected the samurai past in which *sepukku* or ritual suicide was honorable. It was compulsory for warriors to avoid being captured by the enemy. A person could choose suicide because of a private misfortune, out of loyalty to a dead master, or as a protest against the action of a superior. In the Japanese mindset, suicide was more honorable than disgracing oneself by burdening others. The news story that afternoon in the *Aberdeen Daily World* noted that Mr. Saito had been in poor health and that his eyes were failing him. He had "felt worse" that day, and "while Mrs. Saito was telephoning the family physician, he went to the rear portion of the store . . . and ended his life."

Mr. Saito was described as "a merchant, importer and exporter . . . active in commercial affairs of Grays Harbor, [and engaged] in trans-Pacific lumber trade." His body was cremated and his remains placed in an urn in the family living quarters. Perry Hitoshi Saito, who had to behave as oldest son when Lincoln was sent to Japan, was, at fifteen, the oldest man in the household.[37]

Ransaku's youngest son, Morse, who, sixty years later, was still trying to understand his father's action, picked up the story here. Mrs. Saito was left with the problem of supporting three school-age children. She may occasionally have received small sums from Japanese relatives. The family had to choose Japan or America. The children knew only America and insisted Aberdeen was "home." The eldest son, Lincoln, had already said of Japan, "This is no place for us."

Natsu understood. Though she was still immersed in poetry (she wrote *haiku*, *waka*, and *senryu*) and the Japanese music she had studied in Japan, and took pride in being an *edokko* (a child of old Tokyo), she knew she had deliberately and intentionally raised a family of Americans. She decided to keep the gift shop and ship chandler businesses going. They moved to a storefront one block west, between the Aberdeen Drug Co. and the Smoke Shop, under the bowling alley, and across Heron Street from a women's clothing store and a third-run movie house.

Morse recalled: "After my father's death it was impossible to get credit from the wholesale people. So after a few months [probably the summer of 1936], my mother packed us all into the car and we went to the Japanese town in Seattle, staying in the best Japanese hotel and going to movies, eating at the best Japanese restaurants—all of us kids got complete fall outfits—and putting on the dog. I still remember a Nelson Eddy-Jeanette MacDonald movie."

At the time Morse didn't understand his mother's strategy. "I couldn't figure out why since we were actually so poor. . . . We had moved out of a bigger store to a smaller one." The Seattle trip didn't seem right to him.

"After this show of prosperity the wholesale people came running (most were from places like San Francisco) and we made big purchases to get the store going again.[38] By then we were down to the gift shop business and supplying foodstuffs and the like to the freighters." Morse, who had once been a prizewinning bridge columnist, continued: "My poetry-loving high-class mother didn't know anything about bridge but she [knew poker and] once advised me, 'Never draw to an inside straight.'[39] She later described to a grandson her reasoning at this time, "No one will ever feel sorry for anyone in my family."[40]

Living among Caucasians and having many friends, Perry and Morse felt that they were Americans. Until forced to evacuate in the first months of World War II, they considered Aberdeen their home. And only when the list of Japanese to be evacuated appeared in the newspaper in May 1942 did they become aware of a part-Japanese family on Grays Harbor, the Moyers.

AN AMERICAN GROOM

In December 1911 a young American sat at a table in a Yokohama teahouse writing to his oldest sister Jennie in the United States. "Well this is a most delightful country to live in. The weather is lovely and the atmosphere so fresh and clear, one never tires of walking around looking at the sights. Every thing looks strange. . . . The natives are very courteous."[41]

The correspondent from Japan was William H. Moyer, a footloose young man who early felt the lure of foreign places. He was born in 1878 in Saunders County in eastern Nebraska, son of a carpenter who had fought for the Union in the Civil War. At the age of fourteen young Moyer began the journeys westward that didn't end until he'd shipped out on many freighters, crossed the Pacific several times, and brought back a Japanese bride.

Before William left home Jennie had written a poem called "Family Record" describing each of the nine children. Her verse about William, then twelve, was

> The fifth was our second brother Willie
> He is meek and mild and pure as a lily.
> He is good to his parents and causes no trouble
> And I think he will grow to be a man good and noble.[42]

While in Japan, William wrote to Jennie and his parents and sent envelopes of flower seeds for each of his other sisters. The Yokohama letter continues: "The Chinks are still fighting so I feel pretty well satisfied to stay in Japan. When I first landed there was only two noises that sounded familiar to me those were the birds singing and the babies crying. As much difference as there is between the sound of our language and the Japanese, there isn't a particle of difference between their children crying and ours in America."

He later told his children he had worked on many ships as a cabin boy and as a cook and that he had seen opium dens in China and rice terraces carved into the mountains of Japan. Near some of those terraces he met Towa Ishimatsu.

A Japanese man had befriended Moyer in Hoquiam, Washington, sometime in the 1900s, a time when there were only a few Japanese immigrants in western Washington. Moyer may have found this Grays Harbor lumber port by accident, having to disembark from a ship because of a strange fever. While he was in isolation in the Hoquiam hospital, the only person who would care for him was the Japanese man, perhaps an orderly. As the patient recovered, the two became good friends, and the man invited Moyer to visit Japan and meet his family on Kyushu in southwestern Japan. This man was ever after the legendary "Japanese gentleman" who introduced Moyer to his niece, Towa Ishimatsu, who captured Moyer's heart.

Born in 1894, Towa Ishimatsu had been orphaned by her father's death and her mother's remarriage, and was being raised by her grandmother. She lived in what William Moyer described as "one of the warm parts of Japan . . . especially adapted to rice, oranges, silk and tea." Her family's village, Nakatsu, lay some miles southeast of the northern tip of Kyushu Island. William Moyer was the guest of friends, and wrote:

"I am now stopping in a small town called Yukuhashi near the city of Kokura . . . at my friend's house, the one I used to know in Aberdeen eight or nine years ago. . . . Her husband I knew also in America. . . . He has a large factory in this town for making Japanese Sauce.

"I was never treated so kindly in my life before as I have been by these people."

Moyer wrote about rice paddies in every direction, and watching his hostess as she "feeds the little caterpillars, prepares the cocoons, spins the silk thread and weaves it into goods right in her house." He was the only Caucasian living in a town of about five thousand people, though he saw "two white men come through . . . one English Missionary and another Englishman selling bibles."

Moyer made no remarks about the level of development of Japanese towns. He had begun his travels in 1892, a time when farming in America was based on animal power and simple equipment, just as it was in the Japanese countryside. The modernization of many industries had begun in Japanese cities following the opening to the West by Commodore Perry's fleet in 1854. The newly powerful emperor had encouraged people to learn from Western countries in order to prevent being conquered by the West. The government sought to develop a German-style army and a British-style navy. The country's sophisticated political institutions, respect for hierarchies, and a tolerance for bureaucratic rule allowed the orderly adoption of industrial and technological changes, and the citizenry adapted quickly. By 1910, only fifty years after the end of isolation, Japan had modernized to an incredible extent and had successfully fought two neighbors (Korea and Russia) in major military operations. The country Moyer saw from the train window was full of people and intensively cultivated. What caught his attention was that "every thing looks artistic."

In the forty-fourth year of the restored Meiji emperor Mutsuhito, during his pleasant interlude as houseguest in a Japanese home on Kyushu, William Moyer encountered Towa Ishimatsu. He had learned some Japanese. He "made out a great list of words and sentences commonly used," and got an English-speaking Japanese friend to help him write translations—"the list will do for both the Japanese to learn English and me to learn Japanese when I get this list fixed up I will have no trouble getting along any place in this country." Perhaps it was with the aid of this list that he was able to talk to young Towa.

They were married on May 17, 1912, in Yukuhashi, Buzen Province, Japan. William was thirty-three, Towa eighteen. He wore the costume of a Japanese groom: a white robe and sash, a silk kimono, and white stockings. Though he was not a large man, he stood a head taller than his bride. In a traditional kimono and obi, with pompadoured hair, and holding a single large chrysanthemum, Towa could have been a bride from an earlier century in Japan. But her groom was Caucasian (termed a barbarian by the Japanese) and she had agreed to go with him to America.

The young bride would no longer be recognized as a citizen of Japan. Nor would her marriage to an American citizen give her citizenship, the United States Consul in Nagasaki assured the new bridegroom.

The newlyweds arrived at the Port of Seattle on the SS *Enaba Maru* on July 9, 1912. Towa attended a Baptist mission school to learn to speak English and to cook American food. They moved to Hoquiam shortly thereafter, hoping to make a permanent home.

Hoquiam was a thriving place in 1912 and still had a reputation as a rough town, matching that of its sister town, Aberdeen. Hoquiam's share of taverns lined Simpson Avenue near the river. Hoquiam's town site was almost completely surrounded by water. Several forks of the Hoquiam River flowed south from the Olympic Peninsula, through miles of enormous and valuable virgin timber into the North Channel of the Chehalis. The town's riverfronts, three miles downstream from Aberdeen, were lined with sawmills. Where the mills ended on the western flanks of town, mudflats began.

From his earlier visits, William Moyer knew that there would be chances for work in the town or in one of the mills or the shipyard. He renewed his acquaintances, got a job, and later became manager at the Royal Cafe. He and Towa moved into a house on Third Street in Hoquiam facing the First Presbyterian Church, which they later attended. They often saw the masts of oceangoing schooners and heard the whistles of steam vessels berthed on three sides of town. It must have seemed like living in the dockyards of Kokura, Kyushu, near Towa's former home.

Towa set up housekeeping, doing her best to cook the food that she found in the local stores. This town on a rainy seacoast looked a little like the place she had left, but it was colder. She could not see the mountains; there were no terraced fields, no hillsides of bamboo, no teashops, and no seaweed or squid in the fish markets. She may have felt homesick. She and William talked of going back to visit her family in Japan. But then the children came, first Jackson, then Chester, then Madeline. Towa's dream of seeing her home village again remained just that, a dream.[43]

Towa was not the only homesick immigrant on Grays Harbor. Almost everyone had migrated from somewhere. Chinese labor dominated the county's fish-canning industry before the turn of the century because these newcomers were willing to work for less money, were more reliable, did not join unions, and could be hired through a contract-labor system that provided whole crews at a time. The 1890 census indicated 104 Chinese residents but no Japanese for Chehalis County (precursor of Grays Harbor County), whose total population was 9,249.

After the completion of the transcontinental railroad, resentment of Chinese workers developed, resulting in the Exclusion Act of 1882 that forbade the immigration of Chinese laborers including women and children. Many episodes of the violent expulsion of Chinese from West Coast towns followed. Aberdeen's eruption occurred in November 1890.[44] The three local policemen were diverted with a tale of violent fights outside town, while a group of men in masks made a midnight raid to known Chinese houses and washhouses, gathering up the occupants and forcing them onto the ship *Wishkah Chief*. The boat steamed ten miles upriver to Montesano where the men were dumped on the wharf and told to keep going, out of the county. The road led east to Olympia and Tacoma. Few returned.[45]

Eight Japanese, seven of them cooks, were known residents of

Hoquiam in 1900. In the 1910 Grays Harbor County census there were seventy-nine Japanese; for the second decade this group outnumbered Chinese residents. A large number worked as a construction crew for the Northern Pacific Railroad with W. Tuyimoto as foreman; others were cooks or farmers. Some women were seamstresses or servants; one was said to be a prostitute.

By the time Towa Ishimatsu Moyer arrived in Hoquiam, the small numbers of Chinese and Japanese people who remained on the Harbor were expected to work and socialize only with their own kind, or to serve quietly in the kitchens and back hallways of the white world. Towa's babies looked something like her but were Americans. She worked hard to learn English, which her husband and children spoke. Her daughter recalled with pride that as she was growing up she noticed that her mother spoke English better than many of their neighbors who had come from Scandinavian countries years earlier.[46]

Towa's one Japanese friend, her children recalled, was Tinia, a cook in the Frank Lamb household. Son of a New Jersey farmer, Frank Lamb was a botanist and forester who, while studying at Stanford University, had had the good fortune to meet and marry the daughter of wealthy Hoquiam lumberman, George Emerson. Lamb became a successful lumberman in Hoquiam and organized a foundry that produced innovative rigging equipment for the logging operators. William Moyer would later work for the Lamb family's Northwest Lumber Co.

Always an innovator, Frank Lamb designed and built a plains-style mansion on a rise above town, and laid out a large garden. His growing household required domestic help. The Lamb's second and most satisfactory helpers, who followed a Finnish woman, were a Japanese couple identified only as Kay and Tinia. In his memoir, Lamb wrote that Tinia became a good cook and her husband Kay was a fine gardener and handyman.

Towa Moyer visited Tinia often, and occasionally brought along her young children, dressed in their Sunday best.

Lamb visited Japan in 1929 as an officer in the Rotary International and bought stone lanterns and woodwork for a small Japanese building. Kay developed a Japanese garden on the grounds of Lamb's home and installed the teahouse. In midsummer of 1929 Lamb organized a dedication "as a means of promoting better understanding and knowledge of the Japanese by the people of Grays Harbor." He invited the consul and other prominent Japanese from Seattle, whose wives arrived in "their native costumes." Lamb wrote in his memoir: "A troupe of four Japanese dancing girls performed during the evening. Mrs. Saito of Hoquiam in native costume served tea in Japanese style in the little house in the garden." He mentioned an orchestra and an exhibit of Japanese dolls and art objects, and claimed that "everyone in town was invited."[47]

The "Mrs. Saito" mentioned by Lamb was surely Natsu, wife of respected shopkeeper and log buyer, Ransaku Saito, then living in Hoquiam. Ransaku probably had lumber dealings with one of Lamb's operations.

Towa or William Moyer might also have attended Lamb's Japanese celebration. By this time William was working for the Eureka mill, and another son, Billy, was born. In 1928, the year that their fifth child, James, was born, Towa and William bought six acres of land a few miles north of Hoquiam at a place called New London, on the road to Lake Quinault.

New London was homesteaded early because it was at the end of the tidewater on the Hoquiam River, the furthest place early settlers could reach by boat when going upstream from Hoquiam, and hence the jumping-off point for the hard trek into the Humptulips Valley forest. There loggers from the north could dump cedar and fir logs into tidewater to be rafted and towed downstream to the sawmills. Because the land was either heavily forested or swampy, it seemed an unlikely place for a farm.

Some of the Moyers' six acres had been cleared, and William spent years burning out huge stumps to get better grazing land for the family's cow and a couple of steers. They raised chickens and in time had a building that housed five hundred of them. There were often a couple of pigs, and geese that chased the children. With the animals, fruit trees, and a vegetable garden, the family became largely self-sufficient. They traded eggs for what staples they didn't grow. William and the children did the farm chores before work or school. Towa took care of cooking, housekeeping, and pasteurizing the milk. William and Towa taught their children the value of hard work, always reminding them to "do a job you are proud of." This message would be passed on to their grandchildren.[48]

By the end of the 1930s the Saitos and Moyers certainly thought of themselves as Americans; Mrs. Saito and Mrs. Moyer were mothers of American children, and their lives were those of other American housewives. Mrs. Saito and her three schoolage children all worked hard to survive. In his law office a block away from the Saito shop, Karl Bendetson was successfully serving clients and maintaining his status in the army reserve. A quarter-century before Ransaku Saito, Bendetson's father had felt a similar attraction to the timber-rich wilds of western Washington.

Natsuko Tsuzuki [Saito] (in white) poses with her father, three brothers, and sister in front of a painted forest in Tokyo in 1907. Natsu's father was a wealthy banker who may have been an official in the imperial court. (Courtesy of Aylesworth family)

Natsu Tsuzuki in 1915, right, with a friend. Natsu attended five years of high school and two years of music school; after the Pearl Harbor attack she was still proud of being an *Edokko*, a child of old Tokyo, but felt no loyalty to Japan. (Courtesy of Aylesworth family)

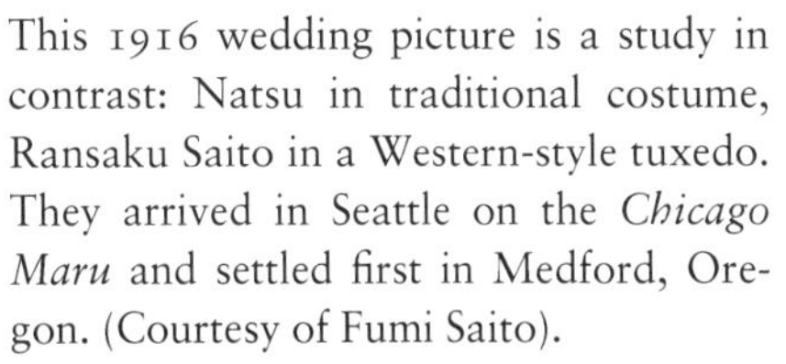

This 1916 wedding picture is a study in contrast: Natsu in traditional costume, Ransaku Saito in a Western-style tuxedo. They arrived in Seattle on the *Chicago Maru* and settled first in Medford, Oregon. (Courtesy of Fumi Saito).

The four Saito children stand in their alley in about 1930. *Back*, Perry and Lincoln; *front*, Dahlia and Morse. Prior to this photo Perry and Lincoln had spent a summer visiting relatives in Japan. (Courtesy of Fumi Saito)

In 1918 the United States was at war with Germany, but Japan was a U.S. ally. As they did in Aberdeen, immigrant groups took part in the Fourth of July Parade in Medford, Oregon. Natsu Saito (carrying parasol and Japanese war flag) and a Mrs. Kanano (in white, carrying American flag) walked with friends and relatives to celebrate their new country's independence day holiday. (Courtesy of Southern Oregon Historical Society, #9107)

Perry snapped a picture of his parents, Morse, Dahlia, and Lincoln enjoying one of their picnics on a "Japanese National Holiday," a quiet spring day, perhaps in April 1932. Perry's camera was confiscated by the police as contraband after December 7, 1941, and was never returned. (Courtesy of Lisa Aylesworth)

Ransaku took a photo while Perry stretched out in his mother's lap on the same picnic. Lincoln (right) was sent in 1933 to Japan for schooling and never returned. The FBI held this against Mrs. Saito when she was arrested in late 1941. (Courtesy of Lisa Aylesworth)

High tides, heavy rain, and wind drove the river onto Heron Street in Aberdeen in the winter of 1932–33. The Saito's Oriental Art Store (as it was then called), third from the left, was flooded along with the others, including the store of Bendetsen's father, which was in the same block. (Courtesy of Bronco Tesia)

View to the west over Aberdeen (near part of urban area on right) and Hoquiam (far part) to the Pacific Ocean. Residents feared the Japanese would invade on the beaches west of town. (Author's collection)

Perry H. Saito graduated from Weatherwax High School in Aberdeen in 1939 at a ceremony during which Karl Bendetson presented an award to the class president. (Inscribed on the back to Rudy Kauhanen) (Courtesy of Rudy Kauhanen)

William Moyer returned from his years at sea with a Japanese wife, Towa. Shortly after their 1912 wedding, they settled in Hoquiam, Washington. (Courtesy of Jim Moyer)

When Jim Moyer, age 13, returned home from Tule Lake, he wrote a paper, "Life in an Internment Camp." He and his family were released from the camp as part of the Mixed-Race Exemption from Evacuation policy developed by Bendetsen. In the next years he played football for Hoquiam High School and served for several years in the navy. (Courtesy of Jim Moyer)

Towa Moyer, Madeline, Jackson, and Chester came to visit friend Tinia, who worked for Frank Lamb. They are shown here in Lamb's garden. Tinia's husband constructed the teahouse that Lamb brought home from Japan, in which Mrs. Saito conducted Tea Ceremonies for Lamb's guests. Hoquiam, late 1920s. (Courtesy of Jim Moyer)

CHAPTER THREE

Karl R. Bendetsen: From Hometown to Nation's Capital

They went after the hills hammer and tongs, with bulls and snorting monsters, with greed and carelessness.

—Edwin Van Syckle, *They Tried to Cut It All*

One sunny day in the last summer of the nineteenth century, a young man stretched out on the grass in front of his seated parents in the yard of their home on East Main Street in Battle Creek, Michigan. Other young people formed a circle behind the group. A photographer captured the progression of the generations, from the Old World to the new, with Lithuanian elders in traditional dress and their offspring in Gibson girl dresses or straw bowlers and checked pants. Albert Mose Bendetson would soon marry the prettiest of the young twins standing in the back, a distant relative who had grown up in their household. He may have had no inkling that he would soon head west to the farthest reaches of the American continent.

In 1900 he worked as a dry goods merchant at Netzorg and Bendetson, the firm that his father had organized. Living in adjoining houses, the extended families of Albert and his Lithuanian-born sister, Anna Bendetson Netzorg, included their parents, his sister Anna's in-laws—also Jewish immigrants from Lithuania—and his wife's father and twin sister. Bendetson's parents and in-laws were among the earliest arrivals in America from the Jewish communities of Eastern Europe.

In 1860 Lithuania was part of Russia, as it had been since the Third Partition of Poland in 1795. In 1791 Empress Catherine of Russia restricted Jewish habitation to the Pale of Settlement, a region stretching from the Baltic to the Black Seas, encompassing much of present day Latvia, Lithuania, Ukraine, and Belarus. Every generation of Lithuanian Jews could find reasons to leave the Pale: economic hardship, political violence, repression, or persecution. In the 1860s in Lithuania, Jews were restricted to living in certain places and limited to certain occupations. In spite of periodic pogroms against them, the Jewish population had expanded greatly in the nineteenth century, and with the Edict of 1861, which freed the serfs, there was much competition from non-Jews even for the traditional jobs such as middlemen between peasants and merchants, tailors, cobblers, carpenters, barbers, fishermen, and porters. At the same time, certain classes of Jews (merchants and professionals) were allowed to move outside the Pale, into some Russian cities. This resulted in further turmoil and more protests against Jews. Also in the 1860s, many Lithuanian Jews were expelled from their villages, called *stetls*, and "forced into urban ghettos, under poverty conditions."[1] Those who could, emigrated from Lithuania. Among these were Samuel and Crena Bendetson and daughter Anna, who came to the United States in 1869 and settled first in Elmira, New York, where Albert M. Bendetson was born in 1873.[2]

Albert's wife, Anna, was born in Minnesota in 1876, one of the twin daughters of Benedict Bentson, also an immigrant from Poland (then part of Russia). After their mother died in a later childbirth, Anna and Lottie spent five years in a Jewish orphanage in Cleveland, Ohio, until their father could again care for them. Later they all moved in with Samuel Bendetson, a distant relative.[3]

By 1906, after the deaths of his parents, Albert M. Bendetson was looking for a new opportunity. He had lost a business in Park Falls, Wisconsin, to fire, and decided to head West, maybe to California.[4] Like others, he was dissuaded from going to San Francisco by the disastrous earthquake and fire of that April. On the westbound train he met a man who talked about the forests of the Northwest coast, the fishing, and the fine harbors. He ended his travels at the westernmost terminus of the northern railroad lines: Aberdeen, Washington.

The town's residents included lumbermen in search of the next wilderness, merchants looking for new customers, laborers hoping for honest work in timber, fishing, or farming, newspaper men, union enthusiasts, anarchists seeking willing followers. Some embraced the new land with a patriotic fervor that surprised those residents who took their citizenship for granted. Naturalization classes in Aberdeen accommodated Finns, Croatians, Germans, Poles, Czechs, Italians, Greeks and Scandinavians. Chinese railroad crews, Japanese cooks, and Chinese cannery workers built lives on the margins, prevented by anti-Asian laws from becoming citizens.

Even in boom times this rough mill town was plagued by labor unrest. The uneven nature of the lumber industry—over-production of logs one month, a shortage of workers the next—caused managers to distrust organized labor. Loggers and sawmill workers wrangled among themselves over which union should represent them and made demands the operators would not meet. The fight for an eight-hour workday would be settled in this area, but not until the federal government intervened in 1918 to ensure availability of the area's fine Sitka spruce for airplane construction. The most radical of the labor groups was the Industrial Workers of the World (IWW), often called Wobblies, whose revolutionary ideas found fertile ground among the stream of migrants who had come to work in timber in the early years of the twentieth century. Aberdeen was recovering from its own disastrous fire of 1903, and building a new, more permanent downtown.

The land upstream grew some of the largest trees man has seen: western red cedar, Douglas fir, hemlock, and spruce. Even the "junk" tree that is first to colonize after a fire, the red alder, grew large enough to have economic value. This was the last uncut place, and it was ready to prosper.

Albert M. Bendetson decided he could do business here. He soon sent for his wife and three-year-old daughter Selma. His wife's father and sister followed shortly thereafter.

In October 1907, when Karl Robin Bendetson was born, his father was running a clothing business with Adolph Karp.[5] The Bendetsons rented a wood frame house in the narrow valley bordering the Wishkah River. The houses in North Aberdeen, or "Finn Town," as it was called, stood on stilts on the tidal land to survive the river's winter highs. The hillsides were ragged from recent logging, and the river ran muddy; its meanders were filled with floating booms of logs, the shore lined with shacks of immigrant Finns and Croatians, and near the bridge to the cemetery, boats bobbed at tiny docks that also served as fish markets.

By 1911 Albert M. Bendetson had his own store in the heart of downtown Aberdeen, two blocks from the tidewater sawmills and close to the "line" of pool halls, taverns, and brothels frequented by loggers and sailors. Bendetson's store catered to city folk as well as to loggers: "clothing from birth 'til death." He even rented funeral clothes suitable for the viewing, to be returned before burial.[6]

Along with many recent arrivals and fellow shopkeepers, Al Bendetson participated in Jewish worship. The county's small Jewish population was not large enough to support a rabbi but would pull together in the coming years to build a synagogue.

There had always been Jews in Aberdeen, just as there had always been Swedes and Greeks, and even some Chinese and Japanese. Among the earliest to arrive and the most nurturing of the Jewish faith was George J. Wolff, who left his poverty-stricken parents in Kempen, Poland, at the age of fifteen. He arrived on the Harbor in 1897 to run a dry goods store for an Olympia company headed by a fellow Kempen Jew. Wolff soon established his own business that grew into "the finest dry goods emporium in southwestern Washington."[7] Wolff loved his adopted country and was an unstinting promoter of civic and social activities in his community. He delighted in horses, and often lead the Fourth of July parade as grand marshal, his horse sporting a silver bridle. He also organized and supported the worship and study of his Jewish religion.

Almost all the Jews who arrived in the first years of the twentieth century were merchants—dry goods, men's clothing, shoes, ladies' furnishings, millinery, jewelry. Al Bendetson's train trip west had ended in Aberdeen in 1906, at about the same time that four Jewish families came north after losing everything in the San Francisco earthquake. A. E. Alexander, Julius and Sid Baer, and Joseph Jacob arrived with their wives and joined the tiny Reform Jewish congregation that Wolff was nurturing on Grays Harbor, as did Al Bendetson. The group at first held services in private homes, then later in rented rooms in such places as the Eagles Hall, Moose Hall, Knights of Pythias Building, and the downtown rooms of the Grays Harbor Business College.

Lay leaders programmed the services. Nis Abrahamson was a regular vocalist. Other groups held services—there were Orthodox families, formerly Russian Jews, and Conservative families, and later several families of Sephardic Jews from Turkey—and sometimes they shared a Seattle rabbi for the high holy day observances or for a funeral. Just before war swept Europe in 1914, twenty Jewish men organized a Grays Harbor chapter of B'nai B'rith, originally an association of German Jews, that established a number of charitable organizations to help the needy. The members included A. M. Bendetson and his close friends Alexander, Jacob, and Baer. George J. Wolff often headed the B'nai B'rith group and traveled up and down the coast, attending its Pacific Coast meetings.

The most learned, and the most colorful of the local Jews was Joseph Jacob, a Frenchman who spoke eight languages including Hebrew (but not Yiddish). He ran a very small shoe store but was not a successful businessman. He preferred to sit in the back of his store reading scripture; he grumbled if anyone came in, and left it to his wife to wait on them. He was a strong leader in the congregation, and taught Hebrew to many of the younger generation, which included Selma and Karl Bendetson, Sylvia and Joel Wolff, Helen Alexander, and Madeline Jacob.[8]

Jacob was sought after as a speaker, and harbored an original viewpoint in support of the League of Nations (he argued that America's Monroe Doctrine was the first example of a successful League of Nations in the Western Hemisphere).[9] In the twenties a ladies' literary group called Friends in Council, made up of wives of doctors, managers, bankers, and newspaper publishers, chose to learn about Judaism, and after weeks of study, invited guests from the Jewish community to speak. On one St. Patrick's Day, in a living room decorated with shamrocks and green leprechauns, Mr. Jacob gave the ladies a talk titled "The Jew."

Jewish religious classes were conducted through the years. Initially taught by Joseph Jacob and the Penn daughters, classes were later taught by Selma Bendetson and Roy Rosenthal, then editor of the *Montesano Vidette*. An active young people's group, which included Karl and his friend Joel Wolff, son of George J. Wolff, presented Purim plays each spring. In 1915–20 the combined Jewish congregation may have numbered seventy-five to a hundred people, drawing from a county that totaled barely eighteen thousand people. Karl and his friends got their first impressions of European history when America joined what was then known as the European War.

HOMETOWN BOYS

Aberdeen's annual Fourth of July parade in 1918 assumed a serious posture, just as it did in Medford, Oregon. Two young boys in khaki uniforms and improvised hats stationed themselves in front of the army's storefront recruiting office to watch the parade, which promised "American soldiers, marines and patriotic organizations" and "a great line of march."[10] Joel Wolff and his friend Karl Bendetson stood still to have their picture taken, then waited for the parade. Detachments of soldiers in khaki, then marines and soldiers from the Harbor's torpedo boat station and the local National Guard unit marched by. At this time more than a million and a half American troops were supporting the European campaign and had shown their worth in the battle of Belleau Woods near the Marne.

The parade continued down Heron Street, with troops from the army's Loyal Legion, the "spruce division" that had been sent into the woods to cut urgently needed spruce logs for airplane construction. Red Cross nurses in long white dresses followed the local ambulance. Many groups marched to show their patriotism and their solidarity with the Western powers in the war. There were "Jugo-Slavs," Czechs, Slovaks, and the Croatian lodge called Zrinsko-Francopan. The Finnish Brotherhood carried a banner reading, "100% Loyal to the USA." Many on the sidewalks tapped their feet to the beat of the Motorship Band. The Polish Society came out in full force carrying a long banner asking for "Liberty for Poland," and noting the number of their boys who had enlisted. Karl and Joel were barely ten years old, far too young to enlist.

During this war some young Jewish soldiers stationed on ocean beaches came to Jewish services in town and were disappointed at not finding any households that kept kosher.[11] With the encouragement of George J. Wolff and other businessmen, the county responded generously to the pleas for contributions to the Jewish Relief Fund to aid Jewish women and children left as refugees in Poland, Galicia, Romania, and Lithuania after the World War. George Wolff often sent money to the old country, and assisted many relatives of Aberdeen friends to come to this country.

Aberdeen was a lumbering hub. Logs came from the woods rafted together in floating booms towed down the rivers; they came by train, and later they came by truck. The mills piled logs or lumber into three-masted schooners and steam ships; after the extension of a railroad link to the harbor, long snaking trainloads of lumber headed east. The Harbor area boasted some fifty sawmills, one of which (Pope & Talbot's Grays Harbor Commercial Corporation) was for a time the largest mill in the world.[12] Belching smoke stacks from pulp mills and sawmills were a sign that all was well. As Karl Bendetson grew up and attended schools in Aberdeen, the woods provided great wealth to hardworking loggers and mill owners and to the businesses that served them. Karl's days were partitioned by the screeches and whistles of the mills, his walks to school dampened by rainfall, his nights brightened by the lines of glowing sawdust burners along the river.

Al Bendetson's business benefited from the burgeoning lumber trade. He turned a disreputable store called the Red Front into a trusted, dependable provider of quality men's clothing and Buster Brown shoes. After some years he bought the store's two-story building on the corner of Heron and G Streets for $37,500, and became landlord for several other businesses. The editor of the *Grays Harbor Post* noted: "The deal marks the permanency and growth of Mr. Bendetson's business and his faith in the city of Aberdeen."[13]

The family moved up the hill (economically and socially a step upward), though always residing close to the center of town and the clothing store. Every few years Al Bendetson bought a new Buick. In February of 1921, Mr. Bendetson took young Karl on a three-week trip to the east, visiting Detroit, Chicago, and Minneapolis.

Anna Bendetson was a good bridge player, and played at the Wednesday night club, often with Bertha Wolff, wife of George J. Wolff. The Bendetsons socialized with other shopkeepers and members of their Jewish congregation, such as the A. E. Alexander family, the Baers, and the Jacobs. In summers, Mrs. Bendetson and Mrs. Alexander took their children to vacation at fashionable resorts at Hood Canal or Offutt Lake.

Karl studied piano, as did his older sister Selma. They both performed for many events, and Karl could play by ear. They each accompanied their father's violin. A. M. Bendetson was a stern taskmaster and ruled a household in which "you weren't to raise your voice," Karl's niece recalled.[14] Karl learned respect for authority. There were cousins and other children of the Reform Jewish community, but Joel Wolff was Karl's best friend. Karl and Joel went to school together, attended Jewish Sunday school, and went to the same parties. Joel's sister Sylvia was one of Selma's good friends.

At the age of fourteen, and not yet in high school, Karl lied about his age to join the Washington National Guard. At one of his first guard encampments he was put in a group with other Jewish boys, in the charge of an older boy, Guard Corporal Earl Thygeson, who had also entered the guard by lying about his age. Thygeson recalled his "tent full of Jew boys," but hadn't minded the razzing he got for having them as his charges—their "Momma and Papa always brought lots of cakes and pies and cookies so we ate real good."[15]

In 1923 Karl was a member of the guard's 489th Company of the Coast Artillery Corps and Headquarters Detachment, First Provisional Battalion. He worked his way through the ranks from private to private first class to corporal by learning to clean, load, and fire the big guns of Battery Benson at Fort Warden, a coastal installation that survived from defenses built along the Straits of Juan de Fuca prior to 1910. He later completed the ROTC course at Stanford, joined the United States Army's Officers Reserve Corps, and was assigned to a reserve infantry division at Fort Lewis, in which he continued until 1940.

Karl attended Miller Junior High and Weatherwax High School, the only choices in this town of some 16,500. In high school Karl took part in all the dramatics that were available—his nickname was "Tut," perhaps from a role in a play. He studied Latin and French, worked on the yearbook and the school newspaper and was a member of the Boy's Chorus. Karl had a taste for flashy shoes and was "well-liked. . . . Definitely a ladies' man," a woman two years behind him in school recalled.[16] He was tall, good-looking, and self-assured— the '25 yearbook said of him, "Oh pretty boy, trust not too much to your good looks." Though he was not a speaker at his high school graduation, he and his father occasionally gave talks or led prayers for their congregation.

On a September evening in 1923, A. M. Bendetson stood in front of the Grays Harbor Reform Congregation gathered for the Rosh Hashanah service in the Odd Fellows Hall at Broadway and Market Streets. He read from a New Year's Eve sermon by Rabbi Moses P. Jacobson:

> However alienated the Jew be from Israel and from Judaism the whole year through, be he ever so disposed to ignore the claims of blood, and be the empire which his ancestral sanctities hold over his soul ever so weak, yet at least tonight he comes seeking a fellowship with all his native brotherhood—a fellowship of race and a fellowship of religion, a fellowship physical and a fellowship spiritual, a fellowship of history and a fellowship of destiny.

His words resonating in the upstairs ballroom, Al Bendetson continued the reading of the Jacobson sermon. "Though a man dwells a solitary Jew in some rural hamlet," he read, "he will find the temple this night. Wondrous event is this annual Rosh Hashanah conclave of Judaism!" The keynote of this day's message is translated to mean, "May you be written for a good year."[17]

ABERDEEN'S BETH ISRAEL CONGREGATION

There were three waves of Judaism in the Grays Harbor community in the first sixty years of the twentieth century, corresponding to the three generations of Jewish residents. In the late 1920s some of the San Francisco people returned to their former homes, while other Jewish families such as those of Ed Reiner, Lou and Cyrus Goldberg, Solie Ringold, and Harry and Ben Matzkind arrived.[18]

In 1930, according to Joel Wolff, "a kind of compromise group—it was definitely Orthodox—built a schul called Beth Israel Synagogue.[19] On February 23, 1930, a Sunday afternoon, members of the congregation gathered at the Eagles Hall, then proceeded to the site of the almost finished building at the corner of Aberdeen Avenue and Division Street to place the Synagogue stone. In a formal ceremony, George J. Wolff wielded the trowel and Rabbi Koch of Seattle delivered a brief address. Many people gathered around to see the stone embedded in the wall of this singular building, the "only edifice of its kind for Hebrew worshipers between Tacoma and Portland."[20]

The Beth Israel Synagogue was constructed at a cost of $5,000 and was ready for use in late March 1930. A formal photograph commemorated its completion. Some sixty men, women, and children stood in front of the unlandscaped building. The simple clapboard building enclosed a single room dominated by three tall, arched windows, each rising to an embedded Star of David.

The small Orthodox congregation had joined with the Conservative group, and because they were less affluent and found it difficult to support the synagogue's mortgage, soon reached out to include the Reform congregation. The synagogue provided a hall for services and the Jewish Sunday school, and was used continuously until it was replaced by a more modern synagogue in 1960.

The combined congregation struggled to hold together three groups with different approaches, backgrounds, and appreciations of what it was to be Jewish. A board of trustees' meeting could spend several hours discussing arrangements for the New Year's service, whether to use the Hebrew Union prayer book, whether to wear yarmulkes, and whether to conduct the service in English or Hebrew. During these years of the formation of the Aberdeen synagogue, Karl Bendetson attended services for the high holy days just before going back to college in the fall.

Though Karl's older sister Selma attended the University of Washington in Seattle, Karl chose Leland Stanford Jr. University (as it was then called), in Palo Alto, California. As his friend Jack Clark had four years earlier, Karl left Aberdeen by train in the fall of 1925 to enroll at Stanford. As an undergraduate Karl studied political science and was active in the Reserve Officer's Training Corps. After trying out for track, where he found himself "running with low class athletes," he gave that up and got to be a junior manager on the football team.[21] During the summers of 1926 and 1927 he worked in the newsroom at the *Aberdeen Daily World*. The former managing editor, Harold Olson recalled: "I thought he was very able . . . very intelligent. I was sure he'd go places."[22]

While at Stanford, Bendetson wrote to his mother daily. Letters to his father were addressed to "Dear Governor." When he was going into the hospital to have his appendix removed he feared his mother would be too worried, so he prepared letters ahead of time that his roommate could mail each day. He didn't tell her about it until afterward.[23]

Five years after Al Bendetson read the sermon for the high holy days in Aberdeen, it was Karl's turn. In September 1928, before returning to college, Karl delivered the sermon at the Saturday morning New Year's service for the Grays Harbor Reform Congregation, perhaps reading the same Jacobson sermon. That sermon closed with the thought, "could my words materialize into powers to control fortune . . . could they enforce their bidding upon the angels of life and death . . . every one of you would be rich, famous, successful, happy. . . . But it is God's wisdom with whom the future is. He will deal out what is best for each of you. May what He ordains for you be even as you pray for. Amen." Karl then returned to Stanford University for his senior year, the year in which, in order to join a fraternity, he denied that he was a Jew.

"I'm quite sure this is a true story," said an admirer, a woman whom he dated just after college.[24] "He had pledged a fraternity and was about to be initiated. He had his pin. Then they discovered he was Jewish, and they were going to take away his pin. Well, my sorority didn't pledge Jews either—at that time people were prejudiced."

"He took it to the [fraternity's] National and won," she recalled.[25] Whatever letter he may have written protesting the fraternity's threat to bar his acceptance has not survived. His name appears in the roster of Theta Delta Chi in the Stanford yearbook of 1927, and not again until the 1931 and 1932 yearbooks. According to records in the fraternity's national office, he was initiated into the Eta Deuteron (Stanford) Charge of Theta Delta Chi on April 6, 1930. By then he was a first-year law student.[26]

Some years later a prominent Aberdeen attorney and acquaintance was asked by the FBI to provide a character reference for Bendetsen. She recalled that "Bendetson's family were lovely Jewish people." She gave her assessment of his years in Aberdeen: "He was somewhat ashamed of being of Jewish faith and wanted to be like everyone else. He even managed to join a non-Jewish fraternity at Stanford University."[27]

It is not possible to overestimate the value to Bendetson of an association with a mainstream (non-Jewish) fraternity. For a young man with ambitions, that tag on his resumé would forever refute any rumor of a different past. Being a member of an organization known to discriminate could open doors that would otherwise be closed.[28]

The stock market crashed in November 1929. Though Aberdeen experienced economic decline ahead of the rest of the country, Albert Bendetson's clothing business endured—loggers had to have heavy clothes and blankets to survive the rigors of wet weather in Grays Harbor's woods, and city folk needed clothes, even in a depression. While many other young people had to give up college, Karl continued at Stanford and in 1932 received his law degree. Perhaps because others had done so, perhaps because of the economic uncertainties caused by the Depression, perhaps because he felt strong ties to his supportive parents, Karl would return to Aberdeen to start his career as a lawyer.

SETTING THE STAGE

After some seven years practicing law in Aberdeen, Karl Bendetson described his hometown to a fellow lawyer: "Grays Harbor is a strange and wonderful community in many respects, particularly in its complex business relationships. In that field it seems to be one big family, but not a very happy one. Everyone seems to know about the others' business. If he doesn't he soon contrives to find out about it."[29]

Aberdeen's business community depended on timber. The 1920s had been boom years for Grays Harbor lumbering. In 1926, a year after Karl graduated from high school, some forty sawmills were running at full capacity and produced 1.5 billion board feet of logs and lumber, enough lumber to build approximately a hundred thousand three-bedroom homes. The annual cut for Grays Harbor was above 1.3 billion board feet for each of the six years from 1924 to 1929.[30]

This frenzy of production and the prosperity that came with it had had its effect on the town. Prior to the stock market crash, everyone, even the shoeshine boy, was playing the stock market, and Aberdeen boasted dozens of timber millionaires.[31] A decline in timber harvests coincided with the market crash. People began to wonder how long the forests would last. In the 1930s nine major sawmills closed and tore down their mills, leaving waterfront sites studded with snags of rotting piling. Companies abandoned their logged-out land to the county, with taxes unpaid. Logging crews worked farther and farther inland, on ever-steeper land. The excesses of the 1920s had "pushed back the timberline and far outstripped nature's ability to keep pace with new growth."[32] The concepts of sustained-yield logging and tree farming were a decade away.

As it did in the rest of the United States, the economic collapse brought labor unrest to Grays Harbor. While Karl Bendetson was attending Stanford as an undergraduate, his high school classmate Robert Cantwell dropped out of college after his father's death and got a job in a plywood factory in Hoquiam. Though Cantwell enjoyed his job as a veneer clipper, he observed how workers were treated and how they felt, and he wrote about it. Cantwell's first novel, *The Land of Plenty*, described a violent confrontation between workers and mill owners similar to those that would actually occur in Grays Harbor and the Northwest in the next few years, with workers often seizing and occupying plants. This influential book, considered an important novel about "class battles of the 1930s," has Cantwell's working-class protagonist win out over "material corruption and fleshly temptation" without destroying American society.[33] Cantwell went on to a distinguished career as an author and journalist.

The Aberdeen that Karl returned to in 1932 was greatly changed from the one he had left in the fall of 1925—it was strangely quiet and the streets were often empty of cars. The remaining mills ran intermittently, the demand for logs was declining, and unemployment was high. The presidential campaign of 1932 pitted Franklin D. Roosevelt against incumbent Herbert Hoover, and the decline in the economy was the issue in the campaign. Shack towns of homeless were called Hoovervilles, and Roosevelt pledged himself to "a new deal for the American people." Roosevelt won with a popular plurality of seven million votes.[34]

After graduation from law school, Bendetson had returned to live with his parents in one of the Roosevelt Apartments, Aberdeen's nicest.[35] During the next two years he studied for the bar exams and worked in the law office of W. H. Abel of Montesano.[36] He dated a popular junior high school teacher, Barbara Tucker.[37] One of the woman's junior high students, Perry Saito's friend Frank Iskra, recalled the class's teasing her about her boyfriend, who impressed the students as good-looking, a "somebody" they noticed and admired.[38]

In 1934 Karl was admitted to the Washington bar. He briefly worked in the office of Clark Adams, a well-established Aberdeen lawyer. Soon he hired a secretary and moved to a fifth-floor office in the Finch Building looking out at Heron Street and the Chehalis River as it turned west.[39] His clients included lumbermen Ed Morley, E. K. Bishop, and Vic Morrison, and William Rosenkrantz, a dealer in mill and logging machinery. Like most lawyers on the Harbor, he took the work that came along—estates, divorces, and property settlements. On Fridays he went to the county courthouse in Montesano to file for recording or to submit motions.

Mary Birdwell, who was the county auditor for many years, recalled him as "very attractive. . . . Always kept himself so neat and clean." She would see him there almost every Friday. "I think everyone in the court house admired him because he was so young and active."[40]

At Morley's suggestion Bendetson joined the Washington State Taxpayer's Association, a conservative group that studied taxes and government and favored "keeping the cost of government within the paying ability of the people governed." He soon became a counsel and trustee for that organization, representing Grays Harbor County.

Important aspects of his Aberdeen upbringing were his loyalty to the town's Jewish congregation as long as his father lived in Aberdeen, and the friendships he established, including those with Joel Wolff, manager of the largest department store in Aberdeen; newspaperman Jack Clark; and lumberman Charles (Chub) Middleton.

When his parents retired and moved to Los Angeles in 1936, Karl took a room in the Elks Club, conveniently located in the center of the downtown. In March 1938 he married his secretary, Billie Jane McIntosh (a Gentile), in a civil ceremony at the county courthouse in Montesano. The couple took a two-week trip, visiting his parents in Southern California, and then set up housekeeping in the Roosevelt Apartments.[41]

Clark Adams practiced law in Aberdeen for fifty years, and once described the legal business in Aberdeen: "The work could be very routine and uninteresting. But every once in a while a case comes along that makes it all worthwhile."[42] For Karl that case came in the spring of 1939. Aberdeen taxpayer John Bayha brought suit against the brand-new Public Utility District (PUD), challenging the right of the entity to buy property and issue bonds without public input or approval. Karl Bendetson became Bayha's lawyer and the suit was supported by the Washington State Taxpayers' Association. Bendetson, along with Seattle lawyer Ernest Skeel and the City of Aberdeen, took the case to court. The local papers noted: "The largest array of legal talent to be assembled in any Grays Harbor court in recent years will take part in the case."[43]

The local court decided in their favor and continued the injunction preventing the PUD's purchase of the Grays Harbor Railway and Light Company. The suit had not opposed the principle of public power, only the "high-handed, secretive and high-priced approach" that the local commissioners had taken.[44] The PUD appealed. In August, Karl argued a similar taxpayer case against the Public Utility District in Skamania County, a little-populated county east of Vancouver along the Columbia River, with the same lawyers from Seattle, and was part of the team of lawyers who argued the appeals.

In addition to his law practice, Karl and his friend Chub Middleton had acquired an income property called the Electric Building at a bankruptcy sale. Located at Broadway and Heron near the Elk's Club, it was on what was at that time one of Aberdeen's best downtown corners.

Bendetson's life in Aberdeen must have seemed settled and peaceful in contrast with the struggles in Europe. Months after the takeover of Austria, and the Munich agreement, Germany had overrun Czechoslovakia, and, in September 1939 attacked Poland. England and France were at war with Germany and it could only be a question of time before the United States would be forced to get involved. Gray clouds and wind-driven rain dominated the Harbor's weather in late December 1939.

Across Broadway from the Elk's Club in the center of town, Joel Wolff's office had a panoramic view of two floors of Wolff's, his department store. As with most Aberdeen merchants, his Christmas revenues had been surprisingly strong, in spite of weeks of gales and worry about the future. The holiday shopping season had been longer because President Roosevelt had moved the Thanksgiving holiday up a week. There had been a flurry of ladies trying on evening gowns to wear to the annual dancing party given by Mr. and Mrs. Clark Adams at the Grays Harbor Country Club; at that party Wolff saw many matrons wearing New York styles that he had selected. The festive spirit encouraged everyone to believe that good times might lie ahead in spite of the news from Europe. Wolff and his mother corresponded with relatives still in Germany, Jews who were targets of Hitler's anti-Semitic laws. They had sent clothing and money to sponsor a distant cousin and her husband, who would be grateful to escape.

A few blocks away, Jack Clark was writing the year-end editorial for his weekly newspaper, the *Grays Harbor Post*. He summarized the hectic year that had begun with labor disputes that idled sawmills and logging camps, and local union leaders' espousing mass struggle and the destruction of private ownership.[45] The year ended with an anti-Communist riot at the Red Finn Hall set off by news of Russian atrocities in Finland, which earned Aberdeen a spot in *Life* magazine.[46] In editorials during this year he had lamented Hitler's easy conquest of Poland and had tried to take the temperature of world. He was not optimistic about peace.

From his office at the foot of Broadway, Chub Middleton supervised his family's logging operations and helped run the huge Anderson Middleton sawmill, which sprawled along the docks on the main channel of the Chehalis River. A bear of a man and an avid hunter, Chub Middleton was continuing the lumbering tradition of his father and grandfathers, who had come to Grays Harbor from the woods of Greenville, Michigan, at the turn of the century and bought one of the best mills in Aberdeen.

Like many young men of the time, Chub Middleton was fascinated by shortwave radio. Jack Clark, Karl Bendetson, and lumberman Herman Hobi often met in the evening in the Middleton garage where Chub kept his radio equipment. While their wives played bridge or helped raise money for the Children's Orthopedic Hospital in Seattle, they rearranged the antennae on Chub's large back lot on the top of Bel Aire hill, swapped out vacuum tubes, decoded Morse code messages and, after dark, talked with people all over the world. Mostly they heard about the war in Europe.

These young men looked after each other. One night in March 1939, Jack Clark and Chub Middleton participated in the mass meeting of business leaders who hoped to solve the problems in the lumber industry. Most of the mills were shut down because of jurisdictional disputes.[47] Union representatives and workers were invited to the meeting only as observers. Resentments were high and violence was always a possibility. Middleton's wife and children were alone in the house on the hill, their son remembered, when "there was a knock at the door."[48] Karl Bendetson, looking smart in his full Army Reserve uniform, complete with side arm, stood on Helen Middleton's doorstep. Just happened to be passing by after a Reserve meeting, he had said, and thought he might like to see the new radio. He sat visiting until Chub arrived home safely.

Meanwhile, down at the Elk's Club, Jack Clark and Hoquiam publisher Russell V. Mack (who in 1947 became Republican congressman for the district) headed the meeting that Middleton was attending and did a masterful job, Joel Wolff recalled, by "getting people respecting each other again and talking."[49] After emotional outbursts and many tirades and speeches, the businessmen passed ten resolutions directed to Congress, local management, and local labor. They asked Congress for tariff protection for the lumber industry, quotas against importation of Canadian shingles, and an embargo on export of "peeler" logs (used to make plywood).

They exhorted management and labor to "get together." They asked that organized labor "put its house in order," urged that they remove "the red element," and force the elimination of jurisdictional disputes."[50] Because the businessmen thought that Harry Bridges, the radical leader of West Coast longshoremen, was the source of Communist influences, they added an eleventh resolution urging his deportation.[51] That first meeting in the lodge room at the Elks Club resulted in a permanent organization of Aberdeen's business and professional people, called the Business Builders. By December 1939 the group boasted two thousand members who hoped to mobilize the "silent majority," and to influence workers to get rid of what many thought was a small, vocal set of radical leaders.

As Clark wrote at the time: "Grays Harbor some years ago was one of the really bright spots on the Pacific slope, with a happy, industrious population. Today we're somewhat below average, but worse than that, outsiders speak of our community as 'Little Russia.' From now on the citizens of Grays Harbor are fighting mad and intend to stay that way until the causes for the 'red label' are removed. A quarter of a century ago good red-blooded men of Grays Harbor took drastic action to clean out the IWWs, who had kept up continual disturbances.[52] If the sincere working men of Grays Harbor can regain control of their own unions, similar action will not be necessary now."[53]

When the Weatherwax High School class was ready to graduate that June, Bendetson was invited to present the Class of 1925 Award to one of the 267 graduates. At the ceremony, the principal presented the Honor Society awards, one of which went to Perry Saito, who was senior class treasurer. A faculty speaker warned that the "present unsettled labor and peace conditions presented a challenge to the graduates of today." The class speaker, Kenneth Price, said, "The youth of today realize the problems confronting them and are determined to conquer them," and declared "world peace [is] desired by all." Bendetson presented the award to Jack Kearney, and the school's prizewinning band, in which Saito played clarinet, rendered Elgar's "Pomp and Circumstance" march.

After finishing his busy court schedule, Bendetson and his wife planned to visit the California World's Fair. The coast enjoyed a dry and pleasant summer brought on by unusually warm air from the onshore Japanese current.

In late December, the state supreme court found against Karl's client, the local taxpayer, and the taxpayer's organization, and in favor of the PUD. Jack Clark wrote about the lost case, noting that the court's findings did clarify parts of the public power law. However, he wrote, "No good is to be gained by further opposition to establishment of the [Public Utility] District."[54]

In his interactions with officers at Fort Lewis during his training stints there, Karl Bendetson became friends with Lieutenant Colonel Harry Auer, judge advocate of the Third United States Army Division. Bendetson said he had listened to many entreaties from Lieutenant Colonel Auer that he should join him in the judge advocate general's department. Though he was close to retirement in 1940, Auer made full colonel and was sent to Washington, D.C., as assistant judge advocate general of the army under Major General Allen W. Gullion.[55] Years later, Karl claimed that he had told Colonel Auer that he didn't want to be on the judge advocate general's staff, saying, "If I'm going to practice law, I would rather go back to my office" in Aberdeen.[56] However, in correspondence in 1941, describing the extensive effort needed to gain appointment to the judge advocate general (JAG) section, Bendetson implied that he had clearly sought the post, and had "no regrets."[57] On December 12, 1939, he accepted promotion to reserve captain in the army's JAG.[58]

In late January 1940 Bendetson and his wife took what he said was a vacation, traveling to New York and Washington, D.C., "to visit friends."[59] He claimed he visited his congressman to lobby for increased appropriations for the army and for enactment of an unprecedented peacetime draft law. What he actually did was go on duty as a reserve officer for five weeks in the judge advocate general's office at the War Department.

Karl and Billie returned to Aberdeen in late February 1940, but only to put his affairs in order. Karl had accepted an appointment in the JAG section of the regular army. Uncertain about how long he would be away, he formed a partnership with J. E. (Jack) Stewart to protect his law practice. He let Jack Clark and Chub Middleton know of his army plans. In a news story, Clark wrote, "Captain Bendetson's appointment to the legal staff of the Army is being regarded by his friends and associates as a flattering recognition of his success in private practice, coupled with his active interest in Army reserve work. . . . Those familiar with the Judge Advocate General's department of the Army consider Captain Bendetson's selection a distinct honor. There are approximately a thousand applicants for [an] assignment to this department of the Army, and to be offered the appointment over the many applicants may well be considered a recognition of ability."[60]

Memories of Bendetson still linger in Aberdeen. He had "an eminent presence," said Jim Middleton, Chub's son. "Karl had a sharp mind. He didn't let anything stand in his way, he knew who to be nice to. When there was something to be done, he got it done," said one observer, capturing the feelings of many.[61]

DRESS REHEARSAL

In May 1940, Bendetson first reported to the headquarters of the Ninth Corps area at the Presidio of San Francisco as news came of the fall of France and the remarkable cross-channel rescue of 245,000 British troops from Dunkirk.[62] He immediately received the order to report to the army JAG in Washington, D.C. He would serve for almost two years as a colleague of Colonel Auer, and the correspondence between these two men during the war would provide insight into Bendetson's ambitions and his sense of his role in the forthcoming evacuation decision.

At the War Department in Washington, D.C., Bendetson discovered that he was the lowest ranking officer on the staff and said later he sometimes felt like an errand boy. He was assigned to the Military Affairs Section of the JAG, which he described as the attorney general's office of the army. "It did not deal with military justice subjects," but rather dealt with broad legal questions: international law, civil functions of the Engineer Corps, administrative law, and the status of army personnel stationed offshore and abroad, for example. Barely thirty-two, and new to Washington, he was set to work as an army lawyer practicing law, preparing and commenting on briefs for Colonel Fred Llewellyn, chief of military affairs. His desk was in the eighth wing of the third floor of the crowded Munitions Building that housed parts of the War Department prior to completion of the Pentagon. He described the neighboring military justice section as "beginning to look like an Elks convention"—desks added everywhere, officers having to thread their way through chairs, spittoons, and desks to get to the hallway at quitting time. He described his workload to a fellow officer who had been moved to the Bermuda Base Command: "We are really snowed under. I believe we are on an average output of more than twelve pieces per day and there are usually at least 50 or 75 cases in the section at all times."[63]

As had happened in Aberdeen, he soon found a case that would attract attention to himself. Legislation similar to that enacted during World War I was going to be needed again, given that men's lives were likely to be disrupted due to the draft and to the activation of reserve units. He drafted and presented to the Bureau of the Budget a bill called the Soldiers' and Sailors' Civil Relief Act. The bill dealt with various kinds of civil actions brought against draftees for debt or mortgage foreclosures or problems of domestic relations. He then defended the legislation before ten individual congressional committees, wrote an article for the *Washington and Lee Law Review*, and spoke before special groups to explain the legislation.

Bendetson claimed that he met then Senator Harry S Truman during this time. Truman was making a name for himself as a member of the Military Affairs Committee of the Senate. Bendetson reported that Truman was interested not only in preparedness but also in protection of draftees and their families, and asked "very intelligent and penetrating questions."[64] His positive association with Truman in these prewar years apparently served him well during Truman's presidency.

Among the officers that Bendetson worked with was then assistant chief of staff of the army, Brigadier General Wade Hampton Haislip, who dealt with many legislative problems. He often insisted that Bendetson, who by then "could recite from memory every line of the National Defense Act and its amendments," should accompany him on appearances before congressional committees.[65]

Anticipating war, the army recreated the office of provost marshal general, with Major General Allen W. Gullion in charge. In April 1941 Bendetson was promoted to major and became Gullion's assistant. In August 1941, when the Selective Service Act of 1940 was about to expire, the War Department's congressional liaison officer, Colonel Wilton B. (Jerry) Persons, asked for Bendetson's help in supporting passage of a reauthorization of the draft. The Senate had passed the extension of the draft, but there was strong opposition in the House.[66] Bendetson claimed that he and Persons practically "'lived' eighteen hours a day on Capitol Hill." The final vote was 203 to 202 in favor of continuing the peacetime draft.[67] The draft bill was approved on August 12, 1941, just two months after the Japanese military, unbeknownst to the War Department, had set into motion the plan for the December surprise attack on the Philippines and Pearl Harbor.

Major Bendetson's travel orders in September took him to the army headquarters in the Territory of Hawaii to discuss the need to intern enemy aliens if there should be a war. He was in Hawaii from September 7–16, 1941. He studied military intelligence activities and inspected possible facilities for internment at the Kilauea Military Camp in the Hawaiian

National Park. It "was one of the pleasantest experiences of my life," he wrote to his army host; he said he hoped he would return, and to insure that he might return "carefully performed the ceremony of casting a lei upon the waters of Pearl Harbor."[68] He scribbled on his trip outline that there were 134,000 persons of dual Japanese/American citizenship in Hawaii, and the "Jap vote controls this very political island. Therefore good Americans who depend on Jap business and votes may give Japs benefit of the doubt."[69]

In November Bendetson traveled to Bendix, New Jersey. Before the trip, he had in his words, "conceived and drafted the executive order, prepared precise operating instructions for and took possession of Air Associates Plant, Bendix, N.J." This was his second such task. Earlier in the year he had drafted similar paperwork for the federal seizure of a North American Aviation plant. These army takeovers were approved by President Franklin D. Roosevelt in order to get strike-ridden plants back in operation to avoid slowdowns in airplane production. Though the United States was not at war, the passage of the lend-lease legislation in March 1941 allowed the country to ship arms, ammunition, surplus tanks, and ships to the British, who, after the fall of France, were alone in the war against Hitler's forces. America's defense industry was given ambitious production goals to replace the "loaned" equipment—to become what Roosevelt called the "Arsenal of Democracy."[70]

Bendetson dramatized the Bendix scene forty-two years later: He was in uniform, a young major sent to take over a manufacturing facility; no one met him at the Newark airport late that November evening.[71] "I got myself driven over to the plant. It was a big plant. . . . The strikers were massed outside the gate. They turned my car on its side. So I got out the side door, pulled myself out, got up on the top of the side, and announced to them that this [plant] was in the possession of the United States by order of President Roosevelt, and they should disband, or [laughs] they would be in serious trouble. And I'll be damned, they did!

"I told them [the strikers] . . . that they'd better disperse, that at 10 o'clock the next morning I would start hiring for the government."[72]

In actuality, according to a report in Bendetson's papers, Colonel Roy M. Jones, Army Air Corps, was ordered to obtain troops and take over the plant. The under secretary of war had "designated Major Bendetson as legal advisor to Col. Jones." The next morning Bendetson "reported by telephone that physical possession had been taken by Col. Jones at 2:00 A.M. on the 31st [of October 1941]." Hence the deed had most likely been done by the time Bendetson arrived.[73] The takeover did help settle the strike.[74] Bendetson was back at his desk in early December, and later, along with Colonel Jones, received a commendation for his effort.

What did not show up in Bendetson's records for this period was any evidence of a trip to the Philippines or Hawaii in the week prior to December 7, 1941, as he would claim years later.[75]

Bendetson was impressed by his superior, Major General Gullion, the provost marshal general, who "had been a Judge Advocate General, although he was a West Point graduate and he was an infantry officer who took law. He was absolutely charming, a splendid man of great intelligence and wit and humor and he knew Shakespeare forwards and backwards and he could recite any part from memory."[76]

During strategy meetings with leaders in the War Department, Bendetson met John J. McCloy, a Wall Street lawyer who became assistant secretary of war to Henry L. Stimson in 1941. Bendetson's work on the handling of aliens and prisoners of war required further association with McCloy, and with Under Secretary of War Robert P. Patterson, throughout 1941. His trip in September, in which he evaluated facilities for internment of enemy aliens, had included a stop at the Presidio of San Francisco, where he met the commanding general of the Western Defense Command, Lieutenant General John L. DeWitt.

Thus the stage was set for Major Karl R. Bendetson, a young lawyer capable of working long hours and of writing clear and decisive position papers, to step into a key role when the time came to evaluate the "Japanese question" in the weeks immediately following the devastating Japanese attack on Pearl Harbor.

Karl Bendetsen's grandparents Catherine (Crena) and Samuel Bendetson immigrated to the United States from Eastern Europe in 1869 with daughter Anna. They were photographed in Battle Creek, Michigan, in 1899 or 1900 surrounded by their children and four Netzorg grandchildren. Albert M. Bendetson reclines on the left holding a straw hat; his brother Arthur lies on the right. Anna Bentson, who is soon to be his wife, stands in the back row, right, beside her twin sister Lottie. In front of them is Anna Bendetson Netzorg, with her husband on her right and son Bendetson on her left. One of the young women standing on the left, Dora Bendetson, married a Netzorg cousin. (Courtesy of Beverly Freedman)

At one year, Karl poses with his parents Albert M. and Anna Bendetson, and sister Selma, age five. Aberdeen, 1908. (Courtesy of Beverly Freedman)

Joel Wolff, left, and Karl Bendetson stand in front of the army recruiter's office on Heron Street in Aberdeen on July 4, 1918, waiting for the Fourth of July Parade to pass by. In later years Karl pretended not to know Joel, who was still proud of his Jewish heritage. (Courtesy of Ruth Wolff)

Troops from the Loyal Legion marched down Aberdeen's Heron Street in the Fourth of July parade in 1918. This "spruce division" was sent to the lumber camps to help settle strikes that succeeded in restricting the workday to eight hours. (Courtesy of Bronco Tesia)

The Fourth of July parade, 1918, passed A. M. Bendetson's Red Front store (in the background, sign illegible) on Heron Street. Many immigrant groups carried banners declaring their loyalty to the United States. This same day Ransaku and Natsu Saito marched in Medford, Oregon's Fourth of July parade. (Courtesy of Bronco Tesia)

Cedar logs waiting on the dock at the Port of Grays Harbor, Aberdeen, Washington. In the late 1920s, steam-powered ships helped transport Grays Harbor's annual output of a billion board feet of logs and lumber, a level of production never again achieved. (Courtesy of Bronco Tesia)

At Weatherwax High School in Aberdeen, Karl Bendetson was active in many organizations, including debate and the school newspaper and yearbook. He also played the piano for the Blue and Gold Melody Men. He is shown here as a senior in 1925 with the Boys' Chorus, on the far right in the front row. Author's father Kearny Clark sits directly behind him. (Author's collection)

While an undergraduate at Stanford University, Bendetson spent the summer of 1928 as an intern in the newsroom of the *Aberdeen Daily World*. (Courtesy of *Daily World*, Aberdeen)

Heron Street at I Street in Aberdeen, a week before the stock market crash in 1929. In the next few years, Mrs. Saito moved her store next to the Aberdeen Drug Co. (right, run by author's grandfather), and Bendetson opened a law office in the Finch Building, the tallest building in the same block. (Jones Photo, Aberdeen)

Karl Bendetson married Billie Jean McIntosh in March 1938. They are shown in front of the court-house in Montesano, Washington. (Courtesy of Beverly Freedman)

Caption from the *Daily World*: "Aberdeen haberdasher Albert M. Bendetson, looking appropriately natty, poses outside his home at 209 W. 5th Street with his new 1936 Buick [$1,995] purchased from M. M. Stewart." (Jones Photo Co., Aberdeen)

PART II

THE JAPANESE QUESTION

CHAPTER FOUR

Specters of Fear

It is not necessary to imitate Hitler by herding whole populations, the guilty and the innocent together, into even humane concentration camps.
—*San Francisco Chronicle*, February 1, 1942, in Grodzins, *Americans Betrayed*

December 7, 1941, dawned peacefully on the island of Oahu, Hawaii. Much of the United States fleet was at anchor and on "weekend" status at the Pearl Harbor naval base. Fighter aircraft were neatly lined up on the ground at Hickam Field in order to guard them from sabotage. When the attack began, an Aberdeen woman who happened to be visiting in Honolulu observed the action from the roof of a tall hotel; she thought she was seeing a demonstration of formation flying and was horrified when the bombs began to fall. She wrote home that the army and navy hoped the Japanese planes would come back: "They are burned up and itching for a chance to even the score."[1]

The attack was devastating. More than half the airplanes at Hickam Field were destroyed on the ground. Eight battleships, three cruisers, and three destroyers were damaged, several beyond repair. A total of 3,500 lives were lost. A shocked America knew only that it was at war.

Blackouts were immediately ordered on the West Coast, and divisions of infantry were sent to defend the beaches, harbors, bridges, and other strategic points. An improvised fleet of yachts, boats, and ships of all kinds rallied to stand offshore to guard against submarines. At the request of President Franklin D. Roosevelt, Congress declared war against Japan the following day, and by the end of the week Italy and Germany had joined the war as allies of Japan. Even before the war declaration, the FBI began arresting "enemy alien" Japanese who had been identified as possible security risks prior to the initiation of hostilities; they went on to arrest previously identified Italian and German aliens soon after.

As it would in towns all across America, the "Our Boys in Uniform" articles in the *Grays Harbor Post* got longer every week. Some reserve units had already been sent to the Aleutians and Greenland. Bendetsen's Aberdeen friends were scattered. Jack Clark, now a Marine Corps captain, was in the Philippines guarding the Cavite Navy Yard in Manila Bay. Ben Weatherwax was stationed in Hawaii. Chub Middleton was preparing to sign up.

Bendetsen was a loyal friend. Concern for his friend Jack Clark and others who were destined to fall into the hands of Japanese forces would loom large in his thinking and perhaps influence his view of "the Japanese question" that he soon would have to consider.[2] Admiration for Chub, and possibly some envy of the Middleton wealth and power, would inspire him to help Middleton get a safe post in the Western Defense Command in the Presidio of San Francisco. And later Karl Bendetsen would adopt, or borrow as his own, Middleton's ancestral history, claiming a long line of English or Danish lumbering men in place of his Jewish forebears.

The attack on Pearl Harbor by Japanese forces and rumors of Japanese ships and submarines roaming the West Coast generated great panic in West Coast residents, particularly those of Grays Harbor. Many in Aberdeen felt that they had already read about this war and they were sure that the Japanese would attack the mainland on Grays Harbor's beaches. They were not imagining this! Such an attack was predicted thirty years earlier by Homer Lea, an eccentric but remarkable young man who had set himself up as a military expert and adviser to Chinese revolutionaries, including Dr. Sun Yat-sen. As the smoke cleared over Pearl Harbor, copies of his prophetic 1909 book, *The Valor of Ignorance*, were unearthed from many a Harborite's dusty bookshelves.

Homer Lea, a "hunchback dwarf" with "an obsession for militarism and war" considered himself to be the "reincarnation of a great historic Chinese warrior called the 'Martial Monk.'"[3] After misadventures in China and Japan, and self-aggrandizing leadership of a Chinese reform movement in this country, Lea wrote his first serious volume, *The Valor of Ignorance*. In florid prose, he developed his theory that Japan was intent on military expansion and that the United States would not be prepared to resist. He predicted that Japan would first "knock out" Manila and Hawaii. Then it would be free to attack America's West Coast (and would do so without first making a formal declaration of war). He noted, "In a military sense Japan is one-third closer to Washington, Oregon and California than [is] the military power of the United States" and "in the debarkation of [Japan's] first expedition [she will select a] . . . landing . . . in

Gray's and Willapa Harbors."[4] He further asserted that the United States, because of what he called its naive preference for peace, would be powerless to defend itself. Using maps and tables, he documented the utter defenselessness that he had observed during his travels on the Pacific Coast in 1907 and 1908.

The book caused a mild furor. International peace movements condemned it. Dr. David Star Jordan, president of Stanford University, a leading pacifist and critical observer of his former student Lea, declared the book worthless. William Randolph Hearst, publisher of numerous newspapers, seized on the book, distorted its thesis to feed growing anti-Asian sentiment, and launched the "Yellow Peril."[5] He planted the fear that Lea's "Jap-American war" would break out in months.[6] Hearst was wrong by thirty years, and Lea was maddeningly right about Japan's military ambitions.

Although *The Valor of Ignorance* went out of print in the United States, it became a best-seller in Japan and a required text for all officers in Japan's armed forces, who declared it "excellent reading matter for all Oriental men with red blood in their veins"—thereby giving the book a means to fulfill its prophesies.[7]

Writing in 1909, Lea asserted that if Japan were to conquer the Philippines and Hawaii, it would then be in a position to attack the Pacific Coast of the United States. Noting the closeness of the Pacific Northwest to Japan, he claimed that the best possible landing place for the Japanese would be Grays Harbor and the beaches north of it from Copalis to Moclips, just twenty-five miles west of Aberdeen. "From there, the invaders would concentrate on the Centralia-Chehalis area (forty-five miles inland), and throw one flank toward the [Puget] Sound and the other to Portland." He went on to describe the takeover of the entire West Coast, which he noted was isolated from the rest of the United States by the natural barriers of deserts and mountains.

In December 1941 Lea's prognoses took on new weight. His prediction of a Japanese attack at Lingayen Gulf on the island of Luzon in the Philippines had proven highly accurate. General Douglas MacArthur, commanding general of the Far East Command, had not expected a Japanese attack until the spring of 1942. In pre–Pearl Harbor staff conferences at MacArthur's Manila headquarters, officers were said to have studied Lea's "invasion map" of the Philippines, and his chief officers later called Lea "clairvoyant to the point of specifying the precise bays and beaches the Japanese would use to debark their troops."[8] By Christmas 1941, the

American and Philippine armies had abandoned Manila to Japanese forces and were retreating to the Bataan Peninsula. They appeared to be fighting a losing battle, just as Lea had foretold.

Residents of Grays Harbor remembered with anxiety Lea's recommendation that their coastline and harbor should be fortified. There was small comfort in the knowledge that several army units had been rushed to the beaches the day after Pearl Harbor. The army's primitive equipment—old mobile canons and the few tanks and guns that had convoyed through Aberdeen—had not looked promising. Japan had attacked Pearl Harbor with modern carrier-based planes and effective torpedo bombers. There seemed good reason to fear a Japanese attack.

"Were people afraid? Hell yes. We were waiting for the Japanese to come in like a wave of ants," said an Aberdeen attorney.[9] Bendetsen's sister-in-law Marilyn McIntosh, then living in Hoquiam, recalled, "Everyone was scared to death the Japs were going to come right on over here and bomb the coast. . . . Pearl Harbor was just such an awful shock."[10]

Washington, December 7, 1941

The nation's capital was enjoying a late autumn Sunday. President Roosevelt was lunching quietly in the White House with his aide, Harry Hopkins. General George C. Marshall was enjoying his Sunday morning horseback ride, touring the site across the Potomac from the Jefferson Memorial where the War Department's new building, the Pentagon, was under construction. The Japanese ambassador was expected to meet with Secretary of State Cordell Hull at 1:00 P.M. Many War Department officers and newspapermen were attending a Washington Redskin's football game. Most Americans would long remember what they were doing when they heard the news of the Pearl Harbor attack.[11]

Bendetsen and his wife were attending a luncheon when news came that the War Department was going on alert.[12] It is likely that Bendetsen drove his wife back to their home on Hesketh Street in Bethesda, Maryland, in their new Buick convertible and then went on to the Munitions building.

Caught in the East at the outbreak of war, Bendetsen's friend Harry Spence, manager of Aberdeen's Radio Station KXRO and a director of the National Association of Broadcasters, observed that people were immediately alarmed, fearing that Germany would strike simultaneously with Japan. On Pearl Harbor Sunday there was pandemonium in New York City for a time as preparations were made for the blackout. Returning to

Washington, D.C., Spence observed the transition in the nation's capital from the peaceful, busy city it had been the previous Friday, to a town bristling with a military presence and heavily guarded government buildings; he was required to show identification everywhere he went. In one day, the capital had gone to war.[13]

News of the Japanese attack "struck with stunning force" in the Munitions Building.[14] Like Bendetsen, many felt outrage and disbelief that the United States forces in the Pacific had been caught on "weekend" status, and were angered at the destruction and loss of life.

On Bendetsen's desk were plans that had been worked out in detail in recent months for compliance with the Geneva Convention as it applied to prisoners of war and the treatment of enemy aliens who were thought to be dangerous, or potentially dangerous, in a wartime situation. He had presented and discussed these plans with the senior commanders at Hawaii's Fort Shafter in September as part of his assignment as chief of aliens. Now he would put the plans into action. At General Gullion's request, Bendetsen had drafted an executive order that would move full responsibility for control of enemy aliens from the Justice Department to the War Department, but Gullion decided to wait until Justice had been given a chance to act.[15]

Some of the aliens referred to in prewar planning were those found to be in the United States inadvertently, such as the crews of foreign ships. The early arrests were confined to resident aliens who had been watched for years and identified by the FBI as potentially dangerous. The leaders of Japanese organizations and communities were placed in this category, as well as persons, like Mrs. Saito, who "trafficked" with Japanese nationals (because she had sold provisions to Japanese ships that stopped in Aberdeen). Some German and Italian aliens were also arrested. It was not until later that all persons of Japanese ancestry became suspect.

It was another forty-eight hours before Karl Bendetsen went home to sleep. His prided ability to work long hours and stay up for several days and nights would be useful and sorely tested in the next months.

San Francisco, California

When the war began, Lieutenant General John L. DeWitt was commanding general of the Western Defense Command and the Fourth Army at the Presidio of San Francisco. Largely experienced as an officer in the quartermaster corps, he had years earlier briefly studied the problem now confronting him. As assistant chief of staff in the War Planning Department, then Colonel DeWitt had laid out the plans for the "defense of Oahu" should the United States find itself at war with Japan, which many army planners, even in the twenties, considered to be inevitable.

The plan detailed by DeWitt in 1923 envisioned the internment of enemy aliens. In order to handle the island of Oahu's civilian population, DeWitt's plan called for a proclamation of martial law; registration of all enemy aliens; internment of those deemed a security risk; and restrictions on labor, movement, and public information. He argued for martial law on the grounds of military necessity and for "the establishment of complete military control over the Hawaiian Islands, including its people, supplies, material, etc."[16]

DeWitt was now responsible for the defense of the Western Sea Frontier. In the first days after Pearl Harbor, while the editorial writers cautioned against panic and urged tolerance for law-abiding Japanese Americans, General DeWitt's staff gave out reports that Japanese planes had "reconnoitered the San Francisco Bay area and other sections of California." The reports, and all later "sightings," proved false. Major General Joseph W. Stilwell, who was then the corps commander in charge of Southern California, described the Presidio reaction to the false alarms as "kind of jittery" and criticized DeWitt's intelligence units as amateur and irresponsible. He thought worse of General DeWitt on December 13 when it appeared that he might declare a general alarm based on a rumor: "What jackass would send a general alarm . . . under the circumstances."[17]

When asked by a reporter if he had read Homer Lea, General DeWitt reached to a table nearby and held up a recently republished copy of *The Valor of Ignorance*. He had read it in 1909, and since then "had used it often" in his lectures. Asked about the war games of 1940, based on Monterey Bay and in western Washington (in Grays Harbor), he replied, "Let us just say that I had read Homer Lea before we planned the war games. . . . [Except for the effect of air power] Lea is still militarily sound."[18]

The newspaper also reported that General DeWitt "had the prime attributes of real leadership: the ability to take suggestions from others."

Aberdeen, Washington, December 7, 1941

Heron Street was quiet on a Sunday morning. The children had gone to church early to rehearse the Christmas program.

Mrs. Natsu Saito was almost ready to join them at the eleven o'clock service at the First Methodist church when news of the Japanese attack interrupted a song on the radio. One imagines her taking off her coat and hat and sitting down. She would have thought of her oldest son Lincoln who was in Japan.

Through the Japanese consulate in Seattle a month earlier, she had received a letter from Lincoln that was reported in the local paper: "Hoping there will be no war between the United States and Japan, Lincoln Saito, twenty-two-year-old former Aberdeen student, has decided to remain in Tokyo to pursue his studies for the ministry." Also quoted in the paper was Perry, who noted that his brother realized that "relations [were] strained" between the United States and Japan but hoped "that war [would] not come. Perry said that Lincoln was "very anxious to complete his studies at Presbyterian College in Tokyo and [had] decided to 'take his chances' on war in order to finish the course."[19] Natsu Saito must have wondered what would happen to him now.

She may then have walked through her small apartment to the doorway to the shop. It was the only Japanese import store on Grays Harbor and she and her children were the only Japanese in this West Coast port. Perhaps she picked up a duster from behind the counter, and began absently dusting salt and pepper shakers of a dozen different shapes. Her husband had had such hopes when they moved here. The town was big enough, the downtown was coming alive after the slow years of the depression. Japanese ships came to buy logs. Their buyers quickly found her husband to serve as interpreter, broker the sale and with his help, replenish their larders. Evenings when he and the buyers came back for tea or saki and talked for hours did she imagine being back in Japan? She did like the United States, she told anyone who asked.[20]

She may have wondered if the United States government would still remember that by acting as interpreter, she had helped authorities break up a ring that handled stowaways. That was several years ago.[21]

Aberdeen was home to her children. Morse and Dahlia were still in school and working hard. Perry graduated with honors two years before and had just transferred to the state college. He was what you called "popular," someone at church told her once. Did she recall the years when the boys brought their friends home to play billiards with their father, proud of his skill? That was before his sight had begun to fail.

An urn containing her husband's ashes stood on a table in a small alcove. Did she sigh as she set down the duster? Looking out through the glass storefront she could watch a few cars drive past. She put on her coat and hat and drove up the hill to church.

It had been calm in Aberdeen the previous week. Town matrons put on the annual Orthopedic Bazaar, a fund-raiser for the Seattle children's hospital. The Morck Hotel ballroom bustled with women selling puppies; tables were loaded with garden items, cake and cookies, candies, Christmas items, baby things, and a treasure chest for children.

Mrs. Arthur B. Langley, the governor's wife, was a guest at a Pro American tea at which a Civil War history by Margaret Leech, *Reveille in Washington,* was reviewed. The Presbyterian Church choir presented Handel's "Messiah." The Sunshine Kids' annual Christmas fund-raiser was under way, seeking to "make every Christmas a happy one." Nelson Eddy and Rise Stevens were appearing in the *Chocolate Soldier* at Warner Brothers Theatre.

The ferocious attack on Pearl Harbor broke the spell. In the editorial in the *Grays Harbor Post*, Kearny Clark wrote,

> WHEN BOMBS FELL ON HAWAII . . . the inevitable clash between two world powers was set grimly into motion. . . . The very nature of the lightning attack on Army and Navy bases in the [Hawaiian] islands, was Japanese. In carrying out their surprise attack on the apparently unguarded key of our Pacific defenses, the Japs only followed the course which they have pursued in every other war. In fighting, the Japs are fanatics. . . .
>
> The thing boils down to one fact. This is *our* war, and to win it *we're* going to have to do more than listen to the cheers of the boys in Washington, D.C., because Japan is no economic or military "pushover" as far as Uncle Sam is concerned.[22]

Civil defense leaders quickly organized neighborhood teams, householders contrived blackout curtains, and everyone looked westward anxiously.

Morse and Dahlia Saito went to school as usual in the days after Pearl Harbor. Dahlia, a sophomore, was a member of the glee club. Morse was in the last year of junior high. They didn't know what to expect. They were Americans; they knew that. Their names attested to that. Their immigrant father had been so pleased with his new country that he named his sons after Americans he admired: Abraham Lincoln; Commodore Matthew Perry, who induced the Japanese to open their ports to Western ships; and Samuel F. B. Morse, inventor of the telegraph. Dahlia, whose name recalled the courtship cartful of flowers, was called Dolly by her many friends.[23]

Two days after Pearl Harbor Sunday, at 1:15 P.M., two strangers in dark raincoats and hats walked across Heron Street, past Pete Nielsen's drugstore, into the Saito's Oriental Gift Shop. Nielsen's youngest daughter, a classmate of Morse Saito, watched from the safety of the druggist's doorway.[24] After some time, the men came out, one on each side of Mrs. Saito.[25] A small woman, she could be mistaken for a child in her Sunday best going on an outing with two uncles. She did not know where she was being taken, nor when she would get back. She left no note.

Major General Allen W. Gullion had groomed Major Karl R. Bendetsen for this moment. Bendetsen was a competent lawyer now versed in enemy alien law, and a westerner with contacts in the army's Presidio of San Francisco. He was an officer in the provost marshal general's office. He was just the right person to be sent to the command of Lieutenant General John L. DeWitt, a nonlawyer, to help the general understand his options in controlling enemy aliens. Bendetsen spent much time with DeWitt, a man who "often seemed to be the creature of the last strong personality with whom he had contact."[26]

In the weeks prior to the war, Bendetsen had collected opinions relating to the handling of enemy aliens during wartime. In August 1941 an assistant to the judge advocate general had asserted that "if the President finds that subversive alien influences operating in the Western Hemisphere threaten an invasion . . . he may lawfully use the Army to restrain aliens whose freedom of action is inimical to the national interests." This was a prerogative General Gullion, and his willing subordinate Major Bendetsen, hoped to take to its logical extreme.

Immediately after Pearl Harbor, President Roosevelt issued proclamations "declaring all nationals and subjects of nations with which we were at war to be enemy aliens."[27] These proclamations allowed the Justice Department to arrest "dangerous enemy aliens" and to confiscate enemy property declared contraband, as well as to declare prohibited zones from which enemy aliens could be excluded or allowed by permit only. The FBI began rounding up the aliens whom they had earlier identified as potentially dangerous to the United States. Those arrested were selected by the FBI from one of three lists of persons suspected of showing allegiance to the enemy. Called the "ABC lists," they included category "A," Japanese aliens who led cultural or assistance organizations, consular officials, and fishermen; category "B," slightly less suspicious aliens, and category "C," members of, or those who donated to ethnic (Japanese) groups, Japanese language teachers, and Buddhist clergy.[28] Similar lists led to the arrest of numbers of German and Italian aliens. For aliens, getting on the suspect list depended on one's status, rather than on having committed a subversive act. At the insistence of Attorney General Francis Biddle, the arrests were orderly; no citizens were to be apprehended without probable cause that a crime had been committed. By December 10, 1942, the FBI had in custody 1,291 Japanese, 847 Germans, and 147 Italians.[29] Otherwise, the Justice Department was slow to issue administrative regulations, directives, and instructions to allow local officials to implement the proclamations with regard to aliens, which soon put it in conflict with DeWitt.

On December 11, 1941, Army Chief of Staff General George C. Marshall declared the Western Defense Command a "Theater of Operations."[30] This declaration "created the legal fiction that the Coast was a war zone," which contributed to DeWitt's sensitivity to the presence of Japanese Americans in his command.[31]

In late December, DeWitt seemed to believe every rumor about an underground network of Japanese saboteurs and felt hampered by the Justice Department's failure to issue the necessary instructions to implement the president's proclamations referring to the Japanese and other aliens. From the provost marshal general's office in Washington, D.C., Bendetsen prodded the Justice Department and on Gullion's behalf frequently notified DeWitt of the impending promulgation of the desired regulations. DeWitt cabled back, "CANNOT OVEREMPHASIZE URGENCY FOR IMMEDIATE PROMULGATION [OF] THESE REGULATIONS STOP CONFISCATION OF ARMS RADIOS CAMERAS AND SO FORTH MUST NOT BE DELAYED LONGER . . . FURTHER DELAY PROLONGS DANGEROUS SITUATION."[32] Finally, on December 30, 1941, the attorney general authorized the issuance of warrants for search and arrest in any house in which an alien enemy lived (upon representation by any FBI agent that there was probable cause that contraband would be found on the premises), and Bendetsen set out by plane to San Francisco to support DeWitt in his conflicts with the Justice Department.

General Gullion hoped to press his own agenda on General DeWitt. He had already made a formal request, which was ignored by his superiors, to transfer the enemy alien program to the War Department, and he had telephoned DeWitt to urge that the West Coast commander recommend a mass roundup of alien and citizen Japanese.[33] On December 26, DeWitt, who had taken a similar stand on December 19, was eloquent in his refusal: "I'm very doubtful that it would be common sense procedure to try and intern 117,000 Japanese in this theater. . . . An American citizen after all, is an American citizen. And while they all may not be loyal, I think *we can weed the disloyal out of the loyal* and lock them up if necessary."[34] [Emphasis added.] His seemingly reasonable views on the potential of weeding out disloyals and on citizenship would be transformed in the next eight weeks.

Many newspapers tried to exert a calming influence. The *Aberdeen Daily World*'s editor cautioned readers, "The FBI can take care of the fifth columnists; is doing so already, in fact. . . . If you believe you have reason for suspicion, tell it to the police; do not whisper it. . . . They can be used, these whispers, against any American—regardless of his forebears—used to ruin a competitor or to serve a private grudge. They are part and parcel of the Hitler method and do not belong in this country."[35]

Bendetsen later recalled this time:

> I was sent out to the headquarters of General DeWitt to confer with him as a representative of the War Department. I made many such trips in December and January. I became a 'commuter.' My assignment was to gather facts and convey General DeWitt's analyses to his superiors in Washington.[36]

At the Presidio, Bendetsen became General DeWitt's chronicler and soon put onto paper in lucid, numbered statements DeWitt's insistent demands for strong action to control aliens and his immediate and total dissatisfaction with the handling of the enemy alien problem by the Department of Justice. Throughout 1941 the War Department had sparred with the Department of Justice over who should be responsible for the custody of alien enemies in the continental United States. The determination of which aliens should be permanently interned was a function of the Justice Department. But DeWitt, backed by Bendetsen, wanted a freer hand and wanted to be the one to decide who should be interned.

As he waited for Bendetsen to arrive at DeWitt's command, Gullion attended a meeting on December 31, 1941, with Assistant Secretary of War John J. McCloy, and Assistant Attorney General James R. Rowe, Jr., and Edward Ennis of the Justice Department, in which Rowe and Ennis, while promising more efficient cooperation, "very frankly admitted the shortcomings of their Department thus far."[37]

On January 1, 1942, V. Ford Greaves of the Federal Communication Commission in San Francisco reported to DeWitt that his offices were cooperating with military authorities in the enforcement of the President's proclamation regarding the use, control, and closing of radio stations. He noted in particular that he had no active cases on file indicating the possession of radio transmitters by any enemy aliens. It became evident from DeWitt's conversations with Justice representatives and others in the weeks to come that he did not believe Greaves.

California attorney general Earl Warren began to be pressured in letters like the following by agricultural interests who wanted to get rid of Japanese competition: "We trust that your office will make a sincere effort to eliminate as many of these undesirable aliens from the land of California as is possible at this time."[38] This view was shared by many groups, such as the American Legion, who expected to support Warren's candidacy for governor in the fall.

The first memorandum that Bendetsen wrote for DeWitt was a planning paper for the impending conference with Assistant Attorney General Rowe. Rowe, who was number three in the Justice Department after Attorney General Francis Biddle and Solicitor General Charles Fahy, was sent to DeWitt's command to attempt to resolve the contention between the Justice and War departments. Bendetsen's memorandum spelled out DeWitt's "Immediate Alien Enemy Control Requirements": decentralization of authority that would allow the FBI special authority to issue alien enemy apprehension warrants, and authority to the military commander of each theater of operations to prescribe restricted areas; he further urged the attorney general immediately to provide the regulations mentioned in presidential proclamations of December 7 and 8, 1941, including complete registration of all alien enemies as a basis for a "pass and permit system" and for a "continental" travel-regulation system. Pulling no punches, Bendetsen concluded for DeWitt that if the attorney general was not prepared to approve and initiate the above recommendations, the War Department must reserve the right to seek a transfer of authority for control of enemy aliens from Justice to the secretary of war. With Bendetsen's help, DeWitt appeared determined to get for himself in 1942 the power he had planned for a hypothetical military commander in Hawaii almost twenty years earlier. And perhaps, by supporting Gullion and DeWitt in this power struggle, Bendetsen, who would soon get a double promotion to colonel, began to hope he might move on to a bigger job and a general's star.[39]

On January 4, 1942, Bendetsen took part in a discussion in the office of DeWitt in which Assistant Attorney General Rowe attempted to understand what DeWitt wanted. Rowe was accompanied by Nat Pieper of the

FBI. DeWitt did most of the talking. He complained that he had to protect his very large theater of operations, which included eight states as well as Alaska, with only 240,000 troops. He felt the presence of 288,000 enemy aliens (including Italians and Germans) was a great threat and said, "I have little confidence that the enemy aliens are law-abiding or loyal. . . . Particularly the Japanese. I have no confidence in their loyalty whatsoever. I am speaking now of the native born Japanese.[40] In less than a week DeWitt had already begun to lump the Japanese American citizens into the term "Japanese."

DeWitt stated, "We have got to be able to enter their homes and premises, search and seize immediately without waiting for normal processes of the law—obtaining a search warrant to make an arrest." DeWitt asserted that the president's proclamation requiring regulation of cameras, radios, and firearms owned by aliens had scarcely been implemented by the Justice Department. He was concerned that the registration of enemy aliens had not begun and wanted to be able to conduct blanket searches of all households suspected of harboring an illicit radio whether or not an alien resided in the household. DeWitt said, "It doesn't mean a thing, Mr. Rowe, that a Jap has turned in a receiving and transmitting set. . . . He could still have another." Rowe argued for the Justice Department that a search was permitted only when an alien was present.

DeWitt asserted, without proof and without being challenged, "I personally am convinced that there is a portable sending set operating in the Monterey Bay area." DeWitt insisted that every ship that had sailed from the Columbia River "since the outbreak of war [had] been subjected to submarine attack." That meant just one thing to him, "that there [was] a boat watching . . . with communications with a submarine at sea."[41]

Bendetsen's summary of the discussion outlined DeWitt's wishes and demanded cooperation from the Justice Department. Bendetsen reported, "It should be stated at the outset that the Army has no wish to undertake the conduct and control of alien enemies anywhere within continental United States. Impressions to the contrary notwithstanding, the Army would accept transfer of such responsibility and authority with great reluctance."[42] Reluctant or not, DeWitt was putting Justice on notice that if they did not satisfy DeWitt's requirements, he and his superiors would go over their heads to get full control of enemy aliens.

Tensions may have arisen in the many meetings between War Department officials and representatives of the Justice Department because of strong underlying political differences. Rowe was a New Deal Democrat, and had until recently been a close aide to President Roosevelt. Bendetsen, according to Joseph D. Roberts, a former Republican state legislator from Seattle, was "a brilliant and personable young attorney from Grays Harbor, who was always on the right side of the political fence in these woods."[43]

Bendetsen and Rowe have been described as "key and mutually antagonistic figures in the bureaucratic struggle over the fate of the West Coast Japanese."[44] James Rowe exerted a moderating influence on DeWitt by appealing to his cautious nature. But DeWitt was easily influenced by strong personalities. Though Bendetsen could not always be sure that he knew the general's intentions, he became the general's voice when discussing the "Japanese problem."

Sending Bendetsen to the West Coast as a liaison between Gullion and DeWitt bypassed the army's normal chain of command. On matters concerning control of enemy aliens, DeWitt, the commanding general of the Western Defense Command, found himself communicating with General Gullion, who as provost marshal general commanded no troops and was responsible for the Army War College, military police, and civil affairs. By February, DeWitt would also be held directly accountable to the War Department's civilian leaders, Assistant Secretary of War John J. McCloy and Secretary of War Henry L. Stimson. In Washington, D.C., Army Chief of Staff George C. Marshall was focusing on bigger military questions and was largely unaware of what was happening on the West Coast; he would ultimately be forced to accept the removal of all Japanese aliens and their citizen children, which the army's civilian leaders would endorse without his concurrence.

In reply to the understanding reached between Rowe and DeWitt, recently appointed Attorney General Francis Biddle sent a teletype to DeWitt requesting information. In order to approve restricted areas either for search and seizure, or for exclusion of aliens, he stated that the army should provide Justice with the reason for the recommendation, as well as the size of the alien population, the number of houses or businesses affected, and "detailed plans for any evacuation and resettlement of the aliens removed, and their ultimate detention."[45]

The army refused this request on January 5, 1942, in a memorandum written by Bendetsen. He wrote that the attorney general's request "apparently envisions a mass exodus of alien enemies from large areas," but that the "Army does not contemplate action of this type" and therefore would provide only general information, such as stating that an area includes a military base; the reason would be given "in general terms only," such as "presence of alien enemies endangering national defense."[46] In answering questions from James Rowe about warrants to search the premises of aliens, FBI Director J. Edgar Hoover reiterated the Justice Department view that search warrants must be obtained for premises of persons other than alien enemies. He further stated, "At present all American citizens including dual citizens are citizens and cannot be apprehended unless under charge of specific crime. Suggest Army submit any specific facts of disloyalty of citizens and report disloyalty to FBI."[47] The army made no such submissions.

As early as January 5, 1942, with Bendetsen's help, DeWitt was proposing to declare restricted areas "in which no alien enemy will be permitted under any conditions," called Category A areas. Many of these were being drawn around strategic military establishments, such as naval bases, and also around important defense industries, such as Boeing (Seattle) and Consolidated (San Diego) airplane factories. According to Bendetsen, "Most of the areas which will be cleared of alien enemies do not now contain inhabitants which must be moved."[48] In addition, DeWitt proposed to designate Category B areas in which alien enemies may be permitted by pass or permit. This plan did not indicate a mass exodus of enemy aliens, since the zones encompassed vacant coastal areas adjacent to sensitive military bases and industrial facilities. Implicit in DeWitt's thinking about restricted areas was the need to exclude enemy aliens physically, though details of what such exclusion would involve or what would happen to the excluded aliens were not discussed until some weeks later. Bendetson had inspected potential facilities for internment of aliens in Montana and Hawaii prior to the war, but these would not accommodate large numbers of people and were already filling up with the aliens apprehended according to the FBI's "ABC" lists.

In the next few days, the Department of Justice agreed to accept a set of restricted areas that DeWitt would designate. The assumption at this time was that the Department of Justice would then issue the orders and make plans for whatever evacuation would be necessary. Justice was told that these areas would be limited.[49] The process of defining restricted areas took time, and the number of persons to be evacuated depended on the extent of those areas. DeWitt was not able to complete detailed descriptions of the restricted areas in California until late January, and soon after, he demanded that the evacuation include citizen Japanese, that is, the Nisei. The Justice Department would not agree to imposing restrictions on American citizens, and rather than arguing on constitutional grounds, made the mistake of trying to deflect the request by saying that they did not have the personnel for such a large action.[50]

In mid-January, Bendetsen was back in Washington, D.C., catching up with his mail. He wrote to Aberdeen timber baron and former client E. K. Bishop, thanking him for a Christmas gift, "the package of good things from the sea," adding, "On sampling I am filled with a nostalgia for home."

To friend Edwin C. Matthias in Seattle, he wrote that he was "assigned to this thoroughly wartime establishment. I find the work plentiful and interesting. In short, in my bailiwick, we work like hell and like it."[51]

Santa Monica Republican Leland Ford, who in December had spoken on the floor of Congress to oppose taking drastic measures against the American Japanese, now agreed with the many opinions arriving in telegrams and letters to Congress suggesting removal of all Japanese and Japanese Americans from the West Coast. In a letter to Secretary of War Stimson, he suggested, "All Japanese, whether citizens or not . . . [should be] placed in inland concentration camps." He argued that any native-born Japanese willing to go to a concentration camp was a patriot; unwillingness to go was proof of disloyalty to the United States.[52]

In a memorandum to Gullion dated January 16, 1942, Bendetsen pulled together some forty pages of information summarizing his actions while assigned to temporary duty at DeWitt's headquarters to work on "the West Coast Alien Enemy Program." Much of the résumé concerned the failure of the Justice Department to implement the presidential proclamations of December 7 and 8, 1941. Though DeWitt and James Rowe had several memoranda of understanding, a response from the Justice Department in Washington had not been issued.[53]

Bendetsen stated that "unity of command" was required in order to conduct the alien enemy program properly. He argued that the army should obtain a presidential order to transfer authority from the attorney general to the secretary of war, with power of delegation to the military commander of the Western Defense Command. Bendetsen said that DeWitt concurred but would delay making this recommendation until "there is a conclusive demonstration of further failure on the part of the Justice Department properly and fully to implement the Presidential Proclamations."[54] Bendetsen almost never split an infinitive.

John B. Hughes, Los Angeles news commentator for Mutual Broadcasting System, growing impatient with what he saw as government inaction, in many broadcasts in January "dwelt at length on the dangers of Japanese American sabotage."[55] Hughes also wrote to Attorney General Biddle, "Persons who know the Japanese on the West Coast will estimate that ninety percent or more of American-born Japanese are primarily loyal to Japan. . . . The Japanese are a far greater menace in our midst than any other axis patriots. They will die joyously for the honor of Japan."[56]

Bendetsen wrote a memorandum on counterespionage for the chief of staff of the War Department. Though he admitted he was "not sufficiently informed on the general methods to submit any specific recommendations," he did assert that "an effective counter espionage agency in the field would be required, necessarily to operate in part in a clandestine manner. . . . While it may not be possible . . . to prevent his [the enemy's] ascertaining important information, it may become possible to prevent its ultimate communication to the enemy." Such an organization might also "place false and misleading information in the latter's hands."

In this memo, Bendetsen repeated DeWitt's assertions that every seagoing vessel that left a Pacific Coast port was met by an enemy submarine, and that unlawful radio transmitters were not being shut down.[57] He hoped to make the case that the army needed a counterespionage service to apprehend spies. In reality, none of the existing surveillance organizations (FBI, naval intelligence, or army intelligence) was ever able to confirm shore-to-ship communication by any Japanese alien or Japanese American or any other person. What was known was that a number of Japanese submarines had lurked offshore in the first days of the war and could easily have observed all sailings out of well-known West Coast shipping channels. Harassment of shipping could have occurred without aid from the shore.

General DeWitt received G–2 periodic reports weekly from his intelligence officer, reports that noted the possible presence of a small number of hostile submarines in the waters "off the Pacific Coast, including lower California and Alaska" in the first week of January. Reports confirmed that one Japanese submarine had been sunk by the coast guard ship *Hermes* off Cape Montara and mentioned the possibility of reinforcements from Japan, Formosa, and other locations in the western Pacific joining the submarines. A surprise attack was "considered a possibility" though no potential complement of Japanese carriers or other large ships was reported to be anywhere in the eastern Pacific. These reports never indicated the existence of a real threat to attack the West Coast in January or February. Rather, they noted a decline in enemy submarines in the weeks after

Christmas 1941, and reiterated week after week that "no hostile operations . . . [were] conducted within this theater of operations."[58]

In a letter to Congressman Ford that was widely circulated, Edwin C. Matthias, attorney for Great Northern Railway Company in Seattle, advocated the "removal of all Japanese, both American born and alien, on the West Coast to concentration camps." He talked of the fallacy of the American melting pot, saying that for an American-born Japanese, "a belief in the sanctity of his forefathers is so inborn that, despite his American birth, his tie is to Japan." Matthias asserted that we must reverse the idea that a person is presumed innocent until proven guilty: "Is it not far fetched to presume that the sympathies of these Japanese are with America rather than with Japan? To prevent another Pearl Harbor on the Pacific Coast . . . [we must stop] this mollycoddling policy we now have toward the Japanese."[59] Matthias's anti-Japanese sentiment struck a responsive chord in many westerners, and encouraged development of the concept of military necessity.

In answer to a question by Gullion, DeWitt again asserted that there was "coordination between the enemy alien on the shore and some higher power outside" and that "they [were] still attacking most of the ships."[60] DeWitt elaborated in a conversation with Bendetsen: "We know there are radios along the coast and we know that they are communicating at sea . . . the fact that nothing has happened so far is, well, let me say, more or less ominous."[61] As noted above, the G–2 reports that he received from his own staff after January 10, 1942, did not support these claims.[62]

The *Roberts Report*, a preliminary review of the attack on Pearl Harbor, was released January 24, 1942; parts of it inflamed public opinion and may have influenced DeWitt.[63] Supreme Court Justice Owen J. Roberts had headed a presidential commission investigating the disaster. Earlier, the *Grays Harbor Post* editor had predicted, "All blame should not fall on Admiral Kimmel and the Army high command. *Maybe* three men could be responsible for the T. H. [Hawaiian] incident of December 7th. We would as well blame the men who passed the first Oriental Exclusion Act, many years ago!"[64] As expected, the *Roberts Report* placed the blame for lack of preparedness in Hawaii prior to the attack on the army and navy commanders in Hawaii (General Walter C. Short and Admiral Husband E. Kimmel). The commission also mentioned that a Japanese espionage network in Hawaii had sent "information to the Japanese Empire respecting the military and naval establishments and [military] dispositions on the island." Then the report asserted, without basis, that in addition to Japanese consular staff, the espionage ring included "persons having no open relations with the Japanese foreign service."[65] Many readers jumped to the conclusion that Japanese Hawaiians were disloyal, giving further fodder to anti-Japanese editorial writers on the West Coast. A few days later, in the first of many such official acts of discrimination, the California State Personnel Board voted to allow the dismissal of "descendants of natives with whom the United States is at war" from civil service positions. Only Japanese American employees were dismissed.

DeWitt was looking forward to the spot raids planned by the FBI, and to information provided by a new FCC (Federal Communications Commission) Radio Intelligence Center to be established in San Francisco. On January 25, 1942, in a letter to the attorney general urging immediate and stringent action, Secretary of War Stimson reiterated and thus perpetuated General DeWitt's claims that ship-to-shore communications "undoubtedly coordinated by intelligent enemy control were continually operating."[66]

Secretary of War Stimson held Representative Leland Ford's letter for about ten days then replied (in a letter drafted by Bendetsen) in seeming agreement with Ford's viewpoint.[67] Stimson said, "The internment of over a hundred thousand people, and their evacuation inland, presents a very real problem. While the necessity for firm measures to insure the maximum war effort cannot be questioned, the proposal suggested by you involves many complex considerations." He implied that the War Department was prepared to provide internment facilities, but that the Department of Justice had the responsibility and authority for determination of the necessity for internment. He assured Ford that the army was aware of the dangers on the Pacific Coast and suggested he send his views to the attorney general.[68] By early February, Representative Ford threatened Attorney General Biddle that if his office not did issue a mass evacuation order, "I would drag the whole matter out on the floor of the House." He said that if the attorney general would not take immediate action, they would "clean the god damned office out in one sweep."[69]

In late January, DeWitt reported to Bendetsen that there was a "tremendous volume of public opinion . . . developing in California, among all classes, against all Japanese."[70] Some of the pressure that he felt came from journalists, such as Henry McLemore, who wrote in the *Los Angeles Times*, "I am for immediate removal of every Japanese on the West Coast to a point deep in the interior. . . . Sure this would work an unjustified hardship on 80 per cent or 90 per cent of the California Japanese. But, the remaining 10 or 20 per cent have it in their power to do damage. . . . You can't tell me that an individual's rights have any business being placed above a nation's safety. . . . Personally, I hate the Japanese."[71]

Having finally received and approved General DeWitt's maps of proposed restricted zones, the Justice Department made the first public, official announcement that some kind of evacuation would take effect after alien registration was completed. General DeWitt's recommendations called for exclusion of aliens from eighty-six restricted Category A zones, and for implementation of a permit system for Category B areas. This was the first time that the public was told what areas would be affected. Many of the A zones surrounding strategic installations contained few residents and consisted of long stretches of unoccupied coastline. Though the numbers were not widely discussed, this proposal would have removed seven thousand aliens, of whom only three thousand were of Japanese ancestry, and would have taken effect on February 24, 1942.[72] At the same, time the Justice Department had assigned Tom C. Clark to assist with the resettlement that would follow upon the declaration of the Category A restricted areas.

An assistant attorney general who had been on the Pacific Coast working on trust-busting activities, Clark (later attorney general under Truman and then an associate justice of the Supreme Court), was assigned as Rowe's representative to the enemy alien unit, presumably in hopes that Clark could moderate DeWitt's strong anti-Japanese stance.[73]

The army was not yet satisfied with the modest proposal of eighty-six Category A areas for which it had gained Justice Department approval. At the end of a January 29 conversation with DeWitt, Bendetsen said: "As I understand it . . . you are of the opinion that there will have to be an evacuation on the West Coast, not only of Japanese aliens, but also of Japanese citizens . . . and that if you had the power of requisition over all other federal agencies . . . you would be willing on the coast to accept the responsibility for the alien enemy program." General DeWitt said, "Yes, I would. And I think it's got to come sooner or later." Bendetsen agreed, "Yes sir, I do too, and I think the subject will be discussed tomorrow at the congressional delegation meeting."[74]

On January 30, 1942, Bendetsen attended the meeting in Washington, D.C., of congressional representatives of the three Pacific Coast states on "handling enemy aliens on the West Coast." Edward Ennis, assistant attorney general in charge of alien control, and James Rowe attended and spoke out against a mass evacuation of Japanese or other aliens. The congressmen asked that the War Department be given control over alien enemies, including United States citizens holding dual citizenship. (Dual citizenship occurred when a child born in the United States to a Japanese alien was registered with a Japanese consulate within fourteen days of birth.) They asked for immediate evacuation of enemy aliens and their families from critical areas. Dual citizens would be asked to resettle voluntarily. Rowe and Ennis saw "plenty of legal problems and no military justification for the evacuation of American citizens of Japanese descent." Bendetsen "violently disagreed" with Rowe and Ennis, and stated: "[W]e did not seek control of the program . . . however, the War Department would be entirely willing . . . to accept the responsibility" for an evacuation provided that the War Department were given full authority "to require the services of any other federal agency and provided that federal agency was required to respond."[75] DeWitt was pleased when Bendetsen told him he had said this. He especially looked forward to getting power over civilian agencies, thinking in particular of the FBI. "In other words," General DeWitt said, "Mr. Hoover himself as head of the FBI would have to function under the War Department exactly as he is functioning under the Department of Justice."[76]

In their discussion of the congressional proposal, DeWitt challenged the use of the dual citizen category, saying "You're never going to be able to prove dual citizenship," and claimed all such records had been destroyed when war was declared. Bendetsen suggested that it wouldn't matter because "out of military necessity some of these areas would be prohibited to everybody concerned, whether they are citizens, white or Jap or black or brown . . . everybody is barred and can only enter on a pass or permit . . . just like a military reservation. I think it's going to come to that." General DeWitt agreed, and referring to the military areas, said, "Now, any Japanese, it doesn't make any difference what he is, who is seen in one of those areas after the 24th of February [the date selected by Justice for the restrictions to take effect] is going to be subjected to suspicion . . . if he's a Jap he's going to be questioned." "In other words," said Bendetson, "as far as the Japanese element is concerned, it's almost self-enforcing." General DeWitt observed that some persons would seem to offer patriotic compliance, "but those are the fellows I suspect the most." "Definitely," said Bendetsen. "The ones who are giving you only lip service are the ones always to suspect."[77]

General Gullion asked DeWitt how far he proposed to move the evacuees. DeWitt said that he didn't know but would have an answer after he studied the congressional proposal.[78]

On January 31, 1942, though he did not yet have any approval from his superiors for a mass evacuation, Gullion initiated planning for the handling of large numbers of people. Bendetsen followed up with cables asking corps area commanders about possible locations in which to house large numbers of persons, saying, "THE EVACUEES WHO MAY BE INVOLVED AT SOME FUTURE TIME WILL IN ALL PROBABILITY BE DOMESTIC JAPANESE INCLUDING WOMEN AND CHILDREN."[79] The president's proclamation of December 7, 1941, provided authority only to apprehend or remove as alien enemies, natives or subjects of a hostile nation "of the age of fourteen years and upwards."[80]

DeWitt gave Bendetsen clarification as to how he would implement the congressional recommendations. He stated that in order to "exercise a controlling influence and preventative action against sabotage," it would be necessary to evacuate all enemy aliens on the West Coast and [force] their resettlement or internment." In answer to Bendetsen's question as to whether he included Japanese Americans, DeWitt said, "I include all Germans, all Italians who are alien enemies and all Japanese who are native-born or foreign-born." When it came to the recommendation that the government provide federal assistance to uninterned alien enemies whose livelihood was affected, DeWitt opposed it. As to complete evacuation and resettlement of aliens, he said, "I am in thorough agreement with this but I think we might as well eliminate talk of resettlement and handle these people as they should be handled. . . . Put them to . . . work in internment camps." He urged the following priorities "from the standpoint of danger of these three groups . . . first the Japanese, all prices [sic] . . . the next group the Germans . . . the third group the Italians." He concluded by saying, "We've waited too long as it is. Get them all out."[81] These were not surprising statements coming from a general who had considered some kind of mass evacuation of persons of Japanese ancestry in a staff meeting as early as December 10. But his conviction would waver in the next weeks.

By the end of January, sentiment from journalists, citizens, law enforcement, and county and civic organizations began to weigh heavily against the West Coast Japanese. The small bursts of support for Japanese Americans that were noted in the weeks after Pearl Harbor had vanished—there were no more reasoned editorials suggesting tolerance and calm, no more pleas that readers not jump to conclusions about the loyalty of their Japanese neighbors. The presence on the West Coast of thousands of Japanese aliens and their citizen children began to be perceived as a threat. Organizations such as the Native Sons and Daughters of the Golden West, the American Legion, the California State Federation of Labor, and the California State Grange continued an anti-Japanese movement of long standing and were soon joined by other groups in Oregon and Washington. Some proposals by these groups included the demand that "all Japanese known to hold dual citizenship . . . be placed in concentration camps."[82] Some commentators also asked for a change in the constitution barring citizenship to children born in the United States to parents of a race "ineligible for citizenship." California Governor Culbert L. Olson said that if evacuation were carried out, "everyone would feel much safer about the alien and the Japanese population."[83]

On the other hand, Agriculture Secretary Claude Wickard had become concerned about the loss of farm production if the Japanese were evacuated, and felt that the campaign against these people was "essentially a conspiracy designed to take over land owned and farmed by Japanese, and to eliminate Japanese competition in agricultural production." Wickard's agents on the West Coast reported that the Japanese rural population was "terrified" and that local officials did not offer to investigate attacks on Japanese or initiate prosecutions in cases in which vigilante actions were said to have occurred. Secretary Wickard proposed to develop a kind of "large agricultural reservation" in the central valleys of California, where Japanese removed from "all strategic areas" could carry on "their normal farming operations" and be given some measure of protection.[84]

Urban Japanese began to feel demoralized and abandoned. Certainly the family of Natsu Saito in Aberdeen felt isolated. The Aberdeen Central Labor Council claimed that there had been "reports of suspicious occurrences on the beaches and at vital coast centers. We feel that these disturbances will disappear if the Japanese are interned."[85] Mrs. Saito was still being held in Justice's alien-detention facility in Seattle, while hundreds of West Coast aliens, most of whom were men, were incarcerated in Fort Missoula and other facilities in the interior. Perry Saito, not quite twenty years old, struggled to support his younger brother and sister.

Prior to the war President Roosevelt sought to expand his intelligence sources and asked John Franklin Carter, journalist, author, and sometime speechwriter, to conduct confidential investigations, one of which was a secret study of the "Japanese situation." At Carter's request, Curtis B. Munson, a well-to-do Chicago businessman, gathered intelligence "under the guise of being a government official." The Munson report was sent to the president on November 7, 1941, and then forwarded to Stimson. Munson had talked at length with many of the professionals in the FBI and naval intelligence who were assessing the possible security threat presented by the large Japanese population, both on the West Coast and in Hawaii and had also interviewed many Japanese. The president may have read Carter's one-page summary only, which did not calm his anxiety regarding the West Coast Japanese.[86] Carter's selection of points from Munson's report obscured its main arguments. His summary stated: (1) "There are still Japanese in the United States who will tie dynamite around their waist and make a human bomb, but today they are few;" (2) "There is no Japanese 'problem' on the coast. There will be no armed uprising of Japanese. . . . There will be the odd case of fanatical sabotage by some Japanese 'crackpot;'" (3) "The dangerous part of their espionage is that they would be very effective as far as . . . movement of troops . . . is concerned;" (4) "For the most part the local Japanese are loyal to the United States, or at worst, hope that by remaining quiet they can avoid concentration camps or irresponsible mobs;" (5) "Your reporter . . . is horrified to note that dams, bridges, harbors, power stations, etc. are wholly unguarded everywhere."[87] Though his confidence in the loyalty of the Japanese community (Munson's main conclusion) was not evident in Carter's summary, Munson agreed with Lieutenant Commander K. D. Ringle, the man who had broken the Tachibana Japanese spy network in Southern California earlier in 1941, that the number of potentially disloyal Japanese was very small and identifiable. An FBI document sent to the White House at the same time reported that suspect Japanese were being monitored and that it was the Japanese consulate that mistrusted Japanese Americans, not the FBI.[88]

Failing to reassure the president of the loyalty of Japanese Americans and wishing to avert a mass evacuation, Carter urged Ringle to write and circulate his own report.

In late January, Ringle submitted his first report to the Office of Naval Intelligence, which was charged by the army to conduct Japanese intelligence. The report soon came to the attention of the War Department. As a naval intelligence officer, Commander Ringle was well qualified to comment on the Japanese question in view of his years as a naval language student in the United States Embassy in Tokyo and his six years' duty as an intelligence officer in Hawaii and Los Angeles where he had moved freely among Japanese vegetable farmers, tuna fishermen, and small businessmen. Ringle's first point was that "[w]ithin the last eight or ten years the entire 'Japanese question' in the United States [had] reversed itself. The alien menace [was] no longer paramount." Ringle wrote that "the 'Japanese Problem' [had] been magnified out of its true proportion, largely because of the physical characteristics of the people; that it [was] no more serious than the problem of the German, Italian, and Communistic portions of the United States population, and finally that it should be handled on the basis of the *individual*, regardless of citizenship, and *not* on a racial basis."[89] He lamented what was happening to the Japanese population in the Los Angeles area (loss of employment, anti-Japanese agitation, personal attacks by Filipinos, cancellation of business licenses for markets, etc.) and predicted that if these practices did not stop there would "most certainly be outbreaks of sabotage, riots and other civil strife in the not too distant future."

In Ringle's opinion, at least 75 percent of the American-born United States citizens of Japanese ancestry were loyal to the United States. The Office of Naval Intelligence "looked with sympathy" on Ringle's report but did not wish to interfere with the army's field of responsibility. Ringle traveled twice to San Francisco hoping to discuss the Japanese situation with Bendetsen. Both times he was unable to see Bendetsen.[90] Had General DeWitt or Bendetsen read the Ringle report, it would have been harder for them to argue that the Nisei were dangerous.

By the beginning of February, General DeWitt seemed to be trying to accommodate everyone when he discussed what to do with the West Coast Japanese. One day he favored the recommendations of the West Coast congressional delegation (calling for a voluntary evacuation controlled by the army); the next day he was prepared to stand aside and let California officials resettle Japanese aliens and their families in inland farming communes. Many times he stated that the evacuation from restricted areas of all Japanese, aliens and non-aliens alike, was necessary to ensure the security of the West Coast; after a warning from McCloy that he should take no position favoring "wholesale withdrawal of Japanese citizens and aliens from the Coast," he would deny that he had taken any position on evacuation.[91] He had at this point not put any recommendations in writing. The writing would be left to Bendetsen.

CHAPTER FIVE

Tightening the Noose

I have come to the conclusion that the Japanese situation as it exists in this state today may well be the Achilles heel of the entire civilian defense effort. Unless something is done it may bring about a repetition of Pearl Harbor.

—California Attorney General Earl Warren,
January 30, 1942

Bendetsen spent the "last three weeks of January and a good deal of time in February" working with the Japanese problem, and though he was still only a major, his presence in some critical meetings appears to have had a marked negative influence on the tenor and the outcome of those meetings. The first such meeting occurred on Sunday, February 1, 1942, in the office of Attorney General Francis Biddle. James Rowe, Jr., Edward Ennis, and FBI Director J. Edgar Hoover of the Justice Department faced Assistant Secretary of War John J. McCloy, General Gullion, and Major Karl Bendetsen. Attorney General Biddle was concerned about the pressure for mass evacuation and about the extreme criticisms directed at him and his department.[1] Hoover had given Biddle a memorandum earlier in the day in which "he attacked the Army's intelligence capability on the West Coast for exhibiting signs of 'hysteria and lack of judgment.'"[2] Biddle asked the War Department representatives to approve a joint press release that opposed removal of citizen Japanese from the coast and stated that further action was not necessary. The War Department representatives would not agree, and tensions were high in the meeting.

Rowe, who, along with Ennis, had disagreed strongly with Bendetsen's statements before the congressional delegation two days earlier, spoke up. He questioned what had changed DeWitt's mind, since he recalled that the general opposed a mass evacuation when Rowe was at his headquarters in January. Rowe made "some uncomplimentary remarks" about Bendetsen, perhaps suggesting that Bendetsen and the western congressmen "were encouraging people to get hysterical."[3] He complained that the western congressmen were "just nuts" on the subject and maintained, as he had in the congressional meeting, that there was "no evidence whatsoever of any reason for disturbing citizens."[4] The details of Rowe's verbal outburst to Bendetsen have not been recorded in any of the many accounts of the meeting, but the consequence is well known; Gullion later reported that he felt "a little sore." A heated argument ensued between War Department and Justice representatives. Biddle stated that he was opposed to mass evacuation and that the Justice Department would have nothing to do with it. Gullion insisted that the military situation on the West Coast was "so precarious that DeWitt might indeed have to 'get all the Japs out.'" McCloy, who had, for the most part, only listened to the exchange, made a shocking statement to Biddle: "You are putting a Wall Street lawyer in a helluva box, but if it is a question of safety of the country, [or] the Constitution of the United States, why the Constitution is just a scrap of paper to me."[5] McCloy appeared willing to defer to the military. In his anger, Gullion said, "Well, listen, Mr. Biddle, do you mean to tell me if the Army, the men on the ground, determine it is a military necessity to move citizens, Jap citizens, that you won't help us?" McCloy insisted that General DeWitt, the commander of the "men on the ground," be allowed to look at the draft press release and, in his first such assertion, said that if DeWitt thought an evacuation was a military necessity, the War Department would go along with it. Biddle agreed to postpone a decision on the joint press release, and the meeting adjourned.

General DeWitt did not agree to the Justice Department's draft memorandum of agreement and did not even want his name mentioned on the press release, fearing that West Coast politicians would think that he had changed his position and would be upset. In telephone conversations with Gullion, DeWitt reiterated that he intended to evacuate "those people who are aliens and who are Japs of American citizenship." Gullion asked DeWitt for a written statement of his position in order to inform and update McCloy, who had not participated in their conversations but would "probably be in any subsequent conference." Bendetsen told DeWitt that it appeared that Justice would go along with a licensing program as "the legal basis for exclusion . . . if we think there is military necessity for that." Licensing programs used the following principle: All persons would be removed from a restricted area and only those persons who were not considered a security risk would be licensed to return to the area. Bendetsen asserted in a letter to his friend Colonel Auer that he had talked his superiors into using this method. McCloy's biographer credits McCloy with coming up with the scheme. On February 12, 1942, Biddle would in fact propose a licensing program in a letter to Stimson. No wonder the method was seriously considered—each thought he had invented it.

Discussing Justice's proposed press release, Bendetsen told General DeWitt that Justice didn't want to be alone: "They apparently want us to join with them so that if anything happens they [can] say 'this is the military recommendation.'"[6] On this occasion, when asked for further views on an evacuation, DeWitt said: "I haven't gone into the details of it, but Hell, it would be no job as far as the evacuation was concerned to move 100,000 people." That he could minimize such a large task, when his staff had still not managed to work out all the details of eighty-eight restricted areas, is interesting if not remarkable. A day earlier Bendetsen had called DeWitt's headquarters to point out an important inconsistency in the declaration of Category A (prohibited to aliens) zones and a Category B (restricted to aliens) zone; the San Francisco-Oakland Bay Bridge had been declared to be in Category B, but all the approaches to the bridge were classified Category A and thus prohibited to people who might otherwise be allowed to use the bridge.

Behind the scenes Bendetsen was preparing reports in order to solidify Gullion's position. Between February 2 and 16, he wrote three position papers that became the basis for the presidential executive order and for the organization of the subsequent evacuation. He also persuaded Assistant Secretary of War McCloy and Secretary of War Stimson, and finally Attorney General Francis Biddle that the declaration of military areas or reservations and the establishment of a pass-and-permit system could be seen as a constitutional way to exclude all persons of Japanese ancestry, even citizens, from the entire West Coast. It is clear from letters and memoranda surviving in his archive that Bendetsen *did* see himself as the architect of military necessity.

On February 3, General DeWitt denied to McCloy that he had favored any kind of "wholesale withdrawal of Japanese citizens and aliens from the West Coast." He said, "Mr. Secretary . . . I haven't taken any position."[7] McCloy (and perhaps also General Marshall) was becoming concerned that DeWitt and the provost marshal general's office were committing their department to a policy that had not been adopted or approved. DeWitt then dictated his editing of the proposed joint press release, removing language to the effect that the two departments do not "at this time require the removal of American citizens of the Japanese Race," and adding a statement that the parties concerned "believe steps taken to date for the control of alien enemies have been appropriate and such additional steps to insure this control will be taken in the future as may be found necessary and advisable."

DeWitt explained that this change in the press release was needed because he was now supporting the proposal by Governor Culbert L. Olson of California, Tom C. Clark, and representatives of the Agriculture Department to set up resettlement projects (the farm communes) in California for alien Japanese and their families. DeWitt described the plan, saying that he would merely be asked to designate areas from which the aliens should be removed. He now seemed willing to stand back and let others take care of the alien problem. The plan called for the citizen Japanese to move voluntarily. McCloy observed "That introduces a new element. . . . The bad ones, the ones that are foreign agents, that are sympathetic with Japan, will not volunteer, will they?" McCloy then talked about the problem of attempting a compulsory movement of citizens, briefly described the military-reservation idea, and suggested that after excluding "all of the Japs" one might permit some to come back if it was "quite certain" that they were free from any suspicion." DeWitt was skeptical of that suggestion, and declared, "Out here, Mr. Secretary, a Jap is a Jap to these people now."[8]

DeWitt expressed optimism that the California officials would succeed with their removal plan, and he agreed to provide "just 23,000 guards from the troops that ought to be gotten back to training." If the plan did not go ahead and the Japanese were not removed, he would expect "to have one complication after another, because you just can't tell one Jap from another." He added, "They all look the same. Give a sentry or an officer or troops any job like that, a Jap's a Jap, and you can't blame the man for stopping all of them."[9] McCloy was sympathetic, but stated very carefully that if the California plan did not go forward, DeWitt should consider the licensing plan that McCloy had described, and he went over it again in detail.

Sometime this same day, February 3, Chief of Staff General George C. Marshall called DeWitt, and asked, "Is there anything you want to say now about anything else?" DeWitt proceeded to describe briefly the limited plan proposed by the governor of California, saying that he supported the resettlement of "the Japanese" to somewhere within the state. "I'm only concerned with getting them away from around these aircraft factories and other places," he said, as if he had no other plan in mind. He said nothing about citizens of Japanese lineage, nothing about the possible size of an evacuation.[10]

At about this time there must have been long faces around the office of the provost marshal general. On February 3, Gullion and Bendetsen met for an hour and a half with their civilian superiors. Stimson and McCloy were moving in a direction that seemed too limited to them. The secretaries were "thinking in terms of creating 'Jap-less' islands of security around a few key installations like the Consolidated-Vultee plant in San Diego, the Lockheed and North American plants in Los Angeles and Boeing in Seattle."[11] And DeWitt, who had been their ally and who could speak of "military necessity" from his post as "the man on the ground" (as commander of a theater of operations) seemed to have abandoned his earlier enthusiasm for mass evacuation. Gullion's deputy, Colonel Archer Lerch wrote, "I think I detect a decided weakening on the part of General DeWitt [on the question of an evacuation], which I think is most unfortunate." Lerch disliked the plan being worked out by DeWitt and California authorities, who planned to gain cooperation from leaders of the Japanese communities, because it "savors too much of the spirit of Rotary and overlooks the necessary cold-bloodedness of war."[12]

General Gullion stated to General Mark W. Clark, who was preparing to attend yet another congressional meeting about the West Coast alien problem, that "the two Secretaries [Stimson and McCloy] are against any mass movement . . . and they are pretty much against interfering with citizens." After telling Clark what McCloy had said three days earlier about the Constitution being a scrap of paper, Gullion noted, "They are just a little afraid DeWitt hasn't enough grounds to justify any movements of that kind." Gullion gave his opinion to Clark that he didn't think evacuation of aliens alone was a good idea. Bendetsen came on the line to describe the California governor's plan to General Clark and volunteered his opinion that the hoped-for voluntary evacuation of Japanese citizens wouldn't work, that the citizens probably would not want to go with the aliens who would be required to resettle in the designated farming camps. Bendetsen then explained to Clark in some detail that the two secretaries might be willing to approve the licensing plan that would require evacuation of about thirty thousand Japanese citizens and aliens from the Category A areas on the West Coast and mentioned that he had just prepared the memorandum showing the details of such a licensing plan. Clark showed no interest in the licensing plan and gave no hint of his own opinion.[13]

However, there was no doubt about Bendetsen's opinion, and no question that his fingerprints were all over the evacuation plan from its inception.

The first paper Bendetsen wrote about the "Japanese problem" was a single-spaced five-page memorandum dated February 4, 1942, addressed to the provost marshal general on the subject "Alien enemies on the West Coast (and other subversive persons)."[14] He equated the alien enemy problem on the West Coast with the sabotage problem, but argued that alien enemies were not the only potential saboteurs or fifth columnists. For discussion purposes, he lumped together in the term "Japanese" both Japanese aliens and American citizens of Japanese extraction or parentage. Large concentrations of these Japanese resided "closely proximate" to strategically critical areas, he asserted, which threatened U.S. security. Removing only alien Japanese from the West Coast would not solve the problem—they were largely old and ill. A greater threat was presented by the Nisei, the second generation, who would be incensed by any seizure of their parents and might be persuaded to become disloyal because they bore allegiance to Japan. He wrote, "The vast majority of those who have studied the Oriental mind assert that a substantial majority of Nisei bear allegiance to Japan and . . . will engage in organized sabotage, particularly, should a raid along the Pacific Coast be attempted by the Japanese."[15] (Bendetsen made these assertions without listening to Commander Ringle, a qualified student of the "Oriental mind.") He gave no evidence of known sabotage nor any proof that there were subversive individuals among the American-born children of Japanese aliens.[16]

He laid out the possible solutions to the "Japanese problem": designation of prohibited areas; designation of restricted areas; designation of military areas, or mass evacuation of all aliens and citizens of Japanese extraction from the entire Pacific coastal frontier. Bendetsen then argued against the use of prohibited or restricted areas because only aliens could be removed. Mass evacuation was a possibility that he said would "largely relieve the necessity for eternal vigilance." He added, however, that no one has "justified fully the sheer military necessity for such action."[17]

In Bendetsen's opinion the best course would be to designate *military areas*, which were islands surrounding vital installations in the Western Defense Command, "from which all persons who do not have express permission to enter and remain, [would be] excluded as a measure of *military necessity*." To address the problem of excluding citizens, he elaborated on the licensing scheme: "The exclusion of all citizens from certain military areas so designated due to *military necessity* by the military authorities excepting those who have permission to enter is justified and does not constitute an arbitrary discrimination by classes." This was the heart of the military necessity stratagem or premise. He continued, "As a practical matter, the undersigned believes that the accomplishment of such steps will involve an evacuation and internment problem of some considerable proportions."

Bendetsen explained that this action should be implemented starting with an executive order giving the secretary of war control of alien enemies and he was prepared to execute his recommendation: "Drafts of the necessary Executive Order [and a] memorandum to the President for this purpose are in the course of preparation."

He detailed how exclusion would work after the declaration of military areas: All persons to whom permits would not be issued to reenter or to remain would be immediately evacuated from the military areas. He proposed temporary internment "for all alien enemies" involved in such a move, with an open offer to the families of such alien enemies to accompany their parents into internment facilities to be provided by the army. This would be followed by resettlement on a merit basis by other government agencies, involving "release from internment of all those persons who could show that they had a bona fide place to go outside of a military, prohibited or restricted area." He estimated that such action would involve approximately thirty thousand people. In this proposal, all persons, including citizens, who could not get permits would be evacuated; what would be voluntary, apparently, was internment.

This memorandum provided the first thoughtful analysis of possible solutions; the most detailed statement of the steps that might be involved in an evacuation; and a large underestimate of the numbers that could be involved. It asserted for the first time that the exclusion of citizens from military areas was "justified and [did] not constitute an arbitrary discrimination by classes." It provided no justification for basing such a drastic action on military necessity. And it was signed by the writer in his new capacity as a lieutenant colonel, a thirty-four-year-old officer now spelling his name "Bendetsen."[18]

Bendetsen's memorandum of February 4, 1942, reflected discussions that took place the day before between Stimson, McCloy, Gullion, and Bendetsen. The licensing plan had been discussed at length and this may have been the occasion for Bendetsen to lay out for McCloy and Stimson his view of how licensing to exclude a whole racial group could be squared with the Constitution.[19] As will be seen, he detailed his licensing argument in a letter to his friend Colonel Auer in June 1942 and described his surprise at how easily he was able to persuade McCloy and Stimson, and later Attorney General Biddle.[20]

In early February the senior officers of the army in Washington, D.C., became aware of the push for exclusion of the Japanese minority on the West Coast, and appointed General Mark W. Clark (brigadier on the general staff, and later commander of the Fifth Army in the European theater) to look into it. On February 4, General Clark was among "an impressive array of military personnel [who] attended the meeting of West Coast congressmen" trying to evaluate the adequacy of Pacific Coast defenses.[21] Admiral Harold Stark, chief of naval operations, stated that "it would be impossible for the enemy to engage in a sustained attack on the Pacific Coast at the present time."[22] General Clark agreed, presenting "the first truly military appraisal of the situation they [the congressmen] had received." He told the delegation that they were "unduly alarmed" and that "at worst, there might be a sporadic air raid or a commando attack or two," and that "while an attack on Alaska 'was not a fantastic idea,' there was no likelihood of a real onslaught on the West Coast states."[23]

Also on February 4, 1942, Governor Olson gave a radio speech calculated to inflame public opinion against the Japanese in California. He repeated DeWitt's assertions that Japanese residents were communicating information to the enemy, or were preparing for fifth-column activities. Referring to a meeting with General DeWitt, Tom B. Clark, and California officials, Olson stated, "At our conference on Monday, general plans were agreed upon for the movement and placement of the entire adult Japanese population in California, at productive and useful employment within the borders of our state."[24] He challenged members of the Japanese community who considered themselves loyal to show their loyalty by cooperating with the authorities to allow themselves to be relocated. He spoke of his hope that this plan would avoid losing Japanese labor in agricultural production.[25] Privately, several California officials noted that by this means they could possibly avoid an influx of Mexican and Negro farm workers in California.[26]

While briefly back in his Washington office, Bendetsen faced a stack of mail. One letter from Fred Friedlander, a friend from Temple Beth Israel of Aberdeen, asked for help for a cousin, a Jewish refugee then in the United States Army, who had been arrested because he was a German.[27] In a letter dated February 5, 1942, Bendetsen assured Edwin C. Matthias in Seattle that he would "see further activities in connection with the Japanese element on the Pacific Coast soon." It was Matthias who had complained of "mollycoddling" the Japanese and urged that they be removed to concentration camps. Bendetsen said of the predicted actions, "I think you will find them to be more satisfactory."[28] He expressed confidence though no program for mass evacuation had been approved at that time. He may have been counting on the pressure from the West Coast congressional delegations and on his own ability to persuade the two secretaries and the attorney general to push forward the exclusion plan he was drafting.

On February 5, 1942, because of his disagreement with what he called DeWitt's new "more lenient" position regarding removal of Japanese from the West Coast, General Gullion wrote a brief memorandum to McCloy proposing that the exclusion zones be changed to "military reservations." This memorandum adopted language suggested by Bendetsen a day earlier and called for internment east of the Sierra Nevada of all Japanese aliens and those citizen members of their families "as may volunteer for internment." He pointedly stated that all citizens of Japanese extraction would be excluded "from the restricted zones without raising too many legal questions," and that resettlement was "merely an idea and not an essential part of the plan." Gullion sent a second version of this memorandum to McCloy that differed only in the first paragraph—a preface stating: "No half-way measures based upon considerations of economic disturbance, humanitarianism or fear of retaliation will suffice—those would be 'too little and too late.'" He discussed his fears of sabotage in the West Coast states, declaring without attribution, "The danger of Japanese inspired sabotage is great." He did not mention DeWitt's changed position.[29]

On February 7, Bendetsen returned a call to DeWitt, admitting that he had missed him the night before because he had gone "home to dinner for the first time in a week." The general had questions about the licensing proposal that Gullion's office was now seriously promoting. DeWitt had come to understand that the plan could "be justified legally on grounds of military necessity," but was concerned about how the military regulations could be enforced. He said, "I see it is a state of modified martial law" and said that he could not intern persons who would be excluded from restricted areas, asserting, "There is no legal sanction for it." Bendetsen agreed and said he didn't think that the president would suspend the writ of habeas corpus (to allow internment of citizens). Bendetsen said, "The first step would be to get out those who are most undesirable. Now as to Japanese for instance, if you were to exclude all Japanese, in effect, from such an area, then it would be more or less self enforcing because he can't hide his identity and everybody in the area would know that he had no business in there."[30] DeWitt said that he would need some legal sanction in case of violation of his orders. Bendetsen said, "I think that would call for a statutory enactment by the Congress which I think could be easily obtained."[31] In the next month he drafted such a bill.

DeWitt was concerned that when the licensing plan was put into effect it could be very cumbersome: it "would present almost . . . tremendous practical administrative difficulties and it might well break down of its own weight." Bendetsen discounted the difficulties, noting that "as a practical matter you could exclude only by class, e.g., all Japanese, and then on an individual basis those persons who were known to be subversive, like, for example, Harry Bridges, or that type of person." Bendetsen noted, however, that the Justice Department was "a little abhorrent of a blanket type of exclusion . . . [but] they are faced with the fact that they can't substitute their judgment for the military judgment of the Commanding General." In another conversation with DeWitt he said that James Rowe told him that he had about decided to ask the attorney general and the White House to transfer the alien problem to the War Department.[32]

Other California officials joined the anti-Japanese clamoring. Senator Hiram Johnson, who had organized a joint congressional effort that successfully eliminated a quota for Japanese in the Immigration Act of 1924, now served as coordinator of the Pacific Coast delegation's effort to get rid of the West Coast Japanese. Johnson claimed that he was simply concerned about the defense of the West Coast.[33]

Los Angeles mayor Fletcher Bowron joined Governor Olson's campaign to move the Japanese into farm labor camps and added new arguments to the campaign: "If we can send our own young men to war, it is nothing less than sickly sentimentality to say that we will do injustice to American-born Japanese to merely put them in a place of safety so that they can do not harm. . . . We [in Los Angeles] are the ones who will be the human sacrifices if the perfidy that characterized the attack on Pearl Harbor is ever duplicated on the American continent." The next day he argued that the Japanese could not be trusted because Californians had discriminated against them. He said, "Undoubtedly many of them intend to be loyal, but only each individual can know his own intentions, and when the final test comes, who can say but that 'blood will tell?'"[34]

In early February, Attorney General Earl Warren presided over a large meeting of law enforcement officers, mostly sheriffs and district attorneys, at which "hysterical thinking" seemed to be allowed free rein, according to an observer, who wrote, "The meeting loudly applauded the statement that the people of California had no trust in the ability and willingness of the Federal Government to proceed against enemy aliens. One high official was heard to state that he favored shooting on sight all Japanese residents of the state."[35] Warren said that it was ominous that no sabotage had yet occurred: "It seems to me that it is quite significant that in this great state of ours we have had no fifth-column activities and no sabotage reported. It looks very much to me as though it is a studied effort not to have any until the zero hour arrives. . . . That was the history of Pearl Harbor. I can't help believing that the same thing is planned for us in California."[36]

It is worth noting that in this meeting, six law enforcement officers described instances of cooperation that they had received from resident Japanese about possible Japanese disloyalty, information that had been turned over to the FBI.[37] Warren acknowledged this fact during the meeting.

In the meeting with law enforcement officers, he urged enforcement of the alien land laws (which allowed neither ownership nor leasing of land to aliens "ineligible to citizenship"), and asked the local officials to provide maps of their counties showing strategic facilities and nearby land owned or controlled by Japanese, suggesting that by so doing they could show that there was a sinister pattern of distribution of Japanese and Japanese Americans in California.[38]

Bendetsen prepared to head back to the West Coast to draft DeWitt's written report, in order to meet Gullion's deadline of February 13, 1942. In the "Aliens files" in the National Archive is an unsigned page dated February 8, 1942, entitled "Japanese Evacuation, West Coast." The page contains a set of statements that reads like a plan of action for someone wanting to implement Gullion's memoranda of February 5 and 6, 1942: "Prepare definite instructions for DeWitt on the following basis: Select key points where danger is great and size not too large. Put them in order of importance. Evacuate everybody, aliens and citizens. Institute system of permits. Whole matter to be handled by the Army Authorities. *Then, as matter progresses, we will soon find out how far we can go.*" [Emphasis added.] This page may have been the outline for Bendetsen's next discussions with DeWitt and for the next position paper that he would write.[39]

When Bendetsen arrived in San Francisco to help DeWitt put together his recommendation for General Gullion, he brought with him a long memorandum that he had written, entitled "Evacuation of Japanese from the Pacific Coast." In his usual lawyerly way he outlined for DeWitt the options available to him. He argued that all Japanese must be placed in the same category regardless of citizenship status, and repeated his claim that American citizens of Japanese ancestry were a greater threat than were aliens. The only question was the scope of the evacuation. He said that the secretary of war preferred an evacuation from selected areas surrounding vital installations only, asserting, "It is highly improbable that the Secretary will accept the recommendation of the entire evacuation from the coastal strip."[40]

The February 10 memorandum contained Bendetsen's personal commitment to a mass evacuation from the entire West Coast. He compared the claims of "military necessity" against competing economic considerations, saying, "If from the military standpoint, the military disadvantage involved in the loss of vegetable production which may result from a complete evacuation from the Pacific Coast is sufficiently great to outweigh the military advantage, then and only then should the recommendation for evacuation be confined to selected areas." Bendetsen assured DeWitt that Gullion was prepared to implement a mass evacuation and was "compiling a list of available shelter in the zone of the interior" for housing Japanese Americans.[41]

Bendetsen and DeWitt talked about the scope of Category A restricted zones. Bendetsen explained the need for expanding the areas by arguing in each case that "if you drew a protective ring around that plant [the Boeing factory in Seattle] you still wouldn't prevent sabotage from all the lines running out from that plant, take for example the trunk line for power and also for water." By extending this argument to every important facility, it could be argued that the entire western half of the West Coast states should have become a military reservation from which persons considered security risks should have been excluded.

Then Bendetsen telephoned Gullion with "the news that General DeWitt was disposed toward the mass evacuation" that he had proposed.[42] McCloy passed this news on to Stimson, who still did not favor mass evacuation but reluctantly agreed that it was time to put the question before the president. Stimson was not aware that Attorney General Biddle had discussed the Japanese situation on the West Coast over lunch with the president on February 7. Biddle had explained to Roosevelt that he considered mass evacuation inadvisable, that there were no reasons for mass evacuation, and that "it was an army job not, in our opinion, advisable." The president had talked about "the dreadful risk of Fifth Column retaliation in case of a raid."[43]

By the second week of February, the future of all persons of Japanese ancestry on the West Coast was being deliberated by at least four groups, each with differing views of the seriousness of the problem and of the appropriate stringency of measures to be taken. The army's general headquarters did not see the need for evacuation, but had not yet expressed an opinion in regard to the mainland's ethnic Japanese; Brigadier General Mark W. Clark would soon propose a very limited version of DeWitt's initial proposal, favoring removal of aliens only from small islands surrounding a few strategic military and defense facilities. California officials and federal authorities were considering establishing agricultural reservations for those Japanese aliens who would be excluded from strategic West Coast restricted areas, and hoped that they could get the Japanese American citizens to move voluntarily with their alien relatives. The Justice Department was becoming concerned that DeWitt's restricted areas, now numbering eighty-eight, would require removing too many people, including citizens, and, rather than opposing on constitutional grounds, was preparing to disassociate itself from the project. General DeWitt was talking up the California plan while at the same time getting deeper into the details of the licensing plan proposed by Gullion and Bendetsen, which would expand upon the eighty-eight restricted areas already proposed, possibly combining them into even larger areas (called military areas) that could potentially encompass the entire western half of the states of Washington, Oregon, and California and the southern half of Arizona. McCloy and Stimson, the civilian leaders of the War Department and ostensibly the managers of the army, would not seek the opinion of the army's general staff (whose unsolicited opinion arrived too late to change the outcome), and were becoming committed to the Gullion-Bendetsen plan.

By mid-February, the FBI had arrested 2,192 Japanese aliens, 1,393 Germans, and 264 Italians.[44] J. Edgar Hoover was satisfied that no further arrests or removals would be needed: when asked for his opinion just prior to the signing of Executive Order 9066 on February 19, he stated that no case had been made to justify mass evacuation for security reasons. In his experience, as in the one prewar case of Japanese espionage in mid-1941, Japan used Caucasians for its espionage. Hoover did not consider the remaining ethnic Japanese on the West Coast, some 110,000 persons, a security threat.[45]

Few of the men considering mass evacuation, except perhaps the two assistant attorneys general, James Rowe and Edward Ennis, fully appreciated the difficulties that could arise in forcibly excluding a minority group from a large area. Not only would the administrative and logistic problems be large, but the question of where to locate, or relocate, the excluded group could be formidable. How could people who were removed as potential security threats in one section of the country be allowed to disperse and live peacefully in any other area? The army and the affected Americans of Japanese ancestry would find an unpleasant answer to this question.

These high-ranking officials who would soon be asking the president for the power to exclude 110,000 persons of Japanese ancestry from the West Coast were a diverse and experienced trio of public servants. Karl Bendetsen claimed later to have persuaded McCloy, Stimson, and Biddle, all lawyers, that the licensing scheme could be a constitutionally acceptable way to remove a large racial minority from their homes and workplaces in time of war.

Henry L. Stimson was a distinguished senior statesman, a respected Republican, and a "fervent internationalist" when he was invited by President Roosevelt in 1940 to become secretary of war.[46] He had served as a cabinet officer in the administrations of Presidents Taft, Coolidge, and Hoover, as a colonel in field artillery in World War I, and in several diplomatic posts. In the years before World War I, he, along with Grenville Clark, had founded a "military preparedness movement" that argued that peace could only be assured by thoroughly preparing for war. His opposition to the Japanese invasion in Manchuria resulted in a policy of American nonrecognition of territories and agreements achieved by aggression that came to be called the Stimson Doctrine. John J. McCloy was among many who admired Stimson and sought to work toward something Stimson called Pax Americana.[47] A Wall Street lawyer prior to the war, Stimson supposedly "was read out of the Republican party" when he joined the Roosevelt administration.[48] Roosevelt clearly had great respect for Stimson.

According to one biographer, Stimson disliked Biddle. Stimson was also susceptible to racial stereotypes. As a presidential adviser, Stimson was "unapologetic about the use of force in what he considered to be a good cause."[49]

Almost a generation younger than Stimson, Francis Biddle had enjoyed a successful legal career as a corporate lawyer after serving for a year as clerk to Associate Supreme Court Justice Oliver Wendell Holmes. He came to government first as chairman of the National Labor Relations Board

(1934–35), served briefly as a judge, and was appointed solicitor general in 1940, and attorney general in 1941. In his autobiography he defended his inability to stop the mass evacuation, saying, "I was new to the Cabinet, and disinclined to insist on my view to an elder statesman whose wisdom and integrity I greatly respected."[50]

John J. McCloy had gained an international legal reputation in the 1920s, when he spent nine years tracking down the activity of German spies during World War I. He succeeded in fixing responsibility on the German government for the 1917 "Black Tom" munitions explosion in Hoboken, New Jersey. According to his biographer, McCloy "possessed a unique combination of predilections that made him particularly vulnerable to Bendetsen's and Gullion's arguments." His experience in the Black Tom case left him believing that an enemy "would inevitably engage in sabotage," and since his college years at Amherst and "his enthrallment with the military preparedness movement," he was susceptible to national security arguments. It was likely that McCloy would find "objections to strong action on civil-libertarian grounds [to be] indications of soft thinking." McCloy's friend and neighbor, Justice Felix Frankfurter, who would later rule on the constitutionality of the evacuation, encouraged him, saying, "He was handling the Japanese American problem with both wisdom and appropriate hard headedness."[51]

When they met in the War Department prior to the war, John J. McCloy was many things that Karl R. Bendetsen was not. He had many connections among the Eastern establishment, in spite of growing up in straightened circumstances; he had renamed himself after his father who died when he was five; and his widowed mother had worked as a "hairdresser in the homes of well-to-do Philadelphia families." He had attended the right eastern private schools, namely Amherst and Harvard Law School, and had been a successful Wall Street lawyer. In the 1930s both men had spent time crafting a national-security philosophy.

McCloy was mild-mannered and smooth, an expert in "yellow-padding." In meetings with contentious groups, he would take notes on a yellow legal pad then effectively summarize "what everyone seems to be saying," and he was respected for his talent for consensus building. He came to the War Department first as a consultant, and when Stimson became secretary of war, became a special assistant, and then assistant secretary of war. In the course of 1941, Bendetsen had often reported to McCloy for assignments within the War Department, such as supporting the Draft Renewal bill and taking over the Air Associates plant at Bendix,

New Jersey, as well as studying plans for the internment of enemy aliens in the event of war with Germany.[52]

McCloy's experience identifying and prosecuting German American saboteurs in the "Black Tom" case gave him justification for assuming that in a different war Japanese Americans could be saboteurs. He argued for the concept of central intelligence but discounted intelligence information gained by groups he did not control, such as the FBI. Harold Ickes, presidential adviser and secretary of the interior, once said of McCloy, he's "inclined to be a Fascist."

Biographer Kai Bird wrote, "McCloy was now psychologically prepared to be a ready believer in all spy rings. . . . Now McCloy would also be skeptical of skeptics."[53] It's easy to understand how such a person could be swayed by the insistent assertions of DeWitt and Bendetsen that the Japanese Americans presented a threat.

McCloy was more or less reconciled to taking some kind of action against the American Japanese by February 3, 1942. His willingness was pushed further by Gullion's "too little and too late" memorandum, and he made the decision to send Bendetsen back to help DeWitt draft his recommendations. On February 10, McCloy and Stimson met to go over the maps of the West Coast containing the large restricted areas from which DeWitt intended to remove both citizen and alien Japanese. Secretary Stimson still had constitutional doubts: "The second generation Japanese can only be evacuated," he wrote in his diary, "either as part of a total evacuation, giving access to the areas only by permits, or by frankly trying to put them out on the ground that their racial characteristics are such that we cannot understand or trust even the citizen Japanese. *This latter is the fact* but I am afraid it will make a tremendous hole in our constitutional system to apply it."[54] [Emphasis added.] He did worry that the Japanese might invade the United States, and recalled Homer Lea's predictions written some thirty years earlier in *The Valor of Ignorance* that changes in power among Pacific nations would occur so that Japan would be capable of invading a lightly populated and barely defended West Coast and would be able to hold the coast to the crest of the Sierra. Stimson had written in his diary, "In those days [Homer Lea's] book seemed fantastic. Now the things that he prophesied seem quite possible."[55]

By early February, the course of the war contributed to the sense of dread and heightened fears of things Japanese. Japanese military forces in the Far East had achieved a series of devastating victories—Hong Kong fell on Christmas, 1941; Manila in early January; they were invading

Malaysia and Singapore (which fell on February 15), and there was no end in sight to the Japanese advances.

On February 11, 1942, McCloy urged Stimson, who was still unsure of his own views on mass evacuation, to see if the president "was willing to authorize us to move Japanese citizens as well as aliens from restricted areas."[56] Secretary Stimson was not able to get a personal interview with the president, so the consultation would take place by telephone. McCloy and General Mark Clark hastily put together draft notes for Stimson, "Questions to be determined re Japanese exclusion," listing several items, including "Is the President willing to authorize us to move Japanese citizens as well as enemy aliens from restricted areas?" and "Should we undertake withdrawal from the entire strip DeWitt originally recommended, which involves a number of over 100,000 people, if we include both aliens and Japanese citizens?" Two lesser steps involved removal of about seventy thousand people, or a smaller removal from restricted islands around critical installations only.[57] From Stimson's notes it seems clear that these less ambitious evacuations were not discussed.

The call from the president came through to Stimson at 1:30 P.M. on Wednesday, February 11, 1942. "I took up with him the West Coast matter first," Stimson wrote in his diary, "and told him the situation and fortunately found that he was very vigorous about it and told me to go ahead on the line that I had myself thought the best."[58] Stimson still had reservations, and favored a limited evacuation plan, "concentrating on areas around the big bomber plants."[59] The president had given no direction on the question of evacuating citizens.

McCloy called Bendetsen at the DeWitt's headquarters at the Presidio of San Francisco shortly thereafter, informing him, "We have *carte blanche* to do what we want to as far as the President is concerned." He said that the president "states that there will probably be some repercussion, but it has got to be dictated by military necessity, but as he puts it, 'Be as reasonable as you can.'"[60]

Bendetsen called Gullion an hour later, relaying news of the "carte blanche" statement, suggesting that DeWitt's evacuation program would involve roughly 101,000 people. (The number would rise to 110,000.)[61] This was his interpretation of reasonable. The battle for mass evacuation was essentially over, though not all the participants, or the press, knew it. And at this point, the only written recommendations for an evacuation based on military necessity were those written by Bendetsen.

On about February 12, General Mark W. Clark completed his own report for general headquarters on the inadvisability of mass evacuation of the West Coast Japanese. In a conversation with DeWitt that day he expressed disbelief that the West Coast commander was proposing a large evacuation to include citizens as well as Japanese aliens. He had reached an opposite conclusion. He gave two reasons for opposing a "mass exodus": "We will never have a perfect defense against sabotage *except at the expense of other equally important efforts*," and "We must weigh the advantages and disadvantages of such a wholesale solution to this problem. We must not permit our entire offensive effort to be sabotaged in an effort to protect all establishments from ground sabotage." [Emphasis added.] He recommended a cautious, step-by-step approach to the problem: Prioritize the list of critical installations (such as Boeing plants, Bremerton Navy Yard), select the most important, delimit small areas around them and eject enemy aliens from those areas; use civilian police as much as possible, urge the FBI to expand its counterintelligence activity, use raids (to seize contraband), arrest and intern ring leaders and suspects, and make it known to the alien group that "the first overt act on their part" would "bring a wave of counter-measures" that would "make the historical efforts of the vigilantes look puny in comparison." He made no mention of restricting citizens. His last point summarized his measured approach: "It is estimated that to evacuate large numbers of this group will require one soldier to 4 or 5 aliens. This would require between 10,000 and 15,000 soldiers to guard the group during their internment, to say nothing of the continuing burden of protecting the [military and industrial] installations. I feel that this problem must be attacked in a *sensible manner*. We must admit that we are taking some chances just as we take other chances in war. We must determine what are our really critical installations, give them thorough protection and leave the others to incidental means in the hope that we will not lose too many of them—and above all keep our eyes on the ball—that is, the *creating and training of an offensive Army*."[62] [Emphasis added.]

General Clark's assessment that the arguable benefits of mass evacuation did not warrant the cost in troops and logistics probably represented the thinking of the general staff. However, the decision-making process did not depend on their views or seek their approval. There is no indication in the record that Generals Clark or Marshall were asked for their views by the president or the civilian leaders at the War Department after Clark's report was issued. Gullion had successfully insinuated himself into the chain of communication between DeWitt and Washington.

While War Department officials agonized, deliberated, and planned, the country's press had not finished with its mastication of the "Japanese problem." Among the journalists who wrote against the American Japanese, the most prominent was Walter Lippmann. Among the arguments put forth against the Japanese minority, the one forwarded by Lippmann was the most shocking and outrageous. Lippmann was a syndicated columnist for the conservative *Herald Tribune*, and his generally liberal opinions were widely admired and discussed. In early February 1942, he had traveled to the West Coast to talk to military officials. In a briefing by General DeWitt during the time that Bendetsen was in his headquarters preparing DeWitt's report to the secretary of war, Lippmann apparently swallowed whole DeWitt's view of the danger presented by the West Coast Japanese. On February 12, 1942, his article entitled "The Fifth Column on the Coast" appeared in papers across America and raised the level of outcry against a group of Americans who had given no cause for action, but merely looked like the enemy.[63]

Lippmann wrote, "The Pacific Coast is in imminent danger of a combined attack from within and without. . . . The peculiar danger of the Pacific Coast is in a Japanese raid accompanied by enemy action inside American territory." As evidence, Lippmann stated that "the Japanese Navy has been reconnoitering the Pacific Coast," and that "communication takes place between the enemy at sea and enemy agents on land." (By early February most of Japan's submarines had returned to waters in the Western Pacific, and only General DeWitt still believed that any signaling was taking place.) Citing the fact that "no important sabotage" had occurred on the coast, Lippmann repeated the time-honored argument of conspiracy theorists, who contended that this is "a sign that the blow is well-organized and that it is held back until it can be struck with maximum effect."[64]

Lippmann lamented that the army and the navy were facing this threat "with one hand tied down in Washington," because they were not being given a free hand to intern citizens as well as those who were "technically alien enemies." He disparaged "legalistic and ideological arguments" over the rights of citizens and made the case for a military solution to the problem: "The Pacific coast is officially a combat zone: Some part of it may be at any moment a battlefield. Nobody's constitutional rights include the right to reside and do business on a battlefield."

Westbrook Pegler, an arch-conservative journalist with a biting pen who wrote for the *New York World-Telegram* and was widely syndicated, amplified and expanded on Lippmann's comments. He accepted Lippmann's statements as fact, and concluded, "The Japanese in California should be put under armed guard to the last man and woman right now and to hell with *habeas corpus* until the danger is over."[65]

Political cartoonist Theodor Seuss Geisel (subsequently well known for his Dr. Seuss children's books) added to the anti-Japanese hysteria the next day with a cartoon entitled "Waiting for the Signal from Home" in which an army of smiling men with slant eyes, glasses, and bowler hats streams through Washington, Oregon, and California to pick up bricks of TNT from a tiny house labeled "Honorable 5th Column," while another grinning, slant-eyed man with a spyglass studies the sea to the west looking for that signal.[66]

Though he himself was not doing well at fending off the army's assault on the rights of Japanese Americans, Attorney General Biddle felt compelled to take Lippmann to task for his intemperate statements, and a week later, in a letter to President Roosevelt drafted by James Rowe, decried the Lippmann column (and Westbrook Pegler's amplification): "My last advice from the War Department is that there is no evidence of imminent attack and from the F.B.I. that there is no evidence of planned sabotage."[67] Urging Roosevelt to speak out against such arguments (and giving him colorful language to use in his coming press conference), Biddle wrote, "It is extremely dangerous for the columnists, acting as 'Armchair Strategists and Junior G-Men,' to suggest that an attack on the West Coast and planned sabotage is imminent when the military authorities and the F.B.I. have indicated that this is not the fact. It comes close to shouting FIRE! in the theater; and if race riots occur, these writers will bear a heavy responsibility. Either Lippmann has information which the War Department and the F.B.I. apparently do not have, or is acting with dangerous irresponsibility." Roosevelt never used these words or any others on behalf of the rights of Japanese Americans.

According to his biographer, Lippmann was not concerned by the criticism of the attorney general or Tom C. Clark, who accused the columnist of making hysterical statements. Even years later, when others, such as Earl Warren (who became governor of California and chief justice of the Supreme Court), "came to deplore the part they [had] played, Lippmann never recanted." After the evacuation was under way he complained that the government had handled the problem incorrectly, that they should have treated it as a problem of military security and not of citizenship: "The legal fiction, which in a matter of this sort is profoundly important, could have been preserved that we were evacuating individuals and not members of a racial group." His biographer concluded that for Lippmann, "public order and national unity were more important to him during a time of crisis than civil liberties."[68] Lippman "accepted . . . the argument that all Americans of Japanese ancestry were potential fifth columnists and should be treated as a class apart from other citizens. It was a rationale the Nazis could have used about the Jews."[69]

What is shocking about Lippmann's attacks on due process is that by putting his imprimatur on DeWitt's justifications, he distorted the public debate. Editorial writers for the Hearst papers, such as Henry McLemore who voiced strong hatred for and fear of the Japanese, could have been dismissed as Western racists who hoped to benefit in some way from removal of the ethnic Japanese. Lippmann brought the debate to the national level, and Westbrook Pegler picked up the beat and turned up the volume.

One could also say that General DeWitt used Lippmann to advance his own agenda, knowing that an aroused public opinion would put more pressure on his colleagues in Washington; it was a clear example of DeWitt's willingness to indoctrinate an influential person with his supposed military expertise.

DeWitt's recommendation was finally put forth in a memorandum for the secretary of war, dated February 13, 1942, and written with Bendetsen's assistance. Entitled "Evacuation of Japanese and other Subversive Persons from the Pacific Coast," it ran more than six single-spaced pages. In the first section, DeWitt detailed "possible and probable enemy activities," including naval attacks on the West Coast, air raids and sabotage of vital installations, and asserted, "Hostile naval and air raids, will be assisted by enemy agents signaling from the coastline," and so on. The justification for this assertion: "*The Japanese race is an enemy race* and while many second and third generation Japanese born on United States soil . . . have become 'Americanized,' the racial strains are undiluted." Asserting that Japanese raised in the United States would fail to be loyal, he echoed Lippmann's words (which he had no doubt inspired): "It, therefore, follows that along the vital Pacific Coastal Frontier over 112,000 potential enemies, of Japanese extraction, are at large today. There are indications that these are organized and ready for concerted action at a favorable opportunity. The very fact that no sabotage has taken place to date is a disturbing and confirming indication that such action will be taken."[70]

The memo, in language very similar to Bendetsen's memorandum of

February 4, recommended that "the Secretary of War procure from the President direction and authority to designate military areas in the combat zone of the Western Theater of Operations (if necessary to include the entire combat zone), from which, in his discretion he may exclude all Japanese, all alien enemies, and all other persons suspected for any reason by the administering military authorities of being actual or potential saboteurs, espionage agents, or fifth columnists." He asked that the executive order use military necessity to control the right of all persons to reside, enter, cross, or be within any military areas using a pass-and-permit basis at the discretion of the secretary of war; he requested the necessary legislation imposing penalties for violation of military orders.

He asked that the military areas encompass all Category A areas previously designated. All persons in the classes selected to be excluded from the military areas were to be evacuated on a designated day and as rapidly as practicable. All Japanese aliens and other alien enemies were to be evacuated and interned at selected places of internment, under guard. At the time of evacuation, the Japanese American citizens would be offered an opportunity to accept voluntary internment, under guard, and those who declined would be "left to their own resources, or, in the alternative, be encouraged to accept resettlement outside of such military areas," with some help from government agencies. Only the fourth group, "other persons . . . suspected . . . to be actual or potential saboteurs," would be treated individually rather than as a class. DeWitt proposed that the Western Defense Command and Fourth Army "be responsible for the evacuation, administration, supply, and guard to the place of internment."[71]

DeWitt recommended that adult males (above the age of fourteen) be interned separately from all women and children "until the establishment of family units can be accomplished." When General DeWitt earlier mentioned this detail, Bendetsen had tried to dissuade him, saying, "Of course, there is a large administrative problem involved in keeping the records straight so that we would not have another Evangeline situation" (in which family members were separated).[72]

DeWitt stated that "mass internment be considered as largely a temporary expedient pending selective resettlement." He estimated the number of persons to be involved in the recommended evacuation would total approximately 133,000 (including 25,000 Japanese aliens, 44,000 Japanese American citizens, 44,000 Italians, and about 20,000 Germans, all from Category A areas). Clearly, this would be a mass evacuation.

DeWitt noted that if the recommended action were approved he would want the flexibility to establish additional military areas, "as . . . necessary" DeWitt's memo shows the fine hand of Bendetsen's legal writing, and is a fleshing out of Gullion's brief recommendation. If, as Attorney General Biddle noted, this is the official "finding" for the policy of "military necessity," one can only conclude that the justification for the concern about persons of Japanese ancestry was largely racial: in DeWitt's words, "The Japanese race is an enemy race."[73]

It is also evident that DeWitt understood that the licensing scheme allowed the army to force Japanese American citizens out of military areas, but would not allow him to order their internment.[74] He also wanted German and Italian aliens evacuated from Category A areas.

Although Bendetsen carried a copy of DeWitt's recommendations back to Washington on February 17, it was not the model for the final plan; the official copy did not arrive in Washington until after the executive order was signed. When DeWitt's recommendation did arrive, the General Headquarters staff conference did not concur and instead recommended that only enemy alien leaders be arrested and interned. The General Headquarters' nonconcurrence was futile, as they would soon find out.

As noted earlier, Colonel Bendetsen felt that he had been responsible for inventing the licensing method based on military necessity. In a June 3, 1942, letter to his friend and mentor Colonel Auer, Bendetsen talked about Executive Order 9066. He wrote, "I was rather amazed that I was able to sell Attorney General Biddle on the idea. There was no difficulty in selling Mr. McCloy within a Sunday afternoon's conference at his home on or about February 15." He said, at that time it was not by any means certain that there was an intention to undertake mass evacuation. . . . I suggested to the Attorney General that it might be constitutional as a matter of *military necessity* to exclude all persons from . . . an island [around a vital installation] and license back on an individual basis those persons whose reentry was found to be necessary to the war effort. This idea after some discussion was pretty largely accepted. I then suggested that in so doing it would be also constitutional to decline to license back into the area persons of Japanese ancestry, admitting perhaps a few 'token' Japanese to preserve the individual licensing idea. The Attorney General agreed to that. I then argued that persons of Japanese ancestry as a group were potentially an enemy group and that in view of the fact that we were at war with the Japanese it would not be arbitrary to decline to readmit all excluded Japanese to such island area. The attorney general finally agreed to this. I then argued that what you could do by *indirection* you could also do by direction, vis., to exclude in the first instance only those persons who would ultimately not be readmitted under the other method. After considerable hubbub, this view was finally accepted and the Executive Order was constructed on that theory."[75]

McCloy had to have been aware that "momentous decisions being made were based on contrary evidence."[76] On February 17, James Rowe drafted Attorney General Biddle's futile letter to President Roosevelt opposing mass evacuation because "'the military authorities and the F.B.I.' had yet to produce evidence of any concrete military necessity."[77] McCloy made a brief entry in his diary: "Dangers too for the reason of yielding to local pressures which demand intelligent action, it is a problem but I'm afraid no easy solution or one which will not be criticized whatever way we move. It is clear, however, we must act with full responsibility and dispatch."[78] At the same time, General Mark Clark was telling McCloy and Stimson that the army's general headquarters was opposed to a mass evacuation and was unwilling to allot to DeWitt any additional troops.

But the decision had gotten away from the general headquarters, and from the Justice Department. Bendetsen had returned from DeWitt's post on February 17 and was included in a War Department afternoon strategy session to prepare for the decisive meeting at Attorney General Biddle's home that evening. Stimson recorded the outcome of the afternoon meeting in his diary: "A proposed order for the President was outlined and General Gullion undertook to have it drafted tonight. War Department orders will fill in the application of this Presidential order. These were outlined and Gullion is also to draft them."[79] As Gullion's legal draftsman, Bendetsen must have had a busy afternoon, since he claimed to have conceived and drafted the executive order as well as the evacuation plan.

At Biddle's home that evening, McCloy, Gullion, and Bendetsen again faced Justice representatives, including Rowe, Ennis, and Biddle, in what became a confrontation. Rowe and Ennis "launched into an exposition of why a mass evacuation of citizens would be unconstitutional." When Gullion pulled from his pocket the evacuation order that he and Bendetsen had drafted that afternoon and read it aloud, "Rowe couldn't believe it. 'I laughed at him,'" Rowe recalled later that year. "'The old buzzard got mad. I told him he was crazy.'"[80] Biddle, however, had given in, saying that he had agreed to support an evacuation order because the president had decided "it was a matter of military judgment." He did not mention that he had spoken to the president that afternoon, and wrote later, "I did not think I should oppose it [evacuation] further."[81] Biddle immediately wanted to get to work polishing the order, to the astonishment of Ennis and Rowe, who were devastated. "Ennis almost wept," Rowe later said. "I was so mad I could not speak at all myself and the meeting soon broke up."[82]

A congressional committee, the Select Committee Investigating National Defense Migration, headed by Representative John H. Tolan of California, was preparing to hold hearings on the West Coast to consider the effect of a probable evacuation order. The War and Justice Departments were asked to cooperate with the committee. On February 18, while waiting for the executive order, McCloy wrote to General DeWitt to suggest that he also appear before the committee. McCloy cautioned him to be careful, saying, "There is no need for any investigation of the military aspect of the problem," and also "you should not give Mr. Tolan the impression that the coast is just on the verge of a 'mass' evacuation." McCloy wished to prepare DeWitt's testimony by making specific suggestions for what he should say: "notify them that an officer [Bendetsen had] just returned to Washington after very thorough study and consultation with you and your staff on the matter of the withdrawal of Japanese from strategic areas; that such officer visited all the critical areas along the Coast and studied each area with officers of your command; and that this officer returned with certain plans and recommendations for the consideration of the Secretary of War and the Chief of Staff."[83] McCloy further cautioned DeWitt that until actual evacuation plans had been made, "it would be improper for you to discuss them." DeWitt should point out that the army was charged with the responsibility for the defense of the West Coast, and "certain dispositions had to be made of enemy aliens and of others who might be potentially dangerous to the defense of the West Coast." McCloy told DeWitt to urge Mr. Tolan to conduct his investigations "with as little publicity as possible" into the dislocations which would be caused by the removal of these elements to avoid stirring up feeling on the Coast "on the matter of Japanese withdrawals."[84]

With the battle over, the Justice Department officials were required not only to help by "polishing up the order" but would have to carry it to the president for his signature. Ennis resisted to the bitter end, "arguing with Stimson and Biddle and getting absolutely nowhere because his own boss was against him." At one point, Rowe said he "had to convince Ennis that it was not important enough to make him quit his job."[85] It was Rowe's task to accompany the order to the White House, and wait for the president's signature, which came on Thursday, February 19, 1942.

Executive Order 9066 authorized Secretary of War Stimson "to prescribe military areas . . . from which any or all persons [might] be excluded."[86] There was no mention of persons of Japanese ancestry, but it explicitly allowed Stimson or his military commander to regulate "the right of any person to enter, remain in or leave [those areas] . . . subject to whatever restriction the Secretary of War or the appropriate Military Commander [might] impose." The order did not bother to embody the licensing scheme that Bendetsen had championed—it simply allowed the military commander to exclude whom he wished. The viewpoint of Gullion and Bendetsen prevailed over that of the highest Justice Department officials, including FBI chief J. Edgar Hoover, and in spite of the misgivings of both McCloy and Stimson.

The president had not had time to meet in person with Stimson and had little time to consider the implications of the executive order. One recent study suggests that the president held the prejudicial sentiments toward ethnic Japanese in America that were common in the United States during his formative years, which made it easy for him to approve the order.[87] He undoubtedly assumed that Stimson, a respected cabinet member, favored the issue he had brought to the president regarding the disposition of the West Coast Japanese. Writing about Roosevelt, Biddle said, "The Constitution has never greatly bothered any wartime President," and, "He [FDR] was never theoretical about things. What must be done to defend the country must be done. . . . Nor do I think the constitutional difficulty plagued him."[88]

The week that the president agreed to and signed the order was a bad one for the civil libertarian in the family, his wife Eleanor. Before Pearl Harbor, Mrs. Roosevelt, who championed the rights of minorities and the downtrodden, had taken an unpaid but working position as head of volunteers with the Office of Civilian Defense, which was originally headed by New York Mayor Fiorello LaGuardia. The conservative press disapproved of some of Mrs. Roosevelt's actions, but mostly opposed her having any position in government. In mid-February she bowed to public pressure and reluctantly resigned from the position. This uproar distracted her from the evacuation decision. At the beginning of the war Mrs. Roosevelt and her husband held opposite views of the threat posed by Americans of Japanese ancestry, and she had argued in favor of Japanese Americans:

"[These people] are good Americans and have the right to live as anyone else," she had told her husband. She spoke out as much as she could and opposed plans for evacuation, but "once FDR signed Executive Order 9066 and internment began, ER fell silent," presumably at the president's request.[89] Troubled by what she considered the unfairness of the evacuation, she wrote in one of her newspaper columns that she "could not bear to think of children behind barbed wire looking out at the free world."[90] Mrs. Roosevelt later visited one of the relocation centers, which the president called concentration camps, observing and reporting on the detainees' many problems, and tried to persuade her husband to end their detention.

In February 1942 Bendetsen probably would not have minded being called the inventor of military necessity. He was convinced that he had persuaded his superiors to accept the licensing scheme to allow the exclusion of West Coast "Japs." The February 13 document that he had helped DeWitt write, which was the finding for the executive order, provided no evidence that any of the ethnic Japanese who would be affected by the order had committed acts of sabotage, treason or subversion. There is no evidence that he and DeWitt had talked to any Japanese aliens or Japanese Americans about their allegiance to America. What Bendetsen and DeWitt asserted can only be called a racial argument, though they would argue strenuously against this view whenever their involvement with the Japanese American evacuation and incarceration was mentioned.

CHAPTER SIX

Taking Full Charge

The Army's job is to kill Japanese not to save Japanese . . . if the Army is to devote its facilities to resettlement and social welfare work among Japanese aliens, it will be that much more difficult for it to get on to its primary task, that of winning the war.

—Lieutenant Colonel Karl R. Bendetsen

Things happened fast after the signing of the executive order. Secretary of War Stimson delegated the authority granted to him by the president's executive order to General DeWitt and requested that as "far as military requirements permit . . . you do not disturb . . . Italian aliens and persons of Italian lineage" unless such persons "constitute a definite danger." Stimson stated that the Italian population was less dangerous and also too numerous to be included in any evacuation.[1]

The War Department was surprised when Attorney General Biddle decided that the order did not require any enforcement legislation. In a memorandum to the president on February 20, 1942, Biddle said that the powers granted to the War Department could be "exercised against the Japanese regardless of their citizenship." Bendetsen was unhappy about the lack of legislation, knowing that only the Congress had the power to back up an executive order. In a conversation reported by Bernard Gufler of the State Department, Bendetsen "displayed great bitterness toward the Department of Justice. . . . [It was] continually writing 'letters for the record' to the War Department and was 'passing the Buck' to the War Department." He implied," continued Gufler, "that the Department of Justice was refraining from taking necessary action and was reserving for itself the position of critic of the War Department's actions."

Bendetsen described to Gufler the army's hope that the evacuation could be orderly, and hoped to avoid bad publicity, which might inspire reprisals against American prisoners of war or others detained by the enemy. He told Gufler that the Army would provide food, shelter, and transportation for evacuees who could not get themselves moved before the voluntary deadline, but did not "desire to advertise the fact . . . for fear that there might be a rush on the part of numerous aliens to take advantage of free living." He pointed out that "the War Department is not a W.P.A. or resettlement organization" and should be training troops to win the war.[2] Was Bendetsen beginning to see the point stressed by General Mark Clark in his memo opposing mass evacuation?

Also on February 20, 1942, McCloy sent DeWitt a brief letter and a long memorandum prepared by Bendetsen that was "a suggested method of procedure" to be used as a guide in planning for the evacuation. It charged DeWitt with the designation of military areas and the promulgation of appropriate restrictive regulations governing access to military areas and asked him to prepare a detailed plan of evacuation, including a timetable. DeWitt was exhorted to make exceptions "in favor of the aged, infirm and the sick" and for bona fide war refugees among the German aliens. He was given military responsibility for processing evacuees, actually evacuating them, supplying and transporting evacuees to points of shelter, and planning for protection of the property of the evacuees, particularly physical property. He was promised the cooperation of other federal agencies to assist in carrying out the executive order.[3]

This was a large program to turn over to the military commander of the Western Defense Command, who in spite of his blustering willingness earlier, already had a large job managing the defense of the eight Western states and Alaska, as well as overseeing training of the 240,000 troops in his command.[4] DeWitt would need an executive for this project. And in the days after the February 19 signing of the executive order, there was an obvious candidate.

Newly promoted lieutenant colonel Bendetsen was ordered back to the West Coast on February 22, 1942, again on temporary duty, "as an observer," he later stated. He was to travel by commercial or military aircraft, was given a flat per diem of six dollars "in lieu of subsistence," and was instructed to draw up a detailed evacuation plan.[5] His task was to perfect a plan for handling more than a hundred thousand persons, including women and children; details would address concerns about transportation, sanitation, food service, education, and even social welfare.

Here is how Bendetsen later told the story of his next assignment: "Shortly after the Executive order was issued, I was again sent to the

Headquarters of the Western Defense Command at the Presidio of San Francisco. While I was there, the Honorable John J. McCloy, the Assistant Secretary of War, and the Chief of Staff of the Army [unlikely] were conferring with General DeWitt.[6]

"I had completed my special assignment . . . had paid my departure respects to General DeWitt's Chief of Staff, General [Allison J.] Barnett, and left for the San Francisco airport. . . . As I was walking up the steps to enter the aircraft, an aide of General DeWitt drove onto the field in a military car and stopped the car right at the bottom of the companionway. He said, 'Bendetsen, you're wanted at the Presidio.'" The aide told Bendetsen, "'General DeWitt and Mr. McCloy are together and they are waiting for you.'"

When Bendetsen was "ushered into the august presence of Mr. McCloy [and] Generals Marshall and DeWitt," McCloy told him that the three of them "feel that you are the best choice to be in charge of this whole program."[7]

In telling this story, Bendetsen not only added General Marshall (who was not in fact present) for greater effect, but also found a way to include McCloy's favorable assessment of his work. Asked whether they had stated why they had selected him, Bendetsen continued, "I had been asked by Mr. McCloy about ten days before to write out for him how such an evacuation might be carried into effect. I then wrote him two letters, a relatively short letter and a very long one. I gave him both." He said that McCloy told him, "Those letters are what hung you, Bendetsen. The Secretary of War and I did not have any choice but to say to General DeWitt that we're going to send Bendetsen out here to be under your command and to take full charge."[8] McCloy referred to these letters in the course of the conversation in the Presidio, stating that he regarded them as "remarkable in their concepts as well as their details of how to proceed if such a decision were to be made."[9]

These letters spelled out in detail the organization of a military hierarchy that would develop and execute an evacuation, so that in addition to conceiving the executive order, Bendetsen could accurately claim that he had "conceived and organized the Civil Affairs Division and the Wartime Civil Control Administration of the Western Defense Command," and had "conceived the method, formulated the detailed plans for, and directed the evacuation of 120,000 persons of Japanese ancestry from military areas of the Pacific Coast."[10]

Telling this story years later, Bendetsen claimed that he could still recount from memory the full text of the order that DeWitt dictated as the group listened: "I hereby delegate to you all and in full my powers and authority under Executive Order 9066"—some three hundred words instructing him to "take this action forthrightly . . . with a minimum disruption of the logistics of military training . . . and preparedness, and with a minimum of military personnel." In his recollection, he was told to "make it known that the Army has no wish to retain them [Japanese persons] at any time for more than temporary custody. . . . These measures are for the protection of the nation in a cruel and bitter war, and for the protection of the Japanese people themselves."[11] In actuality, as he had predicted in his memorandum of February 4, the army was faced with "an evacuation and internment problem of some considerable proportions." This so-called temporary custody—a fiction of his later revisionist memory—quickly evolved into rigid detention.

Bendetsen was immediately designated as assistant chief of staff of the Fourth Army and the Western Defense Command. DeWitt created the Wartime Civil Control Administration (WCCA), which Bendetsen had described in his letter as the main vehicle for managing the evacuation, and named Bendetsen as its commanding officer. As assistant chief of staff for DeWitt he would be expected to issue orders in DeWitt's name to be executed by himself as commanding officer of the WCCA. DeWitt told him, "You will thus have full power and authority to act."

The new job also resulted in a very speedy promotion (really a double promotion): "The following morning [March 12, 1942] I was promoted to the grade of full Colonel with rank from February 1, 1942, which made me the youngest in that grade at that time."[12]

In a written order dated March 15, 1942, DeWitt delegated the powers that had in sequence been delegated by the president to the secretary of war, to the army chief of staff, and to him as commanding general of the Western Defense Command, to Colonel Karl R. Bendetsen.

Though he later claimed that he had not sought the job—that he never even had an opinion on the advisability of an evacuation—Bendetsen was now entrusted with the very job that he had, through his hard work in the preceding two months, created—that is, to organize a bureaucracy to effect a mass evacuation and to construct both temporary and permanent housing for 110,000 persons of Japanese ancestry. In the eyes of his superiors, he would do the job brilliantly and earn a military medal for his labors.[13] But he could never rid himself of the taint of his involvement and enthusiasm for this clear injustice against an American minority.

On February 20, 1942, the day after the executive order was signed, Representative John H. Tolan began the lengthy set of hearings in California considering the "problems of evacuation of enemy aliens and others from prohibited military zones." Prior hearings of the committee had considered questions of civilian morale and the manpower available for war production. Now that the decision to evacuate had been made, the Tolan Committee deliberations could influence only the handling of the incarceration and relocation of the evacuees.

The committee actually received a more balanced set of opinions than had the army. Groups and individuals came forward to speak against the evacuation and on behalf of the loyalty of most Japanese Americans—including Nisei leaders, some academics, churchmen, and labor leaders—although their testimony largely accepted the evacuation as a fait accompli. Some members of the Japanese communities and the twelve-year-old Japanese American Citizens League offered full cooperation with the evacuation as a way to prove the loyalty of their members. Many of the groups that had earlier argued for mass evacuation testified or sent resolutions to the Tolan Committee repeating their statements of distrust and fear of Japanese aliens and citizen Japanese.

Earl Warren's statement to the Tolan Committee included a long, detailed attack on West Coast Japanese and Japanese Americans. As did Bendetsen, Warren lumped together all Americans of Japanese ancestry into the term Japanese or "Japs." Among their offenses, which were largely guilt by vague association, he included their being "very closely organized," noting that Japanese organizations covered every branch of life: Organizations such as the Military Virtue Society of North America, a Japanese school, a Japanese newspaper, and young people's Buddhist organizations shared post office boxes in many communities. He listed "particular points where Japanese are immediately adjacent to strategic points in counties of California." For example, in Marin County, the first entry on the list was "Japs in Sausalito close to Fort Baker, Golden Gate Bridge, with full view of traffic in and out of San Francisco Bay"; another entry read "Jap across the street from boat works." None of the supposedly sinister placements of Japanese were any more explicit than that. Warren reiterated his statement that "the consensus of law enforcement officials of this State is that there is more potential danger among the group of Japanese who are born in this country than from the group of alien Japanese."[14] He expressed satisfaction with the executive order that had been signed, and declared that no Japanese had ever given a law enforcement officer any information on possible subversive activities or any disloyalty to this country by a Japanese, which contradicted testimony he heard at the meeting with law enforcement officers in early February, and added that this absence of informants was another seemingly ominous fact to hold against them. He gave no evidence of actual cases of spying or sabotage by any persons of Japanese descent. The bulk of Warren's lengthy testimony was later incorporated verbatim into DeWitt's *Final Report*, which was prepared by Bendetsen. Warren was elected governor of California that fall.

Prior to his appointment as assistant chief of staff but while he was at the Presidio of San Francisco, Bendetsen had assisted DeWitt by preparing several proclamations designed to pave the way for the actual evacuation. The first in what would be a very long series, was Public Proclamation 1. Issued on March 2, 1942, it designated as Military Area 1 the broad coastal strip including the western halves of California, Oregon, and Washington, and the southern half of Arizona. Military Area 2 took up the remaining areas of the three coastal states. In an accompanying press release, DeWitt declared, "Eventually orders will be issued requiring all Japanese including those who are American-born to vacate all of Military Area No. 1." In the press release DeWitt offered "voluntary resettlement": "Japanese and other aliens who move into the interior out of this area in all probability will not again be disturbed."[15] In spite of this statement, about 5,300 individuals, Japanese aliens and citizens, many of whom voluntarily moved out of Military Area 1 and into Military Area 2 in March, were warned on June 2, 1942, that they were prohibited from further migration and were ordered to await "controlled evacuation" into what was called an assembly center. By mid-August they were all incarcerated.

The newly promoted Colonel Bendetsen set up headquarters for the WCCA in the Whitcomb Hotel at 1231 Market Street in downtown San Francisco. He quickly collected a staff and called meetings of administrators from the other government agencies who would be asked to provide critical services to the evacuation project. These agencies included the Treasury Department, Federal Reserve Bank of San Francisco, a proposed Alien Property Custodian, Works Progress Administration (WPA), Bureau of the Census, Social Security Board, Public Health Service, Employment Service, and Farm Security Administration.[16]

An administrator from the Agriculture Department gave a view of the first days of Bendetsen's tenure. Laurence Hewes had been selected by Milton Eisenhower, a former colleague at Agriculture, to assist in the evacuation.[17] When Hewes reported to DeWitt's headquarters before Bendetsen's office was established, he made the mistake of giving his personal opinion, "I don't like the evacuation. I think it's absolutely wrong to tear 100,000 innocent people from their homes because of their color and the shape of their eyes." An unidentified aide in DeWitt's office, "a burly Colonel," told him in no uncertain terms, "You . . . have been given . . . a properly authorized order, given through official channels in time of war. . . . All I want to know is whether you intend to obey. Before this war is over lots of people will take orders, including orders to go and get killed." Realizing he must swallow his personal beliefs, he said, "Please tell General DeWitt I'm at his service."

Hewes gave this report of his first meeting with the officer in charge, whom he incorrectly referred to as major, though Bendetsen was by then a full colonel:

"On a Sunday morning in mid-March, slender, restrained, beautifully poised, young Major Karl R. Bendetsen stood before a blackboard in a close, smoky, Hotel Whitcomb conference room. This remarkable young man, on whom rested the evacuation's full weight, spoke to a mixed civilian-military group. Like me, the civilians were Government officials ordered to assist the evacuation. . . . Bendetsen was a master; his explanation so clear, his manner so quietly compelling, his command of facts and English so distinguished that without apparent effort he swung his audience to his purpose."[18]

Continuing his praise of Bendetsen's presentation, Hewes wrote, "The effect was almost hypnotic. There on the wall was the map of the Pacific Coast with a new North-South line from British Columbia to Mexico. For our Japanese neighbors, America now commenced east of that line. We Caucasians, patriots by virtue of our skin, could continue to reside west of the line. With the deftness of a surgeon and with somewhat the same reassuring antiseptic quality, the young Major told us of evacuation proclamations to be followed by voluntary evacuation, followed in turn by involuntary evacuation, and *mild detention for three or four years in a Federal institution*. Bendetsen's tones made one think of restful bucolic retirement, not of barbed wire or bayonets." [Emphasis added.]

Hewes listened in awe to Bendetsen's presentation, then noted, "There was a slight alteration in Bendetsen's manner, a more businesslike tone; a faint ring of authority. He began to speak of civilian responsibilities, rapidly sketching the field organization which was to handle the actual work. Within three days the Army would establish forty-eight field stations at locations scattered from Canada to Phoenix, Arizona. One unit in each station was labeled—Agriculture. For a minute I was shocked. How on earth could I find forty-eight crews to staff these offices, much less get them to their stations in three days? I saw that my civilian colleagues were equally shocked. Bendetsen's pleasant smile infuriated me: 'I know, gentlemen, you can't do it, no one expects it. It's just to give you an idea of how fast the Army expects to move on this thing; just get your people on the job as fast as you can—you can take a few days longer if necessary.'"[19]

Hewes was annoyed. "This was just the counterirritant I needed." He swore to himself, "By God! I'll show the Army something about administration." He found a telephone and called the regional official of the Agriculture Department, though it was early Sunday afternoon and ordered the staff to immediate duty. After Bendetsen's meeting ended, Hewes went to the Agriculture office and found most of the staff at work, lining up men to be transferred to the army field stations. To get them there in time, they needed to fly, and to fly they needed priorities, because commercial airlines required that travel orders have official priority. Hewes had the pleasure of tracking Bendetsen down a few hours later to get him to relay the travel requisitions to the Presidio. Agriculture agents were brought in from Boise, Salt Lake City, and Denver to take part in the evacuation. In what became a "game of competing with the Army," Hewes was proud to say that, "at a few places we were ahead of the Army."[20]

The Farm Credit Administration, Farm Security Administration, Department of Agriculture, and the Federal Reserve were charged by Bendetsen with providing services to farmers "(a) with a minimum loss in agricultural production consistent with prompt execution, and (b) with a maximum of fair dealing to all concerned."[21] In actual fact, no alien property custodian was ever appointed, and the Federal Reserve Bank was directed to assist evacuees in disposing of their property only at the last moment; it was "not a custodianship matter at all but a sort of free banking service."[22]

> We trust that our government will treat us as civilian citizens who are voluntarily cooperating in national defense and not as military wards.
>
> —Mike Masaoka, Japanese American Citizens League

In the following weeks, Bendetsen selected more locations needing field stations and finally arranged for as many as ninety-seven civil control stations to regulate the evacuation. The stations performed three functions: to register all persons of Japanese ancestry; to provide services necessary to prepare them for movement from the area, and to direct the actual movement from the area. These stations were short-term operations carefully organized to handle large numbers of evacuees, with waiting spaces arranged between each of the sections. They were in operation only in the week indicated by the applicable evacuation order, were set up and staffed by the Employment Service, and were guarded by armed military police. The Bureau of Public Assistance of the Social Security Board provided trained social welfare workers who registered and interviewed evacuees, described the evacuation procedure, and attempted to determine what kind of help each person would need to dispose of personal property and/or business or farm interests, and the Federal Reserve Bank and the Farm Security Administration provided personnel to assist in those areas. The Public Health Service provided doctors and nurses for medical examinations of all evacuees prior to evacuation. Bendetsen specified the duties and responsibilities of each department. Each station had a control section manager and at least two floormen, an acting provost marshal (a representative of the army sector commander, who could make decisions about possible deferment of evacuation), and "an appropriate number of military personnel to act as guards." A floorman met an arriving evacuee and directed him or her to a receptionist who began collecting information. The first two days of operation involved registration (identifying the evacuee group for the station), and the last three, processing (getting ready to leave). Some bilingual evacuees were hired or enlisted to provide translation assistance, since many of the older aliens did not understand English. The evacuee was given a large packet of forms and directed to other sections for interviews. Evacuees would eventually leave with a tag in triplicate bearing their family number (and tags for other family members), a description of what they were required to take to the assembly center, an appointment for the "medical inspection," and the address to which to report for evacuation.[23]

At these stations the soon-to-be-evacuated Japanese aliens and their children had their first experience with the army bureaucracy, and the press had an opportunity to document the experience. One caption, entitled "Novel Audience," described the scene in an old theater in Seattle that had been converted into a civil control station: "The Japanese passed from table to table and when the 'show' was over they were ready for their trip to the assembly center in Puyallup."[24] Much of the pain of divesting themselves of personal effects had had to be done prior to this last step and largely without the aid of the army—for example, one headline read: "Whites Try to Buy Them Out at Low Price, say Japanese." Classified ads in Seattle papers ("Evacuee offers lease and furniture" and "Grocery—evacuating") alerted sharp purchasers. Shopkeepers faced with costly inventories received offers of ten percent of the stock's value. Because they did not know when they would be evacuated, farmers faced the more difficult decisions of whether to plant and whether to apply for a loan to start a crop that they could not hope to harvest.

To move the civilians assisting with the evacuation, Bendetsen was assigned a four-passenger airplane to be supported by the Fourth Air Force at Hamilton Field, forty-five miles north of San Francisco. Looking after his own interests, on March 19, 1942, Bendetsen obtained a two-week "privileges of the Club House" card from the Bohemian Club of San Francisco.

Secretary McCloy was in close communication with Bendetsen concerning the many details of the evacuation. In the third week of March there was careful planning to supply army escorts for an automobile caravan of a few hundred Japanese families who were voluntarily evacuating from California. Many Japanese who left during this time faced not being allowed to buy gasoline or stay in tourist camps because of their race, and some were turned away at state borders. The voluntary evacuation of persons of Japanese extraction was a failure and was terminated on March 29, 1942. Only about five thousand persons managed to find places to resettle outside Military Areas 1 and 2. The Japanese population within Military Area 1 became immediately subject to a curfew and travel restrictions and was ordered to await the evacuation order for their area. The evacuation schedule was a closely guarded secret.

Bendetsen did not concur in all of the proclamations issued by DeWitt in the first days of his tenure as head of the WCCA. Proclamation 3, which was issued on March 24, 1942, imposed a curfew and travel restrictions on all aliens and persons of Japanese descent who resided in DeWitt's command. Bendetsen told Gullion, "It was issued over my protest, and my protest was put on record very strenuously because it was a proclamation involving a curfew and travel restrictions with no provisions for any exceptions." Several of the proclamations initiated what Bendetsen called "this Tom Clark, Jim Rowe, FBI feud" over how the FBI would get notice of proclamations and exclusion orders, and how the army and the War Department should interact with the Department of Justice and the FBI.[25]

Bainbridge Island, west of Seattle in Puget Sound, was the first area evacuated. Prior to the signing of the executive order, and because of the island's shipyard and an aircraft warning service, the naval commanders of the region had insisted that "all people of Japanese extraction" be removed from the island, hence that the entire island be declared a restricted area. Bendetsen and DeWitt had seemed happy to concur. Rowe, speaking for the Justice Department, noted that his department hadn't "got any jurisdiction." He correctly saw a bad precedent growing if the military wanted to exclude citizens: "If you do that then [in] every area you've already requested, you'll want citizens kicked out too. . . . I don't know that we can do it." In early February the Justice Department had refused to include citizens in any removal order, but their opposition became moot when the army obtained the executive order allowing a mass evacuation. The first exclusion order in late March 1942, uprooted from Bainbridge Island some fifty-five Japanese families composed of ninety-one aliens, largely strawberry farmers, and 180 citizens.[26]

The Tolan Committee decided in March to accept the view of anti-Japanese groups and Secretary of the Navy Knox that because of "what happened in Hawaii" (details of which were guarded as a military secret and in fact did not implicate any Hawaiian Japanese), Japanese Americans could present a threat to the security of the West Coast. The committee did not challenge Executive Order 9066 until months after the evacuation was completed. After receiving testimony indicating that the mountain states might not be hospitable to receiving an influx of persons evacuated from the coast because they were considered to be potential saboteurs or fifth columnists, the committee petitioned the federal government to provide an agency with a civilian coordinator to handle the problem of "forced resettlement or involuntary evacuation." On March 18, 1942, in Executive Order 9102, the president created the War Relocation Authority (WRA), which was empowered to set up and administer the permanent facilities, to be called relocation centers, to which evacuees would soon be transferred for incarceration. Milton Eisenhower, an official in the Agriculture Department and brother to General Dwight D. Eisenhower, was appointed the first director of the WRA.

Enforcement of exclusions under Executive Order 9066 still needed to be addressed. After Justice Department officials declined to do it, Bendetsen prepared a statute to enforce the order. His first draft would have made it a felony for any excluded person to "'enter, leave, or remain in any military area or military zone' in which residence by aliens or citizens was proscribed by military order."[27] This harsh bill, asking for a $5,000 fine and a maximum prison term of five years, conformed to the recommendations of DeWitt that prison terms be mandatory. Bendetsen quoted DeWitt as saying that "you can shoot a man to enforce a felony."[28] McCloy moderated the statute to reduce the severity of an offense to a misdemeanor and limit imprisonment to one year.

The measure, which became Public Law 503, reads as follows:

> That whoever shall enter, remain in, leave, or commit any act in any military area or military zone prescribed, under the authority of the Executive order of the President . . . contrary to the restrictions applicable to any such area or zone or contrary to the order of the Secretary of War or any such military commander, shall, if it appears that he knew or should have known of the existence of the restrictions or order and that his act was a violation thereof, be guilty of misdemeanor and upon conviction shall be liable to a fine of not to exceed $5,000 or to imprisonment for not more than one year, or both, for each offense.[29]

When the bill reached Congress for consideration, Senator John A. Danaher spoke up in the debate "to wonder how a person would know what conduct constituted a violation of the act, an essential requirement for a criminal statute." Senator Robert A. Taft (R, Ohio) spoke against the bill: "I think this is probably the 'sloppiest' criminal law I have ever read or seen anywhere. . . . [It] does not say who shall prescribe the restrictions. It does not say how anyone shall know that the restrictions are applicable to that particular zone. . . . I have no doubt an act of that kind would be enforced in war time. I have no doubt that in peacetime no man could ever be convicted under it."[30] However, there was a war on, and Taft voted for the bill. Even House members expressed doubts about it, noting, "There seemed to be some suggestion that the bill applied to aliens rather than citizens," but it passed and was signed into law by the president on March 21, 1942.[31]

In the next months, administrative duties took up all of Bendetsen's time, at the expense of his personal life. On March 22, 1942, after talking by phone with his wife, who was still in D.C., Bendetsen dictated a letter to "Dearest Billie," giving her written instructions on what she must do in order to move to California. The letter contained detailed wording for an agreement with a real estate firm to handle the rental of their home in Chevy Chase, Maryland. He listed the financial records that she should put into a packet, and instructed, "If you drive, bring it with you in the car." Billie had spoken of a young lady with a civil service rating who was looking for a position. "If in your judgement she is capable, I am sure there is a place for her here as there are new arrivals joining the staff each day." He warned that "this may not be a permanent establishment," and added, "I hope she is good looking!" Showing concern for his wife, who had recently recovered from surgery for an ulcer, he wrote, "By all means hire help to do that part of the packing you feel you should do and have them do it instead of you."[32] A few days later, and ten days after the tax deadline, Bendetsen wrote to the Internal Revenue Service office in Tacoma, Washington, noting that his legal residence was in Aberdeen, Washington. He requested the ninety-day extension on filing his income tax because, "On February 24, 1942, I was sent to the Pacific Coast [from his Washington, D.C., duty] on a special assignment under Lieutenant General J. L. DeWitt. I have been placed in charge of the program to evacuate enemy aliens and persons of Japanese descent from the military zones on the West Coast. . . . Due to this and the fact that all of my books and records are physically located in Chevy Chase, Maryland, I was unable to file my income tax return on the due date."[33]

His wife arrived by car in early April. "A very amusing thing occurred," Bendetsen told Gullion. "I spent Tuesday night in Salt Lake [at the governor's conference] with my wife, but neither of us knew the other was there."[34] They set up housekeeping on North Point Street, in the Marina District adjacent to the Presidio of San Francisco.

At about the same time in April, Bendetsen's good friend, Chub Middleton of Aberdeen, accepted a wartime commission and joined Bendetsen's military command. His wife and children joined him at the Presidio the following summer. Middleton, who was a lieutenant colonel by the end of the war, was put in charge of property and contraband, and also traveled to Alaska for the Western Defense Command.[35] Bendetsen was conscientious about writing recommendations, especially for friends, and within months, Herb Lane of Aberdeen also found a post with the army in San Francisco.

The magnitude of the evacuation and incarceration task might have daunted a lesser man. His Civil Affairs Department and WCCA office was open seven days a week. For Bendetsen it was the kind of challenge he seemed to relish. By June, when the first phase of evacuation was complete, he described this duty in a letter to his friend Colonel Auer: "This assignment has been most trying . . . but at the same time the challenge presented made it a problem of such absorbing interest that I would scarcely wish to have traded the experience."[36]

Auer had written to Bendetsen in May asking for information because he was working on a study of the "Exercise of Military Power in respect to Civilian Activities and Rights in time of War." He was interested in the army's taking over the plant in Bendix, New Jersey, and in the reasoning behind "the Evacuation of Japs from Defense Areas." Auer wrote, "When I last talked to you, I recall you had some doubt (probably influenced by Dept. of Justice as to the power to remove Japs who were citizens of U.S.)." Auer wrote about a means to justify the executive order: "The Doctrine of urgent necessity *salus populi suprema est lex*.[37] I know the tenuous nature of this, its danger to abuse resulting in tyranny—but where the necessity is real, and the safety of the state is ultimately involved, I have no doubt of the power to act to remove citizens and non citizens."[38] In June, Bendetsen answered this letter, explaining how he persuaded his higher-ups to base the licensing scheme on military necessity.

Years later, Bendetsen described his part in setting up the camps, mentioning the temporary assembly centers "which I selected and established along the West Coast. . . . I also selected the sites for the ten Relocation Centers. The whole program was carried out under my direction. I not only had a hand in it, I selected them."[39]

Each of the fourteen assembly centers was generally a major expansion of existing facilities in a fairground, racetrack, or livestock exposition facility, with the addition of large numbers of barracks-type housing similar to units being built on army bases. The ten relocation centers, originally called reception centers, were almost entirely new constructions on vacant plots of land obtained from various government agencies such as the Indian Service, the Bureau of Reclamation, the Farm Security Administration, and the City of Los Angeles, although some required the purchase of adjacent private land. The army constructed the initial facilities "necessary to provide the minimum essentials of living, viz., shelter, hospitals (all medical facilities), mess, sanitary facilities, administration buildings, housing for non-evacuee staff of the Center, post office, store and warehouses, essential refrigeration equipment, and military housing."[40] The completed relocation camps would be turned over to the War Relocation Authority, headed by Milton Eisenhower, as the evacuees were transferred to them.

While the assembly centers were all within Military Area 1 and were relatively close to the original homes of the evacuees, the relocation centers, with two exceptions (Manzanar and Tule Lake, California), were outside both Military Areas 1 and 2, and except for the two Arkansas camps, were located in arid, barren lands with harsh climates compared to the temperate zones from which the Japanese evacuees came. The permanent relocation centers were Central Utah (Topaz), near Delta, Utah; Colorado River, at Poston, Arizona; Heart Mountain, Wyoming; Gila River, southern Arizona; Granada, southeastern Colorado; Minidoka, north of Twin Falls, Idaho; Jerome and Rohwer, eastern Arkansas; Manzanar, Inyo County, California, and Tule Lake, northeastern California. Manzanar, Colorado River, and Tule Lake Relocation Centers began accepting some evacuees in June 1942. Statistical summaries in the *Final Report* carefully account for the number of evacuees by date and camp and also chronicles the demographic characteristics of the incarcerated groups. The bulk of the evacuees had been moved from temporary assembly centers by September, but others had to wait until October or November when the Granada, Jerome, and Rowher centers were completed.[41]

The structure of Bendetsen's evacuation plan "was to designate evacuation zone control areas—we had the demographic data. I called upon *all* of the Federal Agencies for assistance, including the Federal Reserve."[42] It seemed clear that census data was available for the Western Defense Command, because Bendetsen was able to divide the West Coast Japanese population into 108 areas and schedule an organized sequence of exclusion orders addressed to "all persons of Japanese ancestry" living in each of the areas.[43] The sequence of orders was closely guarded "so that the information would not reach any affected person within the area." When an exclusion order was posted, the affected persons were given at most seven days to prepare for the actual evacuation.[44] Even the best property custodian could do little for evacuees with such short notice. In spite of Bendetsen's later assertions to the contrary, most evacuees relied on Caucasian friends to look after their property or sold everything at distressed prices. Only late in the evacuation process were some allowed to ship belongings to government warehouses, and problems relating to property disposal and protection plagued the government and the evacuees for years.[45]

How this evacuation would be treated by the press was of great concern to Bendetsen. He recalled, "I briefed the members of the press in meetings held at principal cities along the West Coast. . . . I told them, 'This is a wartime situation. Please remember that our nationals now in the hands of the Japanese could be grievously tortured and cruelly handled. . . .You will be fully informed of what we do.'" The press was told to be its own censor: "I ask you to avoid publication of sensational photographs. . . . I ask you not to foment what would be the natural antagonistic feelings of these people in the face of this regrettable necessity, many of whom probably are patriotic. We cannot yet tell one from the other. This is the unprecedented tragedy of this wartime situation."[46]

Bendetsen was very aware of what was happening in the western Pacific. Unable to defend the Philippines, General Douglas MacArthur had recently fled to Australia, and the remaining defenders had been pushed back to the Bataan Peninsula and the island of Corregidor. In early April, thirty-six thousand American troops surrendered to the Japanese, including Bendetsen's Aberdeen friend, Marine Captain Jack Clark.

Sometime in April, Bendetsen made an informal appearance before the Tolan Committee to give "a general resume of the over-all plan of evacuation." In reporting on this appearance to the assistant secretary of war he said he had given "the highlights of the means employed for the protection of evacuees' property, for the maintenance of the family units, for the preservation of community balance and for the protection of evacuees and communities adjoining resettlement projects." The committee wondered whether this West Coast action would set a precedent for actions to be taken on the East Coast, and Bendetsen explained that with respect to military necessity, General Drum, commander on the East Coast, would not necessarily face the same situation as had the West Coast commander, and thus would not necessarily make the same decision. He declined to speak for DeWitt or the War Department on the question of using "Loyalty Boards" as a basis for exempting individuals from blanket exclusion orders; such boards would be used to evaluate many Italian and German aliens in the coming months.[47]

On April 7, 1942, Bendetsen accompanied Milton Eisenhower, first director of the War Relocation Authority, to a meeting in Salt Lake City with governors or representatives of ten western states (but not California) to determine whether these states would accept Japanese evacuees.[48] Some attendees hoped to employ evacuees for harvesting. The governors were almost unanimous in opposing any free movement of Japanese aliens in their areas. Governor Sidney Osborn of Arizona had already spoken for many: "We do not propose to be made a dumping ground for enemy aliens from any other state. . . . I cannot too strongly urge that such aliens be placed in concentration camps east of the Rocky Mountains."[49] Herbert B. Maw, governor of Utah, said that the WRA was being "much too concerned about the constitutional rights of Japanese American citizens. . . . The constitution could be changed."[50] Only Governor Ralph Carr of Colorado offered to cooperate, saying at one point, "If Colorado's part in the war is to take 100,000 of them [American Japanese], then Colorado will take care of them." Other Coloradoans did not agree with him and he was defeated in the next election.[51] It became clear that relocation of the evacuated persons of Japanese descent was not going to be easy. Milton Eisenhower was "impressed with the futility of getting general acceptance for any plan for free colonization" and was left with the task of keeping the Japanese in the relocation camps. He assured the conferees that the WRA "would be tolerant, patient, and considerate in handling this human problem of wartime migration and resettlement."[52] Eisenhower would not stay long in this position.

After Bendetsen returned from the Salt Lake City conference, there was still conflict with the Justice Department about how the FBI would get notice of proclamations and exclusion orders, and how the army and the War Department should ask for cooperation from Justice. Bendetsen requested that Gullion ask Justice to settle who can be "the point of contact for immediate and continuous liaison" with the FBI and with the United States attorneys. He told Gullion, "You can't seem to find out what the Justice department wants, you can't satisfy them," and asked Gullion to try to get them to "tell us in writing and we'll do what they say, but point out the need for immediate action."[53]

Bendetsen reported what he called "some very disturbing news": Although FBI agents and local police officers had arrested a large number of persons caught in the act of violating exclusion orders under Public Law 503, the attorney general would not prosecute, and directed their release. "That's some more of Jim Rowe's sabotage perhaps," Bendetsen said. Gullion said he thought that "[Tom] Clark was very friendly and very cooperative on this resistance to the writ." Bendetsen said he was glad to hear that, that he had had to move fast and hadn't gone through Clark, and said, "He was hurt about it for a while. . . . He wrote kind of a nasty letter to the General about me without clearing it with me first."[54] In a conversation with Nat Pieper of the San Francisco FBI office, who by this time had become something of a friend, Bendetsen lamented, "It's been pretty strenuous now, up until the last night, and I went to Salt Lake, it's been 8 A.M. to 2:30 A.M. steadily every day, Saturday and Sunday. . . . And probably one meal a day—I'm just chained to this ___ desk." Pieper commiserated. They then discussed enforcement of the evacuation and curfew orders and the "feud" with the Justice Department, which was requiring that Bendetsen channel all information through Tom Clark. Pieper said that his agents were griping that they first heard about the new evacuation proclamations in the newspapers. He asked Bendetsen to let Agent Kennedy know at the same time that he informed Tom Clark. Pieper suggested that he keep up the proprieties with Tom Clark, but cautioned, "You want to make damn sure that the law enforcement officers get it, and get it right and get it in a hurry, you let us in on it and we'll get it done for you."[55]

In a conversation with McCloy, Bendetsen said, "I understand there's some tendency to weaken on the part of Rowe and Ennis. . . . They now say that the Public Law 503 is not constitutional, in their view." McCloy said, "Yes, they say there was some point of delegation about it." Bendetsen said that Justice insisted that they be allowed to review all orders before they were issued, hence "they would actually have a veto power on the military commander's discretion." McCloy said that he told Justice: "Insofar as we must look to them, for the application of sanction on any violations of military orders, that we do have to consult with them on the military orders." He noted that this applied to curfew orders but not to exclusion orders. Bendetsen said, "We get out an exclusion order every day or so now, we're rolling along pretty well on that, but that involves something that they will have to enforce." He gave the example of a man coming back into an area from which he is excluded by order—Bendetsen wanted the civilians to enforce the order, and he feared that the Justice Department would delay enforcement.[56] He and Pieper had discussed the problem of Justice's making exceptions for certain curfew violators. Pieper felt that he was unable to enforce the general's proclamations because of Justice's intervention.

Bendetsen also reported to McCloy that he was "having a good deal of trouble . . . with Congressman Elliott . . . down at Tulare. I've got to take the day now and go down and see him. I can ill afford it, but I just have to do it." Elliott was the secretary of the county fair, and had a personal interest in the fairground property. "We took it over, along with eleven others for an assembly center. We've gone into all eleven, and nobody's let out a peep—everybody's satisfied, and thinks that the engineers have done a fine job and been very careful . . . everybody but Congressman Elliot—who thinks he's a privileged character. Now he wants to be able to say that we're throwing the tax-payers money around and we don't need assembly centers." Bendetsen said Elliott had made a campaign promise to put on a fair the next fall "in spite of hell or high water" and that he would have to explain to him that DeWitt had barred such gatherings "for fear of choking the road net."[57] The Tulare fairgrounds housed 4,900 evacuees until the end of August 1942.

In a meeting on April 20, 1942, in DeWitt's office, Bendetsen, Tom Clark, and Nat Pieper, with the help of Brigadier General J. L. Bradley, DeWitt's chief of staff, and Colonel Joel Watson, judge advocate, hammered out procedures for the liaison between the War Department, the Commanding General, Western Defense Command, and the Department of Justice regarding enforcement under Public Law 503. Bendetsen agreed to notify Assistant Secretary of War McCloy by telephone of each order and proclamation to be issued under Executive Order 9066, and McCloy would obtain clearance from Assistant Attorney General James Rowe, Jr. When an order was approved, Tom Clark, special assistant to the attorney general, could then notify the appropriate United States attorneys. Justice Department officials were to enforce the penalties prescribed in the statute. Army sector commanders were authorized to communicate directly with the FBI, and impending exclusion orders would be transmitted to Pieper.[58] Perhaps the feud was finally settled.

With the Justice Department agreeing to a set of procedures for enforcing Public Law 503, Bendetsen went forward with the evacuation. In the spring of 1942, though there was by then no threat of invasion, some 117,116 West Coast Americans of Japanese ancestry—men, women, and children—were processed like criminals and methodically uprooted from their homes.[59] Fewer than five thousand had managed to leave the West Coast during the voluntary migration period in March. The rest were transported to assembly or relocation centers to be detained behind barbed wire indefinitely. Bendetsen's hometown would not be spared.

PART III

INCARCERATION

CHAPTER SEVEN

A Painful Time

Secret arrests since Sunday of nine Grays Harbor Japanese and suspected pro-Nazis were announced today by the FBI . . . names and details were withheld temporarily.

—*Aberdeen Daily World,* December 11, 1941

Mrs. Saito was arrested on December 9, and no one knew where she was taken. Rumors ran rampant on Heron Street. Mr. Saito was supposed to have had a searchlight in his chimney, pointing to the sky—it would direct "Jap" planes to the town, they said. Mr. Saito had been dead for five years.

Perry Saito dropped out of Washington State College in eastern Washington where he had just begun the term, to come home to be with his young brother and sister. He got back his job as elevator operator in the Becker Building, worked in a Christmas tree lot, and tried to find out what had happened to their mother. The three young people tried to keep the gift shop open.

Morse later wrote of this painful time: "The FBI had ransacked our house and store. My brother Perry, sister Dolly and I were subject to a military curfew at sundown to prevent us, we were told, from flashing signals to Japanese submarines or aircraft. If anyone of Japanese ancestry had even a firecracker it was assumed they were spies armed with signal flares."[1]

Mrs. Saito's banker, Mr. C. A. Pitchford, wrote maliciously of her later, "Her place of business here was the rendezvous of Japanese officers on lumber ships frequently calling at this port." With a "son in Japanese forces," he distrusted what he said was "her Pro-Japanese attitude."[2] There was fear that the "Japs" would invade through Aberdeen and many assumed that Mrs. Saito would welcome them. In her detention cell, Mrs. Saito had no idea how her son Lincoln, who would seem Americanized and thus a threat to the Japanese, would fare in wartime Japan. But she was sure that he was not in the Japanese army. And it would be at least a year before she received any news of him.

After her arrest, forty-two-year-old Natsu Saito discovered that she had been under surveillance for months prior to the start of the war. She was distrusted because she was fluent in both Japanese and English. She was suspect because she made contact with officers of Japanese ships. Her mail had been monitored, and it was reported that she got letters from Japanese persons in this country and from Japan, and also from the Japanese consul. She was suspect because she had a typewriter and because it appeared that the business of her store "amounted to practically nothing." She was considered dangerous because "she made mysterious late night contacts with white men." Her pool table was in the back room, and it was "impossible for prying eyes to see into this part of the store." She was under suspicion because she got letters *for* captains of Japanese merchant ships—was she a communication center for the enemy?

She was questioned extensively several times while held in the Aberdeen jail, and all these suspicions were thrown at her as accusations. Had she not been asked by a captain of a Japanese ship to provide him with maps or newspaper articles of value to Japan? Mrs. Saito "denied very emphatically any compliance with the aforementioned request." An FBI agent wrote, "subject was very incoherent and her sincerity is seriously doubted."[3] Morse recalled later that an agent even accused her of having "patriotic ties to Japan." She didn't know what the agents were talking about. "Finally someone blurted out, 'Celebrating all those Japanese national holidays!'"[4] After a week she was taken to Seattle for detention and was scheduled for a parole hearing. Her family still knew nothing of her whereabouts as Christmas approached.[5]

Perry's friend Dick Tuttle, the stepson of Aberdeen's Methodist minister, finally located Mrs. Saito. Dick, who was a student at the University of Washington in Seattle, was allowed to see her in an immigration office; their conversation was monitored. Word got back to her family and church friends: The FBI was accusing Mrs. Saito of being a spy.[6]

Morse recalled that Christmas years later:

> As a boy in Aberdeen, Washington, Christmas was wonderful. We had one business left, a gift shop. Months of red ink were made up by a whopping December. We had cause to celebrate.
>
> In 1941, all that changed. Mom was nabbed by the FBI and held incommu-

nicado. Finally, we found out she was at the Immigration Building in Seattle. Visiting days: Mondays and Thursdays. December 25 was a visiting day. We dressed in our best clothes and drove the 112 miles to the big city. My brother Perry told me not to cry when we saw her or make things tougher for her. I was insulted. I was a big 15, y'know!

Perry went first. At the door, he talked to the guard for a long time. Then he looked upstairs and waved, after which the guard sharply told him to walk away and not look back. "Jap spies might be watching us."

Back in the car Perry told us, "No visiting hours. Christmas!" It was a long drive home.[7]

The Immigration and Naturalization Service (INS) center was located on Airport Way, at the east end of what was then the fairly large Japanese district in Seattle to which Mrs. Saito had brought her family for their conspicuous outing after the death of her husband. Thus she and the many Japanese aliens who later were interned at Fort Missoula and other Justice Department camps spent their first months of detention maddeningly close to former haunts.

Mrs. Saito had little time to prepare for her hearing and no way of knowing all the accusations that she would face. She had had to give permission to the arresting officers, a police captain and an FBI agent, to search her store and house, and they took away a bag of Japanese books, magazines, pamphlets, diaries, letters, and papers written in Japanese, and four medals "of apparent significance." Most of the books contained Japanese poetry. She knew that the medals were mementos of her husband's military career of some thirty-five years before, but they seemed sinister to the FBI agent. Prior to the hearing Natsu filled out a 117-page questionnaire.

The hearing may have been more pleasant than the earlier interrogation sessions. Mrs. Saito was allowed to have an "adviser" in attendance, in the person of Reverend Rudy A. Anderson, pastor of the First Methodist Church in Aberdeen. Reverend Anderson brought with him twelve notarized letters from Aberdeen businesspeople, supporting Mrs. Saito's character and declaring her to be a worthy and desirable member of the community.

During the questioning conducted by a panel of three citizen members of the Alien Enemy Hearing Board, Natsu stated that her son Lincoln had gone to Japan to be eligible as oldest son to be an heir, that he was a student in a Presbyterian seminary, and that he had hoped to return to the

United States. She was questioned at length about the ship captain who had asked her to save newspaper articles and maps that might be of interest to the Japanese government. She said she told this man, whom she had known for more than ten years, "No. . . . I am sorry. I can't help anything Japan. I do not wish to get in a jam."[8]

The three examiners accepted her denial: She "was very frank and . . . she emphatically declined to undertake to furnish any information [to the ship captain]." They found "no evidence" that "she expressed herself as favorable to Japan or [had] been in any sense disloyal to the United States." She was not sympathetic to the Japanese government, hated the way they had started the war, and indicated that she was willing to "give her son who is in this country to the United States in its war with Japan." The FBI questioner, who had the reports from the Aberdeen postmaster about mail she had received, asked her about some of this but did not uncover anything that bothered the hearing board. The recommendations from the board were quite reassuring, but she would not get off too easily.

The board concluded that nothing in her conduct or attitude would justify internment (which would have required sending her to one of the Justice Department camps, which at that time held few, if any, women), "but due to the fact that she naturally retains a mother's affection for [her son in Japan] and also to the fact that she has profited by selling supplies to Japanese boats from time to time," the board recommended that she be paroled without bond. This decision was given on January 13, 1942, but she did not receive the signed papers from the attorney general until April.[9] She spent the long wet winter of 1942 behind bars in Seattle.

In the next weeks Morse went to his school principal to ask for a letter recommending his family as loyal citizens. He had been in the same class with the principal's daughter since elementary school. The principal declined to help. "He gave all sorts of reasons why he could not write such a letter: he REALLY didn't know us." Years later Morse could joke about this and the reason that he didn't have the best grades at that time: "Ahh, it wasn't [junior] high school I minded so much . . . it was the *principal* of the thing."[10]

Trying to keep the store running without their mother, Perry and his siblings had to put up with the few unfriendly shoppers and dwindling inventory. Morse recalled that soldiers in the area came in to "buy things Japanese, if we had any. . . . I didn't think about it at the time, but they may have been intelligence people, too, because they seemed to know things about Japan, and were interested in wood block prints. Nice customers."

Perry's children tell the story that none of the Saito young people knew how to cook, so while their mother was incarcerated, they lived on doughnuts. Perry's good friend Dick Tuttle recalled, "Oh how Perry loved donuts," but thought they managed better than that. His parents, Reverend Anderson and his wife, were solicitous, inviting the young Saitos to dinner and looking after their needs. However, Morse remembered "a lot of egg salad sandwiches. You could make them go longer by adding a lot more mayonnaise. Maybe that's why I still don't like egg salad sandwiches."[11]

After the draft was reinstated in 1940, Dick Tuttle and Perry spent many hours exploring "social issues and the things that were right and wrong in our society." Tuttle was a pacificist and planned to be a conscientious objector if war came. "Perry was also a conscientious objector," he said. "We both had walked through some of that ground together." Four years older than Perry, Tuttle had to face the imminent possibility of being drafted. "I think I was an influence on Perry." Tuttle's stepfather Rudy Anderson had become pastor at Aberdeen's First Methodist Church in 1940. Though there were many ministers in Washington State preaching pacifism, Tuttle's stepfather could not be one of them. Tuttle explained, "Aberdeen was an armed camp. . . . He was in a very precarious position himself for preaching pacifism because . . . the streets of Aberdeen were filled with military vehicles, and he had a lot of military people in the church."

Tuttle described the climate in Aberdeen: "You had all your shades down at night and the traffic lights had little slits in them and you couldn't drive down toward the beach at all with headlights on at night, it was a very . . . you see Aberdeen was considered an invasion point along with San Francisco. . . . There was a lot of feeling and of course that only intensified toward Japanese Americans; I think there was only one other family beside the Saitos in Grays Harbor county, and you know the story how people came into the store, their little gift shop, and would run their hands across the counter and knock all the trinkets and glass things on the floor and spit in their face and walk out."[12]

The curfew was declared in March. Perry, who had many friends and had been well accepted in high school, began to suffer rude comments at work. On at least one occasion on the job as elevator operator, he was subjected to an insulting comment from a passenger who "didn't think a 'Jap' should be allowed to work there."[13]

Perry's friends recalled that he didn't acknowledge that the curfew applied to him. He continued to go out with friends in the evening. The Aberdeen police would get calls: "That Japanese fellow is walking down the street past his curfew time." The cops, parents of his friends, would pick him up and take him home. In his mind he was an American—why should he have a curfew?

After almost four months' confinement in the Seattle INS detention center, Natsu Saito was put on parole for "the duration of the war," released by the Department of Justice, and allowed to return to Aberdeen. Her children had also been subjected to investigation by the FBI. Mrs. Saito would be required to report twice monthly to the INS, and once a month to a district parole officer. The Justice Department examiners had been impressed by the "many letters from a wide segment of the population of Aberdeen, all indicating a community interest in and affection for both the subject and her family."[14]

On the second anniversary of his mother's death, Morse wrote of this time:

> Mid-April 1942 was a special time in my life. Aberdeen, Washington, was still in a rainy winter-spring where we saw 113 inches of rain.[15] The early confusion of the war was receding and the FBI finally released my mother on the day after Easter. My widowed mother was pronounced safe and at fifteen I have my first security clearance.
>
> Being 100 percent plus loyal Americans we were law abiding good citizens. I was so loyal I was proud of the fact I knew so little Japanese. Ignorance, I believed, meant I was that much more American. For us the melting pot equaled cultural assimilation which meant being white Anglo-Saxon in looks, outlook and thinking. Schools taught being "American" was not a matter of race and I believed it.
>
> By April, 1942 I knew this was not quite true. Americans of Japanese ancestry were being sent to "Assembly Centers" like state fair grounds where animal stalls were the "temporary" homes for thousands. We joked about "running at Puyallup or Tanforan or Santa Anita [racecourses]" or some other exotically named place. They all held too many things in common: they smelled, they were inadequate for housing families, they were substandard in terms of U.S. federal prison standards.[16]

Morse continued:

> Since the FBI had cleared us, I was naive to think we might not be evacuated. We were 'safe' and even the lame excuse for the coming evacuation, "it is to protect those of Japanese ancestry" had no meaning for us. Aberdeen was our home. We belonged. In fact, if evacuated many would think, "Ha! They must have done something otherwise they would not have been sent off." Evacuation implied guilt.
>
> Our loyalty was proven by the FBI clearance and her [Mrs. Saito's] release.[17]

Perry never dreamed that the evacuation would apply to him. When he first saw the posters in Aberdeen: "Civilian Exclusion Order No. 89," a notice ordering that "all persons of Japanese ancestry, both alien and non-alien, be excluded" from Grays Harbor County, in Military Area 1 by noon on June 1, 1942, he felt sorry for "those poor people" who were going to have to leave their homes.[18] Then he realized that even though he was born in America and had been cleared by the FBI, he had become one of the despised "non-aliens." And he was offended that the notices were posted all over his town. There were so few Japanese, really just his family, that the army could simply have brought the notice to their store and avoided public embarrassment.[19]

Perry, Morse, and Dahlia Saito, whose father had made them memorize all four stanzas of "The Star Spangled Banner" in addition to the Preamble to the Declaration of Independence, because he was proud of his adopted country, would soon be ordered to take only what they could carry and leave with their mother for an unknown destination.

The Saitos did not know that all along it was their former neighbor, Karl Bendetsen who was orchestrating the evacuation, writing the proclamations and exclusion orders over General DeWitt's signature (though notice of Bendetsen's promotion to full colonel had appeared in the local papers). Orders prepared by Bendetsen would soon send them to a "relocation" camp and change the course of their lives.

As head of the WCCA, Colonel Karl Bendetsen spent a lot of time talking to the press. He announced each of the evacuation orders in DeWitt's name and responded to rumors. In March, announcing the end of voluntary evacuation, Bendetsen stated, "The 'freezing order' prepares the way for an Army-regulated program of removal and does not alter curfew regulations, nor any other existing regulations.

. . . General DeWitt has warned the Japanese they must settle their affairs immediately. Any neglect of crops is sabotage."[20] Charles Ross, field officer for the Wartime Farm Adjustment Program, threatened Japanese farmers who are "lying down on the job of producing a crop. . . . We intend to seeing that alien Japanese and American-born are given fair and decent treatment, and that they are not cheated. But we won't tolerate for a moment any sabotaging of food production." Such persons "will have cause to regret their refusal to cooperate" and asked Northwest residents to report those guilty by calling his Seattle office. Farmers were expected to plant their crops, possibly incurring debt to do so, and got no assurance that they could remain on the land for the harvest.[21]

Laurence Hewes, Jr., regional director of the Farm Security Administration as well as Agriculture Department liaison to the army, issued detailed instructions to his offices, noting that "keeping Japanese lands in production is a basic war measure." He reported that from 35 to 50 percent of vegetables in California were produced by Japanese farmers, largely as truck farm operations, but that the army was controlling the order of evacuation "with military considerations always uppermost."[22] By his own admission, Hewes and his coworkers had gotten the reputation of being "Jap-lovers," and he provided positive leadership for his department.[23]

On April 4, 1942, Bendetsen issued a press release as "a final warning" to West Coast Japanese that the army would not relax its regulations or allow anyone to remain in the military zone. "For the last time, the Army is warning evacuees to make arrangements for disposition of their property. . . . If any evacuee hopes to retard the entire evacuation program because he has not taken steps to dispose of his property or settle his other problems, he will be disappointed."[24]

Government assistance for the prospective evacuees in the disposition of property came slowly; especially in the early days of the evacuation, many were victimized by opportunists. The Federal Reserve was not granted authority to intervene in the handling of evacuee property until March 5, 1942, and then its program was limited and inadequate. The army and local officials appeared to be more interested in the mass removal of all Americans of Japanese descent, rather than in protecting their property.[25]

In April and May, as Bendetsen issued further exclusion orders, he stated several times that there was "no basis of fact in rumors that Japanese in rural areas [would] not be removed until crops are harvested." He further stated, "Military necessity is an unrelenting taskmaster and the harvesting of crops or other agriculture tasks cannot be allowed to retard the evacuation program."[26]

In May the Seattle and Tacoma newspapers featured photos of well-dressed Japanese and Japanese Americans sitting at tables and waiting in line to register for evacuation in a temporary WCCA registration office: "Almost in the happy mood of Saturday-night patrons lined up in wait of a seat at a motion-picture theatre . . . the registrants were gay, apparently resigned to any eventuality caused by the war."[27] Though there were photos later of sad farewells, the press seemed to prefer happy scenes, such as photos of the "Cheerful exit" from Tacoma: "More than 400 Tacoma Japanese laughed and joked Monday afternoon as they boarded a train at the Union depot for an evacuation camp in California."[28]

Not only would farmers have to leave their crops, and city people their homes and businesses, but persons of part-Japanese extraction were required to go. Towa Moyer and her five children were ordered to evacuate. In addition, Japanese families, such as the Saitos, whose American children had always lived in Caucasian communities would be ordered to leave their homes.

While the Saito family enjoyed their last days of freedom, their former neighbor, Colonel Karl Bendetsen stood at the podium before members of the prestigious Commonwealth Club of San Francisco to deliver a speech entitled "The Story of Pacific Coast Japanese Evacuation."[29] It was May 20, 1942, and an audience of 344 had gathered in the ornate and well-appointed Rose Room of the Palace Hotel to hear the young colonel. The press was barred from this "off-the-record" talk; Bendetsen reviewed what he saw as the principal dangers, saying that the Japanese community presented a "high potential for action against the national interest [and] persons of Japanese ancestry might possibly engage in sabotage, espionage or fifth-column activities."[30]

He distinguished between Caucasian Americans and the evacuees this way:

> If you and I had settled in Japan, raised our families there and if our children and grandchildren were raised there, it is most improbable that during a period of war between Japan and the United States, if we were not interned, that we would commit any overt acts of sabotage acting individually. Doubtless in the main, and irrespective of our inner emotions, you and I would be law abiding.
>
> But when the final test of loyalty came, if United States forces were

> engaged in launching an attack on Japan, I believe it is extremely doubtful whether we could withstand the ties of race and the affinity for the land of our forebears, and stand with the Japanese against United States forces.
>
> To withstand such pressures seems too much to expect of any national group, almost wholly unassimilated and which has preserved in large measure to itself, its customs and traditions—a group characterized by strong filial piety.

Though many persons of Japanese ancestry are loyal to the United States, he asserted, "many are not loyal." He reasoned that one can assume there are such disloyal people because, contrary to other national or racial groups, "in no single instance has any Japanese reported disloyalty on the part of another specific individual of the same race." Thus, repeating Earl Warren's lie, he called this supposed fact "a most ominous thing."

He cautioned against "chasing specters of fear"—the army and the nation must be realistic. "The contingency that under raid or invasion conditions there might be widespread action in concert—well-regulated, well-disciplined and controlled—a fifth column, is a real one. As such, it presented a threat to the national security and therefore a problem which required solution."

Using information then attorney general Earl Warren had presented to the congressional Committee on National Defense Migration in February, he noted that "substantial numbers of the Japanese coastal frontier communities were deployed through very sensitive and very vital areas."[31]

Bendetsen presented no facts to support his charges against persons of Japanese ancestry—he gave no examples of acts of disloyalty, no incidents of signaling to enemy submarines, no notice of charges of any kind being brought against the countless Japanese aliens who were arrested in the first days of the war, no documented conspiracies to engage in sabotage. One might wonder on what grounds he or the army based their distrust and suspicions.

The story of Pacific Coast Japanese evacuation, as presented by Bendetsen, sounded like a success story with a happy ending. Almost all the 113,000 persons of Japanese ancestry had been removed from their homes on the western sea frontier and put into guarded enclosures called assembly centers.[32] The construction of these temporary facilities in fairgrounds, racetracks, and other public facilities, and the entire evacuation, had been accomplished in ninety days under the direction of only thirty-five army officers led by Colonel Bendetsen. The evacuees would soon be transferred to permanent enclosures run by a civilian agency, the WRA. These would be the relocation centers where they would "live and work for the duration of the war." Under restricted conditions, some Japanese (he almost never said Japanese Americans) would be permitted to leave assembly or relocation centers for private employment. He did not mention that all the camps, which he insisted be called "centers," would be surrounded by barbed wire, guard towers, and armed troops of the United States Army (as were the assembly centers).

In this talk, Colonel Bendetsen revealed a little-known fact that created headlines the following week: The army had been prepared to execute a complete evacuation practically overnight.[33] Plans existed for a mass movement "of the 113,000 Japanese into already established Army cantonments," preparing against "the possibility of fifth column activity, or for any outbreaks of anti-Japanese feeling."

No emergency mass movement was ordered, so it must have been the case that neither the fifth-column activity nor the anti-Japanese feelings occurred. The organized, gradual, but unrelenting evacuation of the entire West Coast ethnic Japanese population had continued on schedule without incident and without further consideration of its appropriateness, though the tide of the war may have seemed ready to shift in America's favor. By May 1942 Doolittle's raiders had successfully flown sixteen B–25s from aircraft carriers to bomb Tokyo and vicinity, and though the Philippines had fallen, Japanese forces invading the West Coast began to seem less likely, especially after the destruction of a large part of the Japanese fleet at Midway on June 5, 1942. Admiral Isoroku Yamamoto's predicted six-month romp was over.[34] But the West Coast's Americans of Japanese ancestry were by then behind bars, their homes lost, their reputations tarnished.

Bendetsen gave an interview with the press in June 1942 answering four questions and giving his view, at that time, of what the evacuation and relocation program involved.

> 1) Colonel Bendetsen, the impression is still widely held that these evacuees are to be regarded with suspicion as actual or potential enemies of the country. Will you please set us straight on this point?
>
> ANSWER: I dislike generalities, and that question covers too much ground, both in what it says and in what it implies. It is not true that "most" of these evacuees are to be regarded as actual or potential enemies. It is true that "some" of them are. But because 1. It was impossible to distinguish between the suspects, and the non-suspects, and because 2. So many "more than

113,000" were concentrated in vital military areas, no other course was open to us than the one we took.

2) Then it is wholly incorrect to regard them as prisoners, or to call these relocation centers prisons, or concentration camps?

ANSWER: It certainly is. There is confinement, that is true. This is a time of war, and it has to be that way, but Relocation Centers are not prisons and they are not Concentration Camps. They are areas that have been set aside for the establishment of new homes and communities for evacuees *for the duration of the war*. [Emphasis added.] Families are kept together. What we have tried to do, so far as it has been possible to do it, is to continue neighborhood life—the same sort of neighborhood life that existed prior to the outbreak of war.

3) Have the Japanese, both citizens and aliens, cooperated effectively during the Evacuation?

ANSWER: They have cooperated very effectively. As I have already pointed out, more than 113,000 of them were living in vital military areas on the West Coast. That was less than three months ago. Today, by comparison practically all are [illegible]. This [illegible] mass evacuation, by far the greatest in our history, was undertaken by the Army. The Army was supported by various Federal Agencies, and both, the Army and the supporting Agencies, were helped by the Japanese. In fact, the evacuation has been accomplished as smoothly as it has due to the cooperative attitude of a majority of the Japanese. Great credit is due them in this regard.

4) Can you give us any definite idea as to what action may be taken on the East Coast with respect to possible evacuation of any aliens or others?

ANSWER: I am authorized to state on behalf of the War Department that no further mass evacuation is contemplated on either the West Coast or East Coast.[35]

"So many 'more than 113,000'" is a distortion of the magnitude of the "Japanese population" on the West Coast. The Bureau of the Census reported 112,985 persons of Japanese ancestry in Washington, Oregon, California, and Arizona in 1940.[36] Bendetsen would have had to tap the Japanese populations of Idaho, Montana, Nevada, and Utah to have more than that number. These inland populations were generally not disturbed.

On June 15, 1942, the *New Republic* published an angry article by Ted Nakashima, a young architectural draftsman from

Seattle, who was incarcerated in the Puyallup Assembly Center. Entitled "Concentration Camp: U.S. Style," the article contained Nakashima's detailed complaints about conditions in the Puyallup Center (bad food, curfew, broken sewer), laments about his loss of freedom, complaints about leaving his comfortable home, and resentment at being distrusted: "What really hurts most is the constant reference to us evacuees as 'Japs.' 'Japs' are the guys we are fighting. We're on this side, and we want to help."[37] Within days, Bendetsen wrote a long, critical response to the magazine refuting the points made by Nakashima: "A few—and very few—of Mr. Nakashima's statements are true. There are towers and there are guards in the towers armed with machine guns. This is war. These centers are located in military areas, in a combat zone. In time of war it is the duty of the Army to protect the nation from all possible danger without its borders; and from all possible enemies within its borders. It may be true that many Japanese are loyal; it is also true that a great many of them, citizens as well as aliens, are not loyal." He claimed that the impossiblity of determining who is loyal was based on *military knowledge* and was not "an expression of editorial opinion."[38]

Bendetsen went on to minimize Nakashima's claims about the conditions, noting that the former stables "were thoroughly renovated and made suitable as dwellings before occupancy" and stating that most evacuees were "housed in standard 'theater-of-operations type' troop barracks, adapted to the purpose, with separate rooms provided." He stated that many of Nakashima's complaints described conditions during the first ten days of operation—for example, dry rations were served "because of short notice given in the orders of evacuation," but said that these were "the same rations that are served American soldiers when they are on duty in the field." He asserted that the food had improved, and "to say that coffee and tea are dosed with saltpeter is not true. To say that 'dirty unwiped dishes and greasy silverware' are the order of the day should not be true because cooking as well as washing dishes are jobs done by the Japanese themselves."

To Nakashima's complaint that he had left behind "a fine American home built with [his] own hands" and a "life of highballs with [his] American friends on weekends" and "a stack of defense houses" for his draftsman's pencil, Bendetsen wrote: "Well, a good many American boys, several millions of them, left their homes to eat the same food about which Nakashima now complains; left their homes not to sleep in barracks, but on the ground; dropped their pencils to pick up rifles; quit their jobs to die on Bataan that Nakashima might someday be able to return to his 'little bathroom with light coral walls . . . [and] the pretty shower curtain.'"

Bendetsen then took the editors of the *New Republic* to task: "This is a time of war, war with Japan! American soldiers, American sailors and American Marines are prisoners of Japan. . . . Do you think the publication in your periodical of an unverified and sensational report makes the lot of these Americans easier to bear!" He gave vent to more frustrations:

"As the officer principally responsible, on the ground, for the evacuation of the Japanese, I can assure you that we have gone to extraordinary lengths in seeking to assure the well-being and the comfort of the Japanese in our care. Humane considerations alone would have dictated such a course. But hundreds of times, during a peculiarly difficult and delicate task, I have asked myself, 'Is this the way I would wish it to be for Americans in Japanese custody?' Every step we have taken has met that test. I only hope that the Japanese will be constrained to equal our standard."[39] He seemed to feel that he was handling Japanese prisoners of war, rather than long-term residents and American citizens who had not been charged with any offense.

In its reply, the *New Republic* offered to print the facts about the Puyallup Center given in his letter, but Bendetsen declined permission.[40] He had been fully aware of problems at the Puyallup camp long before the Nakashima article appeared, in fact from the day the camp opened. Stories in the Seattle press had described how quickly the center had been prepared for occupancy: "United States district army engineers had completed the seeming miracle of building quarters for a city of 8,000 in just seventeen days." (The original contractor had quit after deciding that it would be impossible to meet the army's deadline, the story noted.)[41]

A newspaper in Tacoma, Washington, "broke a story" on April 28, 1942, featuring statements by the Pierce County Health Director who warned residents of Puyallup Assembly Center that "Meeker Ditch and Clark Creek must be considered as open sewers." The Health Department complained that it had protested to army engineers that the sewer construction was not adequate. Mr. T. W. Braun, in reporting this news, suggested to Bendetsen that he should have the army engineers prepare a statement containing their opinion that the sewer installation was completely safe or would be made safe.[42]

On April 30, 1942, A. J. Muste, secretary of the Fellowship of Reconciliation (FOR) in New York, sent a telegram to President Roosevelt calling attention to "EXCEEDINGLY BAD CONDITIONS IN SOME CENTERS OF DETENTION

FOR JAPANESE, ESPECIALLY AT STATE FAIR GROUNDS AT PUYALLUP NEAR SEATTLE." Copies of the telegram proliferated like a chain letter working its way through the Washington bureaucracy and finally got to the officer in charge in San Francisco. Bendetsen wrote a letter to Muste, signing General DeWitt's name, stating that the sewer problem would be taken care of.

On April 22, 1942, Bendetsen wrote to the director of the WRA (Milton Eisenhower) urging rapid selection of relocation sites and speedy acquisition and construction of more permanent facilities, noting that assembly centers were "not designed to provide suitable semi-permanent housing and other facilities."[43] He said, "They are temporary in nature" and said it would be too expensive to improve them "given that permanent facilities were planned. . . . Long residence in an assembly center is bound to have a demoralizing effect."[44]

As a response to Bendetsen's criticism, the *New Republic* sent someone to evaluate Nakashima's charges, and in January 1943 reported that "things were not as bad as Nakashima said, but were in the nature of temporary hardship."[45] By January 1943 all the evacuees had been moved from temporary assembly centers into the ten permanent facilities managed by the WRA. News stories from the latter centers would say little about the comfort of the facilities, but rather would focus on news of strikes, shootings, conflicts among evacuees, and, in the months to come, the turmoil caused by the effort to determine the evacuees' loyalty.

Though they were surprised and concerned by the Pearl Harbor attack and the beginning of the war, William and Towa Moyer had not felt any more threatened than other residents of Hoquiam. Their three adult children had responsible jobs in the community. Many associates were not aware that they were half Japanese. Jackson Moyer, the eldest son, had been a member of the Washington State Guard's Company "K" since the company was mustered into service on July 18, 1941. Though she was an alien, Towa Moyer had lived in Hoquiam for thirty years, and her children were American citizens. They were shocked to learn in April 1942 that Towa and her children, even the adults, would be required to evacuate. They decided to appeal to their congressman, not knowing that DeWitt and Bendetsen were giving almost no deferments of the evacuation order. In the great push to evacuate all persons of Japanese ancestry from the West Coast, the only exceptions being made were supposedly for "Japanese in hospitals too sick to be moved, Japanese children in orphanages . . . [persons] in institutions who required special attention . . . and those who were imprisoned."[46]

William Moyer and his son Jackson, who was accountant and office manager for Spoon Automotive, spoke to many friends and employers, who rallied to their support. The mayor of Hoquiam, the Aberdeen postmaster, a plywood company executive (Madeline's employer), a druggist, and the local draft board all wrote letters requesting that Mrs. Moyer and her children be exempted from the evacuation. Several of their supporters had known Karl Bendetsen and felt that he might help. Among the letters written on behalf of Towa Moyer and her family was the one Walter D. Davis of Sunset Life Insurance sent to "My dear Karl" [Bendetsen] at his office in San Francisco. Davis wrote eloquently of the Moyer children, particularly twenty-eight-year-old Jackson. " [He is] a very high type American boy. . . . It would seem to me a crime to take a fellow of his character and put him and his brothers and sisters in a concentration camp, when they do not read, write, speak or mingle with Japanese." Davis assured Bendetsen that he was not making this appeal based on their friendship, and wrote, in reference to the Saitos, "As you know, there is only one 100% Japanese family on Grays Harbor, and after investigation, I am absolutely satisfied that there has never been any friendship between the two families."[47]

A flurry of letters went to Martin Smith, the Moyer's congressman and former neighbor. He gathered as much supporting information as he could and sent it to Colonel B. M. Bryan, the officer holding Bendetsen's former job as chief of the aliens division in the provost marshal general's office in Washington, D.C. Mr. Smith did warn Madeline Moyer's employer, M. M. Pattison of the Harbor Plywood Corporation, that "members of Congress do not have the deciding voice in these matters, they are wholly within the jurisdiction of the military officers and I am informed they are adhering to the regulations very strictly."

Mrs. Moyer received prompt letters from Bendetsen's office as well as from Fort Lewis, the nearest army base, denying an exemption: "There will be no deferment for persons of Japanese ancestry where the persons are parties to mixed marriages."[48] In the next week, Towa Moyer and her five children had to register for the evacuation. When Jackson, Madeline, and Chester had to quit their jobs, their employers expressed willingness to rehire them if they should return soon. William Moyer remained in Hoquiam and feared that he might have to give up his job at the mill, even though it was considered critical because of wartime labor shortages, to tend his farm single-handedly.

In their last days of freedom, Jim and Billy Moyer were honored with a going-away assembly at the Hoquiam junior high and were presented with pens with which to write to their friends. According to the *Aberdeen Daily World*, the Moyers drove to Olympia, fifty miles to the east, "to find out if possible, whether their five children . . . also would have to be evacuated"; the paper noted, "Two of the half-Japanese children are students at Hoquiam schools."[49] The departure was also reported in Hoquiam's newspaper, the *Washingtonian*, naming Towa Moyer and her five children. The Grays Harbor group, including the Saitos, would be required to meet "a special train to enter Tule Lake, the second largest concentration camp on the West Coast."[50]

After her release from the immigration center, Natsu Saito had little time to prepare her family in case they should be separated again. This *yakudoshi*, a year of calamity, was not over.[51] Evacuation notices were posted on telephone poles in Aberdeen and Hoquiam.[52] She would have to endure another wrenching change. According to a news story, "Mrs. Natsu Saito, proprietor of an Aberdeen novelty store, was registering at Raymond for herself, two sons and a daughter." Raymond was the small town seventeen miles south of Aberdeen, at which numbers of Japanese oyster workers from Willapa Harbor also registered. Registering as head of the family she brought back tags with a family number for each of her children and then prepared to leave for an unannounced location on June 1, 1942, giving her barely eight days to sell a business inventory and a car, pack up a household, and prepare her children for a forced move.

Morse later wrote: "We would not have to go to an 'Assembly Center' and live in a filthy animal stall like the Puyallup [Western Washington] State Fair grounds near Tacoma. We were told to show up at Olympia, Washington, where armed guards took us to the darkened, dirty Tule Lake bound train. We could take 'only what you can carry.' Everything else was to be put up in storage where anything of value simply disappeared. Years later we got our 'stored goods' [for] which we had to sign a release unseen. What could we do with one-fourth of a bed?"[53]

Morse Saito recalled a patriotic parade of friends bearing gifts, accompanying his family onto the bus in Aberdeen; Dolly's friends recalled crying together for three days when they found out she had to evacuate. The Saitos and the Moyers joined the train in Olympia.

Morse recalled "one thing more that irks me about June 1942. In spite of the consequences, I would willingly face arrest on one key point. Never again would I *pay my own bus fare* from Aberdeen to Olympia to be interned. I would fiercely growl, 'Come and get me.'"[54]

INDIVIDUAL EXAMINATION AND INDIVIDUAL EXCLUSION

Once the schedule for evacuation of the West Coast Japanese population was set and the first assembly centers were in operation, Bendetsen began working on establishment of policies for further action under Executive Order 9066, which meant developing concepts for individual examination and individual exclusion to handle Italian and German aliens on the West Coast. Sometime in February, McCloy had hired Alfred Jaretzky, Jr., as a part-time consultant to help with this problem on a national scale. In recommending him to Bendetsen, McCloy said of Jaretsky, "He has a wide knowledge of aliens in this country." A member of a Wall Street law firm, Jaretsky represented a refugee organization, the American Federation of Jews from Central Europe.[55] When he first met Bendetsen, Jaretzky recommended several "former German lawyer[s]" who might be helpful.

It was expected that only a few Italians would be apprehended and excluded. Bernard Gufler of the State Department summarized Bendetsen's view of the Italian problem: "A large proportion of the aliens concerned are of Italian nationality. It now appears to the Army that these persons are not as dangerous as was at first thought. Many of them are apparently loyal to the United States and have no longer any real ties with Italy but have merely neglected to take American citizenship. In this connection Colonel Bendetsen mentioned the DiMaggio family."[56]

As he began evaluating the German and Italian aliens for possible exclusion, Bendetsen, perhaps at DeWitt's insistence, defined a new category, "non-enemy aliens," as a group that would be exempted. After recommending that all German and Italian alien enemies resident in Military Area 1 be excluded under federal supervision, Bendetsen excepted from this group "Italian and German nationals . . . in certain classes who, subject to good behavior are to be regarded as non-enemy aliens." This new category included persons expatriated by the present German or Italian governments who declared an intention of becoming citizens of the United States; persons who failed or were denied citizenship because they lacked mental or educational qualifications; persons who had served in the armed forces; the parents, spouse, or minor children of persons honorably serving in the forces of the United Nations since September 8, 1939; and persons earlier exempted from the curfew.[57] Added to this non-enemy alien category were mixed-marriage groups "where the alien spouse is o.k.'d by the Intelligence service," foster children, wholly dependent daughters, and religious orders, "always subject to good behavior and approval by the Intelligence services as to the latter."[58] In other words, Italian and German aliens would be examined individually and given the benefit of the doubt. First-generation descendants of Italian and German aliens were not considered dangerous as a class. Bendetsen estimated that this reduction by exemptions would result in an evacuation of "considerably less than 10,000" un-exempted German aliens. He was willing to expand internment facilities to accommodate such numbers.[59] DeWitt felt that "failure to take such action [might] entail serious consequences [, . . .] that the probability of retaliatory raids on the West Coast [grew] strong[er] as each week passe[d], and that the removal from the coastal frontier, particularly of German aliens, [was] an essential war measure."[60] DeWitt provided no proof to support any of these assertions.

Bendetsen recommended that once the Japanese evacuation was complete, the curfew on German and Italian aliens be lifted. While persons of Japanese ancestry could not hide their race (making a curfew against them enforceable), a curfew on a European group would require the creation of an identity-card system, which the president opposed.

General DeWitt was opposed to removing the curfew on aliens.[61] His continued insistence that aliens were a threat in spite of a lack of evidence, and his later refusal to make exceptions requested by the civilian heads of the War Department put a strain on relations between DeWitt and his superiors that possibly shortened his tenure as commander of the Western Defense Command.

In a telephone conference in late April, Jaretsky and Bendetsen discussed the severity of the threat presented by German and Italian aliens. Jaretzky said that he didn't think that they should be trying to find large numbers of people to exclude. "There are not a lot of dangerous people," he said. Bendetsen disagreed, saying, "I'm inclined to think there are a lot." Jaretzky moved to the question of what to do if the army decided to issue individual exclusion orders for large numbers of Italian and German aliens. He worried about another relocation job: "We feel if there's any sizeable evacuation from the West Coast it's going to inflame public opinion generally against this group."[62] Agreeing, Bendetsen feared that General Drum (of the Eastern Defense Command) was thinking of excluding groups from some areas in his command, and "if he does, he's going to run into more headaches than he's ever had in his life before, because moving the people across the street is absolutely out the window. That *will not work*. . . . If you really want to profit by our experience out here. . . . Who you consider to be so dangerous, that you cannot permit him to stay at point 'A'—point 'B' will not accept." Jaretzky said that he appreciated what Bendetsen was telling him. In the course of the conversation Bendetsen admitted that in the Western Defense Command, (and in spite of DeWitt's unwillingness to remove the curfew now that the persons of Japanese ancestry were all incarcerated), "We're not announcing it. . . . We haven't told Justice, and we don't want to—we're actually exempting hardship cases [that is, Italian and German aliens] from that curfew." In answer to Jaretzky's question, he said that the sector commander issues permits, stating, "If a man has to go someplace, he gets a permit."[63]

It is interesting to note that DeWitt and Bendetsen proposed to sort through a large alien population of West Coast Germans and Italians and possibly identify ten thousand to be interned. They had consistently opposed the idea that it was possible to conduct an individual examination of persons of Japanese ancestry to determine loyalty, and this insistence, which appeared to be based on a racial stereotype, would, forty years later, cause the courts to reconsider Fred Korematsu's wartime conviction for violating the exclusion order.[64]

In spite of attempts at formal agreements, the disagreement between the Justice Department and the War Department over enforcement of the president's proclamations was never really resolved. In a phone conversation, Bendetsen, who was then in Washington, D.C., told General DeWitt that the lack of support from the attorney general was familiar—"that takes us back to the point where we were when you first asked the provost marshal general to send someone out and I came out." DeWitt said, "I've just reached the end of my rope."[65] DeWitt described the enforcement as a farce: The FBI had arrested sixteen Italians because they possessed contraband, and then they were released. He asserted that Justice was flouting the president's proclamation. DeWitt could not accept the practice of many arrests but few convictions, though he was cautioned by Mr. Jaretzky that this was "altogether proper," and that "the arresting officers would be remiss in their duties if the arrests they made did not far exceed those that may ultimately be held."[66]

On June 1, 1942, the State Department sent Bendetsen a list of 539 names of Japanese individuals, entitled "Japanese Nationals Sailing First Voyage S. S. *Gripsholm*." These people had been selected by the Japanese government to participate in the first wartime exchange for Americans held in Japan. The individuals who would agree to accept repatriation were to leave from Ellis Island on June 11, 1942. Because the train trip from the West Coast to the East Coast required five days, Bendetsen and the WCCA had fewer than seven days to identify, locate, contact, and obtain agreement from the designated persons. In addition they had to locate the families of some men interned by the Justice Department, and for all persons, they had to get their signatures either on a "Declaration of Declination" or on the "Individual Request for Repatriation." Only about a fourth of the persons on the list (plus thirty-four dependents) were found to be in WCCA jurisdiction. In the *Final Report*, Bendetsen wrote, "Operating under considerable pressure because of this imposed time limit, and carrying on all correspondence with Centers and other points by teletype, telegram, and telephone, 101 of the 176 persons were located and their decisions obtained." (Of the 101 found, 41 declined and six were found to be ineligible.) The details of handling repatriation were extensive, and few ground rules existed to guide Bendetsen and his aides. Bendetsen managed to develop a set of rules concerning what kinds of property the repatriates could take, how much money they could take, how to transfer frozen assets, whether there would be inspections by Customs or the Internal Revenue Service, and, not least, which family members not on the State Department list would be allowed to accompany repatriates.

The source of the list was held in close confidence, and few evacuees were aware that their names were included. In the second repatriation effort in the fall of 1942, some evacuees' first notice came in a letter from Bendetsen. Several internees were incensed and indignant and replied in strongly written letters of refusal.[67]

In the last hours of preparations to get the June repatriates onto trains, Bendetsen spoke frequently with Colonel Tate, who was in Washington, D.C., and in contact with the Special Division of the State Department. Every person presented some complication, and one of the last was a case of possible mistaken identity. Yoshio Shinohara was #367 on the State Department list. Bendetsen had a Yoshitaka Shinowara in WCCA jurisdiction, who desired repatriation and who asserted that he was the person on the list.[68] Bendetsen needed Tate's help to get a decision to allow the man, who had been manager of Sumitomo Bank in Sacramento, and had a wife and three children in Japan, to take the place of the missing Shinohara. Tate doubted the man's story. Bendetsen said, "I am getting slant eyes myself here" and asked Tate to help with this case. "We've got to load him on the train. He is in Sacramento. . . . We have got another 9 hours . . . 7 hours. The train goes right through Sacramento."[69]

Bendetsen's problems in locating willing repatriates paled in comparison with those of the Special Division of the State Department, which was attempting to accomplish a simultaneous exchange of Japanese nationals for American nationals detained in the Far East.[70] To put together an exchange of "hostages," the Special Division began with a list of desired persons that Spanish diplomats (who acted as intermediaries for the government of Japan) had obtained from the Japanese. They then had to consult various security agencies, such as the FBI, Office of Naval Intelligence, the Justice Department, the Military Intelligence Division, and other parts of the War Department, all of whom had strong views about which persons on the lists should be allowed or denied repatriation. Little time was left to locate persons on the list. Although the first exchange was accomplished in about six months, the second required negotiations of more than a year and was finally resolved only because General Gullion persuaded someone to persuade the Justice Department that the exchange, to include persons against whom there were objections, must go forward not only to bring home another two thousand or so American nationals but also to gain shipment of relief supplies to the American prisoners of war in the Far East.[71]

Bendetsen wrote of his part in this whole repatriation episode in the *Final Report*: "The many problems which arose, their solution, the human interest aspects, if narrated in detail would occupy a volume of considerable extent itself." The first group finally entrained from the assembly camps on June 6, 1942, consisted of fifty-four persons. Tate had apparently failed to "raise anyone at the State Department." Yoshitaka Shinowara was not among the passengers boarding the train in Sacramento.[72]

In the next months, several additional lists of potential repatriates came to Bendetsen's desk. Based on his experience with the first list, Bendetsen wrote up a formal set of policies for handling repatriation, which he labeled "Warning Order Relative to Possible Repatriation of Japanese Evacuees." He also drafted "General Instructions for Persons Seeking Repatriation," and, ever the bureaucrat, created a set of multipart forms to cover all eventualities. During this time, evacuees were being transferred out of the assembly centers and into the jurisdiction of the WRA as the relocation centers were completed. The question of whether the policies he had outlined would be used by the WRA to handle repatriation began to bother Bendetsen. He discussed this with Colonel Tate. "If it is going to be done through this WCCA proposition then within the policies described by the War Department and the Commanding General, I want to be boss." Tate said that he thought that could be arranged: "I rather judge that [Dillon] Myer would be rather glad to have you be boss." Bendetsen pointed out that what was important was to have a uniform approach, "doing it the same for all evacuees because as you know, some families are separated and they write to each other."[73]

When Milton Eisenhower resigned in June 1942 to take a job with the Office of War Information in Washington, D.C., Dillon S. Myer, a Department of Agriculture colleague, took over as director of the WRA. Eisenhower had had great hopes of avoiding long-term incarceration of the evacuated Japanese Americans, but had been overwhelmed by the negative political climate at the Western Conference of Governors in Salt Lake in April. He found the job as jailer to thousands of Americans of Japanese ancestry repugnant. Laurence Hewes encountered Eisenhower on Market Street in San Francisco. Eisenhower was "in a downcast mood." He said, "I'm getting out of all this. I guess I'm not a grassroots boy. I know my Washington, but out here I'm lost."[74] It had become clear that resettlement of the evacuees in the interior was going to be difficult. Eisenhower later recalled that he "had lost a year's sleep in ninety days."[75] When Myer was considering whether he should accept the job, Eisenhower is said to have told him, "Yes, if you can do the job and sleep at night."[76] Eisenhower's negativity and the hasty transfer of responsibility of the WRA to Myer became sore points with Bendetsen, and he later claimed these as reasons that the relocation effort was largely unsuccessful.

By June 1942 Bendetsen probably knew that his friend from Aberdeen, Jack Clark, had been captured when Corregidor fell, and was among the thousands of Americans imprisoned by the Japanese in the Philippines. His son recalled that Bendetsen had many times said that he always had in mind the view that his treatment of the Americans of Japanese ancestry could possibly influence how well American citizens and American military prisoners would be treated by the Japanese army, and that the marine unit from his hometown was among them.[77] He also had to have known in early June 1942 that the few Japanese Americans from Grays Harbor were en route to Tule Lake Relocation Center.

CHAPTER EIGHT

Tule Lake, June 1942

This is our barracks, squatting on the ground,
Tar-papered shack, partitioned into rooms
By sheetrock walls, transmitting every sound
Of neighbors' gossip or the sweep of brooms
. . .
The floor is carpeted with dust, wind-borne
Dry alkali, patterned by insect feet.
What peace can such a place as this impart?
. . .
Routines, must now adjust within the heart.

—Toyo Suyemoto Kawakami, quoted in Daniels, *Japanese Americans*

In Olympia, Perry Saito, his mother, and Morse and Dahlia found the train bound for Tule Lake. The Moyers from Hoquiam were also among the 151 persons ordered to evacuate from the northwestern counties of the state of Washington that week.

It was Jim Moyer's first train ride. And it was on this memorable trip to Tule Lake that the youngest Moyer recalled first meeting the Saito family. Jim was nervous while they waited at each stop.[1]

Evacuees heading for Tule Lake Relocation Center did not know what to expect as they traveled for hours or days in dingy trains with window shades fastened down, "blindfolded," one evacuee observed, guarded by armed military police.[2] They arrived at the train station in the small farm town of Newell, California, and were bused into a vast empty valley. Heading south, they saw no sign of a lake. They were approaching what looked like "thousands of black barracks standing stark in the flatland, no trees, no color except for the dull gray and pale red of lava beds."[3] The camp tract comprised 7,400 acres of dry lakebed covered with sagebrush or desert grass, but the "colonists," as the government referred to the camp residents, were restricted to the enclosure, which was an area of about one and a quarter square miles encircled by barbed wire and guarded by military police in watchtowers along the fence.[4]

From the dusty enclosure, evacuees could identify two nearby landmarks, Abalone Mountain to the southeast, and Castle Rock, across the highway to the southwest. They were in the rain shadow of Mount Shasta at four thousand feet above sea level, but views of the mountain were partially blocked by Castle Rock. Out of sight was the remnant of Tule Lake and extensive lava beds.[5] The barren windswept plain seemed inhospitable, especially to people arriving from the rainy Pacific Northwest. The accommodations, barely finished army-style barracks with no running water and little furniture, seemed no friendlier.

Only 446 evacuees had reached Tule Lake when the Saitos and Moyers arrived. Eight thousand five hundred "aliens and non-aliens" arrived in the month of June, and another six thousand in July. The camp's peak population was 18,789. Only the Colorado River Center, at Poston, California, was larger. Both families from Grays Harbor found themselves surrounded by Japanese faces in a world that they scarcely knew, but for the Saitos, the strangeness would be tempered by a reunion; Morse tells the story: "[June] 1942 found us in Tule Lake War Relocation Center. Assigned to block 18, we were met by our Medford, Oregon, relatives who had saved us a real nice end-of-a-barrack apartment next to their smaller apartment in block 14. This bothered me but not my mother. She assumed it should be this way."[6] Thus the Saitos did not go to block 18, to which the Moyers were assigned.[7]

Perry later described their accommodations: "My mother and my younger brother and sister and I were assigned a compartment in a tar-papered barrack . . . approximately 20' by 25' in size. In the compartment were one canvas cot, a straw-filled mattress, and an army blanket for each member of the family, and a pot-bellied stove. There were no chairs or table, no partitions, curtains, floor coverings, and only one electric light hanging from the ceiling in the middle of the room."[8] Morse recalled cracks around the windows and in the floorboards, saying, "We could do little to keep out duststorms except to try and plug up the cracks."[9] Perry and his family were always aware that "civilian and diplomatic prisoners of war and prisoners in federal penitentiaries received better treatment and facilities than the inmates in Relocation Centers."[10] However, the association with other Japanese was what they especially remembered. "In 1942," Morse wrote, "we were lucky in the desert Tule Lake camp. We made many lifelong friends and my brother Perry met his beautiful wife, Fumi. I got a job which trained me for my eventual release from camp. I put in 48 hours a week (washing dishes) and later got a pay raise from the original 8 dollars to 12 dollars . . . a month."[11]

By the time he arrived at Tule Lake Relocation Center, twenty-one-year-old Perry Saito had cultivated many skills that would help him find a niche for himself in camp and later find a job that would ease him back into American life. He had had many friends in high school, had served as an officer of many student organizations, and had lettered in baseball and tennis. He had played clarinet and oboe in the high school band and orchestra and sung in the chorus. He had been president of the Aberdeen Methodist Youth Fellowship, had traveled widely in western Washington as chairman of Southwest Washington Christian Youth Council, and had participated in debate competitions for the Junior College. He was used to standing up in front of a large audience to sing, play an instrument, or even preach. Not unexpectedly, he became a recreation leader for young people.[12]

The Saitos from Aberdeen had arrived at Tule Lake shortly after the evacuees from the North Portland and Puyallup assembly centers, and from southern Oregon (the southern group included their "cousins" from Medford). Several ministers came with these groups and began to organize a Christian church in the Tule Lake camp. Reverend Andrew Kuroda, a Methodist minister from Salem, Oregon, soon chose Perry Saito to lead the young people's service.[13]

Many groups of Buddhists organized services as well, since the majority of evacuees were Buddhists. Though some Buddhist priests were held in Justice Department camps for a year or more, many others were evacuated with their communities. All the Buddhist priests then in Tule Lake participated in the funeral for Shoichi James Okamoto who, in May 1944, was shot by a sentry. At least nine thousand people attended the ceremony.[14]

As the camp filled up with arrivals from the Sacramento and Florin areas of northern California, and later from Los Angeles, more Christian ministers arrived.[15] By fall the Christian community had adopted a Union church concept; the church was called Tule Lake Godo Kyokai (Tule Lake Union Church). Six of the ministers were Methodists, including Kuroda and Reverend Shigeo Tanabe from Sacramento. Reverend Daisuke Kitagawa, an Episcopal minister from Seattle who was among the last to arrive, said of his old friends Kuroda and Tanabe: "It was evident that these two were the powers moving everything, and I joined them to complete a trinity." Kitagawa and Kuroda led the Ward church that the Saitos and

FumikoYabe attended.[16] Reverend Tanabe's sermons, always limited to thirteen minutes, were popular with camp audiences seated on backless benches.

Some Sundays Perry would preach to as many as 650 high school students. It wasn't like a youth meeting at home. The group met in a rough barracks hall heated by several coal stoves. The barrack was one of many set in endless rows inside the barbed-wire fence. And rather than facing a Caucasian audience, as he had in the Pacific Northwest, he faced a sea of faces like his own.

Perry Saito, the recreation leader with the wonderful smile and a sparkle in his eye, was asked to organize teams of young people to stand near the gate of the Tule Lake camp to welcome the first arrivals from California, evacuees from the Walerga assembly center near Sacramento. Among this group was Fumiko Yabe.

The future had looked bright for the young Sacramento woman. She had sung before many audiences and her press notices were glowing. As a student at the Pease Music Conservatory, she won an age-group singing competition in 1939 at the San Francisco World's Fair auditorium on Treasure Island. At eighteen she was a featured coloratura soprano for the annual concert of the Sacramento Junior College Symphony for which she had prepared to sing "Un Bel Di" from Puccini's *Madame Butterfly*. The concert in the college auditorium opened at 3:00 P.M. on December 7, 1941.[17]

She was surprised to be asked to sing the national anthem before the concert, and asked why. Her next question, echoed that day by many Americans, was, "Where's Pearl Harbor?" This opening song was the event featured in the *Sacramento Bee* the following day: "Japanese Girl Leads in Singing of US Anthem." Her appearance eclipsed that of the orchestra and clarinet trio. According to the *Sacramento Bee*, "An American girl, Sacramento born, of Japanese parentage, was the guest soloist . . . and . . . led the audience in the singing of "The Star-Spangled Banner." Her name is Fumiko Yabe, and as she stood there beside the flag she seemed to symbolize the thousands of other 'Americans with Japanese faces' whose only allegiance is to the land of their birth."[18]

A year later Fumiko Yabe demonstrated "her varied talent, rare among Nisei singers" to a capacity audience at "#2508," a barracks social hall in the fenced and guarded Tule Lake Relocation Center.[19] She sang arias by Gounod, Verdi, and Puccini and some light opera selections to an enthusiastic audience of fellow evacuees who had no idea how long they would be confined by the WRA in this desert camp.[20] For all they knew, they would be detained for the duration of this war or even beyond that. Though they didn't think it probable, they had to wonder about other dire possibilities: after all, they had not expected that they would be subject to mass arrest and held under armed guard just for being different looking.

Fumiko had grown up a few blocks from the California capitol building in a community that included many Japanese families. Her parents were born in Okayama, Japan.[21] Kazuto Yabe came to Wyoming as a young man to work on the railroad. When he had enough money, he went back to Japan, married, and brought his wife by boat and train to Sacramento. There he found all sorts of work—short-order cook, landscaper, fruit picker, any work he could get. Fumi's mother, Tomoko Shiyomi Yabe, was a seamstress and housewife. Fumiko was born in December 1923 in Sacramento. She and her two younger sisters attended Lincoln School, then Sacramento High School. After school she attended *Nichiren* and other kinds of Buddhist schools, where she studied Japanese, although in 1942 on a camp questionnaire she rated her mastery as only fair.[22] Though her family was Buddhist, she sang at Christian conferences in Berkeley that were attended solely by Nisei. She attended the junior college and did part-time typing for Dr. Mendelssohn, a dentist, until she was evacuated.

On the eve of Pearl Harbor, the Japanese community of the greater Sacramento area was the fourth most populous in the mainland United States and included a large Japanese business district and several farming communities. At evacuation, the community was divided at the center into four sectors, each sent to a different assembly center. The Yabe family was sent to the center at Walerga, the site of a former migratory labor camp on the northern outskirts of Sacramento. At first, Fumiko and many of the other young people thought of the evacuation as a temporary situation. "Mentally all of us that were 17 or 18 thought, 'Oh, this is a nice vacation; we're going to go home in a couple of months.' I know that's what I thought."[23]

After six weeks of uncomfortable confinement in the hastily constructed camp, the family was not going home, as Fumiko had hoped, but rather was ordered to move farther away. When she heard that her family would be sent to a relocation camp at Tule Lake, California, she ordered a bathing suit. Fumiko, her sisters Shigeko (fifteen) and Kazuko (nine), and her parents packed their few belongings and boarded the train along with about 4,600 other evacuees. It was a slow, hot ride up the Central Valley and through the mountains of northern California.[24] She found out later that Tule Lake had disappeared five hundred years earlier into the Black Hawk Desert, known for dust storms and scorpions. It would be another twenty-four years before Fumiko learned to swim.[25]

When Fumiko and her family arrived, Perry Saito and his family welcomed them. Fumi recalled, "[He] greeted us and that's how we got acquainted. Else we wouldn't have known them." Perhaps because she was impressed by the poise and charm of the tall young man from Aberdeen, Fumiko began attending Methodist youth meetings and was soon converted.

When Perry organized programs and variety shows to break the monotony of camp life, Fumi was invited to sing. "It was a good thing for both of us," Fumi recalled, "It would have been really boring. When you're 18, you're going to have fun. . . . You just had to make something to do."[26]

The other family from Grays Harbor, Towa Moyer and her children, assigned to live many blocks away from the Saitos, were having a different experience.

Tule Lake seemed even more foreign for the Moyers than for the Saitos. In Hoquiam, Jackson, Madeline, Chester, Billy, and Jimmy Moyer had never been singled out for being Japanese. This family of "Caucasian-looking children" wasn't sure they belonged in a camp with people from the Japan towns of large West Coast cities.[27]

Jim Moyer recalled his twelfth summer. "Thinking back—at the time it was just a good experience. . . . We were treated great. I lied about my age and got a job as a dishwasher. The rest of the time I was free to play baseball. Had no chores except dishwashing."[28]

"We lived in barracks, there were two families per barracks.[29] The walls went up to ceiling high and then the gable part was open. I remember the family in the same barracks which we never did see, but we could hear them. They were Buddhists, we could hear them praying, I guess that's what it would be. That was kind of interesting." There had been no Buddhists in Hoquiam or elsewhere in Grays Harbor.

Jim continued, "I remember my mom starting to speak Japanese again. . . . It was kind of odd to hear her speaking Japanese because she never spoke it at home. I thought that was kind of neat."

Jim Moyer also recalled that he had been on a work detail with Morse, the Saito's youngest son, in the camp; they had gone in a truck to pick up scrap lumber outside the fences. In early August, Jim had his appendix removed at the camp's hospital. He remembered the experience: "They took good care of me. . . . I think they had some awfully good Japanese doctors."

Though the Moyers hadn't lived among other Japanese Americans, Jim recalled, "It didn't take long. . . . Actually I was around young people like me and older, like 15, 16, 17. . . . And some of the nicest people I've ever met. . . . There were some in the next block down from where we were. . . . They used to yell at us. I didn't do any yelling. There was yelling back and forth, mostly in Japanese. . . . My friends said that they were kind of a tough bunch. They were . . . from southern California."[30]

Madeline Moyer, who had been a stenographer in Hoquiam, quickly got a similar job in the administration's engineering department. Her older brother Jackson was hired as a procurement clerk and paid $19 per month for full-time work. When they heard "encouraging news" regarding their chances of returning home, Madeline and Jackson wrote to friends at home to get further supporting letters. They learned that the WRA was trying to come up with a plan whereby families like theirs would be permitted to return to their previous homes. "Mixed-blood" families would be required to demonstrate that the family would be self-supporting and not become wards of the government.[31]

Madeline and Jackson were confident that they could gain their release. Madeline said, "The authorities already [knew] from us that we still own[ed] our own home and would be self-supporting." It was a nerve-racking time for Madeline and Jackson because "new bulletins [kept] coming from San Francisco" with different interpretations. She said they were "trying to meet every condition" as it came up.[32]

They worried about their mother; she had never been separated from their father and she was not well. Dr. Watkins of Hoquiam, Towa's physician, had written in May that in his opinion, "to take this woman to a concentration camp at this time, and away from the protection of her home, would cause an early death."[33]

Even as the Moyers tried to adjust to living in a somewhat alien communal society, the camp administration had become concerned about their welfare. Writing in the *Final Report* in 1943 Bendetsen described the problems of mixed-race persons who had been included in the evacuee population: "Most of these people were American-born, had been through American schools, had not developed Oriental thought patterns or been subject to so-called Japanese culture. Because of their Americanization and their awkward social position, life in the Japanese Centers proved a trying and often humiliating experience. The adults were ostracized and the half-caste children ridiculed."[34]

By mid-July 1942 a "mixed-marriage non-exclusion policy" based on the assumption that it was more desirable to assure the unemancipated children of a mixed marriage an opportunity for rearing in "a non-Japanese environment" got Bendetsen's approval. Keeping "mixed-blood" children in a WRA project was thought to "expose them to infectious Japanese thought" and "would . . . compel them to live in an environment from which they [had] sought escape."[35] Certain persons became eligible to return to the evacuated zones: "All mixed-blood (one-half Japanese or less) individuals, citizens of the United States . . . whose backgrounds have been Caucasian," and "families consisting of a Japanese wife, a non-Japanese husband, citizen of the United States . . . and their mixed-blood unemancipated children." Had she not had young children, Towa Moyer would have had to remain at Tule Lake. Her adult children had grown up in a Caucasian environment, had promises of continuing gainful employment in Hoquiam, and under this policy could return home to live with their father William. The only exception to the requirement that a Japanese wife have unemancipated mixed-blood children in order to be released was for "Japanese wives of non-Japanese spouses" whose husbands were serving in the armed forces of the United States.[36]

There were conditions to be met before release would be granted.[37] Madeline and Jackson Moyer were never sure that there wouldn't be one more hurdle to deal with. They had to get clearance from military intelligence and they had to provide evidence that they had bona fide offers of employment. The chief of police had to authorize their residence in Hoquiam. If told that they must leave the WDC area, they would have to reside in states east of the inter-mountain states of Colorado, Wyoming and New Mexico.

In July, William Moyer wrote from his home in Hoquiam to Elmer Shirrell, director of the Tule Lake project, "It will be hard for me to attend to my cows, keep house and hold down this job [at the Polson Lumber Company]. If I could have my wife and children home it would greatly lessen my responsibilities. The four of us would be making over $500.00 monthly, the greater part of which would be invested in war bonds as before and would be for the best good for all concerned."[38]

Internal WCCA memos had warned project administrators not to promise release to mixed-marriage families and mixed-blood individuals. Releases were to be authorized only when the conditions had been met and it was assured "that the releases [would] not in any way be detrimental to the safety or welfare of this nation." A nervous army bureaucrat needed to provide himself a cushion, saying, "In time of war, conditions are constantly fluctuating, new problems are developing, and policies must of necessity be subject to immediate revision."[39]

Towa Moyer and her children were granted a release on August 19, 1942. They received a travel permit on August 21, 1942, and soon returned home on a regular train in time for Jim and Bill to resume school in Hoquiam. In December, Captain Charles Middleton provided the list of mixed-marriage cases released to date, which included the Moyer family and forty-seven other residents of Washington. By the end of 1942, a total of 486 persons had been released to return to their homes in the Western Defense Command, and fourteen moved outside the area, for a total of five hundred persons released, less than one half of one percent of the evacuee population.[40]

In the *Final Report*, Bendetsen wrote, "Execution of the mixed-marriage program has not adversely affected military security, and it has achieved certain benefits: 1. Mixed-blood children are being reared in an American environment; 2. Families have been reunited; and 3. Mixed-blood adults predominantly American in appearance and thought have been restored to their families, to their communities and to their jobs." This was true for the Moyers: Jackson and Chester Moyer got their jobs back, and Madeline, who had been replaced, quickly found another good job.

In spite of McCloy's suggestion and their earlier thoughts that licensing back a few Japanese would forestall arguments that the exclusion was racially motivated, both Bendetsen and DeWitt declined to make exceptions for aliens of any stripe. In his early recommendations for the military necessity of mass evacuation, Bendetsen had argued that they exclude all persons from a "military area" and then license back on an individual basis persons "whose reentry was found to be necessary to the war effort," and that it would be constitutional to decline to license back persons of Japanese ancestry whom, he asserted, were potentially an enemy group. As an aside he had suggested that it might be wise to admit "perhaps a few 'token' Japanese to preserve the individual licensing idea." The five hundred individuals freed under the mixed-race policy included a minuscule number of carefully qualifying alien parents and may have satisfied his idea of "token." Over most of the next year Bendetsen supported DeWitt's refusal to allow *any* Japanese to remain in or return to the exclusion area. DeWitt forced the removal of the army's Military Intelligence Service Language School from Crissy Field in San Francisco to Camp Savage, Minnesota, because he would not allow the army's qualified Issei instructors or students who were Nisei (though servicemen) to reside in the exclusion area.[41]

McCloy wrote Bendetsen several "Dear Colonel" letters urging exemptions for Japanese citizens he thought were all right; for example, the Reverend Keizo Tsuji in April 1942, and Mrs. Riyoko Patell in May 1943.[42] In the latter case he urged Bendetsen and General DeWitt to broaden the mixed-marriage policy. Both Mr. and Mrs. Patell were British subjects who had lived in San Anselmo, California, where Mr. Patell represented a tool manufacturer. Mrs. Patell's loyalty was vouched for by a Department of Justice official, but she had no children. General DeWitt denied an exemption for Mrs. Patell and refused to change the mixed-marriage policy. He said, "The policy itself has been in no sense developed on a loyalty basis," though he noted that no one whose loyalty was in doubt had been released. The policy was rather to allow mixed-race children to be raised in their former non-Japanese environment. He said that his policy was "predicated solely on considerations of military necessity." He was opposed to creating a new class of persons to be exempted from a relocation center, and stated, "This would impair military security and it is on this ground that I deem its adoption unwise."[43] A person's Japanese ancestry was of greater concern than their loyalty, in DeWitt's view.

Jim Moyer had the last laugh: "I was a dishwasher though I was only 13. Got away with it because I was tall for my age. Taller than some 18 year olds. So was Billy. The administrators, when they paid us off . . . thought it was very funny that we were only 13 and 15. When I got home, back in school, I wrote a paper called 'Life in an Evacuation Camp.' I didn't save it. Wish I had." Years later, Madeline commented, "If I'd known that we were going to be there such a short time I wouldn't have gone to work." She regretted that she hadn't had time to take any of the "interesting classes . . . [like] flower arrangements." She described her mother as "the type of person that made the best of it."[44] At home, Mrs. Moyer was heard to comment, "My summer vacation in California is all over."

Mrs. Patell had no mixed-race children to provide her an exemption, and though she was a British subject had to remain in camp. The Saito young people, Perry, Morse, and Dahlia, though they, like the Moyer offspring, had been reared in the Caucasian environment of Grays Harbor, also remained at Tule Lake. They would be allowed to leave prior to the end of the war, but only after gaining clearance and agreeing to settle outside the Western Defense Command.

Though the evacuated population of America's ethnic Japanese may have looked like a homogeneous group to the Americans who had argued vehemently for evacuation, the camp administrators quickly found a wide diversity in the viewpoints and attitudes of their "colonists." There were a few Japanese from Hawaii who were aggressively pro-American and outspoken; there were socialists and even a few "Wobblies."[45] Some seamen and longshoremen caught on the West Coast when war broke out were described by a sociologist observer as "a no-nonsense group nobody fooled with. They were political radicals. Japan was a fascist country. They supported the democratic country."[46] The Nisei were initially pro-American, and for them the camp environment was not healthy. Larry Tajiri wrote: "Evacuation destroyed the 'Little Tokyos' of far-western America. But relocation established racial islands [in the camps]. . . . Instead of Americanizing the aliens, as hoped, there was an indication that the reverse was true. . . . Young Americans were being 'Japanized' through daily and enforced co-existence with their elders and their loss of normal contact with other Americans."[47] The logic of Bendetsen's argument that mixed-race children would be better off outside the Japanese-dominated culture of the relocation centers really could have been applied to a large number of the incarcerated Japanese Americans.

In theory, the evacuees were allowed to govern themselves. The administrators of the camp oversaw the entry and departure of the evacuee population, the facility, the guards, the hospital, and the food supply. The residents were told to elect members for a community council (something like a city council) whose chairman (something like a mayor) would speak for the entire Tule Lake population in its dealings with the camp administration. According to Reverend Kitagawa, himself an Issei, "*Issei* were categorically eliminated on the grounds that this was an American city" because the administration could not accept an alien in a leadership position. For a group of people who had grown up respecting their elders, who normally would accede to the wishes of their elders, this was anathema. And it didn't work. The result was an "abnormal community." The Tule Lake administration was entirely Caucasian; the city council was Nisei. Kitagawa wrote, "The really dynamic part of the population was Issei. . . . Where in the world was there a city, or even a little village, run entirely by young people?"[48] The Issei paid little attention to the council and natural leaders among the Issei gradually appeared; in some camps they would eventually be allowed to participate in camp government.[49]

Tule Lake was never a peaceful camp and it became more turbulent than other relocation centers as the incarceration progressed. The earliest conflicts in Tule Lake occurred in 1942: Farm laborers went on strike on August 15 over the lack of promised goods and salaries, and packing-shed workers did the same in September. Food served in the dining halls was the germ of the next uprising and eventually led to a mess hall workers' protest in October. Many of the problems grew out of the abnormality of camp life. Mothers no longer cooked for their families and children of all ages ran off to eat with their friends, with many spending whole days outdoors out of parental control.[50] According to Kitagawa, "The loss of the family table and family kitchen was not simply a loss of opportunity to teach table manners to growing children, but a forceful symbol of the breakdown of that human institution which transmits values from one generation to another."[51] Eleanor Roosevelt later remarked upon "the breakdown of the traditional family structure" as one of the great injustices of the internment experience.[52] Gangs of youths no longer under the firm control of Issei authority figures sought to establish territories. Unknown previously in the Japan towns of America, "juvenile delinquency" became a concern of many parents.[53]

In addition, a group of people accustomed to relying on their own hard work to survive found little incentive to take on the low-paying jobs that were available. They were guaranteed food and shelter in the camp. Kitagawa wrote, "Issei and Nisei alike ceased to be the hard-working people they had been reputed to be. . . . They had no initiative to do anything for their own benefit. . . . The whole situation was demoralizing."[54] In all the relocation camps, idled people found plenty of time to gossip and criticize the administration and their fellow evacuees.

The Issei men, unable to provide for their families and just as dependent on government support as their wives and children, suffered from loss of respect. Many looked to Japan as their only hope for the future and urged others to do the same. Another contentious faction within the relocation camps was the Kibei, persons of Japanese ancestry born in the United States who were, in DeWitt's words, "educated and indoctrinated in Japan during their formative years."[55] An Issei from Manzanar who had become a block leader wrote to the administration to warn that Manzanar was rife with anti-American sentiment and that the commingling of Issei and Nisei was unhealthy. He wrote, "[The] basis for mob violence and agitation is already laid by the dissatisfied elements, fanned and encouraged by pro-Axis elements. . . . Abuses are heaped upon individuals who defend this country's policies, bodily harm and mob action is threatened [against] those who denounce the anti-American sentiments. The bulk of Nisei, fundamentally loyal Americans, are vacillating and bewildered." He pointed out that Issei and Kibei particularly taunt the Nisei, saying, "Look at your citizenship. Is it helping you any in this camp?" The writer described a meeting of four hundred people led by Kibei at which one of them said to a Nisei, "If you think you are citizens, just try to walk out of the camp past the sentry line. If the sentries don't shoot you, I'll believe you are citizens."[56]

Because of such frictions among the evacuees, McCloy and the WRA began planning to "segregate and sequester disloyal and disturbing individuals."[57] A survey that used "Nisei stooges" to gather information from the relocation camps set out "to determine the amount of subversive activity" at Manzanar in August 1942 and reported that "Kibei, the most Japanized and truculent of the Japs, are gradually assuming unofficial control within the camps" and that "the loyalty of the Kibei is growing more doubtful day by day."[58] Similar groups were creating problems in the Tule Lake camp, and in the next year Tule Lake would be selected as the depository for the least cooperative evacuees.

After hearing these reports, DeWitt became concerned that the Kibei represented "a real danger to national security," and feared that there were many thousands of Kibei "at large in the interior."[59] He proposed that Kibei in relocation camps be separated from other evacuees, that those not under federal supervision be apprehended, and that they all be required to forfeit their U.S. citizenship.[60] The Kibei were the only Japanese Americans that Lieutenant Commander Ringle had singled out in his February 1942 report for any kind of severe treatment—Ringle had suggested that they be treated as aliens and "many of them placed in custodial detention." His estimate of the size of the problem was considerably smaller than DeWitt's. Not all Kibei were a security threat; many Kibei were soon enlisted into the army's intelligence service, where their ability to read and write Japanese was invaluable.[61]

By this time, Bendetsen was largely occupied with the coast's other enemy aliens, the Germans and Italians. Once he had begun organizing individual exclusion hearings for selected Italian and German aliens, Bendetsen again asked DeWitt to allow him to revoke the curfew on the West Coast because it was unenforceable against aliens who were Caucasian. In late June 1942 Bendetsen explained to McCloy that "we have taken the first step in the repeal of the curfew and I had a long talk with General DeWitt Friday and really pressed the matter and he has come around to the view that it should be repealed."[62] A week later, July 5, DeWitt wrote to the army chief of staff (Marshall) that he did not agree with Bendetsen's position but thought that "instead of alleviating the conditions of the curfew and travel regulations and the permits, they should be tightened up and enforced strictly." He argued that the military situation was such that "the activities of enemy German and Italian aliens demand closer surveillance and enforcement of existing proclamations than ever before."[63] DeWitt rejected Bendetsen's arguments that the curfew was too expensive to enforce and caused hardship to aliens who were in no other way cause for concern. Bendetsen replied with an extensive argument for removing the curfew based on the official statement by President Roosevelt on July 11 expounding a new policy to classify aliens, both friendly and enemy, "with a view to greater utilization of their services in war production."[64] Bendetsen pointed out to DeWitt that in spite of past actions to enforce the curfew and travel restrictions, "not a single case of actual or attempted sabotage or subversion has been uncovered," and suggested that a better use could be made of the government's time and energy.

In spite of Bendetsen's pressure, DeWitt held firm until the attorney general ordered the exemption of Italian aliens from compliance with the provisions of the general enemy regulations. Finally on December 24, 1942, Public Proclamation No. 15 rescinded all travel and curfew provisions of Public Proclamation No. 3. DeWitt did not give in gracefully. In the *Final Report* was a statement specifically attributed to him: "The need for the curfew no longer exists as other security measures have now been provided. Among these measures is the Individual Exclusion Program under which persons who are found, after hearing, to be dangerous or potentially dangerous to the military security of the West Coast are excluded. I desire to make it plain, however, that there will be no retardation of the program to rid the West Coast of such persons."[65]

In July, Bendetsen answered General Gullion's request for his frank expression about the subjects in his commendation file in order to support Gullion's plan to recommend him for a Distinguished Service Medal. Though he felt "completely embarrassed while writing," Bendetsen replied that "while serving under you I made a signal contribution in connection with the development, drafting and processing of Executive Order 9066."[66] In August 1942, in a rare opportunity to catch up with his personal paperwork, Bendetsen prepared a military brief of record, edited in his own hand, which took explicit credit for the executive order and the evacuation. He wrote that he had "conceived, drafted and processed Executive Order 9066, authorizing creation of military areas and control and exclusion of civilians therein" and had "conceived the method, formulated the detailed plans for, and directed the evacuation of 120,000 [*sic*] persons of Japanese ancestry from military areas of the Pacific Coast." In the brief of record he also stated that he had "conceived and organized the Civil Affairs Division and the Wartime Civil Control Administration of Western Defense Command."[67] Much of the wording from this routine army form, including the 120,000 figure, made its way into Bendetsen's first entry in *Who's Who in America*, in the 1944–45 volume. In 1942 Bendetsen was quite willing to take credit for a task that had brought him a double promotion and considerable attention and that would perhaps earn him a medal.

Bendetsen accepted praise graciously. In answering a query from Aberdeen's police chief regarding curfew restrictions on enemy aliens, Bendetsen acknowledged Police Chief Gallagher's comment on his job. "If my contribution during the present emergency is as favorably received by all of my friends and neighbors at home, I shall be richly rewarded indeed."[68]

Five months after the battle of Midway in which the Japanese navy had lost half of its aircraft carriers and any possibility of offensive action against Hawaii or the West Coast of the United States, Bendetsen prepared to give a speech defending the evacuation and detention. By November 1942 all the evacuated persons of Japanese ancestry had been successfully transferred from the temporary assembly centers into one of the ten newly constructed relocation centers. Speaking to WCCA employees, Bendetsen observed that the press, in writing about the evacuation, had noted parallels with "the moving story of vast migrations of peoples" found in literature, such as in "the pages of Holy Writ . . . the verses of Longfellow . . . a tale by Bret Harte and . . . John Steinbeck's novel," though he made no attempt to give the evacuation "its place in history."[69] Of the transfers of evacuees to assembly centers he said, "Observers noting the ease of the transfers said that the Army handled the movement as if it had been dealing with so many tourists." He concluded, "With the evacuees out of strategic military areas, the Army has discharged its obligation."[70]

That November he was awarded the Distinguished Service Medal on the recommendations of Major General Allen W. Gullion and Lieutenant General John L. DeWitt.[71] A *Grays Harbor Post* editorial noted that "Bendetson has been rightly distinguished by the U.S. Army" for handling "what was probably the toughest military problem of the West Coast." A photograph of Bendetsen appeared on the front page captioned with the new spelling of his name; his Aberdeen spelling appeared in the article, which noted that he "made full colonel early this year . . . one of the youngest men ever to attain such a rank in the Army."[72] *Time* magazine quoted General DeWitt: "[The evacuation] was completed within the designated time, without mischance, with minimum hardship and almost without incident." Of Bendetsen, *Time* said that the thirty-five-year-old colonel had "finished his seven-day-a-week job" by placing "all his charges in the care of the civilian War Relocation Authority."[73] It also observed "an embarrassing sequel to the Japanese migration: when a young Japanese American citizen violated curfew regulations, Oregon's Federal Judge James A. Fee ruled that the curfew law covered aliens only, that General DeWitt had no power over citizens."[74] DeWitt's actions seemed questionable because martial law had not been declared on the West Coast. *Time* prophetically observed that this finding would cause problems for DeWitt and possibly lead to court challenges by citizen Japanese "who may construe from Judge Fee's ruling that they are illegally held in camps." In fact, a habeas corpus petition had been filed in the courts in July on behalf of Mitsuye Endo, a Nisei and former California civil servant who was confined in Tule Lake Relocation Center.

Bendetsen continued as assistant chief of staff to General DeWitt and as director of the WCCA into 1943. He faced serious challenges as DeWitt's interpreter and as author of the *Final Report* in the months that followed. Meanwhile, turmoil reigned in the so-called relocation camps.

Perry and Morse Saito maintained their pro-American outlook, and experienced harassment: They were denounced as spies and called *inu* (dog) and physically threatened. Morse felt that their precarious position (they were on the pro-Japan faction's hit list) helped them to be among the first to get permission to leave Tule Lake in 1943, but the release would not come quickly.[75]

One of the ways that Perry got himself into trouble was by organizing a Nisei theater group that strove not just to entertain, but to help evacuees acquire "cultural refinement," where culture was construed as that of the American society that had allowed the incarceration. Perry and friend Sada Murayama organized "the internment's most prolific theater group," what was called "barrack theater's greatest flowering."[76] Morse took part as an actor, and later described the experience: The troupe selected "serious plays which they felt [were] real dramatics and fine literature."[77] In monthly productions of three one-act plays (always a comedy, a tragedy, and a fantasy) presented for every block in the camp, they enacted plays by Eugene O'Neil, Booth Tarkington, Anton Chekov, A. A. Milne, and others. Most members of the theater group were Americanized and, as Morse recalled, were often in conflict with "the pro-Japan Kibeis [who] tried to stop all such 'frivolous' activities of the rec[reation] department and even threatened to break up Little Theater performances."[78] Tensions were great during "the registration fiasco of 1943," and the theater ended its run shortly after Perry gained his release from Tule Lake. It was later replaced by Issei-produced kabuki presentations.[79]

Though Perry spent much time through the summer and fall of 1942 organizing activities for camp residents, his main focus, as it was for most of the college-age evacuees, was to find a way to get out of camp. Many Christian groups such as the Quakers and other Protestant churches came forward to assist the student evacuees in the relocation centers.[80] By fall Perry was corresponding with the National Japanese American Student Relocation Council (NJASRC), which was willing to provide him with financial support to attend Ohio Wesleyan University in Delaware, Ohio. He agreed with his Medford "cousin" Nani Saito (Yahiro) that "camp life is not for the young. You begin to just deteriorate. Because you lose your ambition, there's no future."[81]

At the time of mass removal and detention of the West Coast Japanese Americans, most of the Nisei college students were attending schools in the evacuation zone.[82] Only 216 of these students gained quick permission to transfer to colleges outside the Western Defense Command in 1942. To pursue their education, the thousands of detained students and prospective students in the camps faced red tape, restrictive leave policies, and reluctance by colleges in the interior to accept students of Japanese ancestry. The NJASRC worked with the WRA to help applicants overcome the hurdles, which also included anxiety on the part of some young people at leaving the confining but relative security of the relocation camps for an unknown and possibly difficult experience.[83]

In early August 1942 Bendetsen wrote a long letter to Colonel Tate explaining why "we do not trust a good many of the representatives of the National Student Relocation Council." He meant the NJASRC. He was concerned that some of the group's representatives argued that the evacuation was political, that other groups "had persuaded the Army to do by force what some had been seeking to do politically for many years."

Bendetsen objected to the group's having meetings with students that did not include anyone from the War Department, and set about creating instructions for the conduct of the NJASRC relating to press releases and the conditions under which the group could speak to prospective students in the relocation camps. He recounted to Colonel Tate the many ways that the NJASRC had violated these instructions and had "distributed printed literature, or information that borders on the subversive." He singled out members of the Friends Society and of the Fellowship of Reconciliation (which he said "consists largely of conscientious objectors") as among the most threatening. "There existed the idea of discrediting the whole evacuation program. The active presence of interlocking membership with the Fellowship of Reconciliation would indicate something even more sinister—the discrediting of the Army itself."[84]

Policies to allow students or other evacuees to leave the relocation centers developed slowly and were not well explained to the evacuees because of conflicts between the civilian WRA and the army. In his speeches and plans, Bendetsen stated that the Japanese Americans would be confined for the duration, but he insisted that "while they [in the assemblies] were detained, they were not imprisoned," and stated, "They were improperly called internees."[85] The WRA was finding that Bendetsen had been right in observing that once a group of people was identified as dangerous and removed from one location, no one else wanted to accept them. Relocation would not be easy.

Perry hoped to start at Ohio Wesleyan in October 1942. However, he still had to get leave clearance from the camp. He recalled, "Since I got the scholarship, I knew that if I could prove to the government that I had never done anything wrong, that I was an ordinary American, [then] I could be released."[86]

Thinking his scholarship was a magic "get-out-of-camp" card, he marched over to the administration barracks. The administrator laughed at his request and handed him what he said were "45 different forms, [each] between 4 and 6 pages long to be filled out in triplicate." The forms asked for information about everywhere he had lived or worked, all travel he had made outside the country, what magazines he read, what organizations he had joined, whether he could speak Japanese, and where he had gone to school. A page and a half of questions asked about any possible connection with Japan, and whether he had registered with the Japanese or Spanish consuls.[87] He was required to list some references and told, "Good Caucasian references may be particularly helpful."

Perry filled out the forms, then waited for the approval. "Ten days, two weeks" was the interval he was told to expect.

Two weeks later he quit his job, preached a good-bye sermon to the young people, packed a suitcase, and went to the administration building. The approval had not arrived. "That night I opened my suitcase, took out my pajamas and went to bed. In the morning I folded my pajamas nice and neat and put them in the suitcase." At the administration building, he found that his papers had not been returned. This sequence was repeated for many days, and eventually, fearing the government had lost his forms, Perry filled out a second set. Still the clearance did not come, and he missed the chance to enter the fall term at Ohio Wesleyan. At least, he said, "I was getting smart. . . . I left my suitcase home."[88]

Although Perry never saw them, the letters sent to Tule Lake on his behalf were supportive. His Methodist church contacts wrote about his leadership abilities. Bertha Pease, the executive secretary of the board of education of the Methodist Church, Pacific Northwest Conference, praised Perry's good judgment, tireless zeal, and enthusiasm. "Under war tension I have not known his spirit to falter from that of cheerfulness and goodwill. Indeed, he has gone 'the second mile.'" Another Methodist, Margarita (Rita) Irle, also wrote on Perry's behalf in her capacity as a member of the National Conference of the Methodist Youth Fellowship. She emphasized, "As his was the only American-Japanese family in Aberdeen, he has become completely Americanized." She noted that he "is a good singer, recreation leader and has a friendly excellent personality."[89]

Irle's friendship was to prove key in getting Perry's eventual release from camp. By 1943 Margarita Irle, whom Perry had met when she was a student at the College of Puget Sound, had moved to Chicago to marry Herman Will, Jr., a lawyer for the Fellowship of Reconciliation who was working to assist evacuees in relocating. When the Fellowship wanted to find a fine young man to represent and speak out for the incarcerated American Japanese, she knew whom to recommend.

Lieutenant General John L. DeWitt is shown addressing troops in the field on July 9, 1941. General DeWitt oversaw the army's war games during the summer of 1940 at Monterey Bay and in western Washington in 1941. After Pearl Harbor, DeWitt was commanding general of the Western Defense Command and the Fourth Army headquartered at the Presidio in San Francisco. (Courtesy of U.S. Army Military History Institute)

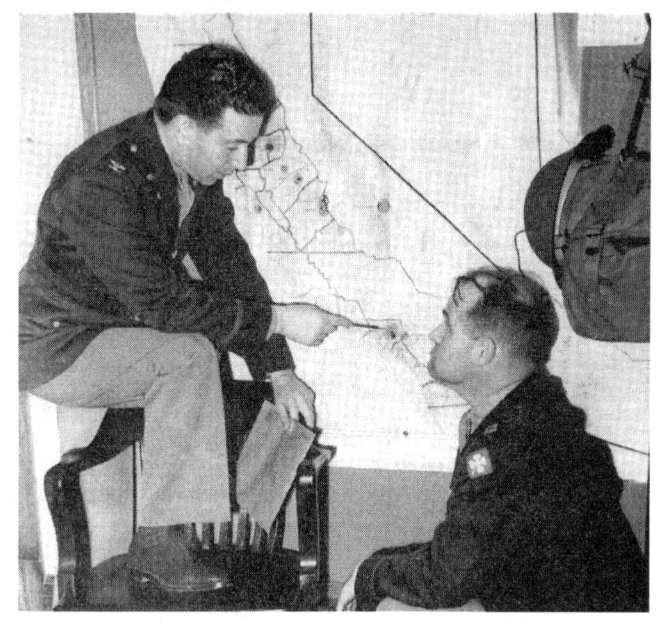

The *Stanford Alumni Magazine* in June 1942 captured Bendetsen on the job as head of the evacuation, pointing out a feature on the map of the Pacific Coast areas "from which Japanese [had] been evacuated under his direction." Another Stanford grad, Hugh Fullerton, at right, served on Bendetsen's staff. This article about Bendetsen made no mention of his having been a representative to General Douglas MacArthur the previous fall, which he alleged in later biographical articles. (KRB Papers, Hoover Institution)

Bendetsen (*left*) brought Milton S. Eisenhower and Tom C. Clark to the Western Conference of Governors on April 7, 1942, to try to persuade inland states to accept the evacuated Japanese. April 8, 1942. (Microfilm of *Salt Lake Tribune*)

John Abbott (*left*), Milton S. Eisenhower, Tom C. Clark, R. M. Neustadt, and Bendetsen at the Western Conference of Governors called by Bendetsen. Almost all governors opposed free movement of Japanese aliens in their states, fearing their states would become "dumping grounds." Years later, Bendetsen argued that the conference had been successful. April 7, 1942. (Microfilm of *Salt Lake Telegram*)

Bendetsen (third from left, in uniform) accompanied a group of United States attorneys on a visit to Alcatraz on June 25, 1942. He headed the evacuation operation from offices in the Whitcomb Hotel in San Francisco. (KRB Papers, Hoover Institution)

This formal portrait of Bendetsen may have commemorated his double promotion to colonel in February 1942; at 34, he was possibly the youngest in his rank. He was assistant chief of staff for Civil Affairs under General DeWitt, and director of the Wartime Civil Control Administration. In these two capacities he issued directives pertaining to the evacuation, and saw to it that they were executed. (Courtesy of Beverly Freedman)

Bendetsen's son was born on May 2, 1943. A distinguished group gathered on the steps of the Presidio chapel to commemorate the "Christening of Brookes McIntosh Bendetsen" in summer 1943. Front row from left, Bendetsen, Mattie and Brookes, Billie Bendetsen, Mrs. Moffitt, Molly and Helen Middleton, and Myrna Schweitzer. Back row, Captain Charles Middleton, Major A. H. Moffitt, Jr., Major Harold W. Schweitzer, and an office secretary. (Photo courtesy of Molly Middleton Tuohy)

Billie and Brookes Bendetsen were left behind and spent the war years in Hoquiam, Washington. This may have been the photo Bendetsen carried with him when he went overseas in the fall of 1943. (Courtesy of Beverly Freedman)

'So Proudly We Hailed'

Symbolizing the loyalty of the "Americans with Japanese faces," Fumiko Yabe, 17 year old Sacramento born singer, yesterday led the audience in the Sacramento Junior College Auditorium in the singing of The Star Spangled Banner, at the opening of the annual concert by the junior college symphony orchestra.
Bee Photo

Japanese Girl Leads In Singing Of U.S. Anthem

Junior College Symphony Concert Audience Is Swayed By Fumiko Yabe

For a few minutes yesterday afternoon, Sacramento musical folk brushed aside the grim realities to attend the annual concert of the Sacramento Junior College Symphony Orchestra in the junior college auditorium—and were rewarded with a beautiful program which symbolized the ideals of Christianity and of racial tolerance for which America stands.

An American girl, Sacramento born, of Japanese parentage, was the guest soloist—and at the invitation of Director David L. Burnam she led the audience in the singing of the Star Spangled Banner. Her name is Fumiko Yabe, and as she stood there beside the flag she seemed to symbolize the thousands of other "Americans with Japanese faces" whose only allegiance is to the land of their birth.

The orchestra opened with the lively and colorful March and Procession Of Bacchus by Delibes, and the impression of a notable improvement in balance and tone and general musicianship was confirmed by the following performance of Schubert's lovely Unfinished Symphony, No. 8. The student group never has excelled in recent years its work in this composition, either in the playing of the various sections, the unity of the ensemble, or

The *Sacramento Bee* asserts that Fumiko Yabe symbolized the loyalty of "Americans with Japanese Faces" as she sang the national anthem hours after the attack on Pearl Harbor. Soon thereafter the McClatchey newspapers launched an all-out propaganda campaign against Japanese Americans. (Courtesy of Fumi Saito)

Soprano And Clarinet Quartet Will Be On Junior College Orchestra Program

A young Japanese coloratura soprano and a clarinet quartet will be the special student artists appearing tomorrow afternoon with the Sacramento Junior College Orchestra in a concert in the college auditorium. The soprano is Fumiko Yabe, a Sacramento singer who is gaining local recognition. The members of the clarinet quartet are Jack Menz, Herbert Harrison, Kenneth Tucker and Harold George.

In the first half of the program, the orchestra, which is conducted by David Lincoln Burnam, will play both movements of the Schubert Unfinished Symphony. The clarinet quartet, directed by Stewart W. Tulley, will be heard in Alabama Capers by Cohen and Scherzo by Tuthill.

During the second half of the program, which will be in the form of a radio skit with Dexter Rivett as the announcer, Miss Yabe will sing the famous aria for coloratura sopranos from Madame Butterfly, One Fine Day.

An epilogue, The Christmas Story, with Peter Walline Knoles as the announcer, will bring the afternoon's program to a close.

The concert will begin at 3 P. M.

They all blow in unison, these members of the clarinet quartet who will appear tomorrow afternoon on the program of the Sacramento Junior College Symphony Orchestra in the col- ... right: Harold George, Kenneth Tucker, Herbert Harrison and Jack Menz.

"One fine day," sings Fumiko Yabe, coloratura soprano, seen in the oval, who will be a ...

This clipping from the *Sacramento Bee*, December 4, 1942, announced that Fumiko Yabe would sing "One Fine Day" with the Sacramento Junior College Orchestra the following Sunday. (Courtesy of Fumi Saito)

When Natsu Saito was released from INS detention in May 1942, she, Perry, Dahlia, and Morse enjoyed a last light moment in Aberdeen. Within days they complied with the order to transport themselves to a rickety train for the trip to Tule Lake, to be incarcerated possibly for the duration of the war. (Courtesy of Lisa Aylesworth)

As he left Aberdeen, Morse was described by a family friend as an "exceptionally manly little chap." He got out of the Tule Lake camp at 16 and finished high school in West Rockford, Illinois; his winning a national writing contest saved him from flunking out. This photo is from 1950s. He is now a missionary-educator and journalist in Kobe, Japan. (Courtesy of Morse Saito)

Fumiko Yabe [Saito], standing in a firebreak, had ordered a bathing suit when she heard she would be moved to a relocation camp called Tule Lake. Perry Saito was among those earlier arrivals who greeted Fumi's family and other Sacramento evacuees. Fumi did not learn to swim until years later. (Courtesy of Fumi Saito)

CHAPTER NINE

Loyalty Crisis

Loyal American citizens of Japanese descent should be permitted, after individual test, to enlist in the Army and Navy. It would hardly be fair to evacuate people and then impose normal draft procedures, but voluntary enlistment would help a lot.
—Elmer Davis, Office of War Information, October 2, 1942, in CWRIC, *Personal Justice Denied*

The whole premise of the evacuation, as conceived by Bendetsen and DeWitt, that it *was not possible* to determine the loyalty of the evacuees, was severely threatened when the army's general staff decided on January 1, 1943, to reverse its position and support the recruiting of an all-Nisei combat team. This decision required the development of a procedure so that "Japanese Americans of the Nisei class [might] be released from War Relocation Centers," and a decision as to "what disposition [might] be made of them" if released, including whether they might be permitted to enlist in the armed forces or get defense jobs.[1]

Though Secretary Stimson and President Roosevelt supported the plan for a combat team, DeWitt and Bendetsen were firmly opposed to the entire review program.[2] How could a set of questions, many of which had already been asked, be used to establish a nonexistent attribute? They feared that the loyalty reviews would undo the entire justification for the evacuation and detention, causing embarrassment and worse. DeWitt was still convinced that no Japanese, alien or citizen, should or would be allowed to return to the West Coast and that they were still a threat to security. If the loyalty of most evacuees were established, wouldn't they have to be allowed to return to their former homes? This knotty issue soon put both DeWitt and Bendetsen in conflict with the leaders of the War Department.

On January 18, 1943, DeWitt and Bendetsen heard about the proposed

"Loyalty Investigation of Japanese-Americans in War Relocation Centers." DeWitt immediately asked for an opportunity to comment on the plan. He called McCloy to express his disagreement, saying that he felt that it was a sign of weakness and an admission of an original mistake: "Otherwise—we wouldn't have evacuated these people at all if we could determine their loyalty." McCloy did not agree. He said, "Everybody is agreed—at least everybody here is agreed—that you can't keep them in pens forever." It was, as DeWitt feared, the beginning of the end of the exclusion: "I hope they are not going to send any of them back here."[3] Bendetsen reported to Colonel Eugene McGinley, "The War Department is now considering a plan which, in my judgement, bids fair to stir up a troublesome public relations problem. . . . It is now proposed that the War Department undertake to determine the loyalty of all Nisei. . . . It looks much like a confession of original mistake."[4]

Bendetsen tried to get further information from Colonel Scobey, McCloy's assistant, about what was expected of DeWitt's command. Not only did the general staff propose formation of a Nisei combat unit, but they thought that those Nisei who did not get inducted but were declared loyal should have the chance to work in a war production plant. Bendetsen pointed out that the general did not consider the determination of loyalty feasible and did not want to be put in the position of making recommendations on loyalty. Bendetsen reminded Scobey that DeWitt's policies take into account only categories: "Up to this point the CGs policy has been that you can't determine loyalty so that all of the policies have been applied without any exception in the individual case based on investigation."[5]

In this conversation Bendetsen got into an argument with Colonel Scobey about the number of people released from the relocation centers up to that time. Bendetsen asserted that "they have released about 18,000, I think." He talked about the initial program to encourage voluntary migration to the interior. "Now that was stopped only because of a certain hysteria that developed at that time," he said, adding that there were nine or ten thousand who left under voluntary migration and another nine or ten thousand who were furloughed. Scobey replied, "You are a little bit wrong Karl: on January 12th, the WRA advised Mr. McCloy that a total of about 900 persons have been granted indefinite leave to date; of this number 350 have been students, about 74 have been the wives of American soldiers . . . and the remaining 475 have been persons going into employment in the defense work." These latter were working in beet crops. According to the

Final Report, only 4,889 persons had managed to avoid incarceration by leaving the West Coast during voluntary migration.[6] Over the years, Bendetsen persisted in overstating the numbers released from the centers.

An hour later Bendetsen called Captain Hall, another of McCloy's assistants, to discuss the plan to determine loyalty. "The whole thing scares me to death. I mean it really scares me." He wanted to "toss a couple of suggestions out." The first was that the plan seemed to be based on the assumption that the evacuation was due to the fact that there *wasn't time* to determine loyalty. "The record doesn't show that at all. . . . The record shows that . . . it was a concentration of a large number of persons of Japanese ancestry in strategic areas near war plants and all that. And that it could not be permitted. And . . . that you couldn't determine loyalty and therefore you had to take the wheat with the chaff. Not that there wasn't time, but that *you just couldn't*."[7] [Emphasis added.]

Bendetsen also argued that "the War Department should stay out of the Relocation business, in view of the record made up to now by the War Department." He had heard that certain groups such as the Sons of the Golden West were petitioning congress to change the administration of the relocation camps, asking that the army take them over. Bendetsen wanted nothing to do with this. He also told Captain Hall that he couldn't spare Dr. C. L. Dedrick, the statistician from the census bureau who had been on his staff from the beginning, to help with the loyalty program.[8] He said, "We're trying to whip out this *Final Report*. Dr. D. is my editor. I have to go over the whole thing . . . try to push it out, get it off and get through with it. By February 15th we will be through with it."[9] When the first copy got to McCloy in April, Bendetsen would regret his haste.

SO-CALLED LOYALTY QUESTIONS

Two questions on the new registration form devised by the War Department raised the level of dissension and conflict within the relocation centers:

> 27: Are you willing to serve in the armed forces of the United States on combat duty, wherever ordered?
>
> 28: Will you swear unqualified allegiance to the United States of America and faithfully defend the United States from any or all attack by foreign or domestic forces, and forswear any form of allegiance or obedience to the Japanese emperor, or any other foreign government, power, or organization?[10]

WRA administrators also developed a version for women, "Application for Leave Clearance," which asked in Question 27, "Would you be willing to volunteer for the Army Nurse Corps or the WAAC?" Camp administrators did not do a good job of explaining the purpose of the questionnaire or how the results would be used, and gave the impression that the evacuees could be forced to "register" and that they could be penalized for failure to do so.[11]

As part of a special "morale-building week" on the occasion of the opening of the schools in Tule Lake, Reverend Kitagawa expressed the hope that the students would get a general education that enabled them to think for themselves, stand up for their convictions "undaunted by any force, and to uphold the principles of justice, love, and peace against all odds." He said they needed to get "the kind of education which will help to make a Gandhi" of each of them."[12] Perry Saito took this message from his minister to heart.

Because of the delay in getting his paperwork approved, Perry had to fill out a new leave-clearance form in February entitled "Statement of United States Citizen of Japanese Ancestry."[13] In addition to requiring the usual personal information, the form contained the troublesome questions above. Questions 27 and 28 were causing an uproar in detention camps that were already experiencing friction within the evacuee population. Reactions by the evacuees to having to answer these questions were not what the government expected, and gave rise to what came to be called the "loyalty crisis."

The older evacuees, the Issei, feared that by answering the leave-clearance questionnaire, which was referred to as "registration," they would be required to leave what had come to feel like security in the relocation camps. They did not want to do this since they could not go back to their former homes and might have to start over in some possibly hostile interior place. If they answered "no" to the questions, would they be sent back to Japan? Many agonized about the unfairness of question 28. After all, it was America's laws that had prevented them from becoming American citizens. If they answered yes to question 28, they would become men or women without a country. If they returned to Japan, this yes would mean treason, and possibly a death penalty.[14] Many of the Issei had raised children who looked Japanese but were Americans. And the parents had given up their notions of returning to Japan and had come to love the country that had become part of them because it was part of their children. Many an Issei father may have thought "in the dying of the foolish dreams which he had brought to America, the richness of the life that was possible in this foreign county destroyed the longing for the past."[15] Other Issei and Kibei with a pro-Japan attitude, perhaps feeling that Japan was now their only hope, would answer no to the two questions and would exert considerable pressure on many others to do the same. These conflicting forces were very strong in Tule Lake, where the preparation for registration had been notably brief and inadequate.[16] Fumi Yabe was caught up in the swirling sentiments, and her exit was delayed. However, Perry Saito was more fortunate.

"Perhaps if Perry and I had been a bit older we might have been disillusioned enough to have gone the 'No, No' route," Morse wrote.[17]

"We had riots in Tule Lake. That prompted the new administrator [Harvey Coverly] to proclaim his hard line which made things worse and alienated those of us who would have been his supporters. The riots stemmed from the questionnaire which eventually divided the camps into 'Yes, Yes' and 'No, No' groups ('Loyal' v. 'Disloyal')."[18]

Why were there so many disloyal Japanese and riots in Tule Lake? Morse: "The camp went from a very good administrator (Elmer Shirrell) to . . . [one] who was not going to be soft on the Japs. Plus lousy food, the variety of evacuees in Tule—we came from the northernmost tip of Washington state down to San Pedro, etc. in southern California; a large rural representation (in some ways the most 'Japanese' because of their isolation), and a smatter of those of us who had been raised in largely (white) American communities. An old Aberdeen friend sent me some hard Christmas candy which I shared with a friend who had gotten a gift of some filbert nuts. Quickly our whole block (250 people) knew about our 'outside' contacts." Morse said that those contacts were viewed with suspicion.[19] In this climate of distrust, Perry had to fill out the questionnaire.

Most young people in camp (the Nisei) had been raised by immigrant parents (Issei) to respect their elders and follow their example, which was usually to try to make the best of the situation. "It can't be helped" was a typical Issei view (*shikata ga nai*, they would say in Japanese). But many Nisei, faced with the loyalty questions, reacted as one might expect, given their American upbringing. How could they answer a question that assumed that they, American citizens, ever felt any allegiance to the emperor of a foreign country? Hadn't their willingness to cooperate in the evacuation been enough to demonstrate their loyalty? Hadn't many of them earlier tried to join the armed forces, and been rejected? They were confused and angry.

But not Perry Saito. All his prewar church work had prepared him for this moment. Perry had associated with a group of progressive church leaders who strongly advocated pacifism and who conducted their lives according to those views. He and his friend Dick Tuttle, stepson of Aberdeen's Methodist minister, had spent many hours talking about what they would do if called by the draft, what they would do when war came.

In fluid, legible script, Perry wrote his answers on the back of the clearance form:

> 27. Due to my religious beliefs, I am a Conscientious Objector and I could not bear arms for any force, whether it be for this nation or any other. I have registered as a CO with my local draft board. I am a pre-theology student (Methodist).
>
> 28. Yes. Insofar as I do not have to bear arms, I do swear allegiance to the United States of America.[20]

Because "conscientious objector" was a legitimate draftee status (though treated punitively by many draft boards), and many of the Caucasian teachers in the relocation camps were conscientious objectors, the administration of the relocation camp had to accept Perry's answers.[21] But still his clearance was not approved. He continued the routine of putting on plays, organizing activities, and preaching sermons, all the while trying to keep out of the way of the pro-Japan group. Conflicts among the residents and dissatisfaction with the camp administration were creating an unpleasant "atmosphere of heightened tension."[22]

Church activities were an important part of camp life during this time, and were well attended. One afternoon a great crowd of people gathered before a camera in the wide firebreak between lines of barracks. People in the front row held up a banner boasting, "Forward with Christ." There were as many as three hundred smiling faces in the photo.

Years later Bill Marutani would try to put names on the tiny dots.[23] He identified Perry H. Saito, "who had answered the call to the ministry." Aki Saito Yasutake (Perry's cousin) identified the rest of the Saitos—Morse; Dahlia; Aki's sister and Perry's cousin, Naoko (Nani); and Fumi Yabe, whom Perry later married. Reverend Kitagawa and Harry Mayeda (first mayor of Tule Lake) stood nearby. In a *Pacific Citizen* article, Marutani gave his version of their family history:

"The two Saito family trees through cousins Ransaku and Kinai Saito had their roots in Gunma-ken, from whence both came. Each married ladies from Tokyo. And although both cousins arrived via Vancouver, from there their paths differed: one settled in Oregon, the other established roots in Washington. In 1942, they and their families were uprooted and thrust into camps. And in 1943, the photo . . . [shows] at least parts of the two branches of the Saitos, rejoined under stressful circumstances.

"Perhaps in the next century, when some blue-eyed blonde bearing the name Saito seeks to trace his/her family roots, this column might serve to provide some clues."[24]

During this difficult period, groups of Issei and Kibei "went around intimidating everybody whom they judged to be pro-American, and branding them 'traitors.'" Kitagawa's friend, Minister Andrew Kuroda, who was also minister to the Saitos, was beaten up. "Another friend, the editor of the Japanese section of the Tule Lake newspaper, had to have sixteen stitches in his head after an unidentified man hit him with a lead pipe."[25] Perry and Morse Saito went to Reverend Kuroda's barrack after the beating, and "his ashen-faced wife" told them to go away. She feared "they might come back." The two stayed past midnight then got others to stand guard. Morse recalls, "I followed a very angry Perry back to the Block 4 mess hall where the Kibeis were still trying to incite everyone to rise up and sign "No, No" or simply riot. Perry got up and told the leader what we had seen . . . a beaten minister who did not fight back . . . the minister of one of the leaders in front of us. . . . Then Perry challenged them to come to 1414-D and we would be there. The shamed leader left the hall to attend to Reverend Kuroda."[26] A few pro-America evacuees were put in protective custody and quietly transferred to other camps. Numbers of young men who were labeled "troublemakers" were put in a guardhouse, known as the stockade.[27] Before Tule Lake closed there would be two episodes of the illegal use of stockades.

Perry was still waiting for his leave clearance. "This is what happened to my forms," Perry later told a New York audience, "They took them to the FBI. They took every answer and went over it and it took several months. . . . After a thorough investigation they filed the application and said, 'Perry Saito has proved himself to be a loyal, patriotic, citizen.' Then they took it to Army Intelligence . . . then to Navy Intelligence."[28]

Perry's Tule Lake records show that his file received the "cleared FBI" status in December 1942, even before he had declared his conscientious objector status. Not until the end of March 1943 did he get the Indefinite Leave Clearance (which was not a Permanent Leave Clearance). Finally in mid-April 1943, after a wait of five months, he got a seven-paragraph travel permit from the army that stated that he would be permitted to travel through evacuated areas only in the company of a Caucasian escort appointed by the WRA. He was one of fewer than two thousand Nisei students granted leave clearance in 1943.[29]

Three hundred and thirteen days after he entered, after preaching one more "farewell sermon," Perry Hitoshi Saito left Tule Lake Relocation Center with a job offer from the Fellowship of Reconciliation in Chicago in his pocket, a Caucasian escort, and those pajamas in his suitcase.

Perry was released in the midst of the loyalty unrest. Morse was surprised that there was nothing in their internment case files about the "riot(s) in Tule Lake and our particular role in that community upheaval. . . .[30] The beatings of Christian ministers and how we were on the blacklist of the militant pro-Japan activists. An obvious group which the FBI must have infiltrated and thus known how Perry was the leader of the pro-America group." (Morse was sure that he was allowed to leave before he was seventeen, in part and "to protect" him because he "was on the 'right' side, namely pro-US."[31])

Perry's new job required him to talk about his experience in camp. He had to process what it meant to him and his family and to the thousands of other American families to have been removed from their homes and businesses and shut away behind barbed wire, distrusted by their countrymen during this war with the country of their parents. His former neighbor, Karl Bendetsen, who was honored for his role in forcing these people into the internment camps, soon admitted that he had enjoyed his assignment.

A GRATIFYING TASK

In early 1943, in a letter to his friend Brigadier General Lawrence Hedrick, Bendetsen described his handling of the evacuation as "a real challenge—one I wouldn't have missed. It was a task of great magnitude and its accomplishment without major incident is most gratifying."[32]

In June 1943 in a personal letter to his friend and mentor, retired colonel Harry Auer, he quoted a section of the Distinguished Service Medal award commentary and said he was "deeply gratified by General DeWitt's comment." He went on to say that he was awaiting a change of assignment, but noted "while the duty here has ceased to be exciting, it is extremely pleasant."[33]

In pondering what Bendetsen's next assignment should be, Auer had thought that maybe Bendetsen should try to get a posting with Auer's former associate, General Joseph W. Stilwell in China, since Auer felt, "It is from China that the death stroke can be given to Japan." He told Karl, "If the good jobs in England are already pre-empted, I hope you will not go there."[34] A month later Auer wrote, "I am still hoping you will not be a BG but an MG (Major General) as the latter better fits the scope of your attainments and usefulness. . . . If you are not selected it will not be your failure, but the failure of higher authority."[35]

Some months earlier, Bendetsen had written to McCloy suggesting that he be allowed to organize some kind of "project unit" for McCloy that would operate in "the twilight zone between the field of military operations and the field of civilian operations related to the war effort."[36] No such job materialized. Bendetsen explained to Auer that his old buddies, Dillon and Lerch, got their stars as brigadier generals after attending the provost marshal general school, which Bendetsen had not had the luck to attend.[37] He did mention that "General Gullion was going to ask for me as his deputy, and that a star would be involved. I do not attach much to this for I do not believe G–1, War Department, would approve the assignment." Bendetsen wrote further that in mid-May he had received notice that he was to be assigned to the European Theater, and then got a reversal of the assignment at the end of May. Also, he had lost out to General Hilldring for the newly created post of Chief of Staff of the Civil Affairs Division on the War Department's general staff—Hilldring was "a more mature man" and there was doubt about whether his health would allow assigning him to overseas duty. Bendetsen thought McCloy and Hilldring had an assignment in mind for him. However, in late June, he wrote to Auer, "The situation regarding myself is SNAFU."[38] Noting that his current situation was tolerable, he said, "I shall wait developments with patience."[39]

For Colonel Karl Bendetsen, as for many in and out of the army, 1943 must have seemed interminable. The anticipated invasion of Europe had been delayed, probably for another year. The dissolution of the WCCA, which Bendetsen had planned for months, was finally scheduled for March 15, 1943, and the civil affairs division of the WDC was reorganized on March 19. Bendetsen and many of his staff moved to the Presidio where he continued as assistant chief of staff for civil affairs. He continued to manage the army's relationship with Executive Order 9066. His division included four branches that oversaw planning, statistics, the Alaska travel control section, special services (including the exclusion section), and a subversive research group. The last group, composed of one Chinese and three Korean professionals, was engaged in a "Japanese translation research project" aimed at determining significant subversive and other pro-Japan activities in the relocation camps. In January 1943, Bendetsen wrote of this group, "It is only now beginning to reflect positive results. It is, perhaps, one of the few sources from which positive information may become available to produce data to justify total evacuation of Japanese."[40] Even so, no charges against evacuees were ever filed. Operations to support the exclusion board remained at the Whitcomb offices (from which Bendetsen had managed the WCCA) until that program was terminated.

The WCCA had served its purpose, but Bendetsen was still busy with his staff position. While he waited for a new assignment, he found himself required to defend the evacuation, trying to make the best arguments to support General DeWitt's stubborn stands. A high point of his time in San Francisco was the birth of a son, Brookes McIntosh Bendetsen, in early May 1943. He shared news of the birth with Gullion, who sent congratulations to him and Billie but expressed grave concern about their dog—"What I'm worried about is Sam! To have his nose put out of joint . . .after having been the sole child for so long. . . . Look out for it."[41] In June, Bendetsen thanked Colonel Auer for his good wishes, noting, "It is now safe to say that the launching was entirely successful. Both mother and son are doing well." Karl and Billie had moved to "very comfortable quarters on the post," on Cantonment Street in the Presidio.[42] For the first time they had time to socialize with their Presidio neighbors, who now included Hal Schweitzer from Los Angeles, as well as his friend Chub Middleton and his family from Aberdeen.[43]

That summer, these friends joined Karl and Billie for the christening of their son at the post chapel in the Presidio. In the commemorative photo, a nurse holds an infant of two or three months in a traditional baptismal dress. Standing on her right, Bendetsen seems to be holding a rolled certificate as well as his hat. The men are all wearing summer uniforms, the women perky hats that accent their outfits. The other officers and their wives smile for the camera. Billie, standing close to the nurse, and Helen Middleton and her daughter Molly are smiling at the baby.[44]

It was at about this time that a story got back to Aberdeen: During a dinner party in Bendetsen's home at the Presidio, another officer went into a lengthy tirade against Jews. What shocked the listeners in Aberdeen, causing the story to be passed along, was that Karl reportedly said nothing to defend his ancestry. He did nothing to stand up for a tradition he had lived in Aberdeen, nothing to honor the culture and values of his parents.

This story was still recalled in the 1990s in Aberdeen.[45] One thing that it may indicate, if true, is that Karl had successfully distanced himself from his Jewish identity and, by having his son christened, claimed acceptance as a Protestant.

Bendetsen worked on many politically sensitive aspects of the Japanese incarceration in 1943 before he was sent to London. He had to cope with problems caused by administration of the loyalty questionnaires, the plans to segregate evacuees into camps for loyals and disloyals, and public relations problems caused by congressional attacks on the administration of the WRA. At times he was asked to compose statements to be released to the press to put the best face on the policies regulating the incarcerated Japanese in the relocation centers, while those policies were undergoing subtle and not-so-subtle changes. He was confronted by the threat that the cornerstone of the evacuation, "military necessity" had been based on a false or indefensible premise—that it was impossible ever to determine the loyalty of the Japanese in America. While DeWitt continued to insist that loyalty could not be determined, Bendetsen began to express doubts, and certainly understood the threats to the program.

One of his concerns was that if the WDC had always planned to determine loyalty, then it was reasonable to ask why they hadn't done it while they had the evacuees in the assembly centers. If they could have done it then, couldn't they have avoided wasting many of the millions they had spent building more permanent relocation centers? Bendetsen discussed how to explain this with his press relations consultant, Mr. T. W. (Ted) Braun, as they worked on the draft of a statement that DeWitt would deliver. Braun commented: "You had them under control [in the assembly centers] but you had not yet moved them inland—you had not yet spent any 80 million dollars—you had accomplished the main thing as to time and space. And at that point, if you could determine loyalty, it should then have been done." Bendetsen observed: "And that will have to be answered." Braun had tried to think of a good answer to that, and Bendetsen reminded him that they hadn't thought that they could determine loyalty then, "and we still don't think so." Bendetsen expressed exasperation, saying, "Maybe our ideas on the Oriental have been all cock-eyed. . . . Maybe he isn't inscrutable."[46]

DeWitt, in particular, feared that a Nisei certified as loyal would demand to be allowed to return to the evacuated area. This would reverse DeWitt's judgment and, as Bendetsen said, would be "confess[ing] an original mistake of terrifically horrible proportions." And Bendetsen argued that if exclusion were not ended, the loyalty review plan would be logically inconsistent. Talking to Captain Hall, Bendetsen said, "How could you keep him [a "loyal" Nisei] out of the evacuated zone if you said he was [loyal enough] to work in a war plant?" Hall suggested that they could argue that "the reasons justifying the original evacuation still exist in certain degree." Bendetsen said, "No, I don't see how they do. . . . The [registration] plan says that you assume that one of the reasons for the evacuation was that there was no time to determine loyalty. One of the primary reasons. So that now that you decide that you can determine loyalty you've erased that reason, haven't you?" To Hall's suggested argument that "we feel he is completely loyal. But because of certain military considerations . . . he should not go back into the evacuated area," Bendetsen said: "Kind of beats the devil around the bush, doesn't it?"[47]

This point was not missed by Dillon S. Myer, head of the WRA. A few months later Myer was arguing with the War Department over the wisdom or ease of sorting and rearranging the evacuees and suggested bluntly to Secretary of War Stimson, "If mass segregation on a fair and individual basis is so simple that the WRA is to be criticized for not accomplishing it, it is difficult to see *why a wholesale evacuation of all persons of Japanese descent was ever necessary*. If the dangerous and potentially dangerous individuals may be so readily determined as your letter implies, it should have been possible to evacuate only the dangerous from the Pacific Coast area." Bendetsen annotated this letter in several places: "Here's where Myer falls on his face again."[48] He discussed Dillon Myer's troublesome ruminations with Ted Braun, who argued that Myer had mixed up short- and long-term objectives. Braun said that the answer to why the army hadn't done it (segregated disloyals) was, "It wasn't your job. . . . It wasn't your business at the time. Your business was to evacuate in an orderly manner."[49]

McCloy did not then press for termination of the West Coast exclusion, but the possibility of gradual resettlement on the Pacific Coast was debated that spring in the War Department. McCloy and some of the army's general staff began to perceive that instead of a Japanese problem, they had a problem general.

DOSSIER ON DEWITT

Officials in the War Department apparently did not appreciate the zeal with which General DeWitt, with Bendetsen's articulate assistance, was determined to uphold the exclusion of the Japanese Americans from the West Coast. Starting in January 1943, his tenacity was becoming a serious problem for Assistant Secretary of War McCloy and Secretary of War Stimson. In order to form a Nisei combat unit by recruiting evacuees from the relocation centers, they and the army's general staff had settled on the questionnaires to determine the loyalty of the volunteers. This exercise had unearthed a crisis not only in the relocation camps, but in the army's leadership. DeWitt steadfastly asserted that loyalty was foreordained by ethnicity, while McCloy and Stimson held the view that loyalty was a matter of individual choice, that loyalty of individual evacuees could be established, and that it had not been done earlier because of the climate of emergency on the West Coast in 1942.

General DeWitt saw any weakening of the exclusion as a challenge to his authority under the executive order. Someone in the adjutant general's office in the War Department saw a different threat and began collecting statements, telephone conversations, and official documents in a file labeled "Dossier on General John L. DeWitt." In those pages, references to DeWitt's insistent statements that no Japanese Americans be allowed to return to the West Coast while he was in charge were underlined.[50]

The dossier, which ultimately ran forty-three pages and included excerpted letters and memos, began with a statement of DeWitt's policy governing the granting of furloughs to soldiers of Japanese ancestry: Such soldiers would be granted furloughs to visit the states of Washington, Oregon, California, and Arizona only in cases of extreme emergency involving serious illness or death of a member of the soldier's immediate family, or in cases that merited special consideration of the commanding general, WDC. Dated October 7, 1942, the policy kept control of travel permits with the commanding general, Western Defense Command.[51] Interpretation of this policy became a point of contention between DeWitt and his superiors.

As the War Department prepared to form Japanese American combat units, McCloy realized that the men who were selected would have to be treated like any other soldier, that they should have the right to a post-induction furlough to go to their former homes and take care of any business. General DeWitt, who Bendetsen often represented in conversations with War Department staff, insisted that a soldier must be in uniform and have a permit from the commanding general, and said that he would allow no travel to their former homes in the exclusion area, *only to Manzanar or Tule Lake Relocation Centers.*

On hearing of plans to conduct thirty thousand or more loyalty investigations in WRA centers, DeWitt called Gullion to say that he "does not see how they can determine the loyalty of a Japanese by interrogation or investigation. . . . There isn't any such thing as a loyal Japanese and that loyalty just can't be determined."[52]

Included in the dossier were documents by Bendetsen. In one, Bendetsen justified DeWitt's permit requirements—that no person of Japanese ancestry be allowed in the evacuated area without a permit or license, and that the army must know where such persons were at all times—on the basis of the terms of the evacuation. Bendetsen also argued that this was for the protection of the Japanese Americans, citing the example of a small group of recruits for an army language school being taken to Los Angeles, escorted by Caucasian soldiers. "It set the whole town on its ear," he said. Reports of hundreds of Japanese at large in Los Angeles caused an uproar that the Los Angeles police and the army had to deal with. Bendetsen and DeWitt cited the incident as an indication of the strong feelings against persons of Japanese ancestry on the coast.[53]

In late January 1943, DeWitt sent a strong memorandum to General George C. Marshall: "*I reaffirm my previous position that no persons of Japanese ancestry should be readmitted to the Pacific coastal frontier (the evacuated zone of WDC) for the duration of the present war.*"[54] This stand did not please his superiors at the War Department in Washington, D.C.

Bendetsen not only had to defend the general's policy but he often had to smooth a path to allow the general's restrictive policy to seem to meet *some* of the intent of the War Department's and McCloy's policies. Bendetsen reiterated that the general would not change his furlough policy *without a formal directive or order from the War Department.* [Emphasis added.]

In February 1943 Colonel Scobey of the War Department told Bendetsen that General DeWitt should interpret the president's public statement (that any American citizen should have equal opportunity to serve in the armed forces if he wants to) combined with the secretary of war's press release (noting that barriers of ancestry shall be removed from the right to bear arms) to be the current War Department policy. As in many other conversations with Scobey, Bendetsen reaffirmed DeWitt's position that he would not relax any of the security measures that he had established under Executive Order 9066.[55]

DeWitt feared that any change of policy for any reason would undermine the entire program. In a discussion with McCloy, General DeWitt presented his fear of "ramifications," that any relaxation of policy would be used "to expand and ramify out in all directions." McCloy told DeWitt that there was beginning to be some sentiment for returning some of "the right kind" of internee labor back into California, and that he felt strongly that if "we are going to send him to North Africa . . . we've got to let him have the same benefits as any soldier." McCloy argued that it had to be assumed that one could determine the loyalty of the evacuees. And if one should make a mistake, and get a couple of "bad actors" who would come onto the West Coast on furlough: "What possible damage can they do as compared to the espionage that is already going on in your area amongst Italians and Germans." Further, "These fellows are going to war. . . . They volunteered to fight for the white man."

DeWitt told McCloy, "I can't see how America is going to determine the loyalty of a Jap on a Jap's say-so on a questionnaire. . . . I don't trust them, and I just can't bring myself around to trusting them."[56] McCloy chided DeWitt, saying, "These fellows, lots of them are Oriental in only one sense—they have that blood in them, but they have been born in California, chew chewing gum and go to American movies, played on basketball teams and when they said: 'We want to take the acid test' [of going to combat areas] we ought to treat them fairly when we do it." McCloy specifically asked DeWitt to remove the restrictions on furloughed soldiers.[57]

That same day, April 3, 1943, General DeWitt called Lieutenant General McNarney, deputy chief of staff, United States Army, to further argue for his view that he must be able to control the entry of soldiers of Japanese ancestry.[58]

The next day DeWitt sent a memorandum to the army chief of staff on the same subject, upholding his prior restrictions. He gave many examples of what "to expand and ramify" could mean. He feared that any exception would generate a precedent: If a Japanese American soldier were allowed, then what about his Japanese American wife, what about a Japanese who is found to be loyal but is disqualified for service, what about a discharged Japanese American soldier, what about his dependents? He stated that he could not provide for the security of the West Coast if the keystone (the removal of all persons of Japanese ancestry) was relaxed. He again made the argument that he could not guarantee the acceptance of Japanese American soldiers, and gave the example of the army's inability "to force the acceptance on certain portions of the United States population of colored soldiers." He suggested that the plan to send Japanese

American troops only to theaters of war in which they would not contact enemy Japanese shows that the troops are not fully trusted. He summarized his opposition on the grounds that "the proposal is opposed to the entire basis on which evacuation was authorized and carried out as necessary to the military security of the West Coast. The proposal will afford the enemy an opportunity to maintain Japanese agents on the West Coast as an aid to attack. He cannot do so now."[59]

The *Final Report* on the evacuation, which was nearing completion in Bendetsen's office at this time, offered the impossibility of determining loyalty of the persons of Japanese Ancestry as the reason for the military necessity of removing all such persons from the western sea frontier. DeWitt held to his position and further challenged the War Department that he would make no exception for furloughed Japanese American soldiers without a directive from the War Department that would modify the authority given to him under the executive order from the president. In several conversations with War Department personnel, Bendetsen defended the general's contention that the executive order gave him the legal upper hand in his struggle with a War Department that wished to relax the exclusion.

Bendetsen argued DeWitt's side in many phone conversations with various colonels and generals at the War Department in April 1943. He had to warn Colonel Meek that DeWitt would not issue travel permits to furloughed Japanese troops except in cases of dire emergency, "unless he is directed to do it." On April 12, 1943, in the conclusion of a conversation with Colonel Wilson at Fort Douglas, Utah, (an army induction center) discussing the same fact, he noted, "*It's an impasse.*" He had instructions from DeWitt that "if any Japanese soldier comes into the area in contravention to his existing proclamations and policy, *'he is to be escorted out.'*"[60] Bendetsen explained to the complaining colonels that DeWitt's office would be very responsive in providing permits, but that they could be used only by furloughed inductees to visit the two relocation projects in the evacuated zone of the Western Defense Command. The War Department did not like the idea of WDC-controlled permits, but on April 13, Bendetsen reported that the general was standing firm.

The next day Bendetsen had a long talk with a Colonel Barber, an aide to General McNarney, who was preparing to issue a directive to DeWitt requiring that he allow entry of United States soldiers of Japanese ancestry into the Western Defense Command. Colonel Barber said that they considered the requirement that each soldier obtain a permit from the WDC unworkable. Bendetsen assured him that permits should be required and that his command could make the requirement work by issuing permits telegraphically if necessary.[61] The directive was finally sent from the War Department in a radio message to DeWitt on April 14, 1943.

That afternoon, General DeWitt spoke to the press at an "off-the-record press conference," and he made the headlines. He told the press that the War Department had decided to do the things that *he had advised against*—to induct persons of Japanese ancestry into the army and to allow these inductees furloughs to visit the evacuated area the same as any other American soldier. Upon questioning by the press, DeWitt admitted his fears and his disagreement with the policy but stated that he would do "exactly as they wish. I pride myself on being a disciplined soldier." He also said that he had told the War Department that "this was an ideal way for the Japanese to infiltrate."[62] It was his next statement that went into headlines: "[A] Jap is a Jap. The War Department says a Jap-American soldier is not a Jap; he is American. Well, all right. I said I have the Jap situation to take care of and I'm going to do it."[63] DeWitt was not going to make it easy for the War Department to rehabilitate the West Coast Japanese. His comments encouraged anti-Japanese elements on the West Coast to rekindle public sentiment against the evacuees.

Papers in the dossier continued to build a strong case against DeWitt. In testimony on April 19, 1943, before the Naval Affairs Committee in San Francisco, DeWitt was asked if there were any problem that the congressmen could help him with. Even though he knew he had to accept the War Department's directive, he said: "I haven't any but one—that is the development of a false sentiment on the part of certain individuals and some organizations to get the Japanese back on the West Coast. I don't want any of them here. They are a dangerous element. . . . We must worry about the Japanese all the time until he is wiped off the map."[64] He spelled out his fear: If the persons of Japanese ancestry would be permitted back, "the danger is espionage and sabotage. . . . Sabotage and espionage will make problems as long as he [the Japanese] is allowed in this area—problems which I don't want to have to worry about."[65]

Written confirmation of the War Department directive came from the office of the adjutant general to General DeWitt and was dated April 19, 1943. It ordered the commanding general of the WDC to prepare a proclamation to implement the War Department's plan to allow the free travel of American soldiers of Japanese ancestry who were in uniform and furloughed, the same privileges with respect to travel in the WDC as were accorded to other American soldiers. The modified policy did not require that soldiers of Japanese ancestry obtain a permit from the commanding general of the WDC, but only that the commanding general be notified of the name, serial number, grade, and so on, of soldiers given authorized furloughs to travel in his command. Although DeWitt's request that soldiers be in uniform was granted, he had lost the battle, at considerable cost to his reputation, and rumors circulated that he would soon be relieved.[66]

During this period, Colonel Bendetsen was heavily involved in completing the *Final Report: Japanese Evacuation from the West Coast, 1942.* On April 19, 1943, while DeWitt was rancorously submitting to the War Department's position on furloughed troops, Bendetsen had his own problems with Assistant Secretary of War McCloy.

He had just a few days earlier mailed to McCloy printed and bound copies of the *Final Report* along with a signed letter of transmittal from General DeWitt. As McCloy read the report on April 19, he telephoned Bendetsen to express his dismay. McCloy had expected to see the report in the galley proof stage, and he was unhappy with what he saw. Bendetsen explained that "This is the report of the Commanding General to the Secretary of War," and quickly added, "this is only a ten copy affair—any changes you feel ought to be made, can easily be made."[67]

McCloy was furious: "There are a number of things in it now which I feel should not be made public—It . . . is a sort of self-serving document on this matter of relocation—too self-glorifying." McCloy said, "I expected to have a crack at the thing before it was made up in the final form . . . so we could together work on something that would be of real value and could be given wide dissemination. Now it is the sort of a document to support the contention that no Jap is ever going to get back into the Western Defense Command. Which was not at all the purpose of the original idea—it was a report on the evacuation and that was all."

McCloy referred to inquiries from California congressmen, and reported that the press had noticed differences in viewpoint between the commanding general and the War Department. He alluded to DeWitt's statements about how long the Japanese are going to stay away, stating: "How a man can make such a recommendation without knowing what developments the war is going to take, I can't see."

McCloy found DeWitt's statements upsetting: DeWitt claimed it was "impossible" under any conditions to determine the loyalty of this "tightly-knit racial group."

McCloy complained that if they had worked together to write the report they "could have flushed the question as to whether or not there was a difference of view," referring to the determination of loyalty. Bendetsen tried to say that there was no change on his side, but McCloy said, "These points have hit my eye." Bendetsen said that there can be differences of view, but once the decision is made "it is carried through with enthusiasm. Just as in the case of this last thing [the furloughed Japanese American soldiers]." Bendetsen said that they would carry through "to see the uniforms are respected and so on," adding, "Well, the Commanding General's viewpoint was different but he feels no different once the decision is made." McCloy, still unhappy, requested that Bendetsen come to Washington, D.C., soon, prepared to spend "three or four days or a week here to go over the whole thing."[68]

In another conversation with Bendetsen later that day, McCloy talked further about his wish that the report had not been rendered: "There's some things in there that are rather stultifying to a commanding officer." He was concerned that the report could not be revised in time to file with the court brief defending the exclusion orders. Bendetsen asked whether he couldn't just take part of the report, since all of it was based on files in DeWitt's office. McCloy wanted to have "some sort of document signed by DeWitt." He said, "I'm afraid that if we file this thing in court now and had some of the things . . . [t]hey'd say: 'What do you mean? This document's not worth anything, because here's a man that attempts to determine what is a matter of military necessity before the event occurred.'"[69] Later, McCloy said, "The suggestion that military necessity is going to require for the duration that every Japanese be kept out of there, they're going to laugh at that. . . . [The court would] be disposed to think that the original determination was not as sound as it might be."[70]

Bendetsen argued that the document did not, as McCloy maintained, argue for permanent relocation or permanent evacuation, though the report said it "will so continue for the duration." Bendetsen found one place in which that was said, but insisted, "That's the only place you find that anywhere in the report." McCloy mentioned another place, saying, "It's a negation of the argument which has been made" about determining loyalty. "Oh, Bendetsen, throughout there's suggestions of that type that I think can be changed, can be well changed." He said that if the document couldn't be changed ("if you don't agree, if DeWitt won't agree with it"), he would not take the document to the court. "I'm quite convinced that you can make a better argument without this document than you can with it, in its present form." Bendetsen offered to render chapter II, "Need for Military Control and for Evacuation," as an official report, if McCloy wished. Bendetsen said, "That was written by me first—and that was set aside, and the work, the sweat—and there was a lot of sweat—was put in on the main part of it, which isn't slanted—it isn't slanted in any direction." When Bendetsen mentioned that the first part of the report had been done in 1942, McCloy said, "Why didn't you let us see it then?"[71]

THE CHALLENGES IN THE COURTS

A good deal of McCloy's concern arose because he had hoped that by helping prepare a report on the evacuation, he would have a document that he could provide to the Justice Department to support the government's side in the court cases challenging the constitutionality of the evacuation and incarceration programs. Soon after DeWitt issued the first exclusion and curfew orders, several individuals, all Nisei, challenged them. Minoru Yasui, a lawyer from Portland, refused to obey the curfew because it "infringed" on his right "as a citizen" to be treated without regard to race. Gordon Hirabayashi, a University of Washington senior and a pacifist, refused to register for the evacuation in Seattle (and had violated the curfew several times). The third person was brought to court for failure to register for the evacuation—Fred Korematsu, a welder from Oakland, had undergone plastic surgery to try to conceal his racial identity so that he could marry an Italian American girl, and had not registered for the evacuation. The fourth case was a habeas corpus petition, filed on July 12, 1942, challenging the WRA to show cause why Mitsuye Endo, a former California civil servant, should not be released from incarceration. ACLU-supported lawyers who often disagreed among themselves represented Hirabayashi and Korematsu, while independent lawyers served Yasui and Endo.

In spite of the fact that the government's lawyers were hampered by the internal conflicts between the Department of Justice and the War Department that were left over from the campaign to exclude the Japanese, they won narrowly argued convictions in the three criminal cases that charged these Japanese Americans with violations of General DeWitt's military orders. The cases went to the appellate court in San Francisco on February 19, 1943, the first anniversary of Executive Order 9066; decisions from this court were appealed to the Supreme Court in March, and the hearing was scheduled for May 10, 1943. Thus, in April 1943 McCloy needed to provide backup for the government's lawyers. But instead of a report on the evacuation that provided useful information, he found in his hand a rendered, dated report from General DeWitt that "at the beginning puts us immediately into a difference of view with the Commanding General." He was concerned that there were parts that should be deleted, "but that is an awkward thing to do; to delete something from a report that is already rendered." And he couldn't "produce in court a part of a document which ha[d] yet to live."[72]

Bendetsen arranged to fly to Washington, D.C., to work with McCloy and his aides, especially with Captain John Hall, a lawyer who was working on the court briefs. However, Bendetsen had trouble persuading DeWitt that his report had to be changed. He called DeWitt's deputy, Brigadier General James Barnett, to pass on the message that War Department officials were insisting on revisions that "went to the fundamental concept of evacuation." DeWitt, who was then in Alaska, wired General Barnett, "My report to the Chief of Staff will not be changed in any respect whatsoever either in substance or form and I will not, repeat not, consent to any, repeat any, revision made over my signature."[73]

Caught between loyalty to his commanding officer and a desire to have McCloy and Hall approve his document, Bendetsen was in a predicament. McCloy told Bendetsen, "I wouldn't want him [DeWitt] to think I was trying to tell him what to say." But he also said, "I would much rather that the report go in to the files and let it go at that."[74] McCloy argued that the president and the secretary of war could not agree with DeWitt's statement in the *Final Report* that it would be "impossible" under any circumstances to determine the loyalty of Japanese Americans." Acting as intermediary between DeWitt in Alaska and McCloy, Bendetsen wrote to DeWitt that the assistant secretary had no objection to saying instead "that time was of the essence and that in view of the military situation and the fact that there was no known means of making such a determination with any degree of safety . . . the evacuation was necessary." Working with Bendetsen, John Hall came up with a compromise version of the sentences in dispute. The original paragraph (the eleventh paragraph in chapter II, "Need for Military Control and for Evacuation") read as follows:

> Because of the ties of race, the intense feeling of filial piety and the strong bonds of common tradition, culture and customs, this population [Americans of Japanese ancestry] presented a tightly-knit racial group. It included in excess of 115,000 persons deployed along the Pacific Coast. Whether by design

> or accident, virtually always their communities were adjacent to very vital shore installations, war plants, etc. While it was believed that some were loyal, it was known that many were not. *It was impossible to establish the identity of the loyal and the disloyal with any degree of safety. It was not that there was insufficient time in which to make such a determination; it was simply a matter of facing the realities that a positive determination could not be made, that an exact separation of the "sheep from the goats" was infeasible.*[75]

Captain Hall replaced the offending sentences (in italics above) with the following:

> To complicate the situation, no ready means existed for determining the loyal and the disloyal with any degree of safety. It was necessary to face the realities—a positive determination could not have been made.

This change altered the meaning of DeWitt's statement, and removed the clear assertion that time was *not a factor* in determining loyalty, as government lawyers would assert in briefs to the court; a number of other, smaller changes and deletions were made.[76] Bendetsen transmitted DeWitt's orders to "call in all copies previously sent to the WD [War Department] less enclosures and to have WD destroy all records of receipt of report as when final revision is forwarded letter of transmittal will be redated."[77] Captain Hall returned to Bendetsen the original report and General DeWitt's April 15 letter of transmittal. Bendetsen then ordered the destruction of records; on June 29, 1943, Warrant Officer Theodore E. Smith submitted to Bendetsen the following: "I certify that this date I witnessed the destruction by burning of the galley proofs, galley pages, drafts and memorandums of the original report of the Japanese evacuation." The remaining records of this episode were then placed in a "confidential" file in Bendetsen's office in the Presidio. Not a single piece of paper was supposed to be left in the War Department to show that an earlier version of the *Final Report* had ever existed.[78] (A description of the alteration of the *Final Report* as well as one copy of the original report were inadvertently stored in the National Archives and would be found in the 1980s.[79])

The altered version was prepared, Bendetsen drafted a new cover letter for General DeWitt, dated June 5, 1943, and the report was submitted to the War Department where it was held with a "confidential" security label. Arguments in the Hirabayashi and Endo cases before the Supreme Court had already taken place. The Justice Department's request for material relevant to these cases, which was made in April, still stood. The revised report was not released to the public or to courts until 1944. Justice Department attorneys were never told about alterations that were made to the *Final Report*, or about the recovery and destruction of the ten copies, or the redrafting and redating of the submission letter.[80]

In May 1943, during the exhaustive conferences with McCloy and his aides, DeWitt's *Final Report* was not the only topic of discussion, or source of disagreements. McCloy had concluded that there no longer existed any military necessity for the continued exclusion of all Japanese from the evacuated zone, and though he would not take any action to end the exclusion, he also would not object if his superiors wished to do so. Bendetsen wrote a three-page argument strenuously objecting to a policy change that would allow Japanese to return to the West Coast. Bendetsen felt such a change would undermine public confidence in the commanding general. He was not overly concerned about the rights of the evacuees: "While there now existed some suspension of the civil rights of the United States born Japanese, it was an *orderly* suspension . . . If Japanese were returned to the coast there would doubtless be rioting and bloodshed with a consequent *disorderly* suspension . . . having the flavor of a race war."[81] The West Coast exclusion policy was upheld for another year and a half.

The brief submitted in the Hirabayashi case was able to argue that the army had lacked sufficient time to conduct loyalty hearings, which clearly would have been seen as a false claim if DeWitt's original report had been part of the evidence. In addition, the War Department suppressed the Office of Naval Intelligence report of Commander Ringle, which countered DeWitt's assertions of disloyalty by Japanese Americans. The decisions released by the court in late 1944 upheld the convictions of Yasui, Hirabayashi, and Korematsu. Mitsuye Endo won her habeas corpus case but the decision was not released by the Supreme Court until December 1944, well after the presidential election, and after the government had issued a statement rescinding the mass exclusion of persons of Japanese ancestry from the West Coast. (The executive order stood until 1974.)

The Yasui, Hirabayashi, and Korematsu decisions were ripe for questioning during the struggle to obtain redress in the 1980s. The facts of the 1943 rewrite would provide the basis for requesting that the court set aside the convictions in these three cases.

Though the War Department had acknowledged the need for a sorting and rearrangement of evacuees among the relocation centers to protect those who were loyal and were being harassed by the pro-Japan factions, Dillon Myer and the WRA did not agree to such a policy until the summer of 1943. The decision was complicated by the loyalty registration, the effort to speed up the release of loyal evacuees, and contention over whether persons declared loyal would be allowed to return to the exclusion zone. Which camp would be declared the Segregation camp was also an issue. Finally the WRA chose Tule Lake, and called on the Army to help with the logistics of moving evacuees. Again, there was an obvious candidate for supervisor of the segregation.

In August 1943 Bendetsen was ordered from the Presidio to temporary duty with the Ninth Service Command at Fort Douglas, Utah (which provided the army's relocation camp guards). He was assigned to "organize, plan and supervise the execution of operations involving the transfer of Japanese evacuees" between the WRA centers "in accordance with its segregation plan."[82] In a report to the commanding general of the Ninth Service Command, he mentioned that he had tried to provide for "every foreseeable contingency" in transporting Japanese men, women, and children to avoid any untoward incident, stating, "If any such incident . . . occurred . . . it [might] profoundly affect the already unfortunate lot of United States citizens in the custody of the Japanese Imperial Government."[83]

On September 3, 1943, he found time to write to Harry and Mary Lou Auer: "I have been on temporary duty at Ninth Service Command headquarters . . . where I am engaged again in moving Japs. This time it is a straight G–4 job. The Army is providing the transportation for the execution of the WRA's segregation plan. The task is one involving reciprocation between the ten relocation centers on a 'sheep from the goats' separation which Congress finally drove the Authority to adopt. I will probably complete my assignment around September 20th." He complained of seeing Billie and Brookes too little. "The war is bound to end one day and then perhaps much can be made up."[84]

He discussed the latest rumors with the Auers: General DeWitt would probably move on to command the Joint Army and Navy Staff College. "There is a possibility I will accompany him as he has several times mentioned his desire to make me the executive of the school. . . . If that came about, I would doubtless be given a chance ultimately to take the course. This would be more than the equivalent of the Command and General Staff School plus Army War College." Though he wasn't "taken with the thought of going to school during war time," he said that "there [was] something to recommend it because it would get the staff school bogy" behind him. He feared, "If I don't go along with that, I will probably be assigned to the European Theater."[85]

Not all the loyal "colonists" would be herded onto one of the trains shuttling between Tule Lake and the other camps. Elmer Shirrell was by then relocation supervisor in the Chicago WRA office, prepared to help "evacuees" resettle. Morse Saito, who was to enter his senior year in the fall of 1943 and was technically too young to be released, managed to get sent alone to Chicago in August, on Shirrell's recommendation. He initially took a job as a houseboy but soon moved to West Rockford, Illinois, and attended West Rockford High School. "Poor grades, working in a hospital and living alone in order to finish," he recalled. Molly Ozaki, who had recently gotten out of camp with her family, also attended West Rockford and recalled that "Morse had big feet, was tall and awkward, and we sometimes called him 'Morse, the horse.'"[86] Morse recalled that he had graduated "180th from the top in a class of 240 students. I had won a national writing contest which really saved me from flunking out."[87]

With the help of Shirrell, Natsu Saito received an invitation to come to Chicago to find work. Shirrell had recommended her for a management job in a Chicago office. The fact that she, unlike most evacuees, had had a formal hearing with the Department of Justice and been paroled in 1942 may have facilitated her release. Roger Axford of FOR agreed to sponsor her. Though released, she was still on parole and had to report her whereabouts regularly to the Immigration and Naturalization Service. She left Tule Lake in September 1943 and was followed shortly thereafter by what had survived of the household goods that she had left in the hands of the government when she was forced to leave Aberdeen.

Among the residents of relocation camps who were moved during the upheavals of the segregation operation were Fumi Yabe and her family, and Dahlia Saito. Like many Nisei, Fumi had not had an easy time during the "loyalty crisis."

Fumiko later called the loyalty registration effort the "Yes, Yes and No, No Time." She was persuaded by her family and the strongly pro-Japan faction in her block to answer "no" to questions 27 and 28. Many others answered similarly, fearing to offend the strong opposition that was fueled by resentment against camp administrators and disgust with a country that had taken away their freedom and caused them to feel ashamed.

Almost immediately, Fumiko knew she had made a mistake. In May

1943 she wrote a letter requesting that her answer to question 28 be changed from "no" to "yes." She explained that her parents had advised the former answer since she was "supposed to take the family name in Japan," because her parents had no son. She wrote, "I sincerely believe that I was wrongly advised because my ideas about living and other customs would not make me able to live in a place like Japan."[88]

After an interview and hearing conducted by the Review Board for Segregation at Tule Lake, Fumiko and her family were given permission to transfer. She would, however, have to face a further hearing in the next relocation center, something called a "Washington Leave Clearance Hearing." At the end of September 1943 she and her family were sent by train to the Minidoka camp at Hunt, Idaho. Fumiko took a job teaching music, as she had at Tule Lake. She taught everything musical, even wind instruments, and was paid $19 a month, close to the highest wage that any internee could earn (Issei and Nisei doctors could earn $21 a month).

In late November at Minidoka, with her parents in attendance, she was again called before two camp administrators to explain why she had decided to change her answer to question 28. She said that she had gone to meetings at which "the block people" talked about the registration. People of her age were confused, she said. "We just had to mind them, or else, too bad for us." She said that the appointed camp speaker, who should have explained the significance of question 28, "was so used to it he rambled on." She now knew she should have answered "yes." "If nobody bothered me, if I had my own mind, own way. . . . We're loyal, that's all."

Asked again about her answer to question 27 (Would you be willing to volunteer for the Army Nurse Corps or the WAAC?), she did not change her negative answer. She said she had sung for the USO, had helped with the Red Cross, and had purchased war bonds in camp. She was not "embittered" or angry about the evacuation program, but "kind of disappointed. We Niseis had to be in camp. . . . Sooner or later, we were going to get out." She said that she thought that she could overcome "the scars of evacuation" and readjust to civilian life again.[89]

On November 30, 1943, the hearing board approved Fumiko Yabe's request for leave clearance. The interviewer wrote, "This girl is thoroughly American. . . . She has a clear record in every respect." The administrative machinery moved slowly. She had applied for leave clearance in February 1943; the FBI report was completed in May; she was told her application was finally approved on February 5, 1944, but her actual leave was not authorized until April 11, 1944, a year after Perry's release.[90]

While waiting for clearance she had been allowed brief leaves, if accompanied by Caucasian chaperones, to attend Christian church conferences and conventions in nearby Idaho towns. With the help of a Quaker organization, she was promised a scholarship that would allow her to go the Curtis School of Music in Philadelphia.[91] She expected to find work as a domestic and attend classes. Her final voluntary statement in the leave-clearance hearing summed up her hopes: "I'd like to go outside and relocate, go on with my musical education. I will do my best for this country. After all I am a citizen of this country and expect to remain here the rest of my life."[92] Years later she recalled, "Well it was good for us and yet it was kind of mean . . . after all we were citizens of this country, thrown into camp, naturally, we wanted freedom . . . especially in Tule Lake, you couldn't get out."[93]

In September 1943 Lieutenant General Delos C. Emmons was named to succeed General DeWitt. While head of the army's defense command in Hawaii, Emmons had taken a more tolerant view of the potential loyalty of persons of Japanese ancestry, and nothing had happened in Hawaii to betray his trust. There was a sense in the War Department that the new commanding general would cooperate more willingly with the slow course of rehabilitation of the evacuees.[94]

In early October, Bendetsen moved to the War Department in Washington, D.C., preparing to be transferred to a post in London. Colonel S. F. Clabaugh wrote to him with suggestions for understanding London and the English, telling him to "get a copy of "Thatcher's Parliamentary Companion"; Clabaugh described many of the Britishers that he would meet and have to deal with. He offered a letter of introduction to Mr. James Sommerville: "His Russian wife and Danish maid have mastered the American style of cooking!"[95] Bendetsen's first post in London was that of acting United States chief of civil affairs for Europe at the headquarters of COSSAC (forerunner of SHAEF), with an office in Norfolk House. His British counterpart was Major-General Sir Roger Lumley.[96] After the Normandy Invasion in June 1944 he moved to the continent and served as deputy chief of staff of the forward communications zone in Normandy and also served with the Twelfth Army group under Lieutenant General Omar Bradley.

It is possible that Bendetsen's loyal service defending General DeWitt in his conflicts with the War Department limited his advancement in the army. His mentor, Provost Marshal General Gullion, remained a major general throughout the war. Gullion and Bendetsen had advocated a project that the army general staff had opposed. Though he held deputy positions close to generals, Bendetsen did not make general. When he left the WDC in 1943, the bulk of the 120,000 evacuees were still in WRA camps; at the end of the war, more than half remained.[97] Though he tried to minimize his responsibility, Bendetsen was never able to live down his most infamous wartime duty.

By the end of the war, thirty-three thousand Nisei had served in the military. Although the War Department had stopped accepting Japanese Americans into the military immediately after Pearl Harbor, they had exempted candidates for the Military Intelligence Service Language School and the army's 100th Battalion. That all-Nisei unit began as part of the Hawaii National Guard, and served with distinction in North Africa and Italy, earning the nickname "Purple Heart Battalion" because of its heavy losses. The 442nd Regimental Combat team was formed in 1943 to accommodate Nisei volunteers coming directly from relocation centers, as well as from Hawaii. After training at Camp Shelby, Mississippi, the team began going overseas as replacements for the 100th. In June 1944 they joined the Italian campaign at Naples. The unit won recognition as one of the war's most decorated combat teams, receiving seven presidential Distinguished Unit Citations and earning 18,143 individual decorations.[98] As he fastened a presidential unit banner to their regimental colors, President Truman commended the men of the 442nd, saying that these Nisei had fought "not only the enemy, but prejudice." The public tributes paid to these two Nisei units at the end of the war would do much to hasten the acceptance of the ethnic Japanese into American life as they were released from the camps.[99]

CHAPTER TEN

Sincere Conscientious Objectors to War

We have no confidence that this war will help to advance or conserve our democracy or internal security. . . . [We fear] that in the name of "peace" and a "New Order" the victors will attempt to establish a world-embracing military tyranny.

—FOR statement, December 9, 1941

Few groups stood up for Japanese Americans in the early days of the war. Those who did, the Socialist Workers Party, the Fellowship of Reconciliation (FOR), the Postwar World Council, the American Friends Service Committee, the Worker's Defense League, and eventually, the American Civil Liberties Union, were distrusted and watched by the FBI. Norman Thomas, perennial candidate for president on the Socialist ticket, spoke out in a pamphlet, "Democracy and Japanese Americans," criticizing the internment, writing that "the method of handling Japanese Americans was neither constitutional nor democratic," and praising FOR for going "all the way in protesting the whole evacuation process."

FOR described itself as an interfaith organization that sought "to replace violence, war, racism and economic injustice with nonviolence, peace and justice." They pursued active nonviolence as "a transforming way of life and as a means of radical change."[1]

Early in Bendetsen's stewardship of the Japanese evacuation, A. J. Muste, secretary of FOR in New York, sent a telegram to President Roosevelt—much to Bendetsen's chagrin—calling attention to bad conditions in some assembly centers. Bendetsen replied to Muste and then asked the FBI to find out about the Fellowship.

A report came back to Bendetsen from consultant Ted Braun indicating that FOR was a national organization founded in England during World War I, that it was primarily a group of "sincere conscientious objectors to war" and was most active on the East Coast; that its Washington State activity centered at the University of Washington, where there were about thirty or forty members; and that "Farquharson, a professor of engineering, was probably the leader of the Seattle organization."[2]

In September 1942, President Roosevelt got at least one more letter from FOR, this time from Mildred B. Potts of Seattle, decrying the fact that Japanese Americans had been singled out because of their race. She urged the creation of hearing boards that could "pass on individual cases and, upon establishing their loyalty and status, release them to return to normal community life." Such hearing boards were a requirement in the handling of enemy aliens held during wartime by the Department of Justice in alien internment camps (Natsu Saito had been paroled by such a hearing board). As already discussed, General DeWitt, backed by Bendetsen, had maintained that it was not possible to determine the loyalty of the Japanese evacuees.

During World War II, FOR was active in protesting "the government's outrageous action" and provided physical and moral assistance to the Japanese American community by, for example, storing furniture and otherwise caring for the property of those interned. FOR secretaries visited the relocation camps (one of these was lawyer Herman Will) while the organization agitated for the release and resettlement of the evacuees. Their refugee committee and local FOR groups helped resettle those who could be brought east from the camps. The Fellowship had a travel loan fund for this purpose and in early 1943 added to its staff "a young Japanese-American who had been interned, to interpret the situation to churches, schools and FOR groups." That person was Perry Saito.[3]

The FBI considered Perry Saito dangerous, and the reports on their surveillance of him provide considerable detail about Perry Saito's activities as a FOR speaker on behalf of the evacuees still in the camps. Perry irritated the FBI in some of his first public appearances by asserting that he had been "cleared by the FBI" and giving the impression that he worked for the government. The FBI employed informants, hired stenographers to transcribe Saito's talks, interviewed young people who had been in Saito's audiences, and informed local leaders that the FBI "would be interested in any seditious statements" made by Saito. One diligent agent listed the eleven car licenses observed parked outside a meeting featuring Perry as speaker. The FBI attempted both to get Perry's leave clearance revoked and to get his home selective service board to prosecute him for not notifying them when he was released from Tule Lake Relocation Center.

Perry Saito reached Chicago in the spring of 1943 and began his work as a race relations secretary for FOR at $15 a week, plus traveling expenses. Herman Will and his wife Rita Irle Will, Perry's friend from Tacoma, invited Perry to stay with them in the home of Herman's parents for a few weeks when he arrived in Chicago. On Perry's twenty-second birthday, in May, a small plastic recording arrived from Fumi. Herman Will recalled, "It was a special record that she had made and sent to him. So he made the whole Will family . . . leave the room. 'I've got to listen to this first myself!'" he had said. When he found that it was not too personal, they were all allowed to hear Fumi's message from Tule Lake. Herman arranged speaking engagements for Perry and accompanied him on one of his first talks. Herman did an introduction and Perry gave a "personal experience sermon." They went to a church in central Illinois, not far from Springfield, where the pastor was a pacifist and a FOR member. "So Perry and I got there, were warmly received by the pastor and his family, went to the church. The service went off fine, and [everyone] seemed happy. We were at the parsonage at dinner, and the telephone calls started coming. Three phone calls came from farm families who wanted to know how they could get a Japanese person to help them on their farm, they were so desperate for farm labor. Illinois has a great grain basis, rich soil. We took all the information down, and went to work trying to make the connection. Perry picked it up from there."[4]

Perry traveled through Illinois and one or two other states during April and May 1943. He often spoke before youth groups and during the summer served on the faculty at fourteen different church camps and conferences, in Vermont, New York, Illinois, Iowa, Missouri, Wisconsin, and Indiana. In September 1943 he began working for the New York office of FOR, traveling throughout the Midwest and East as a lecturer. The FBI first interviewed him in Cortland, New York, in December 1943, after listening to some of his lectures. An agent from Syracuse, New York, initiated a file that ran to thirty-eight closely typed pages, and was kept up to date until February 1944; an additional report of ten pages was made by a Buffalo agent in April 1944.[5] The FBI transcribed articles from local newspapers, including, for example, one in the *Binghamton (N.Y.) Press* entitled "Legion Fights Talk by

Jap."[6] Agents questioned people about the loyalty of individuals who appeared to have invited Perry Saito to give speeches. The FBI interviewed the minister who had brought news of Perry's talk to the attention of the Legion group (and the newspaper). Reverend Darrel Westlake, a Congregational minister, told the FBI that he felt that Perry was "sympathetic with the Japanese in the war," described him as "subversive," and said that he was "very sarcastic in his remarks," and "would commit acts against the United States if he had a chance to do so." He was critical of Saito's remark that the Thanksgiving dinners served in the relocation camps only cost thirteen cents apiece and that they had to sleep on canvas cots. FBI agents interviewed several young students, aged fifteen to seventeen, who had attended a summer camp at which Perry Saito taught. The agent questioned at least one of the young men about Perry's lecture "to determine its effect upon him and upon his coming obligations under the Selective Training and Service Act." Several of the young people said that they thought that Perry showed a "zealous desire . . . to improve what he believes to be the poor conditions in the various internment camps," and that they trusted him because he was selected as a speaker by respected leaders of their summer camp.

An editorial in the *Cortland Standard* entitled "Tell It to the Marines" said, "Two years after Pearl Harbor, a year after Guadacanal, and days after Tarawa, a young man of Japanese ancestry is in Cortland seeking to arouse support of the American people for *his people*." The editor noted that his talks, largely directed to young people, "have stirred much sympathy."

"The intentions of this young man may be honorable and there has been no question brought up as to his citizenship in this country, but this is no time for *such propaganda*. We would not tolerate it from a citizen of this country with a long line of American ancestry." The editor argued that "persons of Jap origin held in detention camps . . . have received far better treatment than the Americans held in Jap concentration camps."[7] [Emphasis added.]

Addressing nine hundred students at a junior-senior high dinner in Cortland, New York, Perry Saito said,

> I like to speak to high school groups and this looks just like my own high school back home. When I went to high school, I was the only person there with a Japanese ancestry. I am an American, not Japanese. . . .[8]
>
> I am working with the Government in trying to get across a program . . . in trying to tell people you can still be an American even though you have a face that looks like an enemy.

> You see we have a couple of people in the American Army whose names are Hitler. They are Americans and proud to be. There are a couple of Tojos. . . . I read [in the newspaper] the names of 34 people, all with Japanese names and all with Japanese faces, who had been killed at Salerno, fighting for this country. Every one of these people has some member of their immediate family in this country behind barbed wires.[9]

He told the story of his father's being converted to Christianity by an Englishman and believing in American principles even though he could not become a naturalized citizen. His father had raised him to be proud of being American. Perry told other stories about his family, his father's death, how the family had been forced into the Tule Lake camp, and how he got out. Then he got to the point of his speech: "There are 93,000 individual Americans behind barbed wires who have been cleared by the FBI and the Navy and Army Intelligence Service, who have been cleared but not released because they don't have a place to go. . . . It is costing the Government millions of dollars to keep them, to feed them, to keep them warm every month." He mentioned the waste of manpower by keeping these people locked up, said that very little was spent on food for the internees (in fact, thirty-nine cents a day per internee), and talked about the conditions in the camps, which were in the middle of deserts. "We are not complaining one bit because we are Americans. If the American soldiers can battle with bullets, we can afford to battle with mosquitoes. We are not complaining because of the physical hardships. All we want is to be recognized as Americans."[10]

The first FBI agent concluded his extensive report with the observation that Perry's supervisor at FOR, John M. Swomley, had heard "the subject speak in Pittsburgh on December 28, 1943, at a banquet in some community house at which time the subject made statements which seemed to him to be exaggerated and that. . . . Mr. Swomley believes that he needs more supervision."[11]

The thirty-eight-page Syracuse report was sent to the director of the WRA's Chicago office and triggered a formal request for further investigation of Perry Saito's status, which could be challenged since he had thus far received only an Indefinite Leave Clearance.

Speaking before a Lion's Club luncheon on March 29, 1944 Perry Saito gave his opinion that Americans of Japanese descent should be freed. He is quoted: "I am an American because I was born in America, I am an American because I believe in America and the democratic way of living. . . . It is your duty to look up the figures and see that the Americans of Japanese descent are doing our part in the war . . . 13,000 of these men fighting in the American forces out of 18,000 young men and women of army age in the country."[12]

"There has been no single act of sabotage in this country or Pearl Harbor," he said. "You can find many statements to this effect by government authorities. We went to relocation centers to avoid being called Japanese, to prove that we are Americans. None went to the relocation centers until six months after Pearl Harbor. [If] there were going to be sabotage there would have been time for it before that."[13] He was quoted further:

> We are not responsible for what the Japanese are doing. American citizens of German descent are not responsible for what the Germans are doing in Europe. Our ancestors came from Japan to this country because they wanted to get away from Japan and to better themselves. My ancestors were here before General Dwight D. Eisenhower's and Mayor Fiorello LaGuardia's. Many of the young folks in the relocation centers are blonde and blue eyed. I urge you to think about us as Americans, and to help resettle the 80,000 now in the centers.[14]

In a lengthy interview with FBI agent John J. Ryan, Jr., in Niagara Falls in March 1944, in which the agent again chided Perry for making the statement that he had been "cleared by the FBI," Perry admitted "the ambiguity of the statement, 'I am working with the Government'" and said that in the future he would make clear to his audiences that he was employed by FOR. On the subject of FBI clearance, "Subject said it was his sincere belief that the FBI had cleared him," but would refrain from saying so in the future. Perry asked the agents "what statement he could substitute for the statement that he had been cleared by the FBI." The two agents apparently said that "they were in no position to offer such suggestions."[15]

Fully half of the paperwork in Perry's internment case file, which was maintained at Tule Lake Relocation Center and later stored in the National Archives, was generated *after* he gained his release from the camp. Unlike his mother, he was not on probation, but like other relocatees, he was still required to notify the WRA of his whereabouts. And he had to go through another challenge to his right to be outside the camp, in part because he was working for FOR. The New York FBI agent had learned of files that revealed that the Chicago and San Francisco Field Divisions (of the FBI) had "pending sedition cases" against the Fellowship of Reconciliation."[16]

On April 10, 1944, Perry was required to appear in Chicago for an Indefinite Leave hearing.[17] Edward Joyce, a relocation officer, conducted the interview and asked questions about Perry and his family. Perry explained that when he was in Chicago he lived with his mother and sister, and then he answered questions that had been asked numerous times at Tule Lake. Joyce had one new question: "How did you get into DeMolay? . . . Wasn't that for the sons of Masons?"[18] Then he directly challenged Perry's answers to questions 27 and 28 on the clearance form, saying of his qualified answer to 28 regarding military service and allegiance, "Your answer was only in part. Your reply to question 28 didn't quite cover the question."[19] This is an interesting challenge by the relocation officer, since the three-part question did not usually require three answers; yes was the acceptable answer to question 28. Perry said of his answer, "I said 'Yes' to all of that inasmuch as I do not have to bear arms. In other words, I will defend the United States in a non-violent way."

> Joyce: Well, suppose the United States were attacked by a foreign country?
>
> Perry : I would use the same technique that Gandhi uses. Non-resistance and pacifism.
>
> . . .
>
> Joyce: Do you suppose that Japan and Germany would listen to Mahatma Gandhi? What do you suppose the outcome would be?
>
> Perry: I believe that the Japanese soldier, to put it another way, I think very definitely that the English soldier is fighting for democracy. I think the American soldier is also. But I would not say the same thing for English leaders. I would say the Japanese soldier, not knowing them at all but knowing that they are human beings, believe that they are fighting for a just cause and that they must believe in the cause they are fighting for. The American soldier and the Japanese soldier should both find out they are fighting for the same reason. I wouldn't say that about the Japanese leaders. Perhaps they are after economic reasons, or for aggression but I believe the Japanese soldier would not carry out an unjust ruling because it is to be advocated that certain soldiers shoot unjustly while others would refuse to do so. Now if I were in Japan, I would advocate the same thing. If America were to come to Japan, I would advocate that the Japanese people not bear arms. I would just as heartily condemn Japan as I would America.[20]

Joyce then asked about charges that his mother had been contacted by representatives of the Japanese government or by officers of Japanese ships, and asked whether Perry had been propositioned by any of the ship's crews. He replied, "No. The reason probably for that was that no doubt I wouldn't know what they were talking about since personally I don't speak Japanese."

Based on this hearing, Joyce made a negative recommendation. He recited the litany of charges (which had never been substantiated) against Perry's mother, asserted that Perry's brother was studying for a naval commission in Japan (a new allegation), and, in particular, remarked that Perry's answers to the loyalty questions:

> are qualified to an extent that indicates to this interviewer a thorough lack of appreciation of the duties of a good American citizen, subject avowedly would advocate . . . [a] non-resistance policy if this country were attacked and invaded. . . .
>
> During this time of war the influence of a man, who is avowedly a conscientious objector and whose connections and associations are not above scrutiny and investigation can only be regarded by this interviewer as being potentially dangerous to the safety and security of the USA and unfairly detrimental to the interest of those *Nisei* who seek a fair opportunity to demonstrate their Americanism by bearing arms for this country and assuming all the obligations as well as the privilege of American citizenship. We do not recommend leave clearance for this subject.[21]

In May 1944 R. R. Best, the Tule Lake project director, wrote to Dillon S. Myer, WRA director, and to Mr. Joyce, that he concurred with the Tule Lake Leave Clearance Hearing Board "that Mr. Saito be granted leave clearance." The hearing board disagreed with Mr. Joyce's recommendation to oppose clearance. They wrote, "There is nothing in Mr. Saito's docket, including the interview given by Mr. Joyce, to indicate that Mr. Saito ever acted as an intermediary in supplying espionage information to Japan. . . . We do not believe . . . that conscientious objection to war constitutes a sufficient basis upon which to deny leave clearance."[22]

Mr. Joyce was allowed to add to his statements concerning Perry Saito. He wrote, "Contrary to the expressed belief of Project Director Best . . . I did not base my adverse recommendation . . . solely on the grounds of his being a conscientious objector." He continued to argue that Perry was guilty of sedition: "It is my opinion that this man could endanger the public peace and security and interfere with the war program by advocating those peculiar philosophies he referred to during his hearing." Obviously angered, he wrote, "To date I have conducted 41 leave clearance hearings and have withheld favorable recommendations in only two cases."[23]

Perry Saito's FBI file was transmitted, in late June 1944, to Dillon S. Myer by J. Edgar Hoover of the FBI. In the meantime Perry's leave file docket was working its way to Philip M. Glick at the WRA in Washington, D.C., who assigned it to a reviewer.[24] On the summary, the reviewer, Russell Bankson, wrote, "we find a young man thoroughly Americanized and most articulate who professes to be a conscientious objector to war." The reviewer acknowledged that since the selective service law provided for conscientious objectors, Perry's answers should be accepted. He went on to say: "Subject is arrogant, somewhat of a rabble rouser, and not prone to stick too closely to facts, but there appears to be nothing in his record which would indicate loyalty toward Japan, or a lack of loyalty for the United States." Bankson noted that federal agents had not brought any action against Perry and though "he is not the type of person to be admired by an America that is at desperate war," recommended he be granted leave clearance, which was authorized on August 19, 1944. This fact was entered on Perry's master file cover sheet at Tule Lake Relocation Center immediately under the notations "Cleared FBI (date) 12-2-42 and 1-2-43."[25]

While Perry was fending off challenges by the FBI and relocation officers, his mother was hoping to use her knowledge of Japanese to rehabilitate herself in the eyes of the United States Army. During a regular visit to the WRA office in Chicago in January 1945, Natsu Saito reported that she was "interested in teaching Japanese at [the] U[niversity of] C[hicago]."[26] The interviewer referred her to Dr. Leeds Gulick who was director of a new section of the army's Specialized Training Program (ASTP).[27]

Dr. Gulick hired her. In the early months of 1945, several hundred enlisted men were enrolled in this intensified Japanese language program at the University of Chicago.[28] The program sought to produce students able to speak Japanese with the language equivalent of a grammar school education in Japan. This branch of the program took on the name "Kanji Kollege" (because students were learning the Japanese character set, called kanji) and was housed for a time at 60th and Ellis streets in a former mansion that had housed a fraternity, then the USO, and was scheduled for demolition in order to build faculty housing for the university. By July some new recruits to the school were housed in the West stands of Stagg Field and classes were held in Hitchcock or Cobb Hall. Three groups of 75–85 men entered the program before it was terminated in January 1946.

Just as had residents of the WRA relocation camps, the "Kanji Kollege" students identified writers and artists in their midst and immediately began publishing a mimeographed paper called the *Geisha Gazette*.[29] Assigned as a teacher for the reading students, Natsu Saito soon gained a mention in the *Gazette*: At a "face showing party" for new students and faculty in early July 1945 that featured singing and a quiz program, Mrs. Saito was described as "Saito-san of the silver voice." During the quiz, she "identified Dr. Gulick with her hands alone," which merited a front-page photo that showed her gestures and dimpled smile.[30]

The AST program balanced military training with regular drills and a fitness component that provided material for the *Gazette*'s sports page. Several early *Gazette* issues featured letters and articles debating whether women students at the University of Chicago should be allowed to wear jeans, which "touched off the campus-wide Blue Jean feud." Many of the graduates of Kanji Kollege expected either to continue their college studies or be sent to Japan to serve during the occupation after the war, possibly as translators for the military police, signal corps, or intelligence.

While Mrs. Saito helped her students fathom the different uses of "postpositions *ga* and *wa*" and decoded kanji for them, her son Perry continued his work for FOR.[31]

Herman Will, who himself was a conscientious objector (CO) during the war and performed alternate service in Puerto Rico, commented that Perry "was certainly outstanding as a pacifist and social concerns person. Most of the COs were not narrowly COs. You might get that among Mennonites or others. They could be a CO and still hold a lot of conventional views. But the conscientious objectors in Methodism usually tended to be very much opposed to any racial discrimination, and they would follow all the progressive positions."[32] Perry was certainly one of these.

In some of his talks to church groups Perry mentioned that on occasion he had been taunted, someone had spit at him or called him a "Jap." He was likely to say, "Does that make you feel better?" and to try to make friends with the person.[33] This ability to turn the other cheek was useful in the second part of Perry's job for FOR.

AN EARLY SIT-IN, INDIANAPOLIS, LATE SUMMER 1943

In a sermon some thirty-seven years later, Perry Saito described that other part, which was "working in the area of human relations, race relations . . . largely between the blacks and the whites, and

I was serving as a sort of go between, a marginal . . . they talk about the piano, the black and white keys, and playing between the cracks; well I [was] the between-the-cracks part of the piano. My job was to try to Christianize other areas of human relations." He described one weekend in late summer of 1943 in Indianapolis: "The civil rights laws in most of the states in the North [laws requiring that in all places of public accommodation the public must be served] . . . were largely being broken." FOR workers held race-relations seminars on weekends in different parts of the country. "There were three of us involved in the leadership of these seminars. One was Bayard Rustin, who [later] organized the March on Washington, and . . . James Farmer, who headed what later became the Congress on Racial Equality (CORE). And thirdly myself.[34]

FOR conducted programs of non-violent direct action on weekends in various communities in the Midwest. On the Friday evening that Perry described, fifty or seventy-five participants in Indianapolis prayed for "courage and for persistence and patience . . . for understanding towards others . . . for good will and peace and reconciliation." He described the beginning of a sit-in: "On Saturday morning after an hour's Quaker silent meditation, we were divided into a dozen teams. My small team of five persons, five reconcilers, one black, three whites and myself, went to a Hookes Drug Store near the Indianapolis train depot. The black man went in first, followed by the white couple, all of whom sat at tables in the restaurant section of Hookes drug store. And then I came in and sat at one end of the fountain and another person, a white man, sat at the other end."

When the waitress came to wait on Perry, he invited her to wait first upon the black man who had entered before Perry. Nothing happened. When she returned, Perry said he was waiting for his turn. She said abruptly, "He's not going to get served . . . because he's a nigger." Perry said this was not right: "First of all for me to be served out of turn was to acquiesce to the notion that I deserved to be served out of turn, that I was more privileged simply because of his race and of mine. Secondly, I could leave, but for me to do so was to see an undemocratic and an unchristian situation and then to pass by on the other side of the road. Therefore, I explained to her, I would simply wait a while, until it was my turn to be served."

Soon a man came and sat down next to Perry at the counter. Perry said to him, "It's a warm day today, isn't it?" The man asked, "Why aren't you eating?" Perry explained that he was waiting his turn. Perry recalled that he had told him that "a war was being fought for freedom and justice and liberty and democracy and equality and against racism and bigotry, and . . . meanwhile that black man was not being served solely on account of his race." That customer left angrily without waiting for his order.

Another man came and sat down next to Perry, who again said, "It's a warm day today, isn't it?" And soon he too asked about Perry's not eating. Perry explained what he was doing, about the black man and about democracy, and then said, "If you're in agreement, please let the manager know your feelings, because he says it's because of his customers that he's not obeying the state law." The man did so. As the morning and then the afternoon wore on, some were in agreement, some didn't react at all, and some argued. And many stayed to see what would happen."

One man, a young GI, said that his train didn't leave for several hours. He wondered if Perry needed any help. He listened, and then he moved to the center of the counter, and, shortly, speaking to someone next to him, Perry heard him say, "It's sure a warm day today, isn't it?" Slowly that drugstore began to fill with people, and the manager was getting excited; he had a lot of customers, but nobody was buying anything, so he called the police.

Perry described how the police came, asked questions, listened as the manager demanded that they arrest "these people" for trespassing. The FOR group's leader quoted the law of Indiana. According to Perry, the police captain offered to arrest the manager of the store, but Perry's group declined, saying, "We want him to change of his own accord." The police left and the restaurant full of people continued to wait their turn. Hours passed.

Eventually, the manager allowed the black man's order to be taken and for him to be served. "When the food touched the table we all burst into applause and we all ended up ordering food."

"That same [police] team had been called out nearly a dozen times that day. . . . They demonstrated that they understood the Civil Rights Law . . . [and] offered to arrest the managers of the drug store, the restaurant, the theater, the skating rink."[35]

Perry described the follow-up: As they left, the group congratulated the drugstore manager for "his change of policy, for his democratic and Christian practice." They then prepared a bulletin enclosure for all the cooperating churches where they listed the names of all the stores that had changed their policy and would now serve persons regardless of race, color, creed, national origin, or ancestry. They urged church members to compliment the stores for their change of policy. And about six weeks later, Perry recalled, they sent another interracial team "to test whether the accommodations were still open, and if they were they got their business, and if they weren't they got a Sit-in."

There were other seminars and nonviolent direct action sit-ins: at a Stauffer's restaurant in Chicago, or in other places in Milwaukee and the Midwest during and after the war. His group set the pattern, developing the model that would be used in the civil rights movement of the 1960s. In his sermon, Perry talked about Martin Luther King, Jr., and told how, after his home had been bombed, King turned to the mob of angry blacks that had gathered, and pleaded with them to love their enemy, to do no violence. "He assured them that love and nonviolence would eventually win out. He had done his proper training at a seminar in Boston, when he was a seminary student working with the FOR program."[36]

Perry was deservedly proud of his contribution to the history of nonviolent direct action in America and maintained his strong support for human rights in his ministry and in his life.

More than fifty years later, many people who had been active in FOR recalled that Perry had been a very effective person for the organization.[37] John M. Swomley, whom the FBI had quoted, recalled Perry as an attractive personality, a good speaker and an important staff member, saying, "He was free to speak on various subjects including Japanese-American relocation, race relations, pacifism, etc. I recall that he and James Farmer and I spoke at least once together at a meeting in or near Pittsburgh."[38] Swomley's wife, Marjie Carpenter Swomley, wrote: "I was also a secretary at the FOR. When Perry would come to New York he always wanted to see a play or musical. I will never forget getting tickets for us to *Othello* with Paul Robeson. It was a rainy night and Perry was carrying my umbrella. As we waited for a train in the subway everyone stole looks at us—a six-foot blonde young woman with an obviously Oriental young man. Finally Perry pulled me behind a wide pole, leaned out around it. Pointing my umbrella as if it were a machine gun, [he] sprayed the whole crowd. Most froze in shock, a few laughed with us.

"A similar episode—or perhaps more than one—indicates his wonderful sense of humor, actually quite daring given the prejudice against Japanese Americans of the time: He was in a restaurant in the Midwest with Caucasian FOR members. Everyone again looked furtively at him. As they left he leaned back around the door, saying with a grin, "Yep, Japanese."[39]

On August 19, 1944, Perry was granted his leave clearance, and he could begin a new chapter in his life. His goal was to finish college and the seminary so that he could continue to be an advocate for Christianity in human relations. He had the satisfaction of knowing that after "being incarcerated . . . behind barbed wires with watch towers and search lights and military police," he had been able to persuade some Americans to help evacuees get out of camp, and he had engaged in some of the first skirmishes in the war for racial equality in America.

PART IV

THE STRUGGLE FOR JUSTICE

CHAPTER ELEVEN

"A Little Hitler"

A person of Bendetsen's prejudiced and undemocratic concepts, if placed in a position of authority in the army, could mean a serious setback to recent efforts to promote racial harmony in the armed forces.
—Mike Masaoka, *Pacific Citizen*, January 28, 1950

Had he sat in the Senate gallery during the session at which his nomination as assistant secretary of the army was brought up for consideration, Karl R. Bendetsen would not have been apprehensive. He was well known to many of the senators. Though the appointment had been delayed for months, his nomination had moved without incident (or public record) from the Senate Armed Services Committee onto the Senate's agenda for January 26, 1950. He was experienced in the ways of Congress and expected to gain approval. For the Japanese Americans who had hoped to forestall his appointment, it would be a day of defeat.

From the first moment in 1949 when the prospect of Karl R. Bendetsen's appointment to a sensitive post in the Department of the Army in Washington, D.C., became known, the Japanese American community mobilized to oppose it. It was almost a reflex action by individuals and groups who harbored animosity toward the army colonel who had so single-mindedly, it seemed to them, pushed for the evacuation. Many recalled with disgust and embarrassment the prejudicial statements made by Bendetsen and his commanding officer, Lieutenant General DeWitt.

While the Japanese Americans and other civil rights groups prepared to write letters mustering opposition to his appointment, Bendetsen was quietly following up opportunities to serve as a civilian adviser to various departments in the Pentagon as he had been doing since the end of the war. In the months following the Victory in Europe of May 8, 1945 ("VE Day"), and prior to his resignation from the army in December 1945, Bendetsen had served on the War Department's congressional liaison staff, and on a number of army boards studying the postwar organization of the army. Several years later, the National Defense Act of 1947 created the National Military Establishment and called for unification of the military services. James V. Forrestal, a former secretary of the navy, was appointed first secretary of defense. In spring 1948, Bendetsen recalled, "Mr. Forrestal phoned me in San Francisco where I was practicing law and said that an emergency was in the making, the Berlin crisis storm was gathering." He was told that "the probabilities were high" that the defense establishment would be asked to respond. "This crisis would require the submission of a unified supplemental budget request to the Congress. . . . I knew enough about unification to know how a unified budget should be coordinate[d] for three armed services and the Marines, [so] he asked me to help."[1] Bendetsen favored unification of the services, but Forrestal opposed it, fearing that one head of the military, "the man on horseback," would become more powerful than the civilian head of government.[2] At the time, Bendetsen wrote to a friend that he was "asked to come back, pitch in and help with respect to the measures requested of the Congress for immediate enactment of temporary Selective Service and UMT [Universal Military Training]."[3] Bendetsen served as acting deputy to Forrestal for about three months, after which he returned to his San Francisco law practice.

His private life had undergone changes during this time. After two years in Europe and six months in D.C., he was apparently unable to rebuild a relationship with his wife. And there was another woman.[4] He returned to Aberdeen after the war only long enough to divorce Billie. Two days after the divorce was final in 1947, he married Maxine Bosworth, who had also been a secretary.

Sometime later, he was again called to Washington, D.C., Bendetsen described this: "I went back on request during the fall of '48 to do a special study for Mr. Gordon Gray whom I had met when I was working for Mr. Forrestal. Gray was then Army secretary. [Perhaps not yet confirmed.] He claimed this study related to control of the Alamogordo, New Mexico bombing range."[5]

Bendetsen continued: "When the Honorable Gordon Gray became secretary of the Army he asked me to become his assistant secretary of the Army. I accepted and left San Francisco. We kept our house; and we took an apartment in Washington, and my name was sent to the White House." However, the nomination was delayed. Bendetsen claimed "a 'personnel' man for the White House" held it up for some months: "He did not let my name go to President Truman because I was a Republican."[6] During this time Bendetsen was special assistant to Gray, and doing the job of an assistant secretary. Bendetsen recommended the creation of the office of general counsel for the army, and was the first to hold that office. He was also appointed by Defense Secretary Louis Johnson to several boards and to the Management Committee of the Department of Defense. He was again moving in high circles of military power in Washington, D.C. Until he was attacked personally, it is clear that Bendetsen's attentions were concentrated far from the struggle for justice by Americans of Japanese ancestry.

Furthermore, the biography that Bendetsen supplied to the Public Information Press Branch of the Department of Defense made no reference to his management of the wartime evacuation of the West Coast Japanese. It acknowledged only that he had been "Assistant Chief of Staff G–5 of the Fourth Army, with headquarters in San Francisco." Thus were eighteen months of his military service completely glossed over. There was no mention of Executive Order 9066 or his post as Director of the Wartime Civil Control Administration that had put him in charge of the evacuation and the construction and organization of assembly and relocation camps for more than 110,000 persons of Japanese ancestry.

Memories of the evacuation and incarceration in relocation camps were still fresh for Japanese Americans in 1949, and the efforts to right the wrongs and to challenge continuing prejudice and discrimination in American society filled the pages of the JACL's publication, *Pacific Citizen*.[7] The JACL had set as its goal for 1949 the elimination of racial restrictions on citizenship, demonstrating that the Nisei, the children of Japanese immigrants, as editor Larry Tajiri noted, "have at last come to realize that their futures were not separate from the lives of the Issei (first generation). If for a time, the Nisei had turned from their parents, they now turned back to them in a common enterprise."[8]

In the years immediately after the war, the former evacuees set about building new lives, many of them in the Midwest. It was not just a matter of leaving the camps and finding a place to live. For some it was a struggle just to be able to participate in American life. The legal counsel for the JACL Anti-Discrimination Committee was Edward J. Ennis, the former Justice Department official who had opposed the evacuation in many meetings with War Department heads, including Bendetsen. Ennis worked tirelessly to oppose enforcement of racially restrictive covenants in housing and to try to end discrimination in employment. Civil rights lawyers helped the Tule Lake renunciants regain their citizenship; lawyers succeeded in persuading some legislatures to rescind restrictive alien land laws, and in California gained repeal of the miscegenation law. A Chicago cemetery refused to bury several Nisei war dead, but eventually Arlington National Cemetery in Washington, D.C., accepted them. The JACL defended the right of a Japanese American professor to live in a neighborhood next to the University of Washington, his employer.

By 1949 some public attitudes toward the evacuation were changing. In February, Drew Pearson declared in his nationally syndicated column: "It hasn't been overly advertised, but a racial revolution has come to the Far West." He gave examples of improved attitudes toward Japanese Americans, and claimed that Japanese Americans had "discovered the true meaning of democracy."[9] After several years of active lobbying by the JACL, Congress enacted, and Truman signed, Public Law 886, which required the attorney general to consider claims resulting from evacuation of "certain persons of Japanese ancestry under military orders," to compensate, at least in a small way "for damages to or loss of real or personal property." Claims were to be filed by 1950. Almost twenty-four thousand claims totaling about $132 million were filed, but they were settled very slowly, and in 1954 it was estimated that evacuees whose claims had been settled had "received on the average no more than ten cents on the dollar."[10] Countless others were unable to make a claim because they lacked paperwork to prove their losses.

PERRY SAITO'S NEXT MINISTRY

After their release from the Tule Lake camp, Perry and his mother, Natsu Saito, had much correspondence with the WRA regarding their household effects, which had been stored in government warehouses, first in Seattle and then in Tule Lake. When their shipment arrived in Chicago, they reported to the evacuee property office that four boxes and twenty-two cartons of their property were missing, but the property managers had paperwork indicating that everything had been shipped and received, papers that Perry had been forced to sign prior to shipment. It probably wasn't possible for Perry or Natsu Saito to file a claim for their losses.

Perry Saito had done well as an interpreter of the so-called relocation experience for FOR. A secretary for FOR recalled meeting him: "He was a tall, handsome, personable, disarming young man, so positive in his outlook on life that looking back, he seemed too good to be true!"[11] While working for FOR in 1944, Perry had applied to Illinois Wesleyan University, which had just "decided to admit two Japanese-Americans from the camps"—a woman whose husband was overseas, and Fumi Yabe, by then engaged to Perry. Perry also applied, but was told that the school "had agreed on two" Japanese students. The school asked: "Can you come around next year?" Perry was surprised and replied, "OK, if IWU admits it has a race quota." Dr. Lowell Hazzard, a professor of religion, put his job on the line, telling the president that "he could not continue at IWU if PHS was not admitted." Perry was admitted and invited by Dr. Hazzard to speak to "the entire student body" after which a poll on inviting more Japanese Americans from camp showed 93 percent in favor.[12] On the day in August 1944 when the government at last granted Perry his final leave clearance from Tule Lake, Perry and Fumi were married so that they could attend the college in Bloomington, Illinois, together. Their first child was born nine months and three days later. By the time Perry graduated in 1946, they had two children. He enrolled at Garrett Biblical Institute (now Garrett Theological Seminary) at Northwestern University along with his Aberdeen friend, Dick Tuttle, and Julius S. Scott, Jr.

Julius, a black man, and Perry were drawn together in part because they were both in the minority at Garrett. They occasionally put on a "race riot" sketch for new students that was shocking enough to break down stereotypes. Perry called Julius "a dirty nigger," then Julius called Perry "a stinking Jap." The routine called for one to seem to hit the other, who clapped his hands, then they'd reverse roles, feinting and name calling. After that they could talk about differences and common values with the full attention of the audience. Perry and Julius shared their commitment to social justice and nonviolent confrontation.

Julius often told the following story to show Perry's patience in dealing with confrontation: "We were [on this bus trip] going from Chicago to Detroit, and he sat in about the third row, and he wanted to sleep so he put his seat back, enough to recline. The guy behind him said, 'You put that seat back up there, you dirty Jap.'

"And so Perry put the seat back up. Then they had these rest stops. Perry got off and went up to the man and said, 'May I buy you a cup of coffee?' And the guy said, 'I don't want you buying my coffee, you stinking Jap.'

"They got back on the bus and sat in the same seats. At the second rest stop, Perry got off with the guy, and said, 'I noticed on the last stop you had a coke. May I buy you a coke now?' The guy said, 'Nah, I don't want you to buy me a coke.'

"At the third rest stop the same identical thing. Perry went up to him and said, 'May I buy you a drink?' And the guy said, 'OK, Jap, you win.' And from there on they sat together and talked. The guy was very bitter about the war."

Julius and Perry were close at Garrett. Sometimes Julius and his friend Pat Barsanti, a tall, blonde, blue-eyed woman, baby-sat, taking Perry's children out for something, maybe ice cream. People stared at the group: "a blonde and a black, with Oriental kids."[13]

Through his contacts at FOR and at the Methodist institutions, Perry was involved with a group of progressive thinkers, people who worked to promote social and economic justice, racial equality, and peace in the world. Concern over these issues was compatible with the Wesleyan emphasis upon the Christian life—faith and love put into practice. Methodism has been known as a denomination involved with people's lives, with political and social struggles having local and international implications. Many of the issues that Perry supported were unpopular, particularly opposing racial segregation in the 1940s.

In 1947 Perry was appointed as an associate at St. Paul's in Chicago. Shortly thereafter Perry was pastor and Julius Scott was associate pastor for the students at the Wesley Foundation near the Chicago Medical Center. In later years Julius and Perry served together on several national boards for the United Methodist Church; in the 1990s Julius was president of Wiley College in Marshall, Texas.[14]

In 1949 Perry served as pastor for the Christian Fellowship Church, a Japanese Methodist congregation, but he still had not been ordained.[15] As the relocation camps emptied at the end of the war, some twenty thousand evacuees resettled in Chicago. Though three-fourths of these gradually returned to the West Coast, Perry and his family stayed in the Midwest.

During his time in divinity school, Perry met Marion Kline, who was also studying for the ministry. She invited him to preach at a church in Kendall, Wisconsin. He brought his wife and two little kids, aged three and four. Marion tells the story: "Well, one of the neighborhoods was having a picnic on Sunday afternoon, so we were all invited . . . out in the yard of one of my parishioners. We were talking. I happened to look over and realize that two of the neighborhood children were in a wagon with Perry's two kids. And they were having a good time, laughing and joking. The parents of the neighborhood children came and grabbed the children out, with anger, pulled them out of there. They shouldn't be playing with Perry's children, because they looked Japanese. Perry saw it. Oh. My parishioner, the hostess, she was just devastated, she thought it was just horrible."[16] Marion said that Perry's reaction to prejudice was "always making friends with the person who was being nasty to him." She thought that Perry understood how the neighbors felt, and it didn't upset him as it did the hostess.

Perry and his family were not the only Japanese Americans who encountered obstacles as they sought to rebuild their lives in the years after the war. The struggle continued in day-to-day encounters and in the courts.

The JACL Anti-Discrimination Committee sent representatives to testify in Congress to support proposed civil rights laws and to urge passage of the equality in naturalization bill before Congress. If passed, such a bill would remove the category of persons "ineligible for citizenship," thus allowing their Issei parents to become citizens. Though the measure did not pass both houses of Congress in 1949, its consideration provided a forum for the Japanese American community to make its case for equity in citizenship, and for many former antagonists to amend their past record.

When John J. McCloy sent a letter to Representative Walter Judd, sponsor of the equality in naturalization bill, "giving tribute to wartime behavior of Japanese American groups," this was page-three news in the JACL's weekly newspaper.[17] McCloy had just been appointed United States civilian high commissioner in Germany, having given up a post as head of the International Bank for Reconstruction and Development. His letter seemed conciliatory, noting that the Judd bill, which would undo the so-called Oriental Exclusion Act of 1924, "is only an appropriate form of recognition for the loyalty which Japanese Americans as a whole evidenced to this country during the war."

McCloy continued, "As you perhaps know, I was very much involved in the movement of the Japanese American population from the West Coast in the early days of the war. The measure which was taken was harsh and very difficult to carry out. It was done, I believe, in the best interest of the country and of the Japanese Americans themselves. Every effort was made that could be made to soften the impact on that population of this forced movement but, with all of the precautions, all of the considerations that were given, at best it was an unfortunate necessity and worked many hardships."

Although McCloy's letter did not go as far as an apology, it resonated well with Japanese American readers. He acknowledged his admiration for the cooperation and exemplary behavior shown by most of the evacuees during incarceration. He also recalled his role in urging the army to form the Japanese American 442nd regimental combat team and the 100th infantry battalion, and noted that he had followed closely the record of these fighting groups. "In every respect they performed their fullest duty to the country. Their casualties were heavy and I think that their conduct and the conduct of the Japanese Americans in Hawaii and elsewhere throughout the United States is the strongest evidence one could ask for of their full loyalty to the country."[18]

Dillon S. Myer, wartime director of the WRA, who had managed the relocation centers, praised the "loyalty of the Japanese in America" in his testimony before the Judd committee. Myer characterized the Japanese as, "in general a loyal, hard-working, law-abiding, self-disciplined people," and argued that if the Judd bill were law before the war "there probably would never have been an evacuation."[19]

Edward J. Ennis also supported the naturalization law on behalf of the Japanese minority, saying, "Through the country as a whole no so-called enemy minority had as fine a [wartime] record of cooperation with our government as the Japanese." He admired the fact that the Japanese Americans gave "complete cooperation with the Government, even though the government mistakenly asked them to suffer the hardship of evacuation." Obviously still troubled by his role in the evacuation, he stated that the "decision to evacuate the Japanese was left entirely up to the military. . . . It has been said that dictators do not dare admit mistakes but that an outstanding feature of democratic government is that it can admit mistakes and do something to rectify them."[20]

In the summer of 1949, editorial writer Larry Tajiri expressed surprise that General DeWitt was "still afraid of Japanese Americans." Apparently DeWitt, by then retired, had not established a home in San Francisco for fear, as Tajiri wrote, that "some evacuees" might "tie up his property through personal suits directed against him," and observed that General DeWitt "has apparently become the victim of a self-imposed exclusion. Although the majority of evacuees [had] returned to the West Coast, General DeWitt . . . remained in the east."[21]

What was important to the editor and columnists of the *Pacific Citizen*, and to their readers, was the willingness of former antagonists, supporters of the evacuation, to admit that they had made a mistake and to apologize, either explicitly, or by supporting legislation for equality in naturalization and immigration, as had the Hearst newspaper chain. The *Citizen* faulted Walter Lippmann, who had "lunged for the racist bait in California. . . . Lippmann has never to this day written a column to admit that he was mistaken in his obviously hurried analysis of the situation on the Pacific coast in February, 1942."[22]

Japanese Americans paid attention to problems of segregation in housing and to efforts to widen the area of employment for members of all racial minorities. They identified with the plight of the Negro and followed with interest the proposal to end segregation in the armed forces of the United States, which had been initiated by President Truman on July 26, 1948 (during his successful campaign to be elected in his own right).[23] In April 1949 Louis Johnson, secretary of defense, directed the air force, navy, and army to put into effect "a policy of equality of treatment and opportunity without regard to race, color, religion or national origin." The army's response, delivered by Kenneth C. Royall, then secretary of the army, was rejected as being too general, and he was asked to submit new plans. Tajiri, editor of the *Pacific Citizen*, expressed the hope that "the country's armed forces [would] soon attain that complete racial democracy so necessary in the units that defend a democratic nation."[24]

In late August 1949, the United States Ninth Circuit Court of Appeals in San Francisco used strong language to condemn the 1942 mass evacuation of persons of Japanese ancestry from the Pacific Coast. Its comments came in a decision reaffirming the American citizenship of three Nisei who had renounced their nationality while at the Tule Lake camp in 1945. The judges declared that the major reason for the mass evacuation was "the Nazi-like doctrine of inherited racial enmity stated by the commanding general (DeWitt)."[25] The court's opinion took the German comparison further: "The barbed wire stockade surrounding the 18,000 people there [Tule Lake] was like that of the prison camps of the Germans. There were the same turrets for the soldiers and the same machine guns for those who might attempt to climb the high wiring." The court condemned "General DeWitt's doctrine of enemy racism inherited by blood strain," and quoted sections of the *Final Report* that had first appeared in documents authored by Bendetsen. There could be no question that Bendetsen would want to conceal his having had a major role in the evacuation.[26]

With the condemnation of the evacuation on racial grounds and the observation that racial equality in the military was making very slow progress, the possible nomination of Karl Bendetsen as assistant secretary of the army became news. The National Democratic Party prepared to oppose the nomination. Galen M. Fisher, a West Coast organizer of the American Principles and Fair Play, "which helped stem the tide of racist prejudice against Japanese Americans during the war," announced that he would oppose the nomination if it were made.[27]

A *Pacific Citizen* editorial explained: "The opposition to Mr. Bendetsen stems from his conduct of his major role in the mass evacuation, in which he displayed a calloused lack of concern for the citizen rights of the Nisei evacuees. At a time when the Army Department has been ordered by Defense Secretary Johnson to abolish race segregation and adopt a new policy of racial equality, it is felt . . . that he will prove, on the basis of his past record, as a deterrent to the successful operation of the non-segregation order." The editorial cited statements in which Bendetsen "misrepresented the loyalty of the Japanese American group," and reminded readers of Bendetsen's argument that the absence of acts of sabotage, espionage, and treason by the Japanese American group should have been seen as "an ominous thing."[28] Noting that "U.S. Commissioner to Germany McCloy and many other War Department officials concerned with the mass evacuation decision later took an affirmative position on the Japanese American. . . . There is no record of a public utterance by Mr. Bendetsen to indicate that he was willing to admit he was mistaken in his appraisal of the Japanese American group in the tense days after Pearl Harbor."[29]

The JACL soon joined the list of opponents of Bendetsen's nomination. Mike Masaoka, legislative director for the JACL Anti-Discrimination Committee, wrote to President Truman in September 1949, speaking for some forty national member organizations of the National Civil Liberties Clearing House: "We feel . . . from a rather bitter association with Mr. Bendetsen, that he long ago disqualified himself from active participation in an administration which has sought as much as you to achieve racial harmony."[30]

The protesters soon found that they might be too late. Reporter Arthur Caylor in the *San Francisco News* observed that Bendetsen "had already accepted the post of assistant secretary of the army when a 'hitch' developed to delay his appointment." Opposition may have delayed the appointment, but Army Secretary Gray said that the problem would be smoothed out. Caylor wrote, "Dope on the nature of the hitch hasn't reached here yet."[31] Caylor observed that Japanese American and Negro groups might mobilize opposition; he wrote further, "Much of the opposition to Bendetsen is based on supposition. His record shows that he did a great deal to soften the blow on relocation. Nevertheless, influential Japanese believe he influenced DeWitt to issue the ouster order in the first place."[32]

In late September, journalist and former evacuee Togo Tanaka elaborated on the reasons to oppose Bendetsen's appointment: "Bendetsen's name is sometimes credited for having been the eyes, ears and possibly the brains behind the DeWitt edict to mass evacuate Issei, Nisei and Kibei from the West Coast. . . . Because of this, Bendetsen's name has an ugly ring in the Nisei consciousness. . . . [His] name is without honor among [former evacuees]."

Tanaka quoted from a letter written to President Truman by Father Hugh Lavery of the Catholic Maryknoll Center in Los Angeles, in which the priest described his experiences with Colonel Bendetsen in 1942: "Colonel Bendetsen showed himself to be a little Hitler. I mentioned that we had an orphanage with children of Japanese ancestry, and that some of these children were half Japanese, others one-fourth or less. I asked which children should we send to the relocation center."

Lavery claimed in his letter to Truman that Bendetsen made the much-quoted reply, "I am determined that if they have one drop of Japanese blood in them, they must all go to camp."[33]

Tanaka quoted statements that Bendetsen made in the speech to the Commonwealth Club of San Francisco on May 20, 1942, and wrote further, "From where we sit, Bendetsen epitomizes the kind of military arrogance that weakens our faith in democratic practices. His appointment to any position of public trust should be weighed in the light of his record."[34]

Sam Ishikawa wrote in the *Colorado Times*: "We urge all Nisei and Issei to protest to President Truman. Bendetsen's appointment to this post would be nearly a condonement of evacuation itself."[35]

On October 15, 1949, John Shelley, president of the California Federation of Labor and former state senator from San Francisco, declared in a letter to Joe Grant Masaoka that he was given "rather definite reassurance by administration officials that the name of former Col. Karl R. Bendetsen would not be revived for appointment to the post of Assistant Secretary of the Army." Shelley, who was a leader in the Democratic party in California, said that he had been offered the appointment and had turned it down. The Japanese Americans must have read the headline: "Bendetsen Nomination for Post Will Not Be Revived" with great relief.[36] They did not know about Bendetsen's strong connections with leaders in the Pentagon, which he had cultivated for years. At about this time, Arthur Caylor reported that "Bendetsen had just been appointed by the Defense Secretary to the policy board that integrates the civilian elements of modern warfare with those of the armed forces. No small job."[37]

Perhaps realizing that they would lose the fight, the *Pacific Citizen* backtracked a bit in December: "It should be noted for the record that the opposition to Col. Bendetsen was predicated on his appointment to a position in which he would have some control over the Army's racial policy, as he would have had as assistant secretary. Col. Bendetsen is undoubtedly a man of considerable administrative ability and there would be no objection to his appointment to a tactical post where his prejudiced racial attitude, as disclosed by him concerning the evacuation, would not be a matter of prime concern." The article claimed that the campaign was not one of personal vindictiveness, but rather an effort to prevent placing a person in an office where his possible prejudices might affect public policy.[38]

For Bendetsen, it may have seemed that the war might never end, and his involvement in the evacuation of all persons of Japanese ancestry from the West Coast might never be forgotten. He now had one more reason to get rid of his past, to continue the renunciations and denials that began when he left Aberdeen. In response to the changing view of what was called the Japanese internment, Bendetsen tried further to reduce the appearance of culpability in the decision and to minimize his role in managing the evacuation.

He was forced to take notice of the charges made by Father Lavery of the Maryknoll Mission of Los Angeles. At the request of Secretary of the Army Gordon Gray, he wrote Gray a lengthy memorandum to try to neutralize Lavery's attack. The tenor of this memo suggests that the public outcry since the war had modified Bendetsen's view of the evacuation and his role in it. In the 1949 memo he claimed, "*I took no part in the decision to evacuate these people*. . . . No assignment could have been more unattractive to me than this. . . . [It was] a distasteful and trying assignment. [Emphasis added.]"[39] This is not the way that he had characterized his job in the era in which he received the Distinguished Service Medal for his efforts.

In his statement to Secretary Gray he claimed that he had recently been asked to state publicly that there had been "no shred of underlying military necessity" at the time of the evacuation of the West Coast population of Japanese ancestry and "that the evacuation was wholly without justification." He said that some persons implied that they would urge others to attack his appointment if he did not make these statements. Nevertheless, he did not do so, and he argued that if he and the other "thoughtful people who labored long and hard to lessen the impact on the evacuees . . . had been guided by the Hitlerian wantonness [as] Father Lavery implies, the record would have been other than it is." He mentioned the oversight of Mr. Justice Tom C. Clark, Mr. John J. McCloy, and the press. "The entire action was constantly subject to the welcome white glare of exacting publicity."

He went on to suggest that Father Lavery's attack was based on bitterness. He claimed, improbably, that Lavery had asked that he grant to Lavery's missionary society "exclusive rights to furnish spiritual service within all of the assembly Centers to all evacuees, regardless of faith," and he had refused. Bendetsen claimed that he had established a policy allowing full freedom of religion to all faiths represented among the evacuees, including the Buddhist faith, for which he was criticized at the time.[40] As noted in the *Final Report*, the number of Catholics among the evacuees was small. The Maryknoll organizations that had catered to Japanese prior to the war were allowed access to the camps.[41]

Still unconfirmed in January 1950, Bendetsen wrote to Gray to express appreciation for "the privilege of serving" him. He continued, "However, because of the atmosphere unavoidably created by these untimely news accounts, I have undergone a most unhappy and frustrating experience."[42] He wrote that he was willing to stay in his present situation for at least six more months, if Gray wished, "whether or not [the] proposed appointment" materialized.

The JACL urged some 250 national organizations to oppose the confirmation. Mike Masaoka, legislative director for the national JACL Anti-Discrimination Committee, asked for letters of protest from the members of such organizations as the National Civil Liberties Clearing House, and from veteran, civic, fraternal, religious, union, agricultural, and educational organizations.

Objections were raised by Americans for Democratic Action and other civil rights groups.[43] Monroe E. Deutsch, vice-president and provost emeritus at the University of California, Berkeley, wrote that "the appointment of a man whose utterances reveal him as possessing racialist points of view analogous to those of Hitler, would be most unfortunate." Deutsch had heard Bendetsen's address before the Commonwealth Club and noted that he "assuredly helped to fan the hostility to American born citizens of Japanese descent."[44]

The chairman of the King County Democratic Central Committee (Seattle) wrote to Washington Senator Warren G. Magnuson: "Mr. Bendetsen was quite prominent in Washington politics in the Grays Harbor area in the '30s. At the time, he was a leader in the "Let the People Vote" campaign and was of great assistance to the private power interests when they attempted to pass Initiative 139. He was quite a chum of Joe Roberts [a Republican legislator] and was violently opposed to Senator Homer T. Bone. . . . He is opposed to most, if not all, of the principles of the Democratic Party." The chairman urged Magnuson: "Get . . . a more worthy State of Washington Democrat."[45]

While he waited for the Senate to consider his appointment, Bendetsen may have thought about his past association with President Harry S. Truman. Bendetsen had met then Senator Truman prior to the war when Truman was investigating the defense program, and had several times been required to testify before his committee.[46] Mr. Gray finally took Bendetsen's appointment to Truman, who apparently said, "'Well, I remember Bendetsen." Bendetsen recalled learning that Truman told Mr. Gray that "his recollections were favorable and he did not see any reason why I should not be appointed."[47] Writing to his former law partner in San Francisco after approval of his appointment, Bendetsen observed, "Although I hold the portfolio of Assistant Secretary I have been in reality functioning as Deputy Secretary." He described his visit to the Armed Services Committee: "I was very courteously received by the Senate Committee which had before it my nomination, and many generous observations were made by the members. As I was confirmed unanimously by the whole Senate two hours later, I can only assume that the Committee chose to give no weight to the protests filed by the Japanese-Americans Citizens League and by whatever other groups the League was able to influence. As you know, I did not turn a hand toward the matter and was in no sense a candidate for this office. The complimentary action of the Senate was, therefore, particularly gratifying to me."[48]

That day on the Senate floor, Senator Millard E. Tydings, (D-Md.), chairman of the Armed Services Committee, spoke briefly in support of Bendetsen's nomination, noting that he was including Bendetsen [in the routine list of nominations] for the following reason: "The law provides that Assistant Secretaries shall serve on boards and commissions. Mr. Bendetsen has been serving on certain boards and commissions by direction of the Secretary of War since last August, but strictly speaking, he is not in a legal status to serve on them, because his nomination has not been confirmed. The Secretary of the Army is anxious to have it confirmed so as, speaking in a humorous way, to make the Secretary of the Army honest and compliant with the law. Mr. Bendetsen has the highest recommendations, particularly from the junior Senator from California [Mr. William F. Knowland], who knows him."[49] Bendetsen's appointment was confirmed in a unanimous-consent request as part of a long block of routine nominations for the army, navy, and coast guard. When he was sworn in on February 2, 1950, Bendetsen was forty-two.

The JACL leaders had lost. Their eloquent protests seem not to have impeded Bendetsen's nomination in any way. The struggle for full citizenship for persons of Japanese ancestry and for redress of the wartime wrongs had to wait another thirty years, until civil rights had been won for blacks, and a new generation was willing to take up the fight. Then both Bendetsen and Perry Saito would have an opportunity to present their (possibly revised) views of the wartime evacuation and incarceration of the Japanese Americans.

Bendetsen married Maxine Bosworth two days after the divorce from Billy was final in September 1947. Here Bendetsen and Maxine pose for a photograph at a function at the Palace Hotel, San Francisco, in 1952 while he was undersecretary of the army. (KRB Papers, Hoover Institution)

Although his appointment was opposed by many groups, including the Japanese American Citizens League, Bendetsen was appointed by President Harry S. Truman as assistant secretary of the army (1950–52) and then appointed undersecretary in 1952. (KRB Papers, Hoover Institution)

Karl, Selma, and their mother at the Los Angeles wedding of Selma Bendetson Brill's daughter Beverly in 1951. (Courtesy of Beverly Freedman)

Autographed photo of the Joint Chiefs of Staff, 1950. Back row, from left: Lt. Gen. R. S. McLain, comptroller; Gen. Wade H. Haislip, vice chief of staff; Gen. J. L. Collins, chief of staff; Lt. Gen. M. B. Ridgeway; Lt. Gen. A. M. Gruenther. Front row from left: A. S. Alexander, assistant secretary of the army; Gordon Gray, secretary of the army; Tracy S. Voorhees, undersecretary of the army; K. R. Bendetsen, assistant secretary of the army. (KRB Papers, Hoover Institution)

Above: In an army photo labeled "VIPs in Korea," Bendetsen stands at attention on the tarmack in October 1952. Bendetsen arrived in Korea with Defense Department heads Frank Nash and William C. Foster. They were greeted by General James A. Van Fleet. (KRB Papers, Hoover Institution)

Opposite, above: Bendetsen receiving the Medal of Freedom from Defense Secretary Charles E. Wilson. 1957. (Courtesy of Beverly Freedman)

Below: On November 5, 1958, Bendetsen received a letter of appreciation from Major General Zwicker on the occasion of his retirement from the army. He had resigned from active duty in the army at the end of 1945. (Courtesy of Beverly Freedman)

By 1962 Bendetsen, Maxine, and daughter Anna Martha had moved to Hamilton, Ohio, when Bendetsen was promoted from manager of the Texas division to president of the Champion Paper and Fiber Co. Though they later suffered the loss of this home in a terrible fire, Bendetsen's World War II papers were not lost. (Courtesy of Beverly Freedman)

Karl married Gladys Ponton de Arce Johnston two months after Maxine divorced him in 1972. At the same time, he stepped down from his position as chairman, president, and CEO of Champion International. Karl and Gladys are shown here, possibly at a party honoring Bendetsen after he gave his détente speech in New York in July 1975. (Courtesy of Beverly Freedman)

On Easter Sunday, 1960, Perry Saito's family posed for a formal family portrait. Front row from left, Fumi, Rebecca, and Deborah Ann; back row: Perry, Patricia, Christine, and Lincoln. Perry was director of the Wesley Foundation of St. Paul's United Methodist Church in Stevens Point, Wisconsin, and soon after became pastor. (Courtesy of Lisa Aylesworth)

Reverend Perry Saito and Fumi enjoy a moment of relaxation at a church function in the 1970s. Ever the pacifist, Perry took part in early sit-ins, was a strong supporter of the Civil Rights movement, and opposed the Vietnam War. (Courtesy of Fumi Saito)

From a brochure supporting Perry Saito's first candidacy for the episcopacy, 1981. At the time, he was senior pastor of the Wauwatosa Avenue United Methodist Church. Perry withdrew after the vote was deadlocked, allowing the election of the first female bishop in the United Methodist Church. (Courtesy of Fumi Saito)

Perry Saito (second from right at witness table) testified before the CWRIC panel at Northern Illinois University on September 23, 1981. He read statements from the General Conference and the Wisconsin Annual Conference of the United Methodist Church and spoke of his family's incarceration experience. (Courtesy of Fumi Saito)

At the CWRIC hearing, Bendetsen held up for the Associated Press a copy of the speech he gave to the Commonwealth Club in San Francisco in 1942. This photo appeared in the *New York Times* over the headline: "World War II Internment Is Defended." November 3, 1981. (From *New York Times* microfilm)

Great-nephew Paul Freedman visited Bendetsen and Gladys about a year before Bendetsen died. Bendetsen spent his last years in an assisted-living center in Washington, D.C., and died in 1989. (Courtesy of Beverly Freedman)

CHAPTER TWELVE

Stories Told in the 1970s

"It is final, conclusive, authoritative and totally accurate."

Karl R. Bendetsen, referring to the *Final Report*, in a letter to Hiroshi Suzuki, June 11, 1976.

The late 1960s and early 1970s were turbulent times. The United States was engaged in a war in Vietnam that it could not win. Consequences of the war overwhelmed Lyndon Johnson's efforts to build a "Great Society" and ended his presidency. Civil rights protests began to merge with protests against the war, and permeated every aspect of American life. Many war demonstrators were moving away from nonviolence; college campuses experienced sit-ins, vandalism, and worse. Some of the strongest protests occurred in Wisconsin, where Perry Saito lived, and where he and Fumi were raising their five children. Perry was not only against war, he was against guns. He would argue, "You buy guns and you belong almost right away to the National Rifle Association (NRA) because of the things they send you." His only son Lincoln once recited to him the motto of the NRA, "Better to have a gun and never need it than to need a gun and never have it," and Perry replied, "It's more important to never have a gun and need it than to have a gun and have your child kill himself or someone else." Lincoln, who had six children, later came to understand that viewpoint and gave up his guns.

However, during the Vietnam War Lincoln did not follow his father's pacifist footsteps; he signed up for the draft in 1966 and went through ROTC. Lincoln would have chosen the Air Force "because being an Asian American during the Vietnam war . . . I wouldn't want to be a ground troop. If I had to leave my foxhole and go jump in someone else's foxhole, I thought, good grief! If I was going to go down I was going to go down with a plane."[1] A football knee apparently kept him out of the service.

When Perry Saito attended his thirtieth high school reunion in Aberdeen in August 1969, he could report to his Aberdeen friends that he had achieved his goal of becoming a Methodist minister. In spite of a delayed ordination, he was completing eighteen years as a United Methodist pastor in Wisconsin and looking forward to being appointed district superintendent for the North Central District, a position of some honor and distinction, a "pastor's pastor." As one would expect, he spoke out against the war and was "an avowed campaigner for human rights."[2]

Unlike most other former evacuees, Perry Saito had talked extensively about his experiences in Tule Lake. But he found that the stigma that the country's incarceration of Japanese Americans had left on his ethnic group was not easily erased.

When he had finished college and theological seminary, he experienced "his most embarrassing moment [which] came when the Methodist bishop asked the Northern Illinois Conference right in front of 2,000 people if anyone was willing to have Saito come to their church as pastor." The bishop "could not find one congregation that would hire a fully-trained pastor of Japanese ancestry, despite the fact that scores of churches were left without pastors."[3]

"The Bishop delayed my final ordination as an Elder until he could guarantee me a pastorate."[4] The bishop told him he could not ordain him because he could "find no church that would accept him." For two years Perry languished in the Chicago area in a sort of limbo. Eventually a church in Wisconsin said that they would be glad to have him. The bishop arranged a hurried ordination so that Perry could accept the post.[5] After a delay of more than two years, Saito was accepted by Reverend Arlie Krussell as assistant pastor of the First Methodist Church in Beloit, Wisconsin. He moved on to pastor positions in Stevens Point, where he helped rebuild the church after a fire, and then to Eau Claire, Wisconsin, where he welcomed an antiwar rally in his church. Fumi Saito recalled, "Perry didn't just preach [against the Vietnam War]. . . . He opened the church to the young people for a rally. . . . We really heard about that."[6]

"In Wisconsin he quickly became one of our most beloved and distinguished pastors, serving nobly in key pulpits, and as district superintendent," according to a fellow minister.[7] Perry also served on many church boards and agencies and on the Governor's Commission on Human Rights, appointed by a succession of governors. A member of the Free and Accepted Masons of Wisconsin, he achieved the thirty-third degree.

Perry worked hard for his parishioners and tried to ignore the stress that might affect his own health. "A pastor who openly admits his problems must have both the humility to realize he is human and the courage to take bricks thrown from congregational members who feel pastors ought not to have problems. . . . There are still people in churches who believe if people trust in God, they shouldn't have heart attacks, or headaches even."[8] In August 1972 Perry survived triple bypass open-heart surgery for which he thanked "God, the Giver of Life and the Sustainer of all health."[9]

A journalist reported that Perry was "especially active in helping his church recognize the needs of minority members of their faith." Because he himself "had faced prejudice brought on by being a distinct minority in a church with relatively few members of Asian heritage," he helped organize the National Federation of Asian-American United Methodists.[10]

He summarized his experience in the ministry: "I have been royally treated and had a great time in the Wisconsin area."[11]

Karl Bendetsen had a smoother course in his career—and while he may have complained about those who revised history, he soon did some revising of his own.

After Gordon Gray resigned, Bendetsen served as assistant secretary of the army under Frank Pace, Jr., handling business and budgetary matters. Pace later described Bendetsen as "a brilliant man . . . [an] indefatigable worker. . . . In the enormously complicated period of the [Korean] war, Karl was really basically indispensable."[12] Among other duties, Bendetsen became director-general of the United States Railroads, which were then under the control of the army; and chairman of the board of the Panama Canal Company, a post he held into 1953; in May of 1952 he was appointed undersecretary of the army.

In 1952 Bendetsen broke his rule of not giving interviews, agreeing to a brief interview with Jacobus tenBroek, a researcher from the University of Califonia who asked him to talk about the evacuation. He told tenBroek that he had written the *Final Report*, and that he had the most complete records on the evacuation "in a wooden box," which he would probably give to Stanford.[13] His record agrees. However, he made numerous assertions to tenBroek that disagree with the record: He asserted emphatically that DeWitt had begun to propose evacuation within a few days of Pearl Harbor; that Stimson and McCloy had deliberated upon these proposals actively from then until the final decision was announced; that General George C. Marshall had been brought into close consultation; that the president himself had considered the subject upon several separate occasions; and that he himself had played no part in the policy determination. Though there is some truth to each of these assertions (except with respect to Marshall and himself), their juxtaposition and simplification is clearly self-serving. In particular he gave tenBroek the mistaken impression that the decision had been "basically a decision of civilians, i.e. they did not merely act as the rubber stamp of the military." TenBroek mentioned Bendetsen's vehement denials of having had anything to do with the decision: "It was fairly apparent that charges and statements to that effect had stung him."[14]

While serving as assistant secretary of the army, Bendetsen enjoyed a trip described by a friend as "kismet." Secretary of the Army Gray one day was unable to attend and deliver a speech at his alma mater, University of North Carolina at Chapel Hill, and sent Bendetsen in his place. Bendetsen found himself "sitting in the stand next to a prominent alumnus. . . . Ruben Robertson from Cincinnati who [was] head of Champion Paper Company, a more or less family-controlled but very large company." The two men chatted and decided to keep in touch.[15]

After thirty-seven months of strenuous service in the Department of the Army, Bendetsen resigned in October 1952 and accepted Ruben Robertson's invitation to join the Champion Paper & Fibre Company as a general consultant. Within three years he was vice-president and general manager of the Texas division of Champion.

By 1970 he had become chairman, president, and chief executive officer of Champion International, a global supplier of paper and forest products, which had just merged with U.S. Plywood.[16] The head of the plywood company was Gene Brewer, formerly of Montesano, Washington, ten miles east of Aberdeen. Friends from Aberdeen were impressed—and wondered how it could be that two Grays Harbor boys would head these two big companies?"[17] One of Bendetsen's Aberdeen friends described the merger that created Champion International: "Karl was chairman of the board, Gene Brewer was president. Karl was smart, he became chairman of the finance committee, got control of the money. Karl was ruthless, didn't have a lot of friends in places. He eased Brewer out."[18] Bendetsen's son recalled, "Gene and my dad, it was kind of a knock-down drag out there toward the end, when that thing was put together. It was not a marriage made in heaven, putting the two organizations together." At this time Bendetsen was also going through what his son described as "a bitter [second] divorce."[19]

Joel Wolff didn't like to talk about his old Aberdeen friend Karl, because of hurt feelings. His wife recalled a scene in the late sixties: "We were at the Washington Athletic Club [in Seattle] having lunch. At another table was Gene Brewer, U.S. Plywood Corp. president, having lunch with Karl Bendetsen. And Joel went over to say hello. . . . Gene Brewer, who knew Joel [and may have seen him first], introduced him to Karl: 'Joel, I'd like you to meet Karl Bendetsen who's head of Champion Paper,' and Karl said, 'I'm happy to meet you,' as if he'd never seen him before. Joel could hardly believe it." Joel said of this scene: "We were little kids together and he didn't want to acknowledge that."[20] Did he not want to remind Brewer that he had been Jewish?

Because of his rising stature as a corporate executive, a new and more detailed biography of Bendetsen was about to appear. Perhaps this is the way that it happened: Bendetsen sat over his morning coffee perusing the *New York Times*. He was planning that day to dictate a new account of his life to submit to the *National Cyclopedia of American Biography*. It was July 17, 1970. An obituary caught his eye: The Prime Minister of Iceland, his wife, and a grandson had died tragically in a fire.[21] The man's name was Bjarni Benediktsson, his grandson was Benedikt Vilmundarson.

Over the years Bendetsen had been heard telling friends about his Danish lumbering ancestors, and he would claim such a lineage in a taped interview with Kai Bird in the 1980s.[22] There must have been that day in 1970 or 1971 when Bendetsen went to his office to flesh out the new biography, which began as follows:

> Bendetsen, Karl Robin, manufacturer, was born in Aberdeen, Wash., Oct. 11, 1907, son of Albert Moses and Anna (Bentson) Bendetsen, grandson of Benedict and Dora Robbins Bendetsen, and great-grandson of Benedict Benediktssen, who came to this country from Denmark about 1815 and lived in Portland, Maine, before settling in Elmira, NY. His father was a schoolteacher and merchant.[23]

Comparing this text to Bendetson family records shows that Karl worried about his heritage. He clearly did not like being a third-generation Jewish American with Lithuanian roots. Perhaps he was trying to be more like his (now deceased) friend Chub Middleton.[24] Why, and why now?

In early 1972 Bendetsen's second wife, Maxine, filed for divorce. They had one daughter. Less than two months after that divorce was final, Bendetsen married Gladys Ponton de Arce Johnston.[25] Gladys was a Washington, D.C., socialite, born in Costa Rica, the former wife of a Panamanian diplomat, and a widow. She had been active on the board of the Washington Ballet Guild and was a friend of Post cereal heiress Marjorie Merriweather Post.[26] Gladys had often visited Marjorie Post in Florida; with his retirement from Champion in the winter of 1973, Bendetsen and Gladys spent time in Palm Beach and joined several exclusive clubs there.[27] His son described Gladys as "the love of his life, really."[28]

For most of his life, Bendetsen declined all requests for interviews or talks about his wartime involvement in the evacuation and incarceration of the West Coast Japanese. When asked, he directed the questioner to the *Final Report: Japanese Evacuation from the West Coast, 1942*, which he wrote and edited in 1943, saying that there was nothing he could add to that material. "It is final, conclusive, authoritative and totally accurate."[29] He made several exceptions.[30] The second is notable because it set the tone and would become the core of all of his later written testimony before government panels.

In 1972, the same year that his new biography was published, Bendetsen gave a three-session interview to Jerry N. Hess of the Harry S. Truman Library, responding to questions, most of which concerned his experience as a civilian administrator in the defense department and the department of the army during the Truman administration.[31] At Hess's request, he first talked at length about the evacuation of the West Coast Japanese.

He started with a Pearl Harbor story, which he could now tell, he claimed, because "applicable classifications had expired." He claimed that he had met in Hawaii with General Short and Admiral Kimmel, and that he had met in the Philippines with General Douglas MacArthur in December 1941, in the week before the Pearl Harbor attack, and had carried secret messages for the chief of staff (George C. Marshall) from them (he was a major at the time). He said General Short wished him to tell the chief of staff that Short feared an attack and wanted to go on alert.[32] Bendetsen claimed that the messages that he carried were too late because his airplane was delayed. At the end of this narrative, he told Hess, "I have never before related to anyone any of the foregoing, either orally or in writing."

He claimed that on December 7, 1941, two hours after his return from Hawaii, "the Chief of Staff sent for me." Bendetsen told him about his dinner with Short and Kimmel the evening of December 5. Marshall supposedly told him in confidence that Marshall had sent messages to MacArthur and Short on December 4 directing all forces be placed on full Red Alert, and had not known until that day, after the attack, that the messages had not been received. And Marshall expressed regret that had Bendetsen's dinner been on the fourth, he might have arrived in Marshall's office on the sixth in time to change history. Bendetsen expressed to Hess his respect and admiration for General Marshall. "In the light of the crushing burdens he bore I was literally overwhelmed that he would take even a few minutes for such extraordinary consideration of a junior officer."

No part of this story agrees with or can be verified in Bendetsen's papers or in the extensive studies of Pearl Harbor. As noted earlier, Bendetsen had traveled to Hawaii in September 1941 and was in Washington, D.C., in the first week of December 1941. He did not go to the Philippines until 1956.[33]

The Hess interview contains fabrications, distortions, and even fantasies, when compared with the *Final Report* and with military records hand-edited and preserved by Bendetsen in a "wooden box." For example, Bendetsen argued that the Governor's Conference in Salt Lake City in April 1942 was a great success in persuading interior states to accept evacuees. He stated several times to Hess that internment was never intended and blamed the WRA for the detention: "No sooner had the WRA assumed responsibility than resettlement stopped. . . . The declared policy was to aid the 'evacuees' and their families to resettle as rapidly as possible. There was an active and successful effort of this nature under way before Mr. Myer took over. Thereafter it was simply moribund." And he blamed the tension in the camps on the WRA: "We had no militants during the Army phase."

As he talked to Hess about the evacuation he argued two major points: that the evacuees' assets and property were protected, and that internment was never intended; he claimed evacuees "were not to be restricted for the 'duration' so long as they did not seek to remain or seek to return to the war 'frontier' during hostilities."[34] He talked at length about the voluntary migration as if it had been an option available and fully supported for a long period of time. According to the *Final Report*, this episode began on March 2 and was terminated on March 27, 1942, and only 4 percent of the identified Japanese minority managed to leave the West Coast voluntarily.[35]

Another story in the oral history: He said that in late 1944 he was in a jeep caught under enemy fire in the Ardennes forest at the start of the Battle of the Bulge. When he finally got back to headquarters, driving the jeep carrying the body of his driver, he asked a general what was needed and duly went out and stole a supply train for General Patton.

Though the train story is somewhat plausible, there are several reasons to think that the MacArthur story is fiction.[36] Bendetsen did not mention any Philippine service in a June 1942 *Stanford Alumni* magazine article or in his Brief of Record in 1943.[37] In a handwritten Brief of Record in 1948 he wrote, "Established Internee program with General MacArthur at Manila and General Short in Hawaii," a statement that does not insist that he had actually gone to the Philippines.[38]

More proof that he did not make a trip to the Philippines in December 1941 was his own memo entitled "Wearing of 'Foreign Service' Clasp on the American Defense Service Medal," which he filed at the request of his superiors on August 2, 1943. Noting that he had been "on temporary duty at Headquarters, Fort Shafter, Hawaiian Department, and on all of the islands in the Hawaiian Group except Maui for a period of approximately two weeks, during August and September 1941," he requested a ruling as to "whether this entitle[d] [him] to the 'Foreign Service' Clasp in question."[39] His son, who traveled with him when he did go to the Philippines on behalf of the secretary of defense in 1956, had never heard either the MacArthur story or the stealing a train for Patton story.[40]

Somehow, giving the interview for the Truman Library broke the ice, and Bendetsen began responding to critics of the evacuation decision. In his third exception, he agreed to a taped interview with historian Kai Bird, who was doing research for a biography of John J. McCloy. In that interview he again told the story of carrying secret messages to Washington from General MacArthur and Admiral Kimmel on December 7, 1941, and asserted that he "had a service pilot's rating" because he'd "always flown." He claimed to have gotten his license by lying about his age in 1924."[41] His son, who had been a navy pilot, was quite sure that this was not true.[42]

A MOMENTOUS MEETING

Morse Saito also had a favorite story, one that his daughter has corroborated.[43] Morse moved to Japan as a Methodist missionary after the war; he met and married Georgia-born Ruth Taylor, and both stayed on as missionary-educators. During a year as a distinguished visiting professor at Morehouse College in Atlanta, Morse had the "privilege of meeting Earl Warren face to face."

It was May 1974, soon after the twentieth anniversary of the *Brown vs. Board of Education* decision that declared unconstitutional the separation of public school children by race. Chief Justice Warren had written for the unanimous Supreme Court that "separate educational facilities are inherently unequal." Warren, by then retired, was invited to speak to the Morehouse graduates, many of whom had benefited from the decision. Morse had mixed feelings about the meeting.

Many Japanese Americans agreed with Carey McWilliams, editor of the *Nation* for many years, that "no one person had more to do with bringing about the removal of the West Coast Japanese during World War II—citizens and aliens alike, men, women, and children—than Mr. Warren."[44] Warren had testified before the Tolan Committee in February 1942: "We believe that when we are dealing with the Caucasian race we have methods that will test the loyalty of them. . . . But when we deal with the Japanese we are in an entirely different field and we cannot form any opinion that we believe to be sound."[45] Morse had many times asserted that after Earl Warren made these devastating arguments against the Japanese Americans, "he rode that into the governorship and almost the presidency."[46] He wasn't sure he wanted to meet the former chief justice.

Morse tells the story: "Morehouse College is all black, it's the school where Martin Luther King graduated; we had 164 graduates. . . . Warren had a bad heart, came in a wheel chair, but he did stand up and march in the graduation procession. A lot of students, graduates, had taken the position that 'What did Warren do that shouldn't have been done a hundred years earlier . . .' This kind of thing. There was talk among the students of boycotting the graduation." These young graduates did not understand the importance of Warren's leadership in getting a unanimous decision. "But they did come and a number refused to stand up after Warren spoke. . . . [While he] got a standing ovation from some of us, the others sat and read newspapers. . . .

"Right after that we had a luncheon for the graduates, and this was also my farewell, so I got [to speak for] 5 minutes. What I had to say was, 'Today we honored, if you look at the entire career, we honored a great person. If you take it only in terms of say, 'my people,' if I had sat this close to this man when I was your age, nearly 21, I would have spit at him.' Someone in the back of the hall shouted, 'Right on!' The President of Morehouse frowned.

"I went on '. . . today we honored a great career together and I am very honored to sit across the table from him.' And so then I sat down and he got up and thanked me and then later made the statement in front of the president of Morehouse, that 'My greatest regret[s] in my career were my actions during World War II.'" Morse felt that Warren could never say this publicly because then somebody would say, "Well, 20 years from now you'll regret the Brown decision."

"My witness to this statement is the president of Morehouse college, Dr. Hugh M. Gloster, Sr. And yet you can see why he [Warren] could never say this. It was just not possible, his whole career, anyone in this kind of position, you can't say 'Well I made a mistake,' it's not that easy, even though you know you did."[47]

Morse had witnessed one of Warren's last public appearances. Two months later he died of a heart attack. Warren's only public acknowledgment of this sentiment appears in his memoirs. In that volume, Warren described the vulnerability of the coast of California, the strong anti-Japanese sentiment among Californians, and the unfortunate consequences of separating the Japanese into the Tule Lake camp. He then wrote, "I have since deeply regretted the removal order and my own testimony advocating it, because it was not in keeping with our American concept of freedom and the rights of citizens. Whenever I thought of the innocent little children who were torn from home, school friends, and congenial surroundings, I was conscience-stricken. It was wrong to react so impulsively, without positive evidence of disloyalty, even though we felt we had a good motive in the security of our state. It demonstrates the cruelty of war when fear, get-tough military psychology, propaganda, and racial antagonism combine with one's responsibility for public security to produce such acts."[48]

For Morse Saito, being incarcerated had been a defining moment. His daughter thought he had been hurt by the experience, that it shaped his political understanding of how this government works, how racism works. She said, "Things like when the FBI came and searched their house and locked up their mother, those were very defining moments."[49] The experience changed his view of being Japanese American, and influenced him to affirm his being an American, to stand up against discrimination as Gordon Hirabayashi had, to speak out, to bring the world's attention to what the United States government had done to its own people, and it influenced him to go to Japan after the war "to get a sense of connection to Japan."[50] In his English-language column in the *Mainichi Daily News* (published in Tokyo and Osaka), he continued to provide an American's view of events in Japan and to talk about the strengths and weaknesses of the United States.

Meeting and talking to Earl Warren was another defining experience for Morse. His daughter attended the Morehouse graduation. "I think that was one of the more significant moments of his life. To have it come back around like that was important to him," she recalled.[51] Even though they spoke only in private, hearing Earl Warren express regret was uplifting and validating, and was perhaps more gratifying than receiving President George H. W. Bush's brief apology or the redress check years later.

Prodded by their grandchildren, who learned to value their ethnicity during the turbulent protest years, many Japanese Americans began to talk about their experience as an excluded racial group during World War II, and out of this sharing of information, a movement to seek redress of the injustice gradually organized.

CHAPTER THIRTEEN

Legacy of History

> Sansei children . . . have asked questions about those early World War II years.
>
> Why did you let it happen? They ask of the evacuation. Why didn't you fight for your civil rights? . . .
>
> As they listen to our voices from the past, however, I ask that they remember they are listening to a totally different time; in a totally changed world.
>
> —Yoshiko Uchida, *Desert Exile*, 1982

The civil rights movement and the protests of the Vietnam era heightened awareness of the rights of ethnic and racial minorities in America. By the 1980s a third generation of Japanese Americans took a new view of the incarceration experience. Far from being people who murmured, as their grandparents in the relocation camps had, "*Shigata ga nai*" (it can't be helped) they were likely to shout, "Justice delayed is justice denied."[1] Many appeared determined to force the United States government to acknowledge that the evacuation and incarceration had been unjust, and to urge the government to provide some form of financial compensation.

Just as there had been factions among the internees during incarceration, there was no unanimity among former evacuees and the Japanese American community about how to enlist public support for redress. The JACL, after meeting with the four Japanese Americans in the United States Congress—Senators Daniel Inouye and Spark Matsunaga, and Congressmen Norman Mineta and Robert Matsui—favored asking first for a congressional study commission.[2] The National Council for Japanese American Redress (NCJAR) urged support for a class-action lawsuit against the United States government on behalf of certain named plaintiffs and all former evacuated and interned Japanese Americans. That suit would assert some twenty-two causes of action, including fifteen violations of constitutional rights, and would sue for $27 billion. A third group opposed the study commission route and supported the bill put forth by Congressman Mike Lowry of Washington, which called for immediate monetary compensation of $15,000 for each internee plus $15 for each day spent in camp. This was the bill that had enraged Karl Bendetsen (he called it "a shameful effort to raid the treasury") and inspired him to speak out for the first time about his role, to seriously revise his account of his participation in the evacuation decision, and to deny the evacuation's negative impact on the evacuees.[3]

When the study commission, the Committee on Wartime Relocation and Internment of Civilians (CWRIC), was approved by Congress, research in the National Archives unearthed serious breaches of the rules of evidence that inspired an unprecedented legal campaign to overturn the wartime convictions of three evacuees.

Thus, in the 1980s the merits of the government's wartime treatment of America's Japanese minority were reconsidered by the congressional study commission, in congressional hearings on implementation of the commission's findings, and in two different kinds of court cases. Perry Saito was drawn into the debates over the best approach to gaining redress, and he and Karl Bendetsen were each called to testify before the CWRIC. Far worse for Bendetsen were the reopened cases on behalf of Korematsu, Yasui, and Hirabayashi, in which he found his name and some of his World War II actions brought to light in an unflattering way.

William Hohri, one of the organizers of NCJAR, was displeased with the way the redress campaign was going, and wrote, "It's déja vu to '42. The JACL has taken a turn on redress which reminds me of March, 1942. The [JACL] National Council voted for redress. The Committee, its creature, overrode that vote by moving for a Study Commission. . . . I do not believe the actions of the JACL national leaders reflect the wishes of their rank-and-file members."[4] Hohri and Perry Saito, fellow Methodists, found themselves on opposite sides in the debate.

In 1980 Perry Saito, by then pastor of a large congregation in Wauwatosa, Wisconsin, was a charter member and national secretary of the National Federation of Asian American United Methodists, a group that sought to empower its members and to encourage self-determination in the United Methodist Church. He was a candidate for bishop in the North Central Jurisdictional Conference, which convened in July 1980. He had worked on the creation of a "Working Description of Racism" document for a World Council of Churches meeting. In April 1980 he was a delegate to the quadrennial General Conference of the United Methodist Church in Indianapolis. At this general conference the two burning issues were Iran and homosexuality. William Hohri described the conference: "Japanese American redress was a minor issue, but it had its moments nonetheless."[5] Of the competing bills in Congress, Senator Inouye and Representative Norman Mineta, both United Methodists, supported the one that would create the commission to study the causes and justification for the evacuation and incarceration. In the Asian American caucus at this general conference, the NCJAR brought forth a resolution that supported the Lowry Redress Bill, and the measure "passed through sub-subcommittee and through subcommittee and through the full committee . . . still surviving with a strong vote in its favor."[6] The general conference was winding up its last session, and delegates had checked out of their hotels. "It was the zero hour," but there were still resolutions on social justice to be considered.[7] The NCJAR petition reached the floor at 11 P.M. under rules restricting discussion and amendments. After a one-minute presentation of the one-page resolution. Hohri wrote, "A delegate stood to be recognized. The presiding Bishop recognized Reverend Perry Saito of the Wisconsin Conference." William Hohri recalled, "Saito made an amendment which gutted our proposed resolution, converting it from support for redress legislation to support for a study." Saito explained his action: "My amendment was to delete from the original resolution all references to specific bills and dates, [because conference resolutions last four, sometimes eight years and,] to add on . . . the statement that evacuation was undemocratic, un-American and unjust." His amendment had four parts, including one that called upon Congress "to support legislation that would determine appropriate remedies."[8] He continued, "I added a resolution urging that the United Methodist Church lead the way in studying the Japanese-American to find out that we were fellow Americans."[9]

Hohri, who was not at the session, was offended that Saito had not made his motion earlier, when he could have argued its merits. Perry recalled, "I was active in another evaluation group having to do with the General Council on ministries."[10] Perry's amendment appeared to support the JACL position to study and educate, and to go through Congress to do it. Hohri wrote, "A few weeks later, the JACL circulated an internal memorandum which crowed about its success at the General Conference and the effectiveness of a single person there."[11] The general conference soon went on record in House hearings in support of the study commission, and in the summer of 1980 Congress approved formation of such a commission. Perry Saito had chosen the winning side, and probably made the right decision. The (CWRIC) commission's hearings and sympathetic press coverage of evacuees who testified before it served to educate the public about the injustice of the evacuation and incarceration, which was a necessary precursor for consideration of financial redress.

Perry's candidacy for the episcopacy was less successful. The voting was very close. Both Perry and the leading candidate had been district superintendants and were well respected by their peers. After twenty-nine ballots, Perry withdrew in favor of a four-foot-eleven-inch grandmother, Marjorie Matthews, who became the first woman to be elected bishop "of any mainline Christian church."[12] Had he been elected, Perry would have been the first Japanese American bishop.

When the CWRIC began conducting public hearings in 1981, Bendetsen became concerned that his and McCloy's unsolicited testimony might be ignored. If that were to happen, Bendetsen wrote, "the record would become an 'historical record' of libelous falsehoods."[13] That summer, Bendetsen cobbled together a seventeen-page statement from relevant parts of his 1972 oral history interview, making small changes and rearrangements, but generally adhering to the earlier text. He submitted the statement, but heard that it was merely set on a table at one of the hearings, and apparently not entered into the record. He modified the testimony slightly and again mailed it to Paul T. Bannai, then executive director of the commission. The modifications, which brought the statement to eighteen pages, had no effect on the factual content of the statement, but were largely efforts to say laudatory things about the other men who took some part in the evacuation decision, as if to shame critics who might impute otherwise: For example, Bendetsen wrote, "It is widely known and appreciated that Justice [Tom] Clark himself was a man of compassion and understanding, not given to rash judgements."[14] And "Franklin Delano Roosevelt, then President of the United States, who made the ultimate decision, was a man of compassion and integrity." Other compassionate leaders were then Senator Harry S. Truman, Earl Warren, and John J. McCloy. He also declared that the Honorable Henry Stimson "was a man of great breadth and tolerance."[15] He wrote to McCloy, "There is neither relevance nor fairness in judging the action of the government taken in 1942 in the perspective of today's myopic vision."[16]

Bendetsen obtained much of his information about the progress of the commission's work from correspondence with Lillian Baker, who headed an organization called "Americans for Historical Accuracy" and who disputed the evacuees' descriptions of the incarceration experience in publications such *The Concentration Camp Conspiracy*.[17] Baker's first husband died in a Japanese prison camp in the Philippines during World War II. (Bendetsen's last public statement on the evacuation appeared as introductory remarks in Mrs. Baker's book *American and Japanese Relocation in World War II: Fact, Fiction and Fallacy*.[18])

Bendetsen was finally called to testify before the commission in early November along with John J. McCloy, Milton Eisenhower, and others.[19] Angus Macbeth, special counsel to the commission, met with Bendetsen prior to the hearing and then sent him copies of his May 1942 speech before the Commonwealth Club in San Francisco (in which he stated that his charges would soon go to "permanent centers where evacuees may live and work *for the duration* of the war") and an archival copy of Bendetsen's memorandum of February 4, 1942, to the provost marshal general (Gullion) in which he recommended the designation of military areas from which citizens, as well as aliens, could be removed due to military necessity. Macbeth said that he wanted to draw the memorandum to Bendetsen's attention promptly "since it clearly contains *recommendations by you on alternatives to mass evacuation* and it seems to me you should have an opportunity to review it before giving testimony."[20] [Emphasis added.]

A critic noted that "some of the things Bendetsen said touched on unreality."[21] In his written testimony Bendetsen said, "It never occurred to me that there would be an evacuation or that I would be assigned to General DeWitt's command. . . . I did not recommend such action."[22] He claimed that the only time that he was asked his opinion was in a meeting with then Senator Truman, which occurred when he was in Washington, D.C., in February 1942 reporting on the Japanese situation on the West Coast before several congressional committees. "Senator Truman asked me to tell him in confidence whether I would be inclined to recommend that Japanese residents be evacuated from the West Coast." Bendetsen said that he told Truman that he was merely presenting the view of others: "If I had reached a conclusion I could not remain objective. He congratulated me."[23]

McCloy, upon reviewing the first draft of Bendetsen's proposed testimony, objected. "I still balk a little at the use of the word 'congratulate,'" he wrote, suggesting, "I think there is the slightest connotation that you disagreed with the measure. . . . I always had the feeling that our positions were substantially identical." McCloy then said, "I wondered about the necessity but never came to a conclusion in my own mind."[24]

> I realize that some who were involved in the original decision to intern us are still defending their actions. I suppose if I had made as big a mistake as they did I would also be reluctant to admit it.
>
> —Congressman Norman Y. Mineta, June 20, 1984

During Bendetsen's rambling statement on November 1, 1981, the audience was hostile. One observer recalled, "When he testified how comfortable the trains were that took the people to their desert barracks, Japanese American victims in the audience had to be gaveled into silence."[25] In spite of the fact that Chairman Bernstein began the session by reminding everyone that the commission was not conducting an inquisition, the questioning by the panel was extensive and probing. Several of the questioners had seemed to want to force Bendetsen to apologize or at least to say that he considered the evacuation and detention had been a mistake, which he did not do.

An interesting interchange occurred between Bendetsen and Arthur Goldberg, a former justice of the United States Supreme Court. Goldberg began by bringing himself to Bendetsen's level.

JUSTICE GOLDBERG: Colonel, you were a real Colonel and I was kind of a desk colonel, so I will ask my questions not as a former justice, but just colonel to colonel.[26]

He then chided Bendetsen for criticizing the commission because it refused to accept his written statement, and got him to agree that it was preferable to have the witness. He asked many questions that Bendetsen did not answer straightforwardly. For example, would he not say that it had been a matter of forceable evacuation to camps? Bendetsen said, "No, that is not so," and went into a lengthy explanation, again, of the effort to encourage "voluntary movement."[27] And when forced to admit that after the voluntary phase was ended, there was compulsory evacuation, he immediately said, "When they were in the centers, they were free to leave."[28]

> JUSTICE GOLDBERG: In your statement you said that I was just a colonel and colonels were a dime a dozen in World War II as you and I both know, if you didn't become a general you didn't amount to anything. In the 15 million persons in the Army.

In your statement as I read it, you said in effect I was a colonel, and I had orders and I followed them, is that correct?

MR. BENDETSEN: Yes, sir.

JUSTICE GOLDBERG: In your *Who's Who*, which all of us write, you know, we are the authors of the complimentary things that are said about us. In the 1940 [he meant 1944-45] edition of *Who's Who*, written by you—as I write my own—it says this, that you conceived the method, formulated the details and directed the evacuation of 125,000 [sic] persons of Japanese ancestry from military areas.

That was as we lawyers say *contemporary evidence as what you conceived your role*. [Emphasis mine.] That is somewhat different from your statement.

MR. BENDETSEN: No, I construed it as I testified, if it were to be done, how it were to be done, voluntarily in the first place, and when it didn't work, I conceived how to go from there. That did not mean I conceived or developed anything else.

JUSTICE GOLDBERG: I'm referring to this *Who's Who*. So was that hyperbole on your part at the time?

MR. BENDETSEN: No, it only refers to what I did conceive.[29]

A version of this testimony found in Bendetsen's papers has a much longer answer that Bendetsen wrote later, which asserted that the statement in question [from *Who's Who*] "has no relation to the decision made by the President in issuing Executive Order 9066," and argued that he did the conceiving "after it appeared that voluntary relocation would not work."[30] The record in his personal archive shows that the conceiving was done in the letters and memoranda written in the weeks prior to February 19, 1942. Voluntary relocation was only possible from March 2 to March 29, 1942.

William Marutani, a Pennsylvania judge and member of the commission, confronted Bendetsen with a transcript of a telephone conversation from February 1, 1942, between several army officials, in which Bendetsen said, "The Department of Justice had agreed, reluctantly, that 'from a legal standpoint' the Army could force the Japanese Americans and aliens to leave the West Coast." Bendetsen is quoted further: "We could also say that while all whites could remain, Japs can't if we think there is military necessity for that." Marutani also challenged Bendetsen's assertions that "'extraordinary measures were taken to preserve [the] property' of those who were removed, particularly crops of Japanese farmers," in the face of testimony from hundreds of witnesses who had reported loss of land, crops, businesses, homes, and personal possessions. One newspaper reported that "under intense questioning by Marutani, Bendetsen conceded that he [had] only 'assumed' the Japanese [had] lost little property."[31]

William Hohri attended this hearing and described Bendetsen's body language: As Bendetsen discussed "reports of atrocities committed by Japanese troops in the Philippines, he was flipping his silver pen"; while discussing how the Federal Reserve Bank protected the inmates' property, "he played with his glasses until one of the lenses fell out," then he "busily tried to place the lens back into its frame." At other times he pushed the microphones away "as though he did not want to be heard." Hohri observed that "his words were often slurred." Although he had been asked to read his testimony, Bendetsen "spoke extemporaneously for sixty-seven minutes" until he was interrupted.[32] Bendetsen ever afterward insisted that the testimony bearing his name in the National Archives files of the Commission hearings (presumably a transcript of the proceeding) is not the testimony he gave, that it was "falsely inaccurate."[33]

Law professor Peter Irons wrote to Bendetsen in January 1982. Irons was doing research for a book on litigation that arose from the evacuation and relocation of Japanese Americans during World War II, focusing on the role of the lawyers in those cases, both those involved in the court cases, and those involved in the relocation program. Irons's letter asked several questions. The first: Was the evacuation modeled on the orders previously issued by the Canadian government (which directed the exclusion of Japanese Canadians from British Columbia), and did Bendetsen meet with Canadian officials in Vancouver prior to the issuance of General DeWitt's evacuation orders? Bendetsen had scrawled "no," and "totally false" beside this question.

Irons's second question: Did Herbert Wenig write the three documents that appear similar (the *Final Report*, the brief amicus curiae submitted to the Supreme Court in 1944, and Attorney General Warren's statement to the Tolan Committee in 1942)?[34] Bendetsen scrawled, "Ennis wrote brief" and "the other way around" beside this question, as well as several no's. Irons also asked whether Wenig wrote sections in the *Final Report* about espionage and the loyalty of Japanese Americans. Another scrawled "no." Irons offered to visit Bendetsen in Washington, D.C.[35]

Bendetsen did not reply to Irons. By refusing to grant interviews Bendetsen had managed over the years to avoid answering any questions this specific. He certainly would not start now.

In fall 1983, as the 493-report of the CWRIC, *Personal Justice Denied*, began circulating, Bendetsen took great exception to a column by Wes Peyton in the *San Jose Mercury News*. Peyton had referred to him as "the Stanford-educated . . . lawyer generally credited with dreaming up the legal justification for America's World War II concentration camps," and suggested that Bendetsen's testimony before the commission tried to put the best light on his participation in the evacuation operation. He wrote, "His extensive testimony seemed directed at ensuring that history wouldn't record him as the lawyer who blew the biggest hole ever in the United States Constitution." Peyton noted,

> Probably it *is* the judgement of history that concerns Bendetsen now because, at age 76, he has or had, about everything else.
>
> He's been chief executive officer and chairman of a $4 billion paper and plywood empire, Champion International Corp. He's served as a director of Westinghouse Electric Corp. And as a member of the board of governors of the New York Stock Exchange.
>
> His public service includes stints as under secretary of the Army, director general of U.S. Railroads, chairman of the board of the Panama Canal Co. and special United States representative (with the rank of Ambassador) to West Germany.
>
> In retirement, he maintains an office in Washington and membership in 16 of the best private clubs from Seattle to Palm Beach (including San Francisco's Bohemian and Pacific Union).
>
> By contemporary standards, Karl Robin Bendetsen is a smashing success. History, which takes a longer view of men and their works, may treat him more critically.[36]

Bendetsen wrote Peyton a long letter, and two subsequent notes, one of which stated that several months earlier he had sent "an accurate copy" of his "actual testimony" to Peyton. "Obviously you have no interest in the truth. . . . You, along with the Commissioners, had your mind made up before you read the facts." In one letter, Bendetsen persisted in exaggerating the impact of the voluntary migration, and amplified assertions made earlier, such as insisting that evacuees could leave the relocation centers whenever they wished: "Many who voluntarily stayed in relocation centers sometimes had jobs within driving distance of the center and their families stayed there throughout the war years with free board, room and medical care, etc. Many of their children were sent *at Federal expense* to colleges and universities and graduated therefrom."[37] [Emphasis added.]

Also that fall, Bendetsen corresponded with Eugene V. Rostow, former dean of Yale Law School. He may have forgotten that Rostow had in 1945 written one of the first and harshest critiques of the evacuation and the Supreme Court's handling of the court cases, in a journal article entitled "The Japanese American Cases—a Disaster." Rostow had urged financial indemnity for Japanese Americans who suffered losses, and suggested that the basic issues of the court cases should be presented again to the Supreme Court to allow it to correct its wartime decisions.[38]

In October 1983 Rostow had written a critical review of Peter Irons's book about the Japanese American wartime legal cases, *Justice at War*.[39] Bendetsen described to Rostow the heckling that he and McCloy had suffered while testifying before the commission, and again argued that no one was interned under Executive Order 9066. Rostow wrote a friendly letter to Bendetsen, thanking him for including his letter to the editor of the *San Jose Mercury News*, but chiding him about internment: "You are of course correct that the order provided only for evacuation and relocation, not internment as such. But evacuation is itself a major restriction on liberty, not to be compared with a curfew; and for most of the people involved, given their circumstances and the atmosphere of the time, *evacuation meant an indefinite period of internment as a practical matter*.[40] [Emphasis added.] Rostow's chiding had no effect on Bendetsen's later testimony.

Perry Saito's testimony before the commission included statements of support from the General Conference of the United Methodist Church and from the Wisconsin Annual Conference, which Perry had helped craft.[41] He questioned whether the Supreme Court could be persuaded to reverse its rulings that had in 1944 declared the evacuation legal. But he felt the evacuation should be challenged as a racist act: "If a patriot who loves his country is liable to imprisonment solely because of his/her national or racial ancestry, then . . . we would have to question whether we all are still 'dedicated to the proposition that ALL persons are created equal.'"

The 1980s had brought Perry more health problems, which may have weakened his second candidacy for the episcopacy. In spite of the Asian American Fellowship's support, he was not elected. He was not greatly disappointed. In his last interview, he said that he considered having "been elected one of the eight ministerial delegates to General Conference for four General Conferences" his most gratifying experience. "That is an honor that if it comes once in a lifetime to a pastor, he should be proud. I am overly gratified and surprised."[42]

On Mother's Day in 1984 he began, "This, my first Mother's day sermon since I became an orphan a few months ago—with the death of my mother. It is a different feeling." He chose the Book of Ruth for his text, recalling the oft-quoted lines, "Whither thou goest I will go," a verse often sung at weddings; he noted that in the Book of Ruth "it is a daughter-in-law singing to an old haggard mother-in-law [Naomi]. 'And your God shall be my God and where you are buried I'm going to be buried.'" He was impressed that this book was even included in the Bible. "Its sole purpose, the only reason for the Book of Ruth being included in the Old Testament is to point out that King David, the greatest Jew that ever lived, had a foreigner for a grandmother." He praised "Booz's lack of prejudice in marrying a foreign woman [Ruth]," and said, "Here is a story that stretches our concept of neighborhoodness, that expands brotherhood and sisterhood and familyhood beyond the boundaries of race and nationality and religion."[43] The sermon served as fitting homage to his Tokyo-born mother.

In 1984, after two ministers in his conference tried unsuccessfully to contribute two years of their own pensions to Perry, the Northern Illinois conference voted to give Perry two membership years of credit because the conference "had delayed ordination and probation . . . for two years, solely on the basis of [his] being an American of Japanese ancestry."[44]

In 1985, at the age of sixty-four, Perry succumbed to heart failure. Speaking at the service celebrating his life, Reverend Lee C. Moorehead observed, "Though on this day in February 1985, the snow is falling heavily from the sky, and though at outward glance one sees that it is still winter, I know that in this midwinter there is an invincible spring. I saw it last night in the Saito home as the children gathered from Alaska, from Japan, from Minnesota, from Wisconsin, and from Illinois. There were beaming smiles, lilting laughter and joys of remembrances. They came to celebrate the wonders of the parenthood from which they were begotten and they rose up to call them blessed."[45]

In his 1981 testimony, Bendetsen had given many justifications for the decision to exclude all West Coast persons of Japanese ancestry, including as justification even Japanese attacks that occurred after February 19, 1942. He never mentioned supposed incidents of signaling to enemy submarines (because these had been totally rejected by investigators in 1942), which was almost the only assertion made in early 1942 to justify an action as drastic as mass evacuation. Neither Bendetsen nor McCloy had made any mention of any information obtained from Japanese coded messages intercepted and decoded during the early days of World War II. The "MAGIC" diplomatic cables were published in 1977 by the Department of Defense.[46] Jack Herzig noted later that Bendetsen, "in some hundred pages of testimony [in 1981], made no mention of the MAGIC cables as a reason to forcibly remove the ethnic Japanese from the west coast."[47]

And the record shows that Bendetsen admitted several times that there had been "no cases of sabotage by the Japanese on the West Coast following Pearl Harbor."[48] In the 1983 interview, McCloy biographer Kai Bird asked Bendetsen about the MAGIC cables (which had still not been brought into the debate over redress). Bendetsen said that he had never seen raw intelligence materials suggesting that there were Japanese networks.[49] He picked that moment to give another version of his background: "My family was in timber and lumber, uh, for generations. My Danish ancestor came over here in 1670, decided he didn't want to be a sailor he wanted to be a farmer so he started up, don't know why he was headed for Maine not very good farm—today; he found out there wasn't any place to plant, the trees were so heavy, so he decided to clear land—*my ancestors have been in timber ever since.* I was born in Washington State because my father came there from Michigan."[50] [Emphasis added.] He went on to describe selling lumber to Japanese ships.[51]

Much to Bendetsen's disgust, the unanimous report of the CWRIC, *Personal Justice Denied*, made five recommendations, and several bills were filed in Congress to implement them: It recommended that the Congress and the President pass a joint resolution recognizing "that a grave injustice was done" and offering "the apologies of the nation for the acts of exclusion, removal and detention." They asked for pardons of persons convicted under regulations associated with the exclusion. Most galling to Bendetsen was the recommendation that Congress should appropriate $1.5 billion for financial redress to those who were excluded, in what he and McCloy referred to as the "great Japanese 'rip off.'"[52] Legislation to implement the recommendations was introduced in both houses of Congress, and in 1984 and 1986 hearings were conducted.

THE INTERVENTION OF MAGIC

In the year prior to the congressional hearings of 1984, David Lowman, a former military intelligence officer, began attacking the report of the commission for not considering evidence from the translated Japanese diplomatic cables.[53] Lowman asserted that "anyone reading MAGIC intelligence during 1941 could easily have concluded that thousands of Japanese-Americans were being organized into subversive organizations."[54] Lowman had inserted a new phrase into the debate: "subversive Japanese agencies" in this country.[55] While other former intelligence officers disagreed with Lowman, pointing out the insignificance of the information contained in the small number of MAGIC cables that actually said anything about Japanese Americans, both McCloy and Bendetsen immediately amended their written statements to include references to the MAGIC cables. They were anxious to counter charges stated in the committee's conclusions that promulgation of Executive Order 9066 was not justified by military necessity, or driven by military conditions, but rather was based on "racial prejudice, war hysteria and a failure of political leadership."[56]

In 1984 Bendetsen was called to testify before the Subcommittee on Administrative Law and Governmental Relations of the House Judiciary Committee, with Sam B. Hall, Jr., of Texas presiding. Jack Herzig, a retired army counterintelligence officer, gave detailed testimony concerning the MAGIC cables, and concluded, "David Lowman's attack on the Commission and on the loyalty of Japanese Americans is a mixture of fact and fantasy."[57] Mr. McCloy had already asserted in his statement to the committee that "the fact that the relocation commission never disclosed the existence of MAGIC is the clear indication of the unreliability of the Commission's so-called investigation." (Couldn't McCloy have brought the MAGIC cables to their attention in 1981, if information from the cables truly had had any bearing on the decision to exclude?) McCloy, who had had some responsibility for the circulation of the MAGIC cables in the War Department during the war, said he did not think that General DeWitt had access to the cables. Edward Ennis, who testified just prior to Bendetsen, said of the MAGIC code, "I think it is a complete red herring. It has been brought in 40 years after the event as an additional justification for the evacuation."[58] He stated that he was sure that General DeWitt did not rely on the MAGIC code, that Bendetsen's statement (which had already been distributed) said that General DeWitt didn't know it, and that it was only known to top officials in Washington.[59]

Bendetsen couldn't let this comment pass: "To say that General DeWitt did not know about MAGIC by my friend [Ennis] is a false statement, totally false." He went on, "The MAGIC intelligence revealed that there were espionage nests among persons of Japanese ancestry on the west coast, hundreds of them. The FBI didn't know that. The intelligence officers of the Army and Navy didn't know it. But that was the basis finally of General DeWitt's recommendation."[60] After another rambling account of the evacuation and the relocation camps including the usual denials of internment, he returned to the subject of the cables: "DeWitt did have MAGIC. He did know about these very dangerous overlapping espionage nets. All other allegations are totally false." He continued, "Now he didn't have the MAGIC intelligence, he had the conclusions of the MAGIC intelligence given to him by the Chief of Staff of the Army. I was the only other officer that I know of who knew about it. I didn't testify to it in front of the Commission because I knew it would be fruitless. Every Commissioner had made up his mind before he was appointed."[61]

During questioning, Mr. Hall asked Bendetsen whether he had knowledge of the MAGIC cables before December 7, 1941. He answered, "No, sir."

Mr. Hall then asked, "Did General DeWitt, so far as you know? Bendetsen answered, "I don't really know, but I would doubt that he had any knowledge of them whatsoever." When asked when he had first heard of them, Bendetsen answered, "After the Battle of Europe [1944–45], which I went through."[62]

The congressmen who conducted the hearing did not appear evenhanded to former evacuees. Donna Rise Omata criticized the committee for questioning "Mr. Ennis, Mrs. Funabiki, Mr. Ohana and Mr. Herzig" (supporters of the CWRIC report) as "rigorous[ly] as prosecutors . . . rather than as statesmen who should uphold the basic principles of the Constitution and the Bill of Rights of the United States." In contrast, she said that "the committee was meek in questioning Mr. Bendetsen's queer statements about the treatment of internees and their properties."[63] An "ex-detainee," Kiku Funabiki of San Francisco, sent Congressman Sam B. Hall, Jr., an addendum to her testimony that challenged Bendetsen's credibility; she offered clarifications and refutations to his testimony that there had been no barbed wire, no watch towers or armed guards, that detainees had "freedom to come and go," and that people had not been shot; citing evidence to the contrary, she questioned "his reliability."[64]

> Ancestry is not a crime.
> —Gordon Hirabayashi, in Irons, *Justice Denied*

Bendetsen would have liked to be remembered for his contributions to the defense establishment of this country. He had chaired a Defense Manpower Commission study during the 1970s. In 1981 Bendetsen and Daniel

O. Graham, a retired general, set up the nonprofit group called High Frontier to study antimissile defenses. They soon began lobbying for a major change in strategic policy, along lines proposed by Edward Teller, who favored defensive use of a proposed X-ray laser and a doctrine of Assured Survival. In early 1982 Bendetsen may have presented the recommendations of the High Frontier panel to President Ronald Reagan.[65] He hoped that these contributions, as he considered them, would be his legacy.[66] But instead, as a side product of the extensive research for the CWRIC, papers were uncovered that gave him more unwanted notoriety. Peter Irons's research produced more than a book; he initiated extraordinary legal proceedings that rewrote the legal history of the incarceration.

As Irons and others probed the archives, they found evidence that General DeWitt excluded from the *Final Report* FBI and ONI reports advising against evacuation (such as the Ringle report); they found evidence that proved that DeWitt knew that the FCC had found no evidence of signaling by West Coast Japanese Americans, though signaling was asserted in the *Final Report*. They noted Ennis's wartime statement, "[The government had] a duty to advise the Court of the existence of the Ringle memorandum. . . . It occurs to me that any other course of conduct might approximate the suppression of evidence."[67] Furthermore, a researcher found in the National Archives the copy of the supposedly destroyed original *Final Report*. This discovery brought to light Bendetsen's cooperation with McCloy in altering the sense of the *Final Report* on the question of whether loyalty of the evacuees could be determined. In all cases, the discoveries laid bare a view of the "findings" for the evacuation that could only be considered racist. This view had been obscured or hidden in the government's defenses of restrictions against Japanese Americans in the wartime arguments before the Supreme Court.[68]

Irons was outraged by what he deemed a "legal scandal without precedent in the history of American law." He contacted Gordon Hirabayashi, Minoru Yasui, and Fred Korematsu, the three Japanese Americans who had been convicted of violating the curfew, exclusion, and internment orders during the war. He and a team of Asian American lawyers decided to employ a little-used legal mechanism of federal law—a "petition for a writ of error *coram nobis*"—to reopen the three cases, charging that "the original trials had been tainted by 'fundamental error' and had resulted in convictions of manifest injustice."[69]

During the years that the three petitions for a writ of error *coram nobis* worked their way through the courts, the long-running Hohri class-action suit suffered several reverses and eventually died because of the statue of limitations. Korematsu's *coram nobis* case was settled in his favor in 1984; the ruling vacated his forty-year old conviction. United States District Court Judge Marilyn Hall Patel wrote, "The judicial process is seriously impaired when the government's law enforcement officers violate their ethical obligations to the court."[70] She could not reverse the Supreme Court opinion of 1944, however, she said, "It stands as a caution that in times of distress the shield of military necessity and national security must not be used to protect government actions from close scrutiny and accountability."[71] A district court vacated Minoru Yasui's conviction but refused to make the findings of government misconduct. He died before the case could be appealed. After a series of appeals and reversals in the Hirabayashi case, United States District Court Judge Donald Voorhees ruled that the suppression of evidence by the War Department was a fundamental error and vacated Hirabayashi's exclusion order conviction, and ultimately, his curfew conviction as well.

Neither Bendetsen nor McCloy were called upon to testify in any of the *coram nobis* proceedings, but the paper trail they had left during the War Department's supervision of the evacuation kept their names, and that of General DeWitt, in the center of the arguments about suppression of evidence and the assertion of statements known to be false or without basis. DeWitt's belief that the "racial characteristics" of Japanese Americans predisposed them to disloyalty (first put on paper by Bendetsen) stood out clearly when the misrepresentations presented in the government's legal briefs were stripped away; racism could be seen as the heart of the case, as it had seemed to the judges who heard the first Japanese Evacuation Claims cases in 1948.

Redress legislation was still pending. With the support of a bipartisan group of Japanese American senators and congressmen, legislation to implement the report of the commission was submitted in every session of Congress starting in 1983 and continuing until it was passed in 1988. The Civil Liberties Act of 1985, H.R. 442, was introduced by Majority Leader Jim Wright, with ninety-nine cosponsors; it had been named in honor of the 442nd Regimental Combat Team; Senator Matsunaga introduced a companion bill, S. 1053, with twenty-five sponsors. Hearings were scheduled.

By 1986 it was clear that Bendetsen should not be speaking in public. His command of basic facts about the relocation camps was tenuous, and his clear desire to discredit the commission's report as a "falsification of history" dominated his rambling testimony. He continued to use the 1944

Supreme Court decision in the Korematsu case as a defense in spite of the fact that Korematsu's petition for a writ of error *coram nobis* was granted in 1984, his conviction was vacated, and the government's lawyers had acknowledged that "today the decision in Korematsu lies overruled in the court of history."[72]

Speaking before the Judiciary Subcommittee in April 1986, Bendetsen still defended the evacuation; he asserted that "many residents of the relocation centers came voluntarily from other States unaffected by the exclusion order of the president. Very many of them came and stayed." (He may have been referring to families of men interned by the Justice Department who had no means of support, a small number.) He argued with a statement of Mike Masaoka, who preceded him, "These were not internment camps whatsoever. That's totally false. Anybody could leave anytime he wanted to with his family. Most of them did not want to." Bendetsen's written statement was largely a jeremiad against *Personal Justice Denied*, and criticized the conduct of the commission's hearings. Mr. Dan Glickman of Kansas asked him to repeat again his assertion that there was no internment, and then asked him to explain "the loyalty review process through which people were released from the camps." He asked, "Wasn't there a loyalty review process before people [could leave]?" Bendetsen replied, "Nothing whatsoever. They just went." Glickman pointed out to him that "immediately following you we have a panel of evacuees . . . that's one of the functions of these hearings—your views on this point are not shared by a lot of folks who had some experience during that time period." Bendetsen: "They are falsely stating the call. If they admitted the truth, they would not receive money."[73]

Brookes Bendetsen recalled his father's condition at that time: "Alzheimer's hit him pretty hard, I think it was really beginning in '86. I went into the Bohemian Grove with him.[74] For the first time, the only time in my memory, he could not remember someone's name. He admitted to me, 'I'm really slipping, you're going to have to help me out here.' His sense of direction was flawless. Every person he ran into, he knew which camp they were in, but he could not remember their names. He always kicked the encampment off with a joke, a classic joke. He got half way through the joke and he forgot the punch line. It was pretty ugly. '86. I'm not sure when the testimony was going on . . . it was ongoing. He was always being asked to grant interviews. At that point in time, his secretary, and Gladys, his third wife, pretty much reined him in. As far as trying to recall or comment on history. And it was down hill from there."[75]

Bills were reintroduced in the One Hundredth Congress, and the House Judiciary conducted additional hearings in 1987. Bendetsen neither spoke nor entered testimony. In April of 1988, his secretary notified Lillian Baker, Mrs. Charlotte Elam, and Bert Webber, all vociferous opponents of redress with whom he corresponded, of Bendetsen's condition. "He has Alzheimer's Disease, and is no longer able to be active in any capacity. It is a devastating illness and perhaps more difficult for Mrs. Bendetsen than for him."[76]

Congress passed the Civil Liberties Act of 1988, and on August 10, 1988, President Ronald Reagan signed it. The Act provided $1.25 billion for individual payment of $20,000 to each surviving internee, with any remainder to go into an education fund. President George H. W. Bush signed the appropriations bill and an apology in 1989.

Bendetsen died in Washington, D.C., June 28, 1989, at the age of eighty-one. A military obituary stated that Karl R. Bendetsen "had a long and illustrious career in business, the practice of law and the military.[77] He was buried at Arlington National Cemetery.

Bendetsen's death was marked in Aberdeen, Washington, by the publication of a lengthy obituary article that recounted the accomplishments of his lifetime. It also spelled out his responsibility for the evacuation and internment, and the fact that he had refused "in hindsight, [to say] that the evacuation was a mistake" and that he had seen no need for apology or reparations.

Perry Saito had argued that if the government were to suffer enough financially, it would cause a president to think again before approving another such abridgement of the Bill of Rights. Representative Robert Matsui wrote of the successful redress effort, "This is a story of the vindication of American values—our ability as a nation to recognize injury and injustice and to set them right."[78] For many former evacuees, the $20,000 payment was humiliating. In Hoquiam, Washington, Jim Moyer recalled that his siblings didn't want people to know they were receiving the money, in part because they were at Tule Lake such a short time. Jim gave his payment to his children. So did Fumi Saito.[79] Morse Saito hadn't wanted to accept the money but finally did; he contributed all of it to a Canadian group supporting orphanages in India and Nepal. Congressman Matsui declined the payment but accepted the president's apology. By the conclusion of the program in 1998, more than eighty thousand Japanese Americans qualified for the redress payment. A Seattle woman said that the $20,000 check was not as important as the official recognition that the civil rights of Japanese-Americans had been violated. "Now the healing can finally take place."[80]

The brief submitted on behalf of Gordon Hirabayashi's petition for a writ of error *coram nobis* concluded with the observation of the awful truth that had permeated Bendetsen's words and actions as he represented the War Department in 1942: "The distinction between citizens of Japan and Japanese Americans which was not made over 40 years ago is still pervasive in our society. Americans did not bomb Pearl Harbor, yet Americans were unjustly deprived of their constitutional rights."[81]

In the Hirabayashi decision, Judge Voorhees wrote in 1986: "If, in the future, this country should find itself in a comparable national emergency, the sacrifices made by Gordon Hirabayashi, Fred Korematsu, and Minoru Yasui may, it is hoped, stay the hand of a government again tempted to imprison a defenseless minority without trial and for no offense."[82]

Weeks before he died, Perry Saito, still the pacifist and a World Federalist, was asked if he had advice for Japanese American young people today. He encouraged them, and "young people in general," not to set up stereotypes about all kinds of people, racial, nation[al], generational, sexual. "It is so easy to cause wars and hate people if you say the enemy is an animal . . . [but] If you think of them as yourself, 'there but for the grace of God go I,' it is much more difficult [to be prejudiced], is much more simple to understand them and forgive them and to literally turn the other cheek and work for peace and reconciliation. . . . Really, I think, the person to person contact has to be the basis of lasting peace."[83]

Judge Voorhees provided some last words: "It is now conceded by almost everyone that the internment of Japanese Americans during World War II was simply a tragic mistake for which American society as a whole must accept the responsibility."[84]

In his "Obligation Fulfilled" speech in November 1942, Bendetsen had alluded to the "moving story of vast migrations," perhaps wanting to suggest that there was something grand and monumental about the forced removal of all Americans of Japanese ancestry from the West Coast, or that by comparing the Japanese Americans with the Acadians (French settlers who were deported from what is now Nova Scotia for not wanting to declare loyalty to Great Britain) the episode would be ennobled.

Karl Bendetsen and Perry Saito did not experience the same war, but the evacuation experience made its mark on each man. For Perry Saito, who had always considered himself an American, it was the burden of finding himself a member of an ethnic group despised and distrusted not for any behavior, but simply for itself, for being Americans of Japanese ancestry. In spite of having been unjustly incarcerated and having to overcome prejudice after the war, Perry Saito is remembered for his constructive outlook and his commitment to the cause of world peace and understanding.

For Bendetsen the evacuation episode was like the blood on Lady MacBeth's hands; no amount of washing could make it go away. He had done a fine administrative job in an unjust program. Bendetsen's performance of that job brought him promotion and prominence, but the dishonor and misfortune visited upon his charges will not be forgotten.

The evacuation experience shattered him, not quickly, as it had shattered the lives of many of the internees, but slowly, as our country recognized the injustice that had been done and the role he played in it. He went to his grave unable to tell the truth about that.

EPILOGUE

My Quest

This is not just a Japanese American story; this is an American story.

—Rod Kawakami, lawyer for Gordon Hirabayashi, quoted in Irons, *Justice Delayed*

I drove away from Seattle on a cold December morning in 1995 full of anticipation. The sky was a jumble of white clouds against blue. The jagged crest of the Olympic Mountains scraped the western skyline, and Mount Rainier dominated the south—sights often obscured by clouds. I was headed for Aberdeen, the coastal town where I grew up. My family had long since moved away, and in recent years I had only passed through on vacations. On this trip I planned to use my recent, modest celebrity as coeditor of a book about Grays Harbor to visit friends and ask questions. I hoped to resurrect memories of Karl Robin Bendetsen, to try to understand where he came from, who he was, and why some old friends in Aberdeen didn't want to talk about him.

My interest in Bendetsen began while doing research for the introduction to *Cohassett Beach Chronicles: World War II in the Pacific Northwest,* a collection of newspaper columns written during the war by family friend Kathy Hogan. To put Hogan's writings into historical perspective I had studied home-front literature and read through the wartime issues of the *Grays Harbor Post*, the small Aberdeen weekly published by my father that was also the source of Hogan's articles.

Bendetsen's name had turned up in several accounts, always associated with the "internment" of the West Coast Japanese during World War II. Here was a name I recognized from childhood—my father had talked about "that swell guy, Karl," his school classmate, with awe and approval. I found his photo on the front page of the *Grays Harbor Post*, November 21, 1942: a lean-faced serious but smiling man who had been awarded a Distinguished Service Medal. I had arranged to talk to several Aberdeen old-timers in the coming week and hoped to find others who had known Bendetsen or his family. My youngest and last surviving aunt had left Aberdeen in 1944. When I asked her what she remembered about Bendetsen, she had said, "Wasn't he Jewish?" By this time I knew that one longtime family friend, another classmate of my father's who is proud of his Jewish heritage, didn't want to talk about Bendetsen. "That's a sensitive point with me," he said. I would discover more people who were reluctant to talk about him. "He is controversial," I'd be told. Driving through McChord Air Force Base and Fort Lewis, I recalled that Bendetsen had started his regular army career at Fort Lewis. I admired the Historical Museum, a handsome, half-timbered structure resembling an Austrian hunting lodge, thinking that Bendetsen had probably been put up there during his induction as a captain in 1940.

My route continued westward. Yesterday's drive from a book signing in Portland had taken me through heavy wind-driven rain that sometimes set the car hydroplaning. Today's clear day seemed a blessing. The remains of a snow squall lingered in the Black Hills, west of Olympia. I watched for familiar corners and listened to descriptions of the impressive blowdown that had occurred in that storm—I had seen several fallen trees near Tacoma. The forecast was for clear, dry weather. Perhaps I would be able to see the mountain from our hill in Aberdeen.

After winding through miles of shady, tree-lined road it was refreshing to come into the open farmlands at Satsop and Brady. Almost home. On the hill to the south two enormous cooling towers idled, haunting remnants of the failed nuclear power project of the 1980s. The Chehalis River was in flood and had invaded willow-edged pastures. Ground fog shrouded fences. This area was the site of a major war game in the wet summer of 1941. I conjured images of sodden foot soldiers following heavy tanks, getting stuck in mud and fences, unable in the mist to see the opposing army. The United States Army's III Corps from Fort Ord was commanded by Major General Joseph W. Stilwell; General George C. Marshall, chief of staff, and Lieutenant General John L. DeWitt oversaw the final truce. The United States's lack of preparedness in 1939 and 1940 were factors that Bendetsen said had inspired him to go to Washington, D.C., to press for greater military spending, and to go on active duty in May 1940 as the Germans overtook France, and the British army was rescued from the beaches of Dunkirk.

A raw clay wall caught my eye. The entry to Aberdeen along the river had been widened. I missed the old route snaking along the base of the mossy Think O' Me Hill bluff that always dripped through a drape of wire mesh and threatened to drop rocks. The harbor opened up in front of me. The river was high, and I could see its mouth to the west. There were no ships along the docks where formerly huge sawmills stacked acres of lumber for export. Only two pulp and paper plants remain. The bend where the Chehalis River enters the bay was outlined in stacks of red logs. An enormous metal barge, the *Sanko Spruce*, headed out of the channel carrying tons of logs bound for Asia.

I noticed many changes as I drove through the downtown to my motel. The building that housed the print shop run by my uncle and then my father is strangely exposed, its neighbor torn down to provide a parking lot and bus terminal.[1] A vigorous mural depicting the Aberdeen train station in its heyday graces the exposed wall. The old Warner's movie theater is home to a revivalist church. The Wolff Building, site of Aberdeen's only department store and the former hub of downtown, is full of dusty antiques and "collectibles." The old Carnegie Library has given way to a modern building, one of ten Timberland Community Libraries in western Washington. I expected to spend research time there.

Settling into my room, I studied the views to the east and west, got out the phone book, and started to plan my quest. Though it was only four o'clock, the sun was close to the Pacific horizon. I thought I could smell the sea.

If I had ever met Karl Bendetsen, it would have been on my uncle's lawn when I was six years old. Bendetsen was a lawyer in Aberdeen and was probably among the friends of Uncle Jack who organized the wedding present that he and his wife Lillian talked about most—everyone brought canned goods with the label removed, filling a large clothes basket with shiny objects. As head of the family's print shop (where my father was the printer), Jack Clark edited the weekly *Grays Harbor Post* and knew everyone in town. He was a great practical joker. The basket of canned goods delighted him; he loved having a friend like Karl, who would organize such a thing.

There were many parties, but those I got to attend were held on Uncle Jack's lawn. The green area on the east side of the big house verged on a wooded gully and sat above the street and the bridge that connected to the next hill; downhill was Aberdeen's downtown. In those days you could see across houses and trees to the river and the wooded hills on the other side. Aunt Lil had laid out food—lots of whiskey, and other bottles wrapped in metal with cartridges that made fizzy water, bowls of olives, and a cabbage stuck with toothpicks—skewering shrimp—and looking like a porcupine. Some of the adults played badminton, which we had learned from one of Aunt Lil's sisters from San Diego. Jack and Chub Middleton and their buddies stood around and made each other laugh. My brother and I ran around the yard, hiding when anyone tried to talk to us. I was Uncle Jack's favorite, and sometimes he would catch me, turn me upside down, and then set me down to be introduced to someone. One of those someones could have been Karl Bendetson. "Miss Fancy-Nancy, I want you to meet my friend Karl," he'd say.

When caught for such an introduction, I'd tilt my head, one foot kicking the ground, waiting to get away. But I imagine Bendetson would have leaned over (he was as tall as my uncle) to ask me something. He would have tried to get me to talk or to make me laugh. Molly Middleton [Tuohy], who is a few years older than I, has many memories of Karl's treating her like a grown-up, and of his being interested in her life. Would he have charmed me? Would I have remembered?

In one of those years before my uncle and his friends left for the war, we watched an eclipse of the sun. My mother took me downtown to her father's drugstore, where he found strips of black exposed film in the darkroom near his prescription workbench. We went out onto the sidewalk as the day darkened to look at the shrinking sun through the strips. On that sidewalk, we were in front of the Saito's Japanese import store (which was also their home), and that may be when I met Mrs. Saito or her children, who were older than I and went to public school. Did my grandfather share the filmstrips with them? My mother loved to look at the trinkets in stores like that, and maybe that's where she bought the fancy doll that I kept in its box, the one with shiny black hair, a red kimono, and flat wooden shoes on stilts.

I didn't think about a connection between Bendetson and the Saito family until years later when I encountered a hostile newspaper column written by Kathy Hogan that appeared in our newspaper (my father was in charge by 1942). By then I was collecting Hogan's columns for the book *Cohassett Beach Chronicles*. Two of them gave such a negative view of Americans of Japanese ancestry that I wondered if I could ever understand a world in which that kind of hostility could be expressed. I tried to comprehend how a woman as urbane as Hogan was when I knew her in later years could have expressed such hatred. She equated the Japanese living in America with the wolf dressed as Little Red Riding Hood's grandmother:

> What to do with some thousands of Japanese citizens of the United States is a moot question on the Pacific coast. They are wearing their caps and glasses very nicely. But their presence here constitutes a dangerous hotbed from which the FBI has dragged many a wolf. Perhaps in due time we can present them with one of the lusher islands of the Japanese Archipelago.

The world must have looked different to people in 1942 than it did to me in the 1990s. I could not imagine such openly expressed dislike and distrust. Our Mrs. Saito who was arrested by the FBI was born to a high-class family in Japan, had studied music and poetry, and sang in the Methodist church choir. I could not believe such hatred justified our country's taking away the rights of some seventy thousand American citizens. In comments in later years, Bendetsen repeatedly said that we couldn't judge the time of the evacuation by today's standards, that you had to have been there. I decided to try to find out what that world was like, how it felt to those people, how Aberdeen might have contributed to the events of 1942.

The threads of my recollections about Bendetsen, my uncle, and the Japanese family began to feel connected and to take on importance when my youngest aunt described the reunion of her Aberdeen high school class of 1944. Since it was their fiftieth, the class had decided to throw a real bash, "a three-day affair," a celebration of reconnecting. More than a hundred survivors of that wartime group converged on Aberdeen for the 1994 weekend. They enjoyed a cocktail party Friday night, and many took part in a golf tournament on Saturday. On Saturday evening, attendees gathered on the steps of the Grays Harbor Country Club in the shade of enormous fir trees for the reunion photo—rows of seniors, now senior citizens, trying to look their best for the occasion and perhaps recalling the excitement of their graduation in the week of the Allied invasion of the Normandy beaches after D-Day. The banquet opened with a wine toast from a classmate who not only did not attend the reunion but also had not graduated with the class. Morse Saito had been forced to leave Aberdeen in June 1942 because of his ancestry. In May 1994 he wrote to the reunion committee that he'd like to "toast the best people in the best place in the world: Aberdeen's class of '44."

"Look at a map," Morse wrote from his home in Kobe, Japan, "and Aberdeen is always somehow kind of out of the way and stuck off in a corner. Corner? In that corner of my heart Aberdeen is a wonderful place which continues to nurture me and my growth." His letter to his classmates recounted his experiences from the time he left Aberdeen, telling of how he got out of Tule Lake, struggled to finish high school and college, and in 1949 had decided to go to Japan, "in search of my roots." He had gone as a missionary for the Methodist Church, and stayed on as an educator and newspaper columnist.

Laila Walli Silva, a member of the reunion committee, recalled Morse from high school: "We just knew one another, and then in '42, when they were taken from town, one day they were here and the next they were gone."

My aunt, Barbara Nielsen de Luna, attended that reunion and was so impressed with Morse's tribute that she sent me his letter. That Morse still valued his years in Aberdeen after what his country had done to him inspired me to write to him. I knew that Bendetsen had been my uncle's friend and that his father's store was on the same block as the Saitos'—all these thoughts roiled in my head, and I began to mold and shape the nucleus that grew to become this book. My interest in Bendetsen was developing into an obsession. Somehow Aberdeen held the key to this story.

Morse Saito wrote, "Describing my 'hometown' is like revealing a love affair. 'Tain't easy. Like so much of 'home' is so personal and intimate . . . so it is with Hometown."

For me, Aberdeen was two sets of grandparents, a print shop, and a drugstore, and scores of aunts and uncles. As the oldest granddaughter, one of the small cohort born during the Depression, I was treated like a little lady and enjoyed and demanded a lot of attention. I lived on "the hill," and though we were not rich, I had nice clothes and felt accepted and respected. During the war years I helped collect tin cans, rubber, and coffee jars—anything to help the war effort, because four of my uncles were fighting the war (and two weren't going to come home).

Morse recalled his wartime experience:

> During the bitterness of early 1943 in Tule Lake it was easy for 15-year-old-me to say my willingness to die for my country. I had many memories of Aberdeen, kids I grew up with, the Methodist church, seeing Aberdeen as one community though recognizing the differences of those who lived up on the hill and our living in a windowless section back of the store. We had friends in the whole community and we did not think about our differences (class? race? ancestry?) as determinants in living together or our future. Sure we knew such things as education would make a difference but these were available to all in Aberdeen. Now THAT's worth fighting for.

Aberdeen had many immigrant groups, but the goal seemed to be to assimilate into the mainstream—did this require giving up differences that mattered? The children of Finns learned to speak English and helped their parents understand American culture. Perry and Morse Saito could not hide the physical attributes of their race, but they could avoid learning Japanese and try to behave like the other kids. And there was no group of Asians for them to join, no "Oriental" club. They were Methodists, good students, and they got along. Especially Perry, who had a great sense of humor and could make fun of himself and of his being different. He had a way of doing something surprising to break the ice, to get you to listen to what he wanted to say.

Morse had a different experience when he was taken away from Aberdeen in 1942. "In Tule Lake it dawned on me how many of my new friends were different from me. They did not have 'Aberdeens' as I had assumed. Those from the rural farm communities of central California and even the city folks from Sacramento had hometowns in the form of their Japanese-ancestry communities. Their hometowns were uprooted with them to Tule Lake. Later as a missionary I met similar people in Kobe: stateless former Russians, overseas Chinese and Koreans in a Japanese culture that would always see them as foreigners. In fact, though my ancestry is Japanese I am seen as a 'strange Japanese' because of my American citizenship which I so highly prize . . . because I have a hometown."

WALKING IN TWO WORLDS

For Perry, as he grew up in Aberdeen, being Japanese had not been an issue, but prior to Pearl Harbor he was warned that he would suffer discrimination because of his race. Nisei growing up in communities with sizable Japanese populations apparently had a more direct experience. The family of Masuo Yasui of Hood River, Oregon, was one such family. (Minoru Yasui, one of Perry's heroes because he protested the evacuation, was one of his children.) An immigrant, Yasui succeeded as a businessman, orchardist, and community leader in Hood River. While they were successful in school, several of his eight children reported that "to be a Nisei was to be two people: a dutiful child of Japan who honored parents and respected authority as well as an adventuresome, independent-minded American youngster who tested limits. . . . To be a Nisei was to participate fully in American life—school, church, sports.

. . . Yet it was also to be told and treated as if you were irredeemably different." The Yasui children "all grew up feeling their 'two-ness.'"[2]

For example, the friends of Michi Yasui, who graduated from Hood River High School as salutatorian in 1939, remembered that she had been "one of the gang," and "just another girl." But when the gang reached dating age, Michi was no longer invited to parties, nor did she go to mixed-gender social events or dances. She accepted this. Her older brother Homer was ever conscious of being a person with a Japanese face and was always mindful of his father's insistence that he be careful about his deportment (they all felt that) around *hakujin* (Caucasians). All the Yasui Nisei, growing up before the war mentioned times when they were left out, called "Jap," denied something, or teased. Perry Saito, who was the same age as Michi, had the gift of humor, and may have been more able to deflect taunts with a joke.

Nisei in the large Japanese communities such as the *Nihonmachi* (Japan town) in Los Angeles experienced more discrimination when they went outside their sheltered community. Richard Nishimoto, a San Francisco Issei, earned an engineering degree at Stanford University in the years that Bendetsen was there. The only Japanese American engineering graduate in his class, Nishimoto was the only Stanford engineer not offered a job during campus interviews; he was forced to find other work, as an insurance broker or tax preparer.[3] During internment, he was an effective leader and researcher in the Poston Relocation Center, but after the war was still unable to find a job that required his engineering education.

At Stanford, Bendetsen could deny or hide his Jewishness and could "pass" as a WASP. It was not so for Nishimoto, nor for Fred Korematsu, the American citizen who resorted to plastic surgery to try to alter his eyelids to avoid the evacuation (and who gained prominence as his case challenging the constitutionality of the evacuation worked its way through the courts).

Perry and Morse Saito had been unique in Aberdeen: Morse recalled, "We were very conscious of being Japanese in ancestry but never felt anything but being 'American.'" Perry's friend Rudy Kauhanen agreed—"We danced with the same girls." Rudy had expected Perry would marry some local Caucasian girl.

Morse wrote, "[the] Yasui's 'two-ness,' I understand very well but not from Aberdeen. For me it came later," as it did for Perry. It had not been easy to get into Illinois Wesleyan University for either Morse or Perry because the school was afraid of getting too many Japanese Americans.

Morse was accepted "on one condition"; he explained, "I was admitted on 'social probation.'" The school official clarified, "If someone from town throws a brick at you, *you* are automatically expelled."

As was true of many other evacuees from the Pacific Northwest, Perry and Morse did not harbor a lot of resentment because of past discrimination. Morse wrote, "Thus in Tule Lake we did not hold the bitterness many others held. One group of the most bitter in Tule Lake kept calling us '*inu*' [dog or spy in Japanese] and we were on a hit list. . . . Perhaps the greatest support we had in Tule Lake was our experiences on 'the outside'—namely Aberdeen." Aberdeen had given them the feeling of having been accepted.

Perry Saito was a man larger than his times, a man proud to be American, a Nisei who loved doughnuts, a man taught by his Japanese father to turn the other cheek and to be upright. He had to revise his worldview as an evacuee suddenly surrounded by Japanese faces. He encountered strong racist views in his work for the FOR, had trouble getting his first job (and couldn't even hope to get a minister's position in the Pacific Northwest). He was happy to go to Wisconsin "as the first 'colored' minister, as a missionary to the Wisconsin conference."

Years of being the only Japanese American in largely Caucasian Wisconsin may have worn Perry down, and he would sometimes assert that because of his experience and how he was treated, he was Japanese (though he was embarrassed when visiting Japan not to be able to speak Japanese). How many times was he told by some stranger in a U.S. town, "Oh, you parked that Subaru expertly, just like an American!"

Bendetsen was a man of his time, a time that accepted racism as the norm. He was a promising young man with ambitions, and he spent his life in an endless quest for preferment and place, and did what was necessary to avoid loss of place. Perry Saito was a *rara avis*, a rare bird, a pacifist among super-patriot Nisei, a man of empathy who could turn a critic into a friend, who could put himself in another's place, who could always say, "There but for the grace of God go I." Bendetsen and Saito undoubtedly had moments when they might have wished that life were other than it was in the America of the 1930s and 1940s. They were each members of a minority in their town. They each may, at times, have had the uncomfortable awareness of not being quite right, like a hyperactive student who has forgotten to take his Ritalin and must struggle to appear to fit in. In a country that talked of justice for all but maintained a segregated army, in a country that would allow naturalization to all immigrants except Asians, a country that tolerated anti-Semitism, how could they find comfort and acceptance?

There were understandable reasons for Karl Bendetsen to revise his ancestry and to deny his Jewishness. Anti-Semitism was widespread and socially acceptable in the United States in the years prior to World War II. Many in America saw the Jews as a distinct race, as a group that kept itself apart, that set up cultural and religious barriers isolating itself from others. This isolation bred prejudice and distrust (as it had for Americans of Japanese ancestry). A Jew could not join many social groups, there were restrictive covenants against Jews purchasing homes in some housing areas, the Ivy League colleges had quotas for Jewish applicants, and many Jewish professionals were denied positions in eastern universities. As a suspect minority, Jews became convenient scapegoats.

Bendetsen could do something about his identity: He denied his Jewish faith to join a fraternity, and he changed the spelling of his name and began asserting that he descended "from a long line of Danish, uh, lumbermen" who moved from Maine to Michigan to the Northwest.[4] He added a Danish great-grandfather to his family tree at about the time that he married his third wife, a woman with socialite friends in Palm Beach.

By the time he changed the spelling to Bendetsen in 1942 he had spent almost two years in Washington, D.C., and may have encountered the more virulent sorts of anti-Semitism that were prevalent on the East Coast at that time. He may have met the Bendetson families of Massachusetts and New York who, like him, were descended from Lithuanians, but who were openly Jewish.[5] Did he fear being linked to that family? I hoped to get some insight into his motivations from his family.

Bendetsen's son, Brookes, a fiftyish stockbroker and former navy pilot, welcomed me into his comfortable San Mateo, California, mission-style home on a bluff overlooking the bay and the San Francisco airport. He was tall and had a long face, but otherwise I didn't see a resemblance to his father, whom I recall only from photographs. He seemed confident but not overbearing, a man who was comfortable with himself. He wasn't sure that he knew anything that would help me. He didn't think his father had anything to do with the decision to evacuate. He said his father had 'this real patriotic bent, he always said he was a nut about that. . . . I think he probably would have liked to have made General. . . . I think Milton Eisenhower was basically instrumental in blocking his promotion." His father, he said, "also blame[d] Milton Eisenhower for what he said was deterioration of the process of internment and the confiscation of their [evacuees'] property."

Brookes described how he learned about the internment experience. He and his wife visited Karl and Gladys in Acapulco. His father had walked around a pool as he talked. "He was basically like a tape recorder, he had this photographic memory on this," as he paced around the pool. His father had said that "he was not in charge of this operation very long, he was in and out. . . . It wasn't my Dad's idea to intern the Japanese on the West Coast to the best of my knowledge. It was not. I really doubt that it was. A lieutenant colonel in the army does not concoct an internment idea.

"My other view on this was that my dad was strongly against revisionist history . . . and that's why he maintained steadfastly that there should not be any reparations." As he paced that pool, his father had talked about "the great concern about Japanese Americans, Japanese who were not U.S. citizens, there was a great deal of hatred at that time toward the Japanese, for what they did at Pearl Harbor and what was done out in the Far East." Even as he talked to his son years later, it was apparent that Bendetsen had not been able to separate the World War II enemy from Americans of Japanese ancestry.

His father insisted that "it was all done with the idea that all the property was protected, nothing was going to be seized, confiscated." Brookes observed, "As it turned out, I guess the process broke down."

Brookes Bendetsen said of his father, "I don't think he had a malicious bone in his body. I know he was not racist in any way, shape or form. Whatever he did at that point in time, I think he believed it was an absolute necessity, and I think governments . . . should always err on the side of national security. I think that was his absolute approach. . . . If he ever had misgivings about it they were never expressed to me." Echoing statements that his father had expressed in many letters and testimony, he said, "You would have had to have been there at the time to really witness, have the feeling of what was going on, and how the army felt about it at that point in time, as to where the policy ever originated.

"But as you said, he was persuasive, any task, he was always on task."

In the course of the interview, I drew his attention to a newspaper article from the *Grays Harbor Post* that included the two spellings of his surname. The article talked of the "Bendetson" who had been a successful lawyer in Aberdeen, then, probably because it was written using the language of the government press release, referred to Bendetsen's receiving the Distinguished Service Medal. Brookes said, "You know, he changed the spelling of the name. As far as I know. At some point, to make it easier, seemingly. Make it easier to, uh, spell."

I did not ask what he knew about his father's ancestry.

Bendetsen was ambitious. From his first experience outside Grays Harbor, at Stanford, he apparently saw that there would be fewer barriers, that opportunities would be greater, the possibilities for success more varied, if he were not Jewish. "He had the right to do what he did. Many do," said Ruth Wolff, the wife of Bendetsen's former good friend in Aberdeen.

Perry Saito and Karl Bendetsen had different views on how to deal with the prejudice of their time. At that lunch counter in Indianapolis, Perry could not let the waitress serve him because that would be showing that he agreed that he was better than the black man who wasn't being served. He could not "pass on the other side of the road." He would have thought less of Bendetsen for giving up being a Jew because of widespread prejudice against Jews in this country. In Perry's Gandhian view, that meant he had gone over to the side of the anti-Semites. For Bendetsen, who found himself in the midst of anti-Japanese racists like General DeWitt, that may have seemed like the least of his problems.

I think Bendetsen's smothering of his background is mainly significant because of the price he paid. He became invested in denial. He could not admit that anything that he had ever done had been an error. He could not give anyone the satisfaction of hearing, "Yes, in hindsight, we made a mistake." In those years, Earl Warren and Tom Clark observed the changed public perception of the incarceration; it had become acceptable, even expected, to admit that Japanese Americans were wrongly detained. Though he did not do so publicly during his lifetime, Warren saw to it that there was an apology in his memoir. For Bendetsen, one denial led to the next. He had to deny the enormity of what he had done in conceiving the executive order and to deny the effect that it had on the Japanese community. He could not give up the crutch of military necessity. In later years he could not even admit that the environment he had carefully put in place in the relocation camps, such as barbed wire fences and guard towers (with the guns facing inward), had existed. Denial (combined with Alzheimer's in his later years) creates a potent amnesia.

What I respond to in the stories about Bendetsen that were told by his son and others is the fact that during his duty on the West Coast, Karl had always remembered that my uncle and the rest of Aberdeen's marine reserve in the Philippines had been captured by the Japanese army in the first months of the war. He felt that what he was doing might affect their well-being. But this idea caused him to equate the Americans of Japanese ancestry (who were not prisoners of war) with those American prisoners, and then to hold the evacuees responsible for the cruelties perpetrated by the Japanese army.

Throughout World War II my child's-eye view of the enemy was shaped by government propaganda programs. I saw the posters depicting the Japanese as monkey-like, sinister, slant-eyed people. I watched newsreels showing images of ferocious Japanese troops defending positions in the Pacific Islands and being defeated. I watched my Aunt Lil and my father wait anxiously for Red Cross letters from the prison camp. I remember the day that the telegram arrived. But somehow I managed to keep separate my recollection of the nice people who had run the Oriental Gift Shop next to my grandfather's drugstore from that enemy in the newsreels. What a shame that Karl Bendetsen could not do the same.

APPENDICES

APPENDIX A

Executive Order 9066

AUTHORIZING THE SECRETARY OF WAR TO PRESCRIBE MILITARY AREAS

"Whereas, The successful prosecution of the war requires every possible protection against espionage and against sabotage to national-defense material, national-defense premises and national-defense utilities as defined in Section 4, Act of April 20, 1918, 40 Stat. 533, as amended by the Act of November 30, 1940, 54 Stat. 1220, and the Act of August 21, 1941, 55 Stat. 655 (U.S.C., Title 50, Sec. 104):

"NOW, THEREFORE, by virtue of the authority vested in me as President of the United States, and Commander in Chief of the Army and Navy, I hereby authorize and direct the Secretary of War, and the Military Commanders whom he may from time to time designate, whenever he or any designated Commander deems such action necessary or desirable, to prescribe military areas in such places and of such extent as he or the appropriate Military Commander may determine, from which any or all persons may be excluded, and with respect to which, the right of any person to enter, remain in, or leave shall be subject to whatever restriction the Secretary of War or the appropriate Military Commander may impose in his discretion. The Secretary of War is hereby authorized to provide for residents of any such area who are excluded therefrom, such transportation, food, shelter, and other accommodations as may be necessary, in the judgement of the Secretary of War or the said Military Commander, and until other arrangements are made, to accomplish the purpose of this order. The designation of military areas in any region or locality shall supersede designations of prohibited and restricted areas by the Attorney General under the Proclamations of December 7 and 8, 1941, and shall supersede the responsibility and authority of the Attorney General under the said Proclamations in respect of such prohibited and restricted areas.

"I hereby further authorize and direct the Secretary of War and the said

Military Commanders to take such other steps as he or the appropriate Military Commander may deem advisable to enforce compliance with the restrictions applicable to each military area hereinabove authorized to be designated, including the use of Federal troops and other Federal Agencies, with authority to accept assistance of state and local agencies.

"I hereby further authorize and direct all Executive Departments, independent establishments, and other Federal Agencies, to assist the Secretary of War or the said Military Commanders in carrying out this Executive Order, including the furnishing of medical aid, hospitalization, food, clothing, transportation, use of land, shelter, and other supplies, equipment, utilities, facilities, and services.

"This order shall not be construed as modifying or limiting in any way the authority heretofore granted under Executive Order No. 8972, dated December 12, 1941, nor shall it be construed as limiting or modifying the duty and responsibility of the Federal Bureau of Investigation, with respect to the investigations of alleged acts of sabotage or the duty and responsibility of the Attorney General and the Department of Justice under the Proclamations of December 7 and 8, 1941, prescribing regulations for the conduct and control of alien enemies, except as such duty and responsibility is superseded by the designation of military areas hereunder."

Franklin D. Roosevelt
The White House, February 19, 1942

APPENDIX B

Classification Questionnaire for Statement of Military Qualifications

BIOGRAPHICAL: Date 7/5/42

Name in full: BENDETSEN KARL ROBIN
(Last name) (First name) (Middle name)

Date of birth: October 11, 1908.

Place of birth: Aberdeen, Washington.
(City or town) (State)

Parent's names: Albert M. Bendetsen

Anna Benson Bendetsen

Education: (Give dates of graduation and specify school)

Leland Stanford Jr. AB, LLB. 1929, 1932, respectively
(University or College) (Degree) (Date of Graduation)

Nearest Relative: BENDETSEN BILLIE McINTOSH (wife)
(Last name) (First name) (Middle name)

Permanent address: 1756 North Point Street, San Francisco, California
(Street and number) (City) (State)

MILITARY:

Rank: Colonel

Serial number: 0-22885

Component A.U.S. (RA)

Organization: General Staff Corps (Assistant Chief of Staff Western Defense Command & 4th Army, Civil Affairs Division)

Date of original entrance into Army: May 3, 1940

Entered Army from: Reserve Corps

Ranks held in Army with dates: Captain, May 3, 1940

Major, April 4, 1941

~~Lieutenant Colonel, February 1, 1942~~

Colonel, February 1, 1942

-1-

Date of marriage March 3, 1938

350

Page two--

Military Schools attended: none

Outstanding performance of duty with citations or decorations:
(List briefly with circumstances)

Commendatory citations received for each military event listed below, on file with The Adjutant General

Serious wounds in line of duty:
(List briefly with circumstances unless given above)

none

Important events in civilian or military career:

As War Dept. Representative; drafted and processed Soldiers and Sailors ~~Civil Relief Act of 1940 through Congress, established Regulations~~

Developed basis for, regulations and organization of new Army Exchange system (abolishing the old share system), the and

As War Dept. Representative, drafted processed and steered through committees and on the floor of House and Senate, the Service Extension Act of 1941.

As one of the original 5 officers comprising it, assisted in establishing and organizing the Office of The Provost Marhhal General. Organized and directed the Aliens Division thereof; the Prisoner of War Information Bureau; set up the International channels for exchange of information on Prisoners of War and Internees; wrote complete new compilation of regulations for handling and processing prisoners of war from point of capture; also for operation of enclosures and camps; initiated and carried out the application of Geneva Convention relative to Prisoners of War and civilian internees by the U.S. and other warring nations.

Conceived, drafted and processed executive order 9066, authorizing creation of military areas and control and exclusion of civilians therein.

Conceived and organized the Civil Affairs Division and the Wartime Civil Control Administration of Western Defense Command.

Conceived the method, formulated the detailed plans for, and directed the evacuation of 120,000 persons of Japanese ancestry from military areas of the Pacific Coast.

Conceived and drafted Executive order and precise operating instructions for seizure of North American Aviation Plant in spring of 1941.

Conceived and drafted Executive order, prepared precise operating instructions for and took possession of Air Associates pla Bendix, New Jersey. Had full responsibility for directing operations and negotiated withdrawal of government without liability for operations.

350

Date for Preliminary Classification Questionnaire
(June 23, 1942)

Karl R. Bendetsen 0-22885
AUS GSC COMPONENT AUS(RA)

Ht. 5ft 10½ in. Weight 160 lbs. Born October 11, 1908

Appointed regular army May 3, 1940

	Captain	Major	Lt.Colonel	Colonel
Date of appointment	T(May 3'40	T Apr.7'41	T(Feb.4,1942	T)March 12,'42
Date of rank in grade	May 3'40	April 4'41	Feb.1,1942	Feb. 1, 1942

Legal residente: Finch bldg. Aberdeen, Wash.

Emergency addressee: Mrs. Karl R. Bendetsen, wife
1756 No. Point St., SF

Education:
High School, Aberdeen High , 1925
College, Leland Stanford Jr. University, AB 1929
" LLB 1932

Born Aberdeen

Parents names: Albert M.
Anna Benson

Note: Although this copy of the brief is hand-edited by KRB, he failed to notice that his year of birth was incorrectly typed as 1908 rather than 1907.

APPENDIX C

Bendetson Family Tree

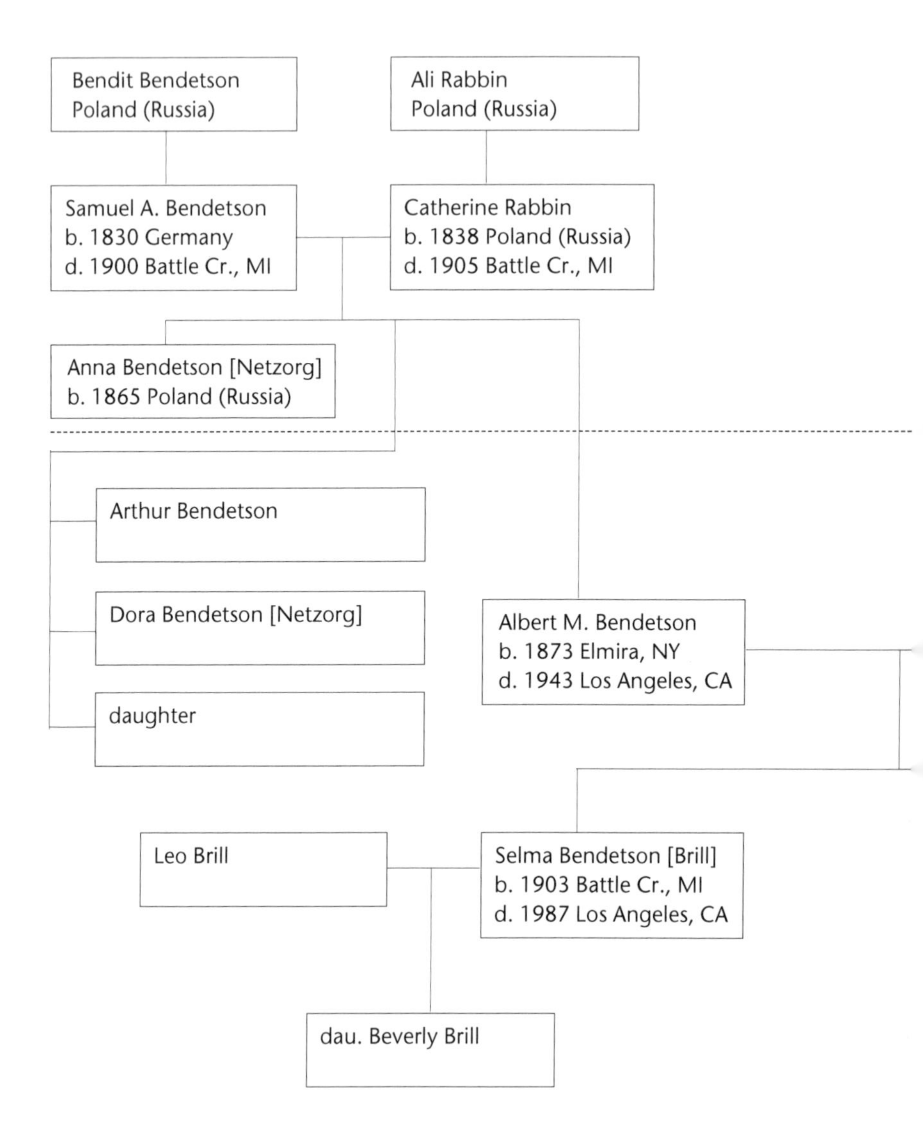

Bendetson dates and places of birth from 1900 census, Battle Creek, MI.
Bentson dates and places of birth from 1880 census, Minneapolis, MN.
Other dates from U.S. vital records and KRB FBI file.
Lithuania was part of the Russian Pale of Settlement in the nineteenth century.

Notes: Anna Bentson Bendetson's death record gives an age four years younger than fact.
Bentson twins were 4 in the 1880 census, and 8 in the 1884 orphanage application.

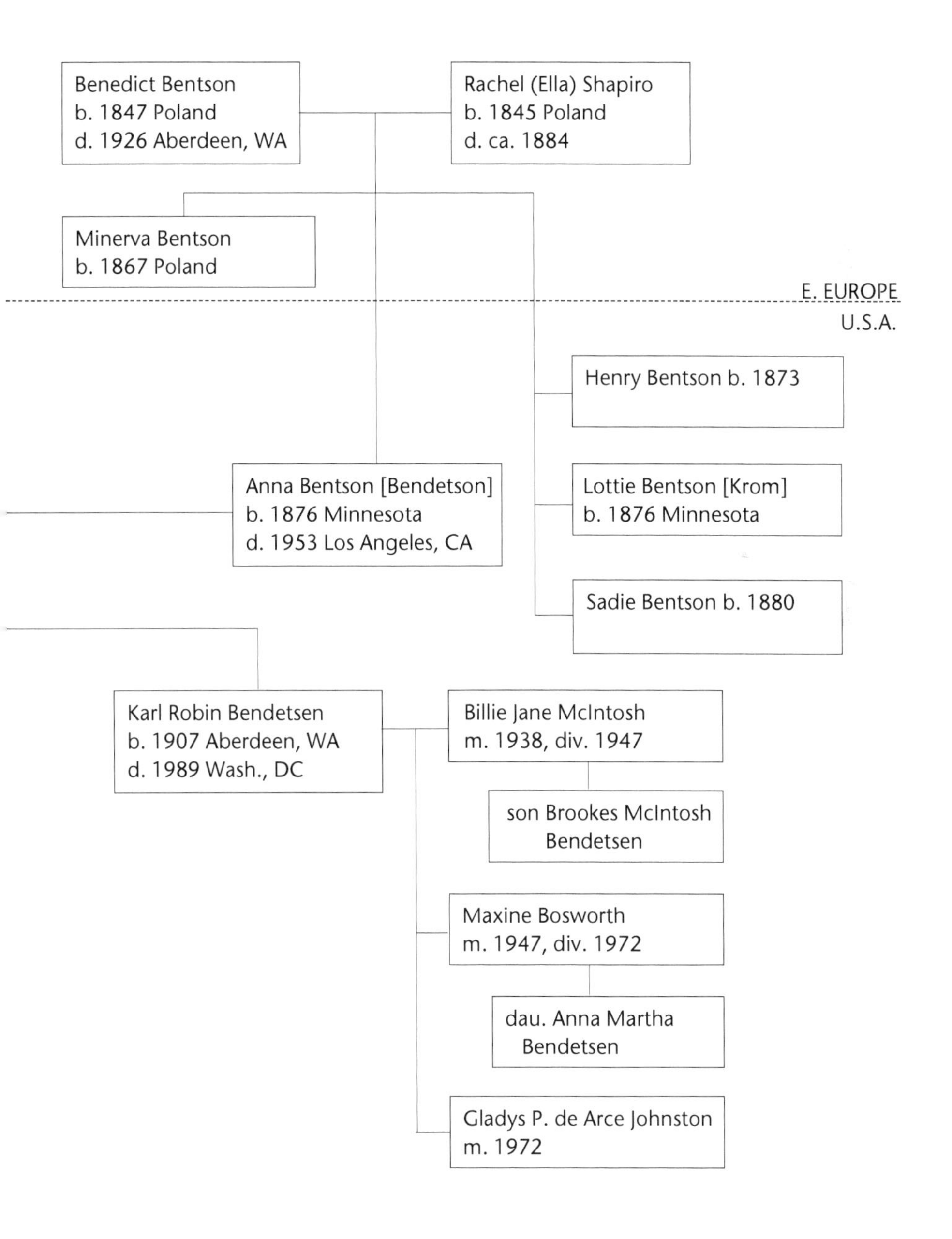
Benedict Bentson
b. 1847 Poland
d. 1926 Aberdeen, WA
Rachel (Ella) Shapiro
b. 1845 Poland
d. ca. 1884
Minerva Bentson
b. 1867 Poland
E. EUROPE
U.S.A.
Henry Bentson b. 1873
Anna Bentson [Bendetson]
b. 1876 Minnesota
d. 1953 Los Angeles, CA
Lottie Bentson [Krom]
b. 1876 Minnesota
Sadie Bentson b. 1880
Karl Robin Bendetsen
b. 1907 Aberdeen, WA
d. 1989 Wash., DC
Billie Jane McIntosh
m. 1938, div. 1947
son Brookes McIntosh
Bendetsen
Maxine Bosworth
m. 1947, div. 1972
dau. Anna Martha
Bendetsen
Gladys P. de Arce Johnston
m. 1972

Saito Family Tree

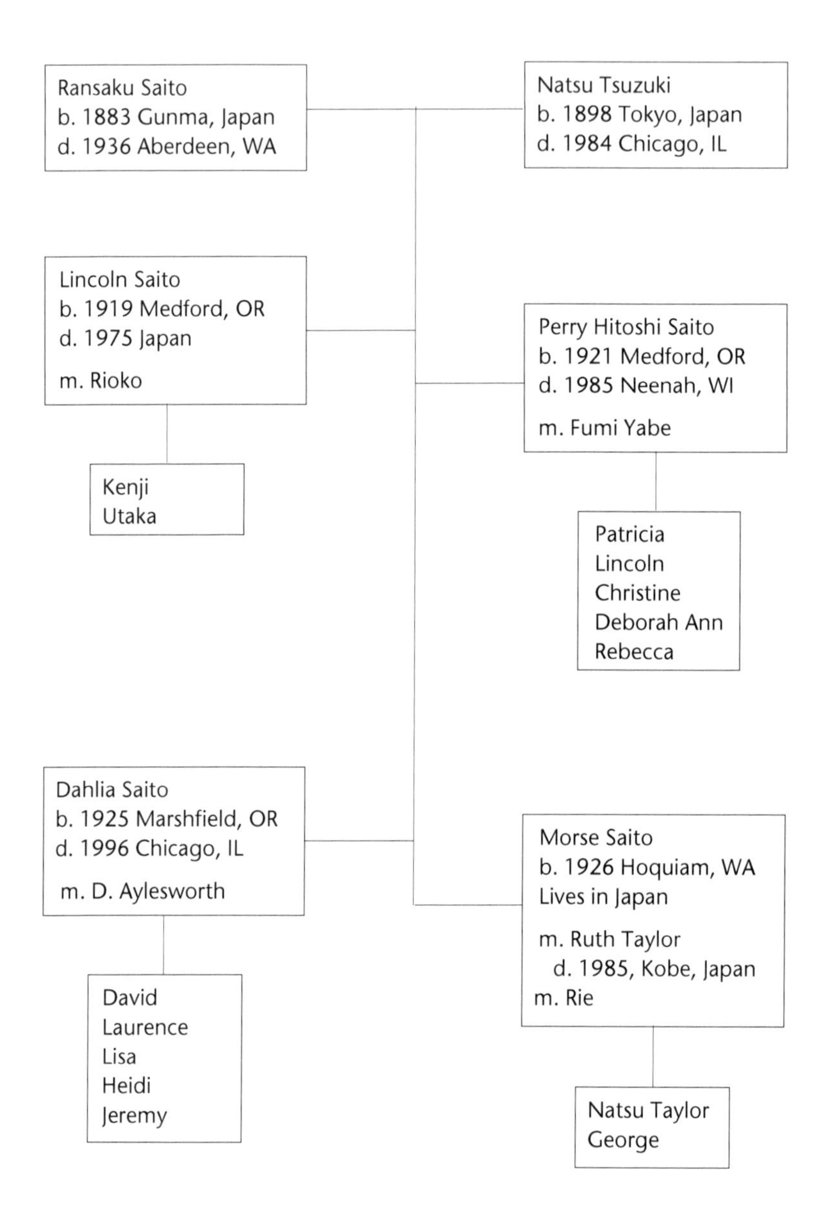

APPENDIX D

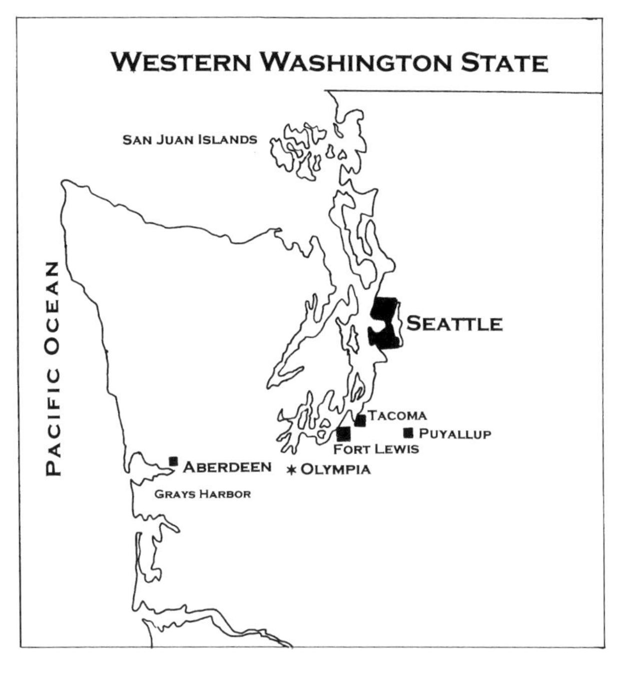
WESTERN WASHINGTON STATE
SAN JUAN ISLANDS
PACIFIC OCEAN
SEATTLE
TACOMA
PUYALLUP
FORT LEWIS
ABERDEEN
OLYMPIA
GRAYS HARBOR

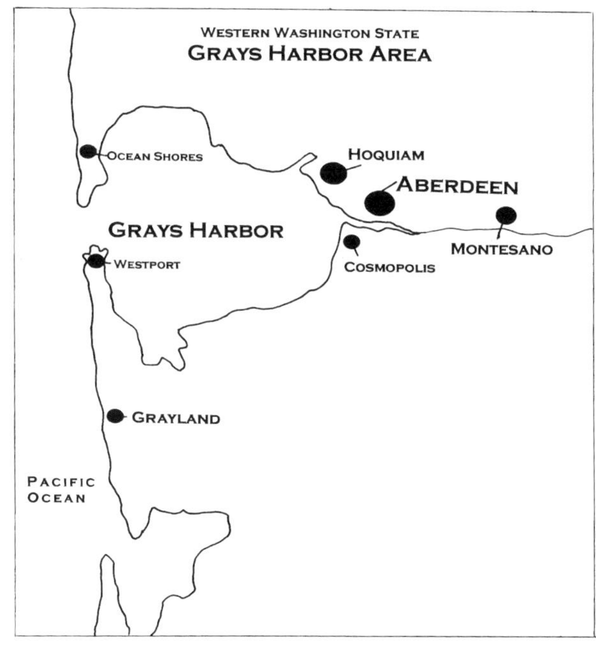
WESTERN WASHINGTON STATE
GRAYS HARBOR AREA
OCEAN SHORES
HOQUIAM
ABERDEEN
GRAYS HARBOR
WESTPORT
COSMOPOLIS
MONTESANO
GRAYLAND
PACIFIC
OCEAN

APPENDIX E

WRA Relocation Centers

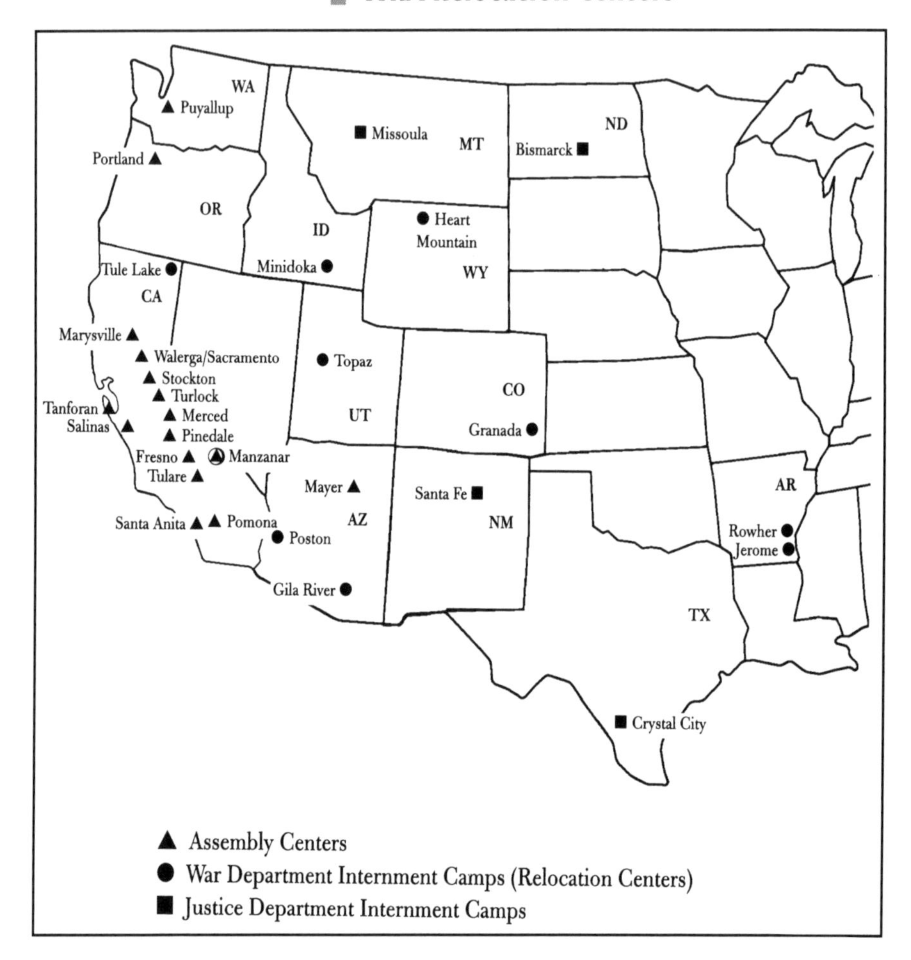

ABBREVIATIONS

ACC i	American Concentration Camps, ed. R Daniels, Vols. 1–10.
ACLU	American Civil Liberties Union
Battling Windmills	Column by Morse Saito in *Mainichi Daily News*, Tokyo & Osaka, Japan
CWRIC	Committee on Wartime Relocation and Internment of Civilians
FBI	Federal Bureau of Investigation
FOR	Fellowship of Reconciliation
HST papers	Papers from Harry S Truman Presidential Library, Independence, Missouri
JAG	Judge Advocate General
JACL	Japanese American Citizens League
KRB papers	Papers of Karl R. Bendetsen in the Hoover Institution Archives, Stanford University, Stanford, California
NJASRC	National Japanese American Student Relocation Council
NCJAR	National Council for Japanese American Redress
Oral History-KRB	Oral History Interview with Karl R. Bendetsen, by Jerry N. Hess, Harry S Truman Library, New York City, NY, October 24, November 9 and November 21, 1972.
PMG	Provost Marshal General
Watanabe	Watanabe Clipping File, Wing Luke Asian Museum, Seattle.
WCCA	Wartime Civil Control Administration
WDC	Western Defense Command
WRA	War Relocation Authority
WPA	Works Progress Administration

NOTES

Introduction

[1] CWRIC, *Personal Justice Denied*, 265.
[2] Weglyn, *Years of Infamy*, 344.
[3] *Nisei* is Japanese for the second generation—the children of *Issei*, the immigrants.

CHAPTER 1: 1981: Revisionism or Redress?

[1] Interview with Brookes M. Bendetsen, son of Karl R. Bendetsen, San Mateo, California, March 5, 1997.
[2] Letter to Harold D. Austin from KRB, December 4, 1979. KRB papers, box 324.
[3] Bendetsen's détente speech was presented in New York, and later in Washington, D.C., reprinted in *Manchester Guardian*, August 1975, KRB papers, box 274; see FitzGerald, *Way Out There in the Blue*, 131–46, Bendetsen's High Frontier group was later and falsely given credit for inspiring President Ronald Reagan's "Star Wars" speech, and see Chapter 13; KRB correspondence with Edward Teller, 1981–82, KRB papers, box 351.
[4] Description from Kai Bird, who interviewed Bendetsen in 1983 regarding his contacts with John J. McCloy, for his book *The Chairman: John J. McCloy, The Making of the American Establishment*. Of the interview conducted on November 10, 1983, Bird noted: "Mr. Bendetsen was well-dressed and seemingly well-occupied, although there was nothing on his desk to indicate that he did much paper work. He wore Presidential-seal cufflinks."
[5] Letter from Caspar W. Weinberger to KRB, January 5, 1981. KRB papers, box 290.
[6] Letter to Philip Tajitsu Nash, March 7, 1980. KRB papers, box 324.
[7] "The Japanese Americans," *Washington Post*, July 15, 1981. KRB papers, box 321.
[8] Letter to John J. McCloy, August 14, 1981. KRB papers, box 321.
[9] During World War II, "Japanese American" was never hyphenated. By the 1980s the term was, as noted in the quote from the *Washington Post*.
[10] Letter to Harold D. Austin, KRB papers, box 324. Harold Austin, son of Doc O. R. Austin, was Kearny Clark's best friend in Aberdeen; after a career with the Washington Highway Patrol, he retired to California.
[11] Hohri, *Repairing America*, 157. See also chap. 13.

[12] *Aberdeen Daily World*, Associated Press story from Washington, D.C., probably from November 3, 1981. The account of Bendetsen's testimony appears under the headline: "Aberdeen Native Puzzles Relocation Panel." Source: Ann Hobi Scroggs, Hood Canal.

[13] *Aberdeen Daily World*, "Aberdeen Native."

[14] Ibid.

[15] Ibid.

[16] KRB papers, box 321.

[17] *Time*, November 30, 1942.

[18] *Who's Who in America, 1944–1945.*

[19] *Who's Who in America, 1986–1987.* KRB's entry of '55–'56 mentions the evacuation but omits the "conceived . . . " language; interview with Brookes M. Bendetsen, San Mateo, California, March 5, 1997.

[20] Gordon Hirabayashi, a senior at the University of Washington, and a Quaker, refused to register for the evacuation and was arrested. His became the second of the five cases challenging the legality of the curfew, evacuation, and/or internment. Fred Korematsu of Oakland failed to report to an assembly center. The cases went all the way to the Supreme Court, which in 1944 affirmed their convictions. The cases were reexamined in 1985. See chap. 13.

[21] *National Cyclopedia of American Biography*, 481–83. See also chap. 12.

[22] "Oral testimony of Perry H. Saito of Wauwatosa, Wisconsin, on September 23, 1981, to Commission on Wartime Relocation and Internment of Civilians." Chicago CWRIC Hearing. Source: Fumi Saito, Stevens Point, Wisconsin. Hereafter cited as Saito testimony.

[23] "Tulelake" was a nearby place in California, but the relocation camp was called Tule Lake and given a postal address of Newell, California; Saito testimony.

[24] Interviews with Fumi Saito and several of their children.

[25] Saito testimony, emphasis in original.

[26] Perry Saito speech transcribed verbatim by confidential informant T–5, December 9, 1943. FBI file of Perry Saito, p. 13. Found in Perry Saito's ICF (internment case file), National Archives; obtained by Fumi Saito, 1997.

[27] Saito testimony.

[28] Marion Kline, who attended ministry school with Perry, described his answer to whether he'd met up with any prejudice: Kline quoted Perry: "When anybody spit in my face, I would just say, 'make you feel better?'" Kline continued, "Very noncommital, without any anger whatsoever. He would say this with an expression on his face. In the first place, why would anybody spit in his face, in the second, why didn't he get mad? Why didn't he hit the guy back. But that was never his response. His response was always to be friends with a person no matter how he treated him." Interview with Marion Kline at home of Herman and Rita Will, Des Moines, Washington, December 1, 1997.

[29] Saito testimony.

[30] *Chicago Tribune*, November 24, 1981.

[31] "Behind Barbed Wire: Love Conquered All During War Years," by Polly Hackett, published in *Wauwatosa News Times* (Wisconsin), 1980. Source: Fumi Saito.

CHAPTER 2: Birds of Passage

[1] Daniels, *Asian America*, 115 and 127.

[2] CWRIC, *Personal Justice Denied*, 29.

[3] Ibid., 21.

[4] Johnson set a precedent. A subsequent publisher, Russell V. Mack, "used the *Washingtonian* as a springboard to Congress in 1947." Van Syckle, *The River Pioneers*, 273. Mack is mentioned in chap. 3.

[5] Biography of Johnson by Roger Daniels, published in *American National Biography*. The Johnson quote is from 1927.

[6] *Final Report*, 368. Report in *Aberdeen Daily World*, May 23, 1942, indicated that the army expected to remove 102 Japanese residents from these counties and only one from Grays Harbor. (Most would come from Thurston County.) The number probably increased because of children.

[7] Ichihashi, *Japanese in the United States*, 78.

[8] Paul Spickard, *Japanese Americans*, 33.

[9] Gunma Prefecture is situated in the northwestern part of the Kanto Region, being bounded on the east by Tochigi, on the south by Saitama, on the west by Nagano, and on the north by Niigata and Fukushima Prefectures. It is bordered by mountains on the east, the west, and the north. The southeastern part of the prefecture belongs to the Kanto Plains, which has many hills, plateaus, ravines, rivers, lakes, and hot springs.

[10] Accent marks, called macrons, are indicated for Japanese names in the section describing the lives of the Saitos in Japan.

[11] In the 1990s, konnyaku was touted as a health food, a high-fiber, low-calorie food good for controlling one's weight, improving digestion, and possibly reducing cholesterol.

[12] Morse Saito writes a newspaper column entitled "Battling Windmills" for the *Mainichi Daily News*, an English-language publication in Tokyo and Osaka. This account appeared in, "Memories of Medieval Japan," *Mainichi Daily News*, July 21, 1997. Morse heard the story in Chicago, just after leaving Tule Lake camp. Also, author's correspondence.

[13] Communications with Morse Saito; FBI file of Natsu Saito.

[14] Ichioka, *The Issei*, 11.

[15] Much of the information about the lives of Ransaku and Natsu Saito in Japan comes from communications with Morse Saito between 1996 and 2000. For Natsu Saito there is also detailed information in her internment case file.

[16] Ibid.

[17] Dahlia Saito Aylesworth's daughter Lisa tells this story. Telephone conversation with Lisa Aylesworth, October 6, 1997.

[18] Tamura, *The Hood River Issei*, 16–17.

Years later, Natsu (as adults, Japanese women often dropped the suffix -ko) talked to a granddaughter about her marriages. Widowed in 1936, she had remarried after World War II. Natsu's granddaughter Lisa Aylesworth recalled: "She said she had to marry Grandpa Saito because her parents arranged it and she loved him in certain ways, but it was not the deep kind of love . . . and she said that her second marriage was a deeper sort of love. Not lustful or anything, but it was a deep love, enduring love." Sadly, that marriage ended after five years when Mr. Orita died of cancer. Telephone conversation with Lisa Aylesworth, October 6, 1997.

[19] Ito, *Issei: A History of Japanese Immigrants in North America*, 41.

[20] Quoted in Linda Tamura, "High Hopes, Subtle Realities.

[21] Tamura, *Hood River Issei*, 54.

[22] Letter from Morse Saito, May 27, 1998. The third child, Dahlia, was born in Marshfield, Oregon.

[23] Telephone interview with Nani (Naoko) Saito Yahiro, March 31, 1998.

[24] Telephone interview with Bill Jones, November 27, 1992. Jones continues to run the family photography business in Aberdeen.

[25] Telephone interview with Morse Saito, January 27, 1998.

[26] Aberdeen residents always said "Sato" rather than "Saito." Even in 1997, Rita Irle Will, who had met Perry before the war, remembered him as Perry "Sato."

[27] One of Perry's granddaughters heard this on a visit to Japan.

[28] Interview with Marvin Reiner, February 7, 1996. Reiner, by then a dealer for Honda motorcycles, visited Japan in the early 1960s.

[29] Correspondence from Morse Saito, January 28, 1998.

[30] Morse Saito, "Changing Images of Christmas," *Mainichi Daily News*, January 25, 1995.

[31] Author interviews with Rudy Kauhanen, February 9, 1996, and March 16, 1997, Aberdeen, Washington; Rudy's collection of school yearbooks.

[32] Some linguists hypothesize that Japanese is related to the Ural-Altaic languages, which would explain some common linguistic traits found in Finnish and Japanese.

[33] Author interviews with Rudy Kauhanen, February 9, 1996, and March 16, 1997, Aberdeen, Washington.

[34] Ibid.

[35] Perry Saito interview in Roger Axford, *Too Long Been Silent*, 77. Perry said that he had never said this before to a non-Japanese, or to any group.

[36] *Grays Harbor Post*, March 1936.

[37] *Aberdeen Daily World*, March 10, 1936. (The evening paper reported that there had been a suicide "this morning.")

[38] Advertisement, *Grays Harbor Post*, December 9, 1939.

[39] Correspondence from Morse Saito, January 28, 1998. Mrs. Saito was trying to draw a whole new poker hand by making the show of prosperity in Seattle.

[40] E-mail communication with Laurence Aylesworth, June 17, 2003. Natsu Saito Orita lived with Dahlia's family and assisted in raising him from 1952 to 1963.

[41] The information on William Moyer came from a family scrapbook maintained by James and June Moyer of Hoquiam, Washington. Two letters that Moyer sent from Japan survive. Interviews with James Moyer on May 19 and December 4, 1997, Hoquiam, Washington.

[42] William's parents, Jackson R. and Mary Dutton Moyer later moved to Falls City, Oregon, where they eventually celebrated their fiftieth wedding anniversary.

[43] Interviews and telephone conversations with Madeline Moyer Kelly and James Moyer on January 16 and 29, 1997.

[44] Story from Polson Museum Chehalis County Nationality Survey, 1848–1915. 1984. Polson Museum manuscript. Early population statistics also come from this volume.

[45] A generation later the author's grandfather, J. W. Clark, sans mask but brandishing a nightstick specially made by the Hoquiam Chair Factory, participated in a similar activity, with Wobbly agitators engaged in Free Speech demonstrations taking the part of the despised Chinese. (The nightstick is labeled in ink: "I.W.W. November 1911 to April, 1912.")

[46] Telephone interview with Madeline Moyer Kelly, February 6, 1998.

[47] "Fifty Years in Hoquiam: Memoirs of Frank H. Lamb, 1948." Unpublished manuscript resides in Hoquiam Public Library. A condensed and restructured version of the memoir, edited by John Hughes, was published in the *Daily World Perspective*, April 25, 1998. Kay, Tinia, and Mrs. Saito of Hoquiam are mentioned on page 163 of the original.

[48] Telephone interviews with James Moyer, March 13 and August 13, 1996, and January 16 and 29, 1997; interviews in Hoquiam, Washington, May 19 and December 4, 1997.

CHAPTER 3: From Hometown to Nation's Capital

[1] Schoenburg, *Lithuanian Jewish Communities*, 27–32.

[2] See the Bendetson family tree in Appendix C.

[3] Correspondence and phone interviews with Beverly Brill Freedman, daughter of Selma Bendetson Brill, October 29, 1997.

[4] Telephone conversation with Earl Thygeson, January 29, 1997. His parents told vivid stories about the Park Falls fire and Mr. Bendetson's loss; the family moved from there to Aberdeen in 1911 when Earl was five.

[5] His middle name honored his Bendetson grandmother's maiden name, Rabbin (or Robbiner).

[6] Many details were obtained from an interview with B. F. (Bim) Morrison in Aberdeen, December 6, 1995.

[7] J. W. Clark, in *Grays Harbor Post*, on the occasion of the opening of Wolff's new store, December 2, 1922.

[8] In the spring of 1920, Joseph Jacob presided as speaker at the funeral for Mrs. Anna Penn, which was well attended by members of the Grays Harbor Hebrew Relief Society.

[9] Many of these details were gleaned from the pages of the *Grays Harbor Post*. Some of Jacob's speeches are printed verbatim.

[10] *Grays Harbor Post*, July 6, 1918.

[11] Sylvia Wolff Epstein, interviewed in 1973 for the Jewish Archives Project, University of Washington: Sylvia, who was a teenager at the time of World War I, recalled these extremely orthodox soldiers. Her mother made a concerted effort to prepare a kosher meal for them.

[12] A wonderful summary of Grays Harbor lumbering can be found in *They Tried to Cut It All: Grays Harbor—Turbulent Years of Greed and Greatness* by Edwin Van Syckle.

[13] *Grays Harbor Post*, October 23, 1920. Editors of Aberdeen papers have without fail touted the potential of the local community, asserting that it will prosper, if not this year, then surely the next. This was true of the author's grandfather; uncle; father; *Aberdeen Daily World* editor Mr. Rupp; and John Hughes, current *Daily World* editor.

[14] Correspondence, October 30, 1997, and telephone interviews, October 29, 1997, and March 3, 2000, with Beverly Brill Freedman, niece of KRB.

[15] Retired circulation manager for the former *Aberdeen Daily World*, Thygeson has an encyclopedic memory of people and events in Aberdeen. In 1998 he was retired and living in San Jose, California.

[16] Telephone interview with Sally McLean of Aberdeen, April 24, 1996.

[17] Printed copy of "A Sermon for Erev Rosh Hashanah," by Rabbi Moses P. Jacobson, found in Joel Wolff archive at University of Washington, #2387–2. Handwritten note on copy: "Mr. A. M. Bendetson Eve Sept. 10 1923." Attached is note from Joel Wolff indicating that his father assigned this sermon to A. M. Bendetson on that date. This is probably the same Rabbi Moses Perez Jacobson who wrote "Is This a Christian Country?" (Shreveport, Louisiana: M. L. Bath Co., Ltd., c. 1913).

[18] Telephone interview with Diddy Goldberg; interview with Jay Goldberg, Aberdeen, May 17, 1997.

[19] Joel Wolff, interviewed in 1974 for the Jewish Archives Project, University of Washington; also interviewed by the author on June 16 and between December 5 and 8, 1995, and on May 20, 1997.

[20] *Grays Harbor Post*, February 22, 1930.

[21] Interview with Brookes M. Bendetsen, March 6, 1997, San Mateo, California, and *Stanford Alumni Magazine*, June 1942. KRB papers, box 349.

[22] Quote is in July 3, 1989, article reporting Bendetsen's death in the *Aberdeen Daily World*. Olson by then lived in Woodburn, Oregon.

[23] Telephone interview with KRB's niece Beverly Brill Freedman, March 20, 2000.

[24] Telephone interview with Barbara Tucker Adams, January 3, 1996.

[25] Ibid.

[26] Stanford Quad collection in Lane Room of the Green Library, Stanford University. Theta Delta Chi information from Sunil Dwivedi, research assistant, in letter, March 6, 1996. Dwivedi found a photo from 1930, which was not in the yearbook, showing Bendetson and other men in front of their new house at 584 Mayfield. Dwivedi wrote, "There may well have been a time when our fraternity, as most others, preferred not to have Jewish members. . . . There is no record of any formal policy in dealing with such issues and it would seem that such racism would not be publicized in the *Shield* or any other national publication." Even a decade later at the University of Washington, Jews were not invited to join most fraternities. Rudy Kauhanen (Perry Saito's Aberdeen classmate) recalled having to tell an Aberdeen friend who was Jewish that he was not going to be invited to join Phi Kappa Psi. Rudy had felt badly and feared the friend thought it was his doing.

[27] Interview with informant (almost certainly Gladys Phillips), FBI file of KRB, October 14, 1981.

[28] Carey McWilliams, *A Mask for Privilege: Anti-Semitism in America*, dis-

cusses social discrimination against Jews in the United States. McWilliams describes an organized policy to exclude Jews from clubs, fraternities, and sororities and many professions and occupations in the 1930s; Ivy League universities and most medical schools had quotas for accepting Jewish applicants, and resisted hiring Jewish faculty, for example. See also Leonard Dinnerstein, *Antisemitism in America.*

[29] In a letter to John J. Long written from Washington, D.C., and dated July 21, 1941, Karl talked about his hometown. New to Aberdeen, Long had asked for help in choosing a lawyer to try to recover money he was owed from one of Aberdeen's large plywood companies. KRB papers, box 349, personal and semi-official correspondence file.

[30] Lumber production data from annual reports of the Port of Grays Harbor.

[31] Recollections of author's mother, Dorothy Nielsen Clark, prior to her death in 1993.

[32] Van Syckle, *They Tried to Cut It All*, 257. For colorful descriptions of the mills' huffing and puffing of the 1920s, see 256.

[33] Preface by Harry T. Moore to *The Land of Plenty*, by Robert Cantwell. A useful starting point for study of labor relations in the Aberdeen and the Northwest is the chapter "Marching Marching," from Hughes and Beckwith, *On the Harbor: From Black Friday to Nirvana*. Cantwell is discussed in the chapter "A Town and Its Novelists." Though he later became a Republican and a respected journalist for *Time*, *Newsweek*, and *Sports Illustrated*, Cantwell supported William Z. Foster, the Communist candidate for president in 1932. He soon after rejected the Communist movement and the idea of a classless society.

[34] Roosevelt won the electoral vote 472 to 59.

[35] By this time his sister Selma, a schoolteacher, had married Leo Brill and moved to Minnesota.

[36] Bendetsen's FBI report of 1981 includes interviews of Aberdeen acquaintances, all of whom mentioned this fact.

[37] Interview with Mrs. Barbara (Tucker) Adams on January 3, 1996, in Seattle.

[38] Telephone interview with Frank Iskra, a retired engineer in Hamilton, Ohio, July 7, 1997.

[39] First Room 523, later Room 421, of the Finch Building. The Finch Building, Aberdeen's first "skyscraper" (of five floors) was finally torn down in 1999. The Becker Building has seven floors and a penthouse.

[40] Telephone interview with Mary Birdwell, January 5, 1998. At ninety, Mary was living in Fife, Washington, the second wife and widow of Jackson Moyer.

[41] *Grays Harbor Post*, March 12, 1938.

[42] Mrs. Clark (Barbara Tucker) Adams, quoting her husband who had died ten years earlier. Telephone interview, January 3, 1996, and interview, Seattle, 1997.

[43] *Grays Harbor Post*, June 24, 1939.

[44] Ibid.

[45] *Grays Harbor Post*, March 11, 1939.

[46] "Communist Popularity Hits Record Low in New Incidents on West Coast," *Life*, December 18, 1939, p. 24. The article featured three photos of the destruction in Red Finn Hall.

[47] At this time the AFL and CIO were competing unions: The AFL preferred to organize skilled craftsmen, while the CIO organized whole industries. The AFL tolerated the Sawmill & Timber Workers, whose membership swelled during the strikes of 1934 and 1935 in Aberdeen and elsewhere. The International Woodworkers of America, a CIO union, was considered a "radical faction," which employers disdained. See Hughes and Beckwith, *On the Harbor*, 80.

[48] Interview with James Middleton, June 5, 1996, in Hoquiam, Washington.

[49] Interview with Joel Wolff on December 5, 1995, in Aberdeen, Washington.

[50] Program adopted, printed in *Grays Harbor Post*, March 25, 1939.

[51] Bridges was an immigrant from Australia who organized the San Francisco local of the International Longshoremen's Association (ILA) and became head of the West Coast ILA; he was denounced by the Dies Unamerican Activities Committee of the United States Congress as a Communist; his deportation was overruled in an important Supreme Court case, and he became a citizen at the end of World War II.

[52] Jack Clark was recalling the time in the winter of 1912 when his father, whom he called "the Boss," joined the posse of several hundred city fathers that rounded up several dozen Wobblies who claimed to be free speech protesters, and ran them out of town. J. W. Clark had come to Aberdeen in 1904 from South Dakota. Though he had been a schoolteacher and superintendent of schools, he found work in Aberdeen as a carpenter and then took over the carpenter union's paper, turning it into the weekly *Grays Harbor Post*. He used the paper to celebrate "the man in overhauls" [*sic*] who did the work and wrote critically of the "timber barons." He insisted that his sons have a trade to fall back on. Jack did not have the same romantic view of the goodness of the workers as his father did—in many of his editorials it sounded as if he had gone over to the side of the "Better Elements." ("Better Elements" is a term used by Murray Morgan in *The Viewless Winds*, a novel based on the unsolved 1940 slaying of the wife of radical labor leader Dick Law in Aberdeen, Washington, to distinguish the business leaders from the working people.)

[53] *Grays Harbor Post*, March 18, 1939.

[54] *Grays Harbor Post*, December 30, 1939.

[55] Colonel Auer retired on May 31, 1942. Harry Anton Auer was from Columbus, Ohio, and earned an LLB and LLM from George Washington University in 1898 and 1899. He served during World War I and was assigned to the JAG in some capacity for most of his military career. He served several brief tours as a foreign service legal officer for the United States Army in China.

[56] Quotes here are from the Oral History-KRB, October and November 1972, pp. 5–7. For the most part, I am using only those parts of the oral history that seem to agree with the contemporaneous record found in the KRB papers.

[57] Exchange of letters between KRB and Harold W. Schweitzer of Los Angeles, March 5 to May 2, 1941, KRB papers, box 349, personal correspondence.

[58] This fact is recorded in the Register of the Army of the United States for 1942. Also included is a complete listing of dates of his two-week reserve stints.

[59] *Grays Harbor Post*, January 13 and February 17, 1940.

[60] *Grays Harbor Post*, April 27, 1940.

[61] Interview with B. F. (Bim) Morrison on December 6, 1995 in Aberdeen, Washington.

[62] Oral History-KRB, pp. 6–7, and *Stanford Alumni Review*, June 1942, pp. 14–16, made this connection. KRB papers, box 349.

[63] Letter to Maj. Charles P. Light, Jr., Bermuda Base Command, May 29, 1941. KRB papers, box 349.

[64] Oral History-KRB, p. 10.

[65] After the war Haislip became the vice chief of staff of the army. KRB served along with him on the Joint Chiefs of Staff in 1950, Oral History-KRB, p. 12.

[66] Colonel Wilton B. Persons later became special assistant to President Dwight D. Eisenhower.

[67] According to KRB, the bill passed primarily because House Speaker Sam Rayburn of Texas watched closely as congressmen approached the well to enter their votes. When he had the winning vote he banged the gavel, cutting off five well-known "doves" just arriving at the cloakroom door. Oral History-KRB, pp. 27–28.

[68] Letter of thanks to Lt. Col. Kendall J. Fielder, acting chief of staff headquarters, Fort Shafter, Territory of Hawaii, October 2, 1941. He addressed Fielder as "My dear Wooch." KRB papers, box 349. Letter of thanks to Lt. Col. Thomas H. Davies, Hdq., October 2, 1941. KRB papers, box 349.

[69] "Points for discussion in Honolulu," attached to radiogram to provost marshal general dated September 3, 1941. KRB papers, box 313.

[70] Roosevelt fireside chat, December 18, 1940.

[71] Interview taped by Kai Bird, November 1983. KRB had said captain, but by then he was a major; it was actually October 31, 1941.

[72] He mentions ninety days to settle. He may have been remembering the North American experience, which could have taken ninety days. Bendix went faster, because he was done by the end of November and was writing summaries of the operation before the Pearl Harbor attack.

[73] Detailed description of takeover, titled "Air Associates, Bendix, New Jersey." This War Department record contains a sequence of events from September 17, 1941, to November 1, 1941, and spells out much of KRB's involvement. KRB papers, box 292.

[74] Bendetson was credited with analyzing the financial state of the company and saving it from collapse. KRB papers, box 349.

[75] Jack Herzig, retired lieutenant colonel who served as counterintelligence officer for the army in Japan and Europe, made some attempt to verify Bendetsen's story but failed to find any confirming evidence. Letter to the author dated December 7–13, 1995. On an FBI form titled "Foreign Countries Visited since 1930," Bendetsen's first entries were his European service from 1948 to 1952. KRB FBI file, 1981.

[76] Interview taped by Kai Bird, November 1983. James Rowe, assistant attorney general in 1942, who regularly clashed with Bendetsen, commented about Gullion: "I never thought [he] was very smart. I mean, as far as comparing him with a man like Bendetsen. He wasn't even in the major leagues." Earl Warren Oral History Project, University of California Archive, March 1, 1971, p. 4.

CHAPTER 4: Specters of Fear

NOTE: Bendetson had not yet changed his name to Bendetsen during this time interval; both spellings appear in these notes because his later papers all bear the latter name.

[1] Letter from Nora Jean Stewart to her parents, *Grays Harbor Post*, December 27, 1941.

[2] Interview with Brookes M. Bendetsen, March 6, 1997, San Mateo, California.

[3] Boothe, "The Valor of Homer Lea," introduction to *The Valor of Ignorance*, by Homer Lea.

[4] Lea, *The Valor of Ignorance*, 265 and 268. Note: Grays Harbor has long since lost the apostrophe that connects the name to the harbor's discoverer, Captain Robert Gray. Gray was the first American to circumnavigate the world. Gray, in the ship *Columbia*, sailed into the harbor in 1792 and named it Bullfinch; he then discovered the huge river he had missed a year earlier and named it after his ship.

[5] The Yellow Peril was a propaganda campaign seeking to blame all the ills of American life on immigrants from China and Japan; it fostered a fear of waves of "coolie" immigrants. For more detail, see CWRIC, *Personal Justice Denied*, 37–38.

[6] Boothe, "The Valor of Homer Lea," 23.

[7] Ibid., 24.

[8] Anschel, *Homer Lea, Sun Yat-sen, and the Chinese Revolution,* 100.

[9] Interview with Jack Close in Aberdeen, Washington, May 16, 1997. On December 7, 1941, he was working in the attorney general's office in Olympia and visiting Grays Harbor to court the woman he later married.

[10] Telephone interview with Marilyn McIntosh, June 13, 1997.

[11] See oral histories, such as Studs Terkel, *"The Good War": An Oral History of World War Two.*

[12] Interview with Brookes M. Bendetsen, March 6, 1997, San Mateo, California.

[13] *Grays Harbor Post*, December 20, 1941.

[14] Oral History-KRB, p. 61.

[15] Archer L. Lerch, Colonel, JAG, Memorandum for the Files, January 1, 1942. Daniels, *Concentration Camps: North America*, 45.

[16] Okihiro, *Cane Fires,* 124.

[17] Daniels, *Concentration Camps: North America*, 36–37. General Stillwell went on to command all American forces in the China-Burma-India theater for much of the war. (See his laudatory biography by Barbara Tuchman.)

[18] *San Francisco Call-Bulletin*, April 9, 1942.

[19] *Aberdeen Daily World*, November 6, 1941. Clipping quoted in Natsu Saito FBI file.

[20] Statement Natsu Saito made to an FBI agent pretending to be a customer in her shop, June 2, 1941. Natsu Saito FBI file.

[21] Ibid.

[22] Editorial by Kearny Clark, *Grays Harbor Post*, December 13, 1941. He took over the paper when his brother, Jack Clark, left with his Marine outfit in November 1940.

[23] On Mrs. Saito's earliest FBI case record, after listing suspicious activities, the

agent mused: The names of the children "made me think—That the great e-man-ci-pater [*sic*] discovered that he would have to telegraph for a flower."

[24] Letter and telephone conversation, Barbara Nielsen de Luna (author's aunt), September 10, 1994.

[25] FBI file of Natsu Saito.

[26] Roger Daniels, *Concentration Camps: North America,* 44.

[27] Presidential proclamations of December 7 and 8, 1941, *Final Report*, 3.

[28] CWRIC, *Personal Justice Denied*, 54.

[29] Ibid.

[30] Daniels, *Decision to Relocate the Japanese Americans*, 16.

[31] Daniels, *Concentration Camps: North America*, 40.

[32] Radiogram from DeWitt, December 26, 1941. Daniels, *American Concentration Camps*, vol. I.

[33] Archer L. Lerch, Colonel, JAGD, Deputy Provost Marshal General, Memorandum for the Files, January 1, 1942. Daniels, *Decision to Relocate the Japanese Americans*, 66.

[34] Daniels, *Decision to Relocate the Japanese Americans*, 14

[35] *Aberdeen Daily World*, December 29, 1941.

[36] Oral History-KRB, pp. 70–71.

[37] Letter from Gullion to DeWitt, January 1, 1942. Western Defense Command records, RG 338; National Archives, College Park, Maryland.

[38] Letter from F. W. McNabb, Western Growers Protective Assn., to Earl Warren, January 3, 1942. Grodzins, *Americans Betrayed*, 22–23.

[39] Bendetsen mentioned wanting to be promoted to general in letters to Colonel Harry Auer, as noted later in this chapter; his son heard him express his regret at not making general.

[40] January 4, 1942 conference in office of General DeWitt. Part of resume of action regarding West Coast Alien Enemy Program, by KRB, to PMG, January 16, 1942. KRB papers, box 349.

[41] Transcript of conference in office of General DeWitt, January 4, 1942. KRB papers, box 349.

[42] Memorandum from DeWitt (by Bendetson) to Assistant Attorney General Rowe, Subject: Alien Enemy Control Requirements, January 5, 1942. KRB papers, box 349.

[43] Letter from Joseph D. Roberts to Adjutant General, July 29, 1941. By this time, Roberts is a first lieutenant and public relations officer at Fort Lewis, Washington. KRB papers, box 349.

[44] Daniels, *Concentration Camps: North America*, 44.

[45] Replying teletype from Francis Biddle, January 5, 1942, Tab D of January 16, 1952, resume to provost marshal general. KRB papers, box 349.

[46] Copy of memorandum, January 5, 1942, "prepared at General DeWitt's direction and handed to Mr. Rowe for transmission to Washington (Atty Gen)" Initialed by KRB, Tab E of January 16, 1952. Résumé to provost marshal general, KRB papers, box 349.

[47] Copy of teletype from Hoover to Mr. James Rowe, Jr., January 7, 1942. Tab F of January 16, 1952. Resume to provost marshal general, KRB papers, box 349.

[48] Copy of memorandum to attorney general, January 5, 1942.

[49] Bendetson's statements in Tab E of January 16, 1952, a memo "handed to Mr. Rowe for transmission to Washington (Atty Gen)." KRB papers, box 349.

[50] Interview with James H. Rowe, Earl Warren Oral History Project, University of California Archive, March 1, 1971, p. 1.

[51] Letters from KRB to E. K. Bishop and Edwin C. Matthias, January 13, 1942. KRB papers, box 349, personal file.

[52] Letter from Ford to Stimson, January 13, 1942, in CWRIC, *Personal Justice Denied*, 70.

[53] Memorandum by KRB, January 16, 1942. Resume to PMG, KRB papers, box 349.

[54] Ibid.

[55] Grodzins, *Americans Betrayed*, 386, n. 28.

[56] Letter from Hughes to Biddle, January 19, 1942. tenBroek, *Prejudice, War and the Constitution*, 74.

[57] Memorandum by KRB to Chief of Staff, January 17, 1942. KRB papers, box 314.

[58] G–2 Periodic Report, Headquarters Western Defense Command and Fourth Army, Presidio of San Francisco, California, signed by D. A. Stroh, Colonel. January 3, 1942, January 10, 1942, January 17, 1942, January 24, 1942, maps accompanying reports. Western Defense Command records, RG 338; National Archives, College Park, Maryland.

[59] Letter from Edwin C. Matthias to Leland M. Ford, Januarry 22, 1942. KRB papers, box 314.

[60] Telephone conversation between General Gullion and General DeWitt, January 24, 1942, Daniels, *American Concentration Camps*, vol. II.

[61] Telephone conversation between Bendetson and DeWitt, January 24, 1942, Daniels, *American Concentration Camps*, vol. II.

[62] In an interview with Jacobus tenBroek ten years later, Bendetsen asserted that the G–2 reports were partly responsible for the final evacuation decision, but since tenBroek didn't know about them, KRB couldn't tell him about them, implying that they were classified.

[63] Roberts visited both Stimson and DeWitt on his return from Hawaii and talked about the danger of espionage, sabotage, and fifth-column activity by Japanese in the islands. CWRIC, *Personal Justice Denied*, 59.

[64] Kearny Clark, *Grays Harbor Post*, December 13, 1941.

[65] Irons, *Justice at War*, 40, and *Roberts Report*, Secretary of War records, RG 107; National Archives, College Park, Maryland.

[66] Letter from the secretary of war to the attorney general, January 25, 1942, Daniels, *American Concentration Camps*, vol. II.

[67] Daniels, *Concentration Camps: North America*, 47, n. 7.

[68] Ibid.

[69] CWRIC, *Personal Justice Denied*, 84.

[70] Telephone conversation between DeWitt and Bendetson, January 28, 1942, Daniels, *American Concentration Camps*, vol. II.

[71] *Los Angeles Times*, January 29, 1942, Girdner and Loftis, *The Great Betrayal*, 22–23.

[72] Conn, *Japanese Evacuation from the West Coast*, 119–20.

[73] Rowe gave no specific instructions to Clark, assuming that he would take a civil liberties view of the Japanese question. Clark, a Texan, was ambitious, and "he was going to go with whatever group had the power," in this case the army. Interview with James H. Rowe, Earl Warren Oral History Project, University of California Archive, March 1, 1971, p. 8.

[74] Telephone conversation between Bendetson and DeWitt, 5:00 P.M. January 29, 1942, Daniels, *American Concentration Camps*, vol. II.

[75] Bird, *The Chairman*, 149; telephone conversation between Major Bendetson and General DeWitt, January 30, 1942, Daniels, *American Concentration Camps*, vol. II.

[76] Ibid.

[77] Ibid.

[78] Ibid.

[79] Daniels, *American Concentration Camps*, vol. II.

[80] Proclamation No. 2525, December 7, 1941, by Franklin D. Roosevelt, reprinted in Roger Daniels, *Decision to Relocate the Japanese Americans*, 61–64.

[81] Telephone conversation between General DeWitt and Major Bendetson, January 31, 1942, Daniels, *American Concentration Camps*, vol. II.

[82] CWRIC, *Personal Justice Denied*, 68.

[83] Tolan Committee hearings, Part 31, p. 11632, March 6, 1942.

[84] Daniels, *Concentration Camps: North America*, 47–48.

[85] *Grays Harbor Post*, January 31, 1942.

[86] Robinson, *By Order of the President*, 68.

[87] Memorandum on C. B. Munson's report "Japanese on the West Coast," November 7, 1941, attached to the report itself. Daniels, *American Concentration Camps*, vol. I. Robinson, *By Order of the President*, 79–84, discusses the Carter intelligence network and the efforts of Carter, Munson, and Ringle to defend and bolster the loyalty of the Nisei in late 1941 and early 1942.

[88] Robinson, *By Order of the President*, 69.

[89] General Correspondence, J. J. McCloy, 1941–45. Secretary of War records, RG 107; National Archives, College Park, Maryland. Emphasis in original.

[90] In May 1942, at the request of Milton Eisenhower, head of the WRA, Ringle expanded his report into a 57-page document, "The Japanese Question in the United States." This document addressed the culture of America's ethnic Japanese, as a guide for relocation center managers. Ken Ringle, "What Did You Do before the War, Dad?" *Washington Post*, December 6, 1981. The original Ringle report was published in *Harpers*, October 1942, with a byline indicating it was authored by "An Intelligence Officer."

[91] Telephone conversation between McCloy and DeWitt, February 3, 1942, Daniels, *American Concentration Camps*, vol. II.

CHAPTER 5: Tightening the Noose

[1] Daniels, *Concentration Camps: North America*, 63. Henry McLemore, a nationally syndicated columnist, put into words the extreme reaction against Attorney General Francis Biddle, "whom Californians . . . had made the chief target of their

ire." Biddle, McLemore reported, couldn't even win election as "third assistant dog catcher" in California. "Californians have the feeling," he explained, "that he is the one in charge of the Japanese menace, and that he is handling it with all the severity of Lord Fauntleroy."

[2] Hoover sent a similar memorandum to Biddle dated February 9, 1942. Biddle said further that Hoover "denied the existence of any information showing that the attacks on ships leaving West Coast ports were associated with espionage activity ashore," and "in no case had 'any information been obtained which would substantiate the allegation that there has been signaling from shore-to-ship since the beginning of the war.'"

[3] Bird, *The Chairman*, 149.

[4] Daniels, *Concentration Camps: North America,* 55.

[5] Daniels, *Concentration Camps: North America*, 55–56. Transcript of telephone conversation between Major Bendetsen, General Gullion, and General Clark, February 4, 1942. KRB papers, box 323. Gullion quoted Secretary McCloy to General Clark.

[6] Ibid. Transcripts of telephone conversations between DeWitt and Gullion, and Gullion and Bendetsen, February 1, 1942, Daniels, *American Concentration Camps*, vol. II.

[7] Daniels, *Concentration Camps: North America,* 57, and transcript of telephone conversation between McCloy and DeWitt, February 3, 1942, Daniels, *American Concentration Camps*, vol. II.

[8] Ibid.

[9] Ibid.

[10] Transcript of conversation between DeWitt and Marshall, February 3, 1942, provided by the chief of staff's office to the secretary of war. Daniels, *American Concentration Camps*, vol. II.

[11] Daniels, *Concentration Camps: North America,* 59.

[12] Conn, *Japanese Evacuation from the West Coast*, 128; Daniels, *Concentration Camps, North America,* 60.

[13] Telephone conversations between Gullion, Clark, and Bendetsen, February 4, 1942, Daniels, *American Concentration Camps*, vol. II.

[14] Memorandum to PMG, Alien enemies on the West Coast (and other subversive persons.), February 4, 1942. KRB papers, box 321. Found in letter from Angus Macbeth, October 31, 1981.

[15] Ibid.

[16] Ibid.

[17] Ibid.

[18] From this date forward, his name was spelled "Bendetsen." His promotion to colonel came five weeks later, with rank in grade retroactive to February 1, 1942. On a form for a security investigation in 1981 (not his first), in a box labeled Other Names Used, he wrote: "My surname Bendetsen has been from time to time erroneously spelled Bendetson." KRB FBI file dated October 14,1981.

[19] Irons, *Justice at War*, 47, attributes the "genesis of this [licensing] scheme" to conversation between Rowe and Bendetsen on January 30, in which Rowe (in an

"offhand comment") said that "military edict might justify the evacuation of citizens from 'prohibited areas.'" Bendetsen attended meetings in Washington on February 3 with Stimson, McCloy, and Gullion, and later wrote that he persuaded McCloy and Stimson of the usefulness of the military necessity argument, and it was on February 3 that McCloy was explaining the licensing scheme to DeWitt.

[20] Letter from KRB to Colonel Auer, June 3, 1942. KRB papers, box 349.

[21] Daniels, *Concentration Camps: North America*, 63.

[22] Ibid.

[23] Ibid.

[24] Radio address by Governor Culbert L. Olson, February 4, 1942, Daniels, *American Concentration Camps*, vol. II.

[25] Ibid.

[26] Daniels, *Decision to Relocate the Japanese Americans*, 36.

[27] Letter from Fred Friedlander to KRB dated February 13, 1942, found loose in KRB papers, box 313. Friedlander had helped his cousin get out of Germany; Bendetsen would have known him in Aberdeen. The cousin, surnamed Werner, was a corporal in the US Army, since perhaps 1938, but had been held for eight weeks in a military prison at Fort Lewis, with no charges. In a February 6, 1942, letter to Friedlander, he wrote, "Am I not Jewish, of all possible enemies of Hitler we are the most logical ones."

[28] Letter to Edwin C. Matthias from KRB, February 5, 1942. KRB papers, box 314.

[29] Gullion, memoranda for the assistant secretary of war, February 5, 1942, and February 6, 1942, Daniels, *American Concentration Camps*, vol. II.

[30] Telephone conversation between General DeWitt and Colonel Bendetsen, February 7, 1942, 1:30 P.M., Daniels, *American Concentration Camps*, vol. II.

[31] Ibid.

[32] Telephone conversation between Bendetsen and DeWitt, February 7, 1942, Daniels, *American Concentration Camps*, vol. II. Rowe later said that his mistake had been to assume that the army would not want or be able to take on such a large project, and that he should have focused on the unconstitutionality of the project, rather than saying that Justice couldn't do it. James H. Rowe interview, Earl Warren Oral History Project, University of California Archive, March 1, 1971, p. 8.

[33] Daniels, *Concentration Camps: North America*, 60.

[34] Ibid.

[35] Ibid., 62 and n. 36.

[36] Grodzins, *Americans Betrayed*, 94.

[37] Ibid., 144–46. Grodzins provides multiple examples of Japanese cooperation with government intelligence authorities. There were no convictions.

[38] Ibid., 96–97.

[39] January 1, 1942–February 19, 1942, archival documents leading up to Executive Order 9066. Daniels, *American Concentration Camps*, vol. II.

[40] Irons, *Justice at War*, 56. This significant memo was missing from Bendetsen's Hoover archive.

[41] Ibid.

[42] Ibid.

[43] Robinson, *By Order of the President*, 104, and the Biddle papers.

[44] CWRIC, *Personal Justice Denied*, 55.

[45] Memorandum from J. Edgar Hoover to Attorney General Francis Biddle, February 9, 1942. Cited in Biddle, *In Brief Authority*, 222.

[46] Bird, *The Chairman*, 18.

[47] Ibid., 19.

[48] *The Columbia Encyclopedia*, 2045.

[49] Hodgson, *The Colonel*, 248–61.

[50] *The Columbia Encyclopedia*, 214, and Biddle, *In Brief Authority*, 226.

[51] Bird, *The Chairman*, 154. Frankfurter later voted with the Supreme Court majority that upheld the constitutionality of the curfew and exclusion orders.

[52] Bird, *The Chairman*, 148.

[53] Ibid., 94–95.

[54] Ibid., 151–52.

[55] CWRIC, *Personal Justice Denied*, 79, and Stimson's diary.

[56] Bird, *The Chairman*, 152.

[57] Irons, *Justice at War*, 57. Memo, February 11, 1942, draft of "Questions to be determined re Japanese exclusion," Daniels, *American Concentration Camps*, vol. II.

[58] Bird, *The Chairman*, 152.

[59] Daniels, *Concentration Camps: North America*, 65.

[60] Bird, *The Chairman*, 152.

[61] Conn, *Japanese Evacuation*, 132.

[62] Memo from Mark W. Clark to General Headquarters, c. February 12, 1942, quoted in Roger Daniels, *Concentration Camps: North America*, 66–67.

[63] Walter Lippmann, *Washington Post*, February 12, 1942. Western Defense Command records, RG 338; National Archives, College Park, Maryland.

[64] Grodzins, *Americans Betrayed*, 286. Grodzins labels these statements *extensio ad absurdum*.

[65] Westbrook Pegler, "Fifth Column Problem on Pacific Coast Very Serious—Japs Should Be under Guard," *New York World-Telegram*, February 16, 1942, quoted in CWRIC, *Personal Justice Denied*, 80.

[66] Minear, *Dr. Seuss Goes to War*, 65. Published in *PM* magazine, February 13, 1942. Minear notes that Seuss (and *PM*) was generally antiracist and progressive, opposed Hitler, and valued individuality. Minear said this view of the American Japanese population was "a blindspot of the wartime New York left."

[67] Bird, *The Chairman*, 153.

[68] Steel, *Walter Lippmann and the American Century*, 393–95.

[69] Ibid. Recalling that Lippmann, a generation ahead of Karl Bendetsen, was also the product of a wealthy Jewish family and had given up Judaism, one suspects that he would not have appreciated this comparison.

[70] Memo from DeWitt (written with KRB), February 13, 1942. KRB papers, box 349.

[71] Ibid.

[72] Telephone conversation between General DeWitt, General Gullion, and Major Bendetsen, February 1, 1942. Daniels, *American Concentration Camps*, vol.

II. *Evangeline: A Tale of Acadie*, a poem by Henry Wadsworth Longfellow, 1847, is the story of innocent Nova Scotia lovers who were separated during deportation by the English and, though never reunited, remained faithful till death.

[73] Biddle, *In Brief Authority*, 218. DeWitt memo, February 13, 1942, KRB papers, box 349.

[74] Ultimately the Supreme Court agreed with him in the Endo decision, delivered in December 1944, which declared that the government could not hold an evacuee in a relocation camp against her will. Knowledge that this decision was pending forced the rescinding of General DeWitt's exclusion orders. CWRIC, *Personal Justice Denied*, 232–43.

[75] Letter from KRB to Colonel Harry A. Auer, Laguna Beach, June 3, 1942. KRB papers, personal Stayback file, Box 349.

[76] Bird, *The Chairman*, 153.

[77] Ibid.

[78] Ibid.

[79] Irons, *Justice at War*, 61.

[80] Bird, *The Chairman*, 153.

[81] Biddle, *In Brief Authority*, 219.

[82] Irons, *Justice at War*, 62.

[83] Telephone conversation between McCloy and DeWitt, February 18, 1942. McCloy was preparing DeWitt for an appearance before the Tolan Committee, Daniels, *American Concentration Camps*, vol. II.

[84] Ibid.

[85] Irons, *Justice at War*, 62.

[86] The full text of the order is given in Appendix A.

[87] See Robinson, *By Order of the President.*

[88] Biddle, *In Brief Authority*, 219.

[89] Black, *Casting Her Own Shadow: Eleanor Roosevelt and the Shaping of Postwar Liberalism*, 142–47.

[90] Ibid., 146.

CHAPTER 6: Taking Full Charge

[1] Letter from Stimson to DeWitt, February 20, 1942. *Final Report*, 25–26.

[2] State Department memo from Gufler, February 12, 1942, reporting on meeting with Lt. Col. Bendetsen. National Archives, College Park, Maryland. The Works Progress Administration (WPA), founded during the Depression, used federal money to provide employment, and developed useful projects of all kinds, from bridges, hiking trails, lodges, and roads, to guidebooks for each state.

[3] Letter and memorandum from McCloy to DeWitt (by Bendetson), February 20, 1942. *Final Report*, 27, and KRB papers, box 349.

[4] Washington, Oregon, California, Idaho, Montana, Nevada, Utah, and Arizona.

[5] Orders, February 22, 1942. KRB papers, box 349. *Final Report*, 28.

[6] It is not likely that George C. Marshall was in San Francisco. This may be one more of Bendetsen's fantasies. General Marshall was reorganizing the War Department because it had become a "huge, bureaucratic, red-tape-ridden operating

agency." He also was heavily involved in negotiations with the United Kingdom, trying to plan offensive strategies and trying to make the best possible decisions on uses of the United States's limited resources to shore up forces besieged by the Japanese in the Pacific. See Pogue, *George C. Marshall,* Vol. II.

[7] Oral History-KRB, p. 75.

[8] Ibid.

[9] This is Bendetsen paraphrasing McCloy's comment. Oral History-KRB, 75–76.

[10] Preliminary classification, edited in KRB's handwriting, dated 7/5/42. KRB papers, box 350. Photocopy shown in Appendix B.

[11] Oral History-KRB, p. 77.

[12] Ibid., 77–78. His tenure as a lieutenant colonel had thereby vanished, and it was thus a double promotion.

[13] The brilliance of the execution of the job would be less obvious to his charges, who would experience "shoddy shanty towns in desert areas" or possibly to American taxpayers who might later realize the effort was a colossal waste of money and done with little regard to the rights of the people evacuated. Comment by Wes Sasasaki-Uemura, 2003.

[14] Hearings before the Select Committee Investigating National Defense Migration, House of Representatives. Part 29. San Francisco Hearings, February 21, 1942. "Problems of Evacuation of Enemy Aliens and Others from Prohibited Military Zones. Testimony and statement of Hon. Earl Warren, pp. 10973–11023.

[15] tenBroek, *Prejudice, War and the Constitution*, 117. One reason that the voluntary evacuation was not successful was that all Japanese assets had been frozen by presidential order in July 1941. Many potential evacuees were unable to leave the coast voluntarily because they were unable to access their savings. CWRIC, *Personal Justice Denied*, 54.

[16] Robinson, *By Order of the President*, describes the conflicting views in the Roosevelt administration on the need for an alien property custodian, and Roosevelt's failure to appoint one.

[17] Hewes, *Boxcar in the Sand*, 182.

[18] Ibid., 164–66.

[19] Ibid.

[20] Ibid.

[21] Ibid.

[22] CWRIC, *Personal Justice Denied*, 110–11. Also Greg Robinson, *By Order of the President*, 142–46, and Sandra C. Taylor, "The Federal Reserve Bank and the Relocation of the Japanese in 1942."

[23] *Final Report*, chap. X.

[24] Watanabe Clipping File. Collected by Yoriko Watanabe Sasaki during evacuation, 1942. Wing Luke Museum, Seattle, Washington, 55.

[25] Conversation between Colonel Bendetson and General Gullion, probably mid-April, 1942. KRB papers, box 312.

[26] There were five Germans in the set of aliens reported to be on Bainbridge during the following conversations: telephone conversation between Major Bendetson and Mr. Ennis, January 31, 1942; and telephone conversation between DeWitt and

Bendetson, February 1, 1942, 1:15 P.M.; Daniels, *American Concentration Camps* vol. II. The actual number of Japanese Americans evacuated from Bainbridge Island by Exclusion Order #1 was 257, and they were sent to Manzanar. This first evacuation was the background for David Guterson's novel, *Snow Falling on Cedars.*

[27] Irons, *Justice at War*, 65.

[28] Ibid., 65 and n. 44.

[29] *Final Report*, 30–31.

[30] CWRIC, *Personal Justice Denied*, 99, cites the *Congressional Record*, March 19, 1942, p. 2726.

[31] Ibid.

[32] Letter from KRB to his wife, March 22, 1942. KRB papers, box 350.

[33] Letter from KRB to IRS, Tacoma, Washington, March 25, 1942. KRB papers, box 350.

[34] Conversation between Colonel Bendetsen and General Gullion, probably in mid-April 1942. KRB papers, box 312.

[35] Correspondence in the mixed-marriage file shows that Charles Middleton was a captain in November 1942, a major on September 28, 1944, and a lieutenant colonel in September 1945.

[36] Letter from KRB to Colonel Auer, June 3, 1942. KRB papers, box 349.

[37] Translation: "The good of the people is the chief law." Attributed to Marcus Tellius Cicero, c. 52 B.C.

[38] Personal letter from Harry A. Auer to Karl Bendetsen, May 31, 1942. KRB papers, box 349.

[39] Saying he selected the relocation center sites may be another of KRB's exaggerations. WRA Director Eisenhower and others participated. Oral History-KRB, p. 78.

[40] *Final Report*, 248.

[41] Ibid., chap. XXVIII.

[42] Oral History-KRB, p. 79.

[43] Roger Daniels, "The Bureau of the Census and the Relocation of the Japanese Americans: A Note and a Document," *Amerasia Journal* (Spring 1982). See also William Seltzer and Margo Anderson, "After Pearl Harbor: The Proper Role of Population Data Systems in Time of War," paper presented at Population Association of America, March 2000, Los Angeles, California.

[44] TenBroek, *Prejudice, War and the Constitution*, 124–25.

[45] CWRIC, *Personal Justice Denied*, 110–11.

[46] Oral History-KRB, p. 79–80.

[47] Memorandum from KRB to the assistant secretary of war: Appearance before Tolan Committee, no date. KRB papers, box 31.

[48] In the interview, Kai Bird asked KRB about Milton Eisenhower going to talk to the governors. Bendetsen said, "I took him out. I wasn't with him, he was with me. I took him around." Tape 2, Kai Bird, November 10, 1983. Tom C. Clark also accompanied Bendetsen, traveling with him in the general's plane. Memo from Tom C. Clark to Bendetsen, April 6, 1942. KRB papers, box 315.

[49] Grodzins, *Americans Betrayed*, 248.

[50] Roger Daniels, "Western Reaction to the Relocated Japanese Americans: The

Case of Wyoming." In Daniels, et al., *Japanese Americans: From Relocation to Redress*, 112–17.

[51] Girdner and Loftus, *The Great Betrayal*, 116.

[52] Ibid., 239, and a letter from Milton Eisenhower, undated.

[53] Conversation between Colonel Bendetsen and General Gullion, probably mid-April 1942. KRB papers, box 312.

[54] Ibid.

[55] Conversation between Colonel Bendetsen and Nat Pieper, 11:15 A.M., April 9, 1942. Clark Dossier, KRB papers, box 315.

[56] Conversation between Colonel Bendetsen and Mr. McCloy, 9:45 A.M., April 11, 1942. Clark Dossier, KRB papers, box 315.

[57] Ibid.

[58] Memorandum for the assistant secretary of war. Subject: Liaison with the Department of Justice regarding enforcement under Public Law 503. Signed by J. L. DeWitt, April 20, 1942. KRB papers, box 349.

[59] *Final Report*, 362. This number included the 4,889 voluntary migrants and 1,022 persons "In Institutions." Of the total, 110,723 persons "Entered a Center."

CHAPTER 7: A Painful Time

[1] Morse Saito, "April 1942," *Mainichi Daily News*, April 21, 1986.

[2] Letter from Pitchford to director of Tule Lake camp, April 24, 1942; internment case file of Natsu Saito. Pitchford had written a notarized letter supportive of Mrs. Saito for the January 7, 1942, hearing; Department of Justice file of Natsu Saito.

[3] FBI file of Natsu Saito, received by author February 16, 1999 from FBI, Seattle.

[4] Morse Saito, "Changing Images of Christmas," *Mainichi Daily News*, December 25, 1995.

[5] Natsu Saito files: FBI file from Seattle; closed legal case files; Department of Justice Records, RG 60; National Archives, College Park, Maryland.

[6] Telephone interviews with Dick Tuttle, January 14, 1998, and August 2, 1996. As of December 31, 1941, there were only nineteen Issei females in temporary detention in the entire INS system (and 1,113 males). On January 15, 1942, twenty Japanese enemy aliens were being held at the INS station in Seattle; three of them were female. Source: E-mail of May 8, 2000, from Louis Fiset, author of *Imprisoned Apart*.

[7] Morse Saito, "Christmas—the Sad Season," *Mainichi Daily News*, December 23, 1996.

[8] FBI file of Natsu Saito, and her Department of Justice file.

[9] FBI file of Natsu Saito.

[10] Morse Saito, "Great Teachers," *Mainichi Daily News*, July 7, 1997.

[11] Telephone conversation with Morse Saito, January 27, 1998; telephone conversation with Dick Tuttle, August 1, 1996, and January 14, 1998; telephone conversation with Rebecca Saito, August 5, 1996.

[12] Telephone interviews with Dick Tuttle, January 14, 1998, and August 2, 1996.

[13] Letter and telephone conversation with Barbara Nielsen de Luna, (author's aunt), September 10, 1994.

[14] Department of Justice file of Natsu Saito.

[15] Annual rainfall in Grays Harbor was typically about ninety inches; Seattle typically saw around thirty-five; a desert, by definition, gets fewer than ten inches.

[16] Puyallup was Western Washington State Fairgrounds; Tanforan, a racetrack south of San Francisco; and Santa Anita, a racetrack in Los Angeles. Morse Saito told this story in "Wider Family Ties," *Mainichi Daily News*, July 15, 1997, and in "April 1942," *Mainichi Daily News*, April 21, 1986.

[17] Morse Saito, "April, 1942," *Mainichi Daily News*, April 21, 1986.

[18] Polly Hackett, "Behind Barbed Wire: Love Conquered All during War Years," *Wauwatosa News Times*, Wauwatosa, Wisconsin, 1980. Fumi Saito collection.

[19] Interview with Natsu Taylor Saito, daughter of Morse, August 14, 1997, Salt Lake City, Utah.

[20] March, Seattle newspaper, Watanabe Clipping File (hereafter, Watanabe), collected by Yoriko Watanabe Sasaki during evacuation, 1942. Wing Luke Museum, Seattle, Washington, 40.

[21] Ibid., 43.

[22] Ibid.

[23] Hewes, *Boxcar in the Sand*, 166–71.

[24] April 4, San Francisco, from Watanabe, 74.

[25] Sandra C. Taylor, "The Federal Reserve Bank and the Relocation of the Japanese in 1942."

[26] Seattle newspaper, undated, from Watanabe, 84.

[27] Ibid., 48.

[28] Ibid., 76.

[29] Karl Bendetsen, "The Story of Pacific Coast Japanese Evacuation," May 20, 1942. Army's printed copy obtained from KRB's niece. Also available from New York's The City News Publishing Company in *Vital Speeches of the Day* 1, no. 1 (October 8, 1934).

[30] Ibid.

[31] Ibid. Note that the location of Japanese communities was so sinister they are referred to as "deployed." Later, cooler heads noted that the distribution of German and/or Italian "deployments" was even denser in sensitive, vital areas and could have been said to be even more threatening. Few German and almost no Italian aliens were interned.

[32] Bendetsen quotes numbers between 110,000 and 120,000 in his various statements.

[33] Watanabe, 100. "Army Prepared for One-Day Evacuation of Coast Japanese, San Francisco," appeared in Seattle paper one week after Commonwealth Club speech. The article stated: "Colonel Bendetsen said that he could reveal the secret now that evacuation was almost completed."

[34] The Battle of Midway was fought six months (minus two days) after Pearl Harbor. Hiroyuki Agawa, *The Reluctant Admiral*. (Tokyo: Kodashana, 1979), p. 191.

[35] KRB papers, box 314, semi-official file. A draft statement was marked "OK by KRB as changed."

[36] *Final Report*, 79.

[37] As quoted in Girdner and Loftis, *The Great Betrayal*, 155.

[38] Letter from KRB to Bruce Bliven of *The New Republic*, June 19, 1942. Reply from *The New Republic* is in the same file. KRB papers, box 349.

[39] Ibid.

[40] Ibid.

[41] *Seattle Post Intelligencer*, April 16, 1942. Watanabe, 67.

[42] T. W. Braun to KRB, Fellowship of Reconciliation folder, National Archives, College Park, Maryland, RG 338; 15; T. W. (Ted) Braun was head of Braun & Company, a Los Angeles management consulting firm that offered its services to the WCCA for a dollar a year, plus direct out-of-pocket expenses not to exceed $5,000 a month. Services provided would be press relations representatives for twenty assembly centers, communications, and transport. (Memo/letter April 22 and May 17, 1942. KRB papers, box 312.) KRB had great respect for Braun, spoke highly of him to General Gullion, and after the war worked for him as a management consultant doing a one-year study of margarine marketing.

[43] Though Bendetsen, in his oral history, asserted that he had chosen the sites for the relocation centers, this letter suggests that it was WRA officials who did so. Milton Eisenhower's memoir suggests the latter as well.

[44] KRB memorandum to Mr. Eisenhower, director, WRA, April 22, 1942. KRB papers, box 350, personal.

[45] Girdner and Loftis, *The Great Betrayal*, 155, paraphrasing *The New Republic*, January 18, 1943. Bruce Bliven reported to Bendetsen that he had General Surles's approval for printing the corrections to the Nakashima article. Letter to KRB from Bliven, January 5, 1943. KRB papers, box 314.

[46] *Final Report*, 145.

[47] Letter from Walter Davis to KRB, May 8, 1942. Jackson Moyer files.

[48] Letter from Herman P. Goebel, Jr., from WCCA, Chief Regulatory Section, May 13, 1942. Jackson Moyer files.

[49] *Aberdeen Daily World*, May 27, 1942.

[50] *Washingtonian*, June 4, 1942. Moyer scrapbook.

[51] "Year of calamity or disaster," *yakudoshi* is a Buddhist or Shinto celebration marking particular years of one's life.

[52] Order 89 was posted in Grays Harbor between May 23 and 24, 1942.

[53] Morse Saito, "Wider Family Ties," July 15, 1997.

[54] Ibid.

[55] Sullivan and Cromwell. Jaretzky was recommended to McCloy by his neighbor, Justice Felix Frankfurter.

[56] Joe DiMaggio had gained prominence in 1941 for a fifty-six-game hitting streak; his success and quiet dignity did much to overcome prejudice against Italian immigrants. His parents were not naturalized. Gufler memo for the files, State Department memorandum of conversation on February 20, 1942. Department of Justice records, RG 59; National Archives, College Park, Maryland.

[57] There was no justice. Many of the interned Japanese Americans met one or more of these conditions but were not exempted.

[58] Memorandum from KRB to the assistant secretary of war, May 11, 1942. KRB papers, box 312, personal file. A memo dated May 10, 1942, has a summary.

[59] Memo for assistant secretary of war, May 11, 1942, by KRB; Secretary of War records, RG 107; National Archives, College Park, Maryland.

[60] Memo from KRB to assistant secretary of war, May 12, 1942. KRB papers, box 312.

[61] Ibid.

[62] Telephone conversation between KRB and Jaretzky, April 27, 1942. Western Defense Command records, RG 338; National Archives, College Park, Maryland. In Oral History-KRB interview, Bendetsen denied having known Jaretzky.

[63] Ibid.

[64] The test cases are discussed in chap. 9.

[65] Telephone conversation between Colonel Bendetson [*sic*] and General DeWitt, May 13, 1942. KRB papers, box 313.

[66] Telephone conversation between KRB and Jaretzky, April 27, 1942. Western Defense Command records, RG 338; National Archives, College Park, Maryland.

[67] For example, Fred M. Tayama, a Nisei who had been beaten up by a gang at Manzanar, and Robert Hosakawa (Minidoka, formerly of Seattle). Western Defense Command records, RG 338; National Archives, College Park, Maryland.

[68] According to Morse Saito: "Anyone with any knowledge of written Japanese would realize they were the same person." However, he wrote, "since names are written in characters (kanji) many times a person will not know the reading of a particular name . . . the official name is simply what is written or officially the seal. No one would know whether Shinohara is Shinowara or not unless he personally knew him." Letter from Morse Saito, January 15, 2001.

[69] Telephone conversation between Colonel Bendetsen and Colonel Tate, June 6, 1942, 6:15 P.M. Secretary of War records, RG 107; National Archives, College Park, Maryland.

[70] What is now referred to as East Asia was at that time the concern of the Far Eastern Division of the State Department, a terminology reflecting Washington, D.C., as the center, and travel to "the Orient" as always going eastward.

[71] The *Gripsholm* set sail on the second exchange voyage to a Portuguese port in India on September 2, 1943. This complex story is told in P. Scott Corbett. *Quiet Passages: The Exchange of Civilians between the United States and Japan during the Second World War.*

[72] Report of Captain Albert H. Moffitt, who accompanied Japanese repatriation evacuees to New York City, June 15, 1942. Secretary of War records, RG 107; National Archives, College Park, Maryland.

[73] Telephone conversation between KRB and Colonel Tate, July 12, 1942. Secretary of War records, RG 107; National Archives, College Park, Maryland.

[74] Hewes, *Boxcar in the Sand*, 174.

[75] Eisenhower, *The President Is Calling*, 123.

[76] Bird, *The Chairman*, 163.

[77] He may have gotten this fear/belief from representatives of the State Department and the Special Division, who espoused it often.

CHAPTER 8: Tule Lake, June 1942

[1] These and following quotes obtained in author's telephone conversations and interviews with James Moyer, August 13, 1996, and January 16 and 29, May 19, and December 5, 1997.

[2] Kitagawa, *Issei and Nisei: The Internment Years*, 74.

[3] Miyakawa, *Tule Lake*, 87.

[4] Thomas and Nishimoto, *The Spoilage*, 28.

[5] Tule Lake National Wildlife Refuge and Lava Beds National Monument (founded 1925) lie to the west of the Tule Lake compound, beyond Castle Rock.

[6] Morse Saito, "Wider Family Ties," *Mainichi Daily News*, July 15, 1997. Morse incorrectly remembered that they arrived in May. Tule Lake opened on May 27, 1942.

[7] They went to Block 14; their center address was 1414–D.

[8] Perry Hitoshi Saito testimony before the CWRIC, September 22, 1981.

[9] Letter from Morse Saito, March 20, 2000.

[10] Perry Hitoshi Saito testimony. Ibid.

[11] Morse Saito, "Wider Family Ties," *Mainichi Daily News*, July 15, 1997.

[12] A block consisted of twelve barracks clustered about the group bathroom and laundry room, kitchen/mess hall, and a recreation building; each block was to house no more than three hundred persons, which meant up to twenty-five people in a building. Thirty-six blocks were needed to accommodate ten thousand persons.

[13] Mrs. Kuroda was put in charge of the Sunday school, and by the end of June, the group had organized a regular schedule for Sunday services that included services in Japanese and English, a women's society, the high school group, a prayer meeting, and a post–high school group meeting.

[14] Suzuki, *Ministry in the Assembly and Relocation Centers of World War II*, 150–57.

[15] Florin was an agricultural community ten miles southeast of Sacramento that was home to many Japanese farmers.

[16] Kitagawa, *Issei and Nisei*, 76. Reverend Kitagawa later served with the World Council of Churches.

[17] *Sacramento Bee*, November 30, 1941, and December 6, 1941. "Un Bel Di" translates, ironically, as "One Fine Day."

[18] *Sacramento Bee*, December 8, 1941. Fumiko eventually dropped the feminine diminutive, 'ko,' as Natsu Saito had done years earlier.

[19] *Daily Tulean Dispatch*, December 17, 1942. Former evacuees recognize that this social hall (with the 08 suffix) was in Block 25; every block also had barracks numbered -01 to -07.

[20] Program published by Tulean Music Department, December 13, 1942; also the *Daily Tulean Dispatch*: announcement, December 8, 1942, concert review, December 17, 1942.

[21] A prefecture midway between Hiroshima and Kobe on the Inland Sea,

Okayama experienced much publicity about the United States in the early 1900s. See Lauren Kessler, *Stubborn Twig.*

[22] Japanese was Fumi's first language, but she didn't keep it up. Perry never spoke Japanese well, according to Fumi. Their son said that Fumi and Perry used Japanese like code. Telephone conversation with Fumi Saito, February 6, 1997.

[23] Fumiko Yabe Saito quotations are from telephone interviews on July 2, 1996, February 6, 1997, and October 2, 1997, and from the leave clearance hearing transcript in her internment case file. Fumi later thought the evacuation was dumb. "None of us could tell Chinese from Koreans or Filipino or any of us." She recalled the example of a Japanese farm couple who didn't read English—they managed to stay in California by keeping to themselves—"people thought they were Chinese or something."

[24] Because the railroads were needed to provide for high-priority transport such as troop movements, Bendetsen commandeered out-of-service railroad cars and put together slow trains with no priority, so they were often shuttled onto sidings.

[25] Polly Hackett, "Behind Barbed Wire: Love Conquered All During War Years," *Wauwatosa News Times*, Wauwatosa, Wisconsin, 1980. Fumi Saito collection.

[26] Telephone conversations with Fumi Saito, July 2, 1996, February 6, 1997, and October 2, 1997.

[27] Telephone conversation with Mrs. Uemura, January 14, 1998. She recalled the Moyers as "Caucasian-looking children."

[28] Interviews with James Moyer.

[29] Letter from Morse Saito, March 20, 2000. Morse wrote: "As to Jim Moyer's 'two families per barracks,' remember he was just 12. Also at first there was probably an empty unit because we had gone to neighboring block 14. Things were confused those early days." There were generally six units per barracks.

[30] Interviews with James Moyer. Morse Saito observed that this shouting was from "the new camp gangs of youths establishing their territory." This was one cost of ignoring the Issei authority figures. Saito letter, March 3, 2000.

[31] Notes saved from this period and drafts of letters requesting help were found in the Moyer scrapbook at the home of James Moyer, Hoquiam, Washington.

[32] Ibid.

[33] Towa Moyer survived only five more years, dying at age fifty-three, Moyer scrapbook.

[34] *Final Report*, chap. XII, "Deferments and Exemptions From Evacuation," 145.

[35] Memorandum from Wilkie C. Courter to Major Ashworth, November 13, 1942, which wondered whether Matsuyo Regasa would have to return to the War Relocation Authority Project when her only unemancipated daughter married. Western Defense Command records, RG 338; National Archives, College Park, Maryland.

[36] *Final Report,* pp. 145–47, and Bendetsen memos, Western Defense Command records, RG 338; National Archives, College Park, Maryland. There were actually eight classifications of families of Japanese ancestry granted exemption from evacuation under the mixed-marriage policy. Towa Moyer was in the first category. Other families included any family with a Caucasian woman and mixed-

blood children, families with a Filipino or Chinese husband, and families with other non-Caucasian heads of family with a Japanese wife and mixed-blood children.

[37] Memorandum from Herman P. Goebel, Jr., to A. H. Cheney, July 12, 1942, regarding release of mixed-marriage families. Western Defense Command records, RG 338; National Archives, College Park, Maryland.

[38] William Moyer to Elmer L. Shirrell, July 27, 1942. James Moyer collection. Chester had also been employed in Hoquiam, in a pharmacy.

[39] Goebels to Cheney, July 12, 1942. Western Defense Command records, RG 338; National Archives, College Park, Maryland.

[40] Papers in mixed-marriage file, Western Defense Command records, RG 338; National Archives, College Park, Maryland.

[41] Later absorbed into Fort Snelling, Minnesota.

[42] McCloy to Bendetsen, April 6, 1942. Western Defense Command records, RG 338; National Archives, College Park, Maryland.

[43] DeWitt letter to J. J. McCloy, June 16, 1943, McCloy to KRB, June 1, 1943. Western Defense Command records, RG 338; National Archives, College Park, Maryland.

[44] Telephone interview with Madeline Moyer Kelley, January 5, 1998.

[45] The most infamous of the labor groups in the early 1900s was the Industrial Workers of the World (IWW), often called Wobblies, whose revolutionary ideas found support among migrants who had come to work in timber in the early years of the twentieth century.

[46] Girdner and Loftis, *The Great Betrayal,* 249.

[47] Ibid., 250, n. 26: Larry Tajiri, "Democracy Corrects Its Own Mistakes," *Asia*, April 1943.

[48] Kitagawa, *Issei and Nisei*, 79.

[49] Some people who would have been leaders were elsewhere—most of the men on the FBI lists were still interned in Justice Department internment camps.

[50] See Houston, *Farewell to Manzanar.*

[51] Kitagawa, *Issei and Nisei*, 88.

[52] Eleanor Roosevelt made a thorough inspection of Gila River Camp in Arizona on April 23, 1943. She also noted the dust, the lack of freedom, and the ingenuity of the residents who were making an American community in what was really a penitentiary. She urged the president to end the exclusion and allow the evacuees to return to their homes. Goodwin, *No Ordinary Time: Franklin & Eleanor Roosevelt*, 427–31.

[53] Letter from Morse Saito, March 3, 2000.

[54] Kitagawa, *Issei and Nisei*, 85.

[55] DeWitt, Memorandum to Army Chief of Staff, War Department, August 23, 1942. KRB papers, box 312.

[56] Report submitted by non-citizen, Block Leader #11, Member Executive Council, 11–6–3 Manzanar, California. KRB papers, box 312.

[57] Scobey memorandum for the commanding general, services of supply, December 23, 1942, Secretary of War records, RG 107; National Archives, College Park, Maryland. Friction among evacuees is well documented elsewhere; for example: Thomas and Nishimoto, *The Spoilage.*

[58] Memorandum to chief of staff by J. W., August 18, 1942. KRB papers, box 312. Tule Lake had similar problems.

[59] According to a statistical table found in Bendetsen's archive, in 1942 there were 540 Kibei in the United States outside the WDC (and 6,360 Kibei inside). KRB papers, box 312.

[60] DeWitt memorandum to army chief of staff, August 23, 1942. KRB papers, box 312.

[61] "Believed most likely to be 'disloyal' during World War II, ironically Kibei were overrepresented in number both in the Tule Lake 'Segregation Center' and in the Military Intelligence Service." Niiya, *Japanese American History: An A-to-Z Reference from 1868 to the Present*, 201.

[62] Telephone conversation between Colonel Bendetsen and Mr. McCloy, June 2, 1942. KRB papers, box 312.

[63] Memorandum from DeWitt to chief of staff, July 5, 1942. KRB papers, box 312.

[64] Memorandum from Bendetsen to DeWitt as commanding general of the WDC, July 14, 1942. KRB papers, box 312.

[65] *Final Report*, 308, apparently quoting General DeWitt.

[66] Personal letter from KRB to Gullion, July 9, 1942. KRB papers, DSM file, box 350.

[67] Bendetsen's brief of record, August 5, 1942. KRB papers, box 350. Although this copy of the brief is hand-edited by KRB, he failed to notice that his year of birth was incorrectly typed as 1908 rather than 1907.

[68] Letter to A. M. Gallagher, Chief of Police of Aberdeen, Washington, October 6, 1942. Western Defense Command records, RG 338; National Archives, College Park, Maryland.

[69] KRB also alluded to other great evacuations, such as the exodus of the Jews from Egypt; the banishment of the Acadians, as described in Longfellow's *Evangeline*; and movement of the "Okies," whose westward escape from the Dust Bowl of the 1930s was hauntingly evoked in Steinbeck's *The Grapes of Wrath* in 1939.

[70] Colonel Karl R. Bendetsen, *An Obligation Discharged: The Army Transfers to War Relocation Authority, a Civilian Organization, Japanese Evacuated from the Pacific Coast.* Delivered November 3, 1942, p. 4. Beverly Brill Freedman papers.

[71] In addition to his handling of the evacuation of the West Coast Japanese, the citation mentioned his meritorious performance of three earlier assignments: authoring and gaining passage of the Soldiers' and Sailors' Civil Relief Act, drafting and gaining passage of the extension of the Selective Service Trainees Act (peacetime draft) in August 1941, and handling the takeover of the Air Associates plant at Bendix, New Jersey, in order to keep the plant operating while a labor dispute was settled.

[72] *Grays Harbor Post*, November 21, 1942. Bendetsen initiated army paperwork to change the spelling of his name on October 15, 1942. KRB papers, box 349.

[73] *Time*, November 30, 1942.

[74] A ruling had come from Judge Fee's court in the case of Minoru Yasui; he ruled the curfew unconstitutional as applied to American citizens, but declared that

Yasui had forfeited his citizenship by working for the Japanese consulate, and so was an "enemy alien" and therefore could be found guilty of violating the curfew; Yasui was fined and imprisoned, and the case was appealed. It would go all the way to the Supreme Court.

[75] Personal communication from Morse Saito, March 6, 1998, and others.

[76] Robert Cooperman, "The Americanization of Americans: The Phenomenon of Nisei Internment Camp Theater,"in *Re/collecting Early Asian America: Essays in Cultural History*. Barrack theater was presented in a barrack that could seat only 150, rather than in the larger auditorium/gymnasium that was used for high school theater presentations.

[77] Letter from Morse Saito to Robert Cooperman, April 4, 1995. Robert Cooperman, "The Americanization of Americans: The Phenomenon of Nisei Internment Camp Theater," in *Re/collecting Early Asian America: Essays in Cultural History*.

[78] Ibid.

[79] Ibid.

[80] For an account of the help Christian churches provided, see Sandra C. Taylor, "'Fellow-Feelers with the Afflicted': The Christian Churches and the Relocation of the Japanese During World War II," *Japanese Americans, from Relocation to Redress*, ed. Daniels, et al.

[81] Telephone conversation with Nani (Naoko) Saito (Yahiro), March 31, 1998.

[82] There were about three thousand Nisei college students when the war began, four thousand high school seniors, and large classes in the grades that would graduate in the 1940s. The average age of Nisei in 1940 was seventeen. See O'Brien, *The College Nisei*.

[83] See also Okihiro, *Storied Lives: Japanese American Students and World War II*.

[84] Letter from KRB to Colonel Ralph H. Tate, August 3, 1942. KRB papers, box 315, Assistant Secretary of War McCloy file.

[85] Colonel Karl R. Bendetsen, *An Obligation Discharged*, 7.

[86] Perry Saito described the delay in getting his leave clearance in a talk to a youth group in New York in December 1943 (transcribed by an FBI informant). PHS internment case file.

[87] Whenever asked whether his birth was registered, Perry answered in the negative, not knowing that his father had registered his birth with the Japanese consulate, which would have made him a dual citizen. He did not find out until years later.

[88] PHS internment case file.

[89] Letters dated February 20 and 22, 1943, found in PHS internment case file.

CHAPTER 9: Loyalty Crisis

[1] CWRIC, *Personal Justice Denied*, 190.

[2] A policy came down from Washington a week later: A questionnaire would be devised to reveal "tendencies of loyalty or disloyalty to the United States." Army personnel would administer the questionnaire to potential recruits at all relocation centers, and copies of the questionnaires for males within the age limits for military

service would be sent to military intelligence to decide who should be inducted. The provost marshal general's office would get the rest of the completed questionnaires for evaluation before sending them on to the WDC for investigation.

A joint board, including representatives of the navy, WRA, military intelligence, and the provost marshal general, would decide whether a person who completed a questionnaire could be released from the relocation center, and, if he were not to be inducted into the army, whether he might be employed in a plant important to the war effort. This step was necessary to avoid duplicate investigations by the provost marshal general and the WDC. The WRA, which had not been party to the planning, recommended that the loyalty determination process be enlarged to cover all persons over age seventeen, including Issei, in order to speed up the existing leave-clearance process, which seemed to be causing needless delays that prevented eligible evacuees (such as Perry Saito) from accepting jobs or other opportunities.

[3] Telephone conversation between General DeWitt and Secretary McCloy, January 19, 1943. KRB papers, box 313.

[4] Letter from KRB to Colonel Eugene McGinley, January 19, 1943. KRB papers, box 312.

[5] Telephone conversation between Colonel Bendetsen and Colonel Scobey, 9:25 A.M., January 18, 1943. KRB papers, box 313.

[6] *Final Report*, 362, and Scobey conversation, ibid.

[7] Telephone conversation between Colonel Bendetsen and Captain Hall, January 18, 1943. KRB papers, box 313.

[8] When he did have to give up Dedrick in March, he wrote a glowing letter thanking him for his contributions, and gave him the highest compliment: "You possess an utter disregard for the length of a normal working day." Letter, March 4, 1943. KRB papers, box 314.

[9] Telephone conversation between Colonel Bendetsen and Captain Hall, January 18, 1943. KRB papers, box 313.

[10] Statement of United States Citizen of Japanese Ancestry, February 12, 1943. PHS internment case file.

[11] For an excellent account of the registration crisis, see Weglyn, *Years of Infamy*, chap. 8.

[12] Kitagawa, *Issei and Nisei*, 93.

[13] The original form was titled "Application for leave clearance." The alternate title may have been selected to avoid the suggestion that filling out the form would force the citizen to leave the center if answers were acceptable.

[14] Letter from Morse Saito, March 20, 2000.

[15] Kenji's father in *No-No Boy*, a novel by John Okada.

[16] Jacoby, *Tule Lake*, 70–90 describes the registration program.

[17] Letter from Morse Saito, November 4, 1998.

[18] Ibid.

[19] Ibid.

[20] PHS internment case file.

[21] There were 42,973 conscientious objectors (COs), less than four-tenths of one percent of all inductees during World War II. Pacifist organizations opened Civilian Public Service camps to which COs could be assigned. Selective Service put

COs to work on rural conservation projects, which seemed less like public service and more like punishment. Fifteen percent of the World War II COs were incarcerated for reasons of conscience. Perry's friend Dick Tuttle did alternate service, as did Herman Will.

[22] Weglyn, *Years of Infamy*, 141. See also Drinnon, *Keeper of Concentration Camps*.

[23] Bill Marutani, "East Wind," *Pacific Citizen*, August 22, 1986.

[24] Ibid. There are several interracial marriages among the Sansei (third) generation of Saitos, but so far no blue-eyed, blond grandchildren.

[25] Kitagawa, *Issei and Nisei*, 120–21. In a January 14, 1998, telephone conversation, Maye Uemura identified the beaten minister as Kuroda.

[26] Letter from Morse Saito, March 20, 2000. 1414–D was the Saitos' camp address.

[27] See Weglyn, *Years of Infamy*, and Drinnon, *Keeper of Concentration Camps*. Also Miyakawa, *Tule Lake*, a fictitious account of the troubles, and the entry on Tule Lake Segregation Camp, in *Japanese American History: An A-to-Z Reference from 1868 to the Present*. Kitagawa claimed he was spared an attack because of a rumor that he was an expert fencer. However, people in his block were concerned for his safety, and "every night a group of young men stayed in my room . . . as bodyguards," and he thought camp security also patrolled his block.

[28] Perry Saito talk in Cortland, New York, December 13, 1943. Transcribed by FBI informant. FBI file, p. 19. PHS internment case file.

[29] In 1943, there were 1,493 college Nisei attending Rocky Mountain and Midwestern colleges. O'Brien, *The College Nisei*, 116.

[30] There was no internment case file on Morse; perhaps because he was under the age of 17.

[31] Letter from Morse Saito, March 6, 1998.

[32] Letter to Brigadier General L. H. Hedrick, February 7, 1943. KRB papers, box 349, Stayback file.

[33] Letter to Harry Auer, June 23, 1943. KRB papers, box 349, Stayback file.

[34] Letter from Harry Auer, May 15, 1943. KRB papers, box 349, Stayback file.

[35] Letter from Harry Auer, June 29, 1943. KRB papers, box 349, Stayback file.

[36] Confidential letter to McCloy, June 11, 1942. KRB papers, box 349.

[37] Archer L. Lerch was fourteen years older than Bendetsen, and was a career army officer who got his law degree in 1942 while he was in the judge advocate general's office.

[38] A wartime acronym translated as "Situation Normal, All Fouled Up." Author is assured by adult survivors of that era that the F in SNAFU stood for a less polite word.

[39] Letter to Harry Auer, June 23, 1943. KRB papers archive, box 349, Stayback file.

[40] Memorandum for Commanding General, WDC, and Fourth Army Abolition of WCCA and Transfer of Civil Affairs Division to the Presidio, by KRB, January 30, 1943, KRB papers, box 314.

[41] Letter from Gullion, May 12, 1943. KRB papers, box 349.

[42] Letter to Harry Auer, June 23, 1943. KRB papers, box 349, Stayback file.

[43] A lieutenant colonel by the end of the war, Schweitzer returned to law practice in Los Angeles and became a Municipal Judge in 1947, then a judge on the superior court of Los Angeles in 1952.

[44] Helen Middleton preserved this photo warmly recalling their time in the Presidio. Source: Molly Middleton Tuohy, Tacoma, Washington.

[45] Story told by Jim Middleton in a December 5, 1995, interview in Aberdeen—it is likely that his parents attended the party and reported the scene to friends in Aberdeen; Ruth and Joel Wolff also told the story in a December 1996 Aberdeen interview; finally, it was also volunteered by Gladys Phillips, an Aberdeen lawyer and KRB acquaintance, in a January 9, 1997 interview. Phillips said, "I have no respect for his memory."

[46] CWRIC, *Personal Justice Denied*, 217. Telephone conversation between Bendetsen and Braun, January 19, 1943. Western Defense Command records, RG 338; National Archives, College Park, Maryland. Also in Daniels, *American Concentration Camps*, vol. II. Braun was introduced in chap. 9, n. 42.

[47] CWRIC, *Personal Justice Denied*, 218. Telephone conversation between Bendetsen and Hall, January 19, 1943. Western Defense Command records, RG 338; National Archives, College Park, Maryland.

[48] Confidential letter from Dillon S. Myer to The Honorable Secretary of War, July 9, 1943. KRB papers, box 312. Emphasis in original.

[49] Telephone conversation between Colonel Bendetsen and Mr. Braun, July 6, 1943. KRB papers, box 312.

[50] "This dossier, found in the files of the Adjutant General, was assembled sometime in 1943, and could have been the basis for an official reprimand—or worse—as it shows General DeWitt in deliberate and insubordinate resistance to War Department policies." At this time Major General J. A. Ulio was adjutant general. Source: Daniels, *American Concentration Camps*, vol. 7. (New York: Garland, 1989).

[51] October 7, 1942, Revision of policy, signed by Major General J. A. Ulio, Adjutant General. Dossier, pp. 2–3.

[52] January 18, 1943, paraphrased on p. 3 of Dossier.

[53] Conversation between Colonel Bendetsen and Captain Hall, January 22, 1943, Dossier, pp. 11–14.

[54] Memorandum from DeWitt to Chief of Staff USA, January 27, 1943. Dossier, pp. 8–9. Emphasis in original.

[55] Conversation between Colonel Bendetsen and Colonel Scobey, February 17, 1943, Dossier, p. 13.

[56] Telephone conversation between DeWitt and Mr. McCloy, April 3, 1943. Dossier, p. 19.

[57] Ibid., pp. 16–21.

[58] Telephone conversation between DeWitt and McNarney, April 3, 1943. Dossier, pp. 21–23.

[59] Memo from DeWitt to Chief of Staff, United States Army, April 4, 1943. Dossier, pp. 24–27.

[60] Telephone conversation between Colonel Bendetsen and Colonel Wilson, April 12, 1943. Dossier, pp. 29–32. Emphases in original.

[61] Transcript of telephone conversation between Colonel Bendetsen and Colonel Barber, April 13, 1943. Dossier, p. 34.

[62] "Off-The-Record Press Meeting Held by General DeWitt," April 14, 1943, Dossier, p. 3.

[63] CWRIC, *Personal Justice Denied*, 222, and transcript of conference between DeWitt and newspapermen, April 14, 1943.

[64] Transcript, DeWitt at Naval Affairs hearing, April 19, 1943. Dossier, p. 38.

[65] Ibid., Dossier, pp. 36–38.

[66] CWRIC, *Personal Justice Denied*, 225.

[67] Telephone conversation between McCloy and Bendetsen, April 19, 1943, 4:45 P.M. KRB papers, box 313.

[68] Ibid.

[69] Telephone conversation between McCloy and Bendetsen, April 19, 1943. KRB papers, box 313.

[70] Ibid.

[71] Ibid.

[72] Ibid.

[73] Irons, *Justice at War*, 209.

[74] Ibid., 209–10, and footnotes.

[75] Ibid.

[76] In all, fifty-five changes and/or deletions were made to the report. DeWitt grudgingly agreed because he did not wish to damage the War Department's position in the court cases. Irons, *Justice Delayed*, 294.

[77] Irons, *Justice Delayed*, 143, and telegram from Colonel Bendetsen to General Barnett, May 9, 1943.

[78] Irons, *Justice at War*, 211. No record of the destruction was found in Bendetsen's personal papers in the KRB papers archive, except for transcripts of the phone conversations.

[79] Irons, *Justice at War*, 388, cites Western Defense Command records, RG 338; National Archives, College Park, Martyland.

[80] The destruction was witnessed by Theodore E. Smith, June 29, 1943. See note in CWRIC, *Personal Justice Denied*, 419. However, one copy was missed, and was found in the National Archive by a researcher for the CWRIC.

[81] Memo from KRB to CG, WDC Notes on Conferences with Assistant Secretary of War John J. McCloy, May 3, 1943. KRB papers, box 314.

[82] KRB commendation report to Commanding General, Ninth Service Command. September 27, 1943. KRB papers, box 315, transfer of loyals file.

[83] Ibid.

[84] Letter to Harry Auer, September 3, 1943. KRB papers, box 349, personal.

[85] Ibid.

[86] Interview with Mollie Ozaki, Chicago, March 12, 1999.

[87] Letter from Morse Saito, September 8, 1997, and his letter to the class of '44 reunion, May 2, 1994.

[88] Interviews with Fumi Saito.

[89] Fumi Saito hearing. Fumi Yabe internment case file.

[90] Ibid.

[91] Possibly it was the NJASRC that was helping her.

[92] Fumiko Yabe internment case file.

[93] Telephone interview with Fumi Saito, February 6, 1997.

[94] General DeWitt had supporters as well as detractors. An article in the *Anchorage Daily Times*, July 30, 1943, criticized "Pro-Japs in High Places" for planning to remove General DeWitt because of the "severity of his measures in evacuating the Japanese on the West Coast," called an "outstanding accomplishment" of DeWitt's administration. The article decried the "powers in high places that would molly-coddle the Japanese and perhaps allow them to return to their homes in the combat zone." KRB papers, box 313.

[95] Memorandum to KRB from Colonel S. F. Clabaugh, October 9, 1943. KRB papers, box 348.

[96] Brief of record, Karl Robin Bendetsen, October 30, 1948. KRB papers, box 363. SHAEF is the Supreme Headquarters of the Allied Expeditionary Forces.

[97] Daniels, "The Forced Migrations of West Coast Japanese Americans, 1942–1946: A Quantitative Note." Daniels, et al., *Japanese Americans from Relocation to Redress*, 72–74.

[98] There were thirty-three thousand soldiers in the unit, and a soldier could receive more than one decoration. The 100th Battalion was incorporated into the 442nd Regimental Combat team in June 1944.

[99] CWRIC, *Personal Justice Denied*, 253–59.

CHAPTER 10: "Sincere Conscientious Objectors to War"

[1] FOR's newsletter, *Fellowship*, July 3, 1995. Letter from Richard Deats, Fellowship of Reconciliation, September 20, 1997.

[2] Gordon Hirabayashi came from this group. Mary Farquharson was a state senator in Washington from 1935 to 1941 and an activist for liberal and Christian causes who encouraged the work of the FOR and the Pacific Coast Committee on American Principles and Fair Play. The professor of engineering at the University of Washington was her husband.

[3] Richard Deats, editor of FOR's newsletter, *Fellowship*, noted this fact in a "for the record" reply to critics, July 3, 1995.

[4] Interview with Rita and Herman Will, December 1, 1997, Des Moines, Washington.

[5] Interestingly, the names of special agents, informants, and interviewees have not been blocked out, which they would be if the files had been obtained from the FBI under the Freedom of Information Act. Fortunately, these files had been included in toto in the PHS internment case file. In 1998, when Perry Saito's FBI file was requested from the Seattle office (the file had been forwarded to them according to the New York paperwork), they replied that the records had been destroyed.

[6] *Binghamton (NY) Press*, December 13, 1943, article quoted on p. 10, FBI file 100–246 VMB, originated at Syracuse, New York, February 22, 1944. PHS internment case file.

[7] Editorial, *Cortland Standard*, December 11, 1943. Quoted on p. 5 of FBI file, PHS internment case file.

[8] This talk was transcribed verbatim by confidential informant T–5, December 9, 1943. FBI file, p. 13. PHS internment case file.

[9] Probably an exaggeration. Most casualties at Salerno were Hawaiian Japanese who would not have had relatives in the camps.

[10] The talk's transcription takes up thirteen single-spaced pages (pp. 12–24). Actually, mosquitoes were most likely a nuisance in the Arkansas camps. FBI file, p. 13. PHS internment case file.

[11] Ibid., 37.

[12] "Says Americans of Jap Descent Should Be Freed," *Niagara Falls Gazette*, March 29, 1944. Ibid., 5–6. (The numbers are puzzling. The mention of women is probably an error.)

[13] Ibid.

[14] One of his exaggerations: LaGuardia was born in New York in 1882; Eisenhower was born in Texas in 1890; Perry Saito's parents arrived in this country in 1918. His assertion about their physical characteristics was also an exaggeration—but it was a wish of many Nisei, apparently; see Houston, *Farewell to Manzanar*. "Says Americans of Jap Descent Should Be Freed," *Niagara Falls Gazette*, March 29, 1944; FBI report, p. 7. PHS internment case file.

[15] FBI report, pp. 9–10. PHS internment case file.

[16] Perry Saito's FBI reports characterized his case as "Security Matter, Sedition, Selective Service." Mrs. Saito's first FBI report initiated in Seattle characterized her case as "Espionage." The label on the reports for the FOR may have been equally free with the characterizing term.

[17] WRA, minutes of hearing, April 12, 1944, PHS internment case file. Six-page transcript of questioning, and a negative recommendation by Joyce.

[18] Perry maintained his membership in the Masons throughout his life and achieved the thirty-third degree.

[19] Question 28: "Will you swear unqualified allegiance to the United States of America and faithfully defend the United States from any or all attack by foreign or domestic forces, and forswear any form of allegiance or obedience to the Japanese emperor, or any other foreign government, power, or organization?"

[20] WRA, minutes of hearing, April 12, 1944, PHS internment case file.

[21] Ibid., 5–6.

[22] Confidential letter from Best to Dillon S. Myer, May 15, 1944. Information in this letter was forwarded to Mr. Joyce by W. W. Lessing, relocation officer, Chicago, May 22, 1944. PHS internment case file.

[23] May 31, 1944. PHS internment case file.

[24] Robert K. Thurber noted, "Many of the factors present in the Hamanaka case are also found here." Memo from Thurber, head of the WRA's leave section, to Philip M. Glick, July 8, 1944, PHS internment case file.

[25] Summary of leave hearing docket, August 19, 1944. Signed by Russell A. Bankson. PHS internment case file.

[26] Natsu Saito internment case file.

[27] Leeds Gulick was the youngest son of Sidney Gulick, a missionary and publi-

cist who championed the cause of Japanese in this country. See Taylor, *Advocate of Understanding: Sidney Gulick and the Search for Peace with Japan.*

[28] ASTP was organized in 1942 in collaboration with civilian educators in order to expand the supply of educated servicemen. The basic phase of the program provided the equivalent of the first one and a half years of a college course. Advanced phases included studies in medical, dental, and veterinary courses; six branches of engineering; marine transportation; personnel psychology; languages; foreign-area study; surveying; internal combustion engines; and numerous other useful curricula. The students in Kanji Kollege were "enlisted men of the Language Company, Det. #3, 3650 SCU–ASTU, University of Chicago."

This program should not be confused with the Civil Affairs Training School (CATS), one of whose sections was also conducted at the University of Chicago. The CATS provided training in Japanese language, social life, and government to mature officers of the army and navy who would then expect to be assigned to the military government in Japan and liberated areas of the Far East. The Japanese language faculty for this program were academic language teachers.

[29] The *Geisha Gazette* was published in mimeograph by students of Japanese at the University of Chicago between 1944 and 1945. University of Chicago archives, Department of Special Collection, Archive Serial, *Geisha Gazette.*

[30] Ibid., July 25, 1945, pp. 1 and 6. According to the *Gazette*, Natsu Saito taught reading for term 6.

[31] Mortimer Shaff, "From Pillar to Postposition," *Geisha Gazette*, June 30, 1945, p. 4.

[32] Interview with Rita and Herman Will, December 1, 1997, Des Moines, Washington.

[33] Interview, Marion Kline, (Garrett classmate of Perry's), Des Moines, Washington, December 1, 1997.

[34] Actually, Perry replaced Farmer and Rustin, but the latter continued to work with FOR on sit-ins.

[35] Sermon by Perry Saito, February 20, 1980, Wauwatosa, Wisconsin. Tape recording obtained from son Lincoln and Perry's widow, Fumi.

[36] Ibid.

[37] Letter from George Houser, November 13, 1997. Houser at that time was interim executive director of FOR in Nyack, New York.

[38] Letter from John M. Swomley, November 24, 1997.

[39] Letter from Marjie Carpenter Swomley, November 24, 1997.

CHAPTER 11: "A Little Hitler"

[1] These and quotes in the next paragraph are from Oral History-KRB, pp. 150 and 156.

[2] Ibid. The result was "triplification."

[3] Letter from KRB in Washington, D.C., to Honorable Harold W. Schweitzer, April 1, 1948. KRB papers, box 350, "Statements before US Senate AFC." This contemporaneous account does not mention working on the budget.

[4] "Who turned out to be Maxine," said Brookes M. Bendetsen in a March 6, 1997, interview.

[5] Gray's tenure as army secretary was from June 20, 1949, until April 13, 1950. Hess, in Oral History-KRB, p. 181.

[6] He said the man was Donald Dawson. Oral History-KRB, p. 182. In a September 19, 2001, telephone interview, Dawson said he has no recollection that politics entered into the decision. Dawson handled the letters of opposition and the FBI investigation. Truman Library, file 1285–B.

[7] The JACL and the *Pacific Citizen* were headquartered in Salt Lake City, Utah. The JACL also had offices in Washington, D.C., Chicago, New York, Denver, San Francisco, and Los Angeles.

[8] Editorial, *Pacific Citizen*, December 31, 1949.

[9] Drew Pearson, nationally syndicated columnist, quoted in *Pacific Citizen*, February 12, 1949, p. 5.

[10] Girdner and Loftis, *The Great Betrayal*, 434.

[11] Letter from Shizu Asahi Proctor, New York City, March 23, 1998.

[12] Letter from Morse Saito, February 25, 2000.

[13] Telephone interview with Julius S. Scott, Jr., October 22, 1997.

[14] Historically a black college, Wiley College is a four-year, fully accredited, liberal arts, Methodist, coeducational institution.

[15] Methodist Church records and brief biographies of Perry H. Saito obtained from Fumi Saito.

[16] Interview with Marion Kline at home of Herman and Rita Will, Des Moines, Washington, December 1, 1997.

[17] *Pacific Citizen*, May 21, 1949, p. 3. McCloy letter, introduced at the congressional hearing on April 19, 1948.

[18] McCloy letter.

[19] *Pacific Citizen*, July 23, 1949, p. 2.

[20] Ibid.

[21] "Nisei USA," *Pacific Citizen*, July 30, 1949, p. 4.

[22] Ibid.

[23] Binkin and Eitelberg, *Blacks and the Military*, 26: "On July 26, 1948, just three months before the presidential election, President Harry S. Truman issued an executive order, which 'declared to be the policy of the President that there shall be equality of treatment and opportunity for all persons in the armed services without regard to race, color, religion, or national origin,' and that promotions were to be based 'solely on merit and fitness.'"

[24] Editorial, *Pacific Citizen*, June 25, 1949, p. 2.

[25] *Pacific Citizen*, August 27, 1949, pp. 1 and 2.

[26] *Pacific Citizen*, September 3, 1949, pp. 1 and 3.

[27] Editorial, *Pacific Citizen*, August 27, 1949, p. 2.

[28] It isn't clear whether Earl Warren, General DeWitt, or Bendetsen said this first. It is clear that they all said it many times.

[29] *Pacific Citizen*, August 27, 1949, pp. 1 and 2.

[30] *Pacific Citizen*, September 17, 1949, p. 2.

[31] Ibid.

[32] "San Francisco," *San Francisco News*, September 12, 1949, p. 11. KRB papers, box 364.

[33] *Pacific Citizen*, September 24, 1949, p. 5. And quoted in Weglyn, *Years of Infamy*, 76–77. This letter was not among those preserved in the file of protest letters to Truman (see note 43).

[34] Ibid.

[35] Ibid.

[36] *Pacific Citizen*, October 15, 1949, p. 3.

[37] "Nisei USA," *Pacific Citizen*, December 10, 1949, p. 4, quoting Arthur Caylor of the *San Francisco News*.

[38] Ibid.

[39] Memorandum from KRB to secretary of the army. September 13, 1949. KRB papers, box 349.

[40] Ibid.

[41] Suzuki, *Ministry in the Assembly and Relocation Centers of World War II*.

[42] Letter to "My dear Gordon" [Gray], January 11, 1950. KRB papers, box 364, personal file.

[43] File 1285–B in Harry S. Truman Library, regarding protest of Bendetsen's nomination, ran to 151 pages; the FBI file cross-reference sheet listed eight items, but the documents are missing; Truman received sixty-two letters or telegrams opposing the nomination, twenty-one of which represented the opinions of groups or organizations. None were form letters. Some letters paraphrased statements in Morton Grodzins's book, which had just come out.

[44] Ibid.

[45] Ibid. Letter dated February 7, 1950.

[46] In the Oral History-KRB, Bendetsen told stories of many conversations with Truman. In particular, he described explaining to him at length how they moved "Japs" by train during the segregation.

[47] Oral History-KRB, p. 184.

[48] Letter resigning from his law firm in San Francisco. KRB to Jesse H. Steinhart, Esquire, San Francisco, February 14, 1950. KRB papers, box 364, personal file.

[49] *Congressional Record*, Senate, January 26 (legislative day of January 4), 1950, p. 956, 81:2 1950–51.

CHAPTER 12: Stories Told in the 1970s

[1] Telephone interview with Lincoln Saito, July 29, 1996.

[2] Polly Hackett, "Behind Barbed Wire: Love Conquered All during War Years," *Wauwatosa News Times*, 1980.

[3] Ibid.

[4] Addendum to the written testimony before the CWRIC by Perry Hitoshi Saito, September 22, 1981. Letter from Morse Saito, March 4, 1999.

[5] Lee C. Moorehead, eulogy for Perry H. Saito, Neenah, Wisconsin, February 10, 1985. From Mary Schroeder, Wisconsin Conference, United Methodist

Church, Sun Prairie, Wisconsin. Until a congregation accepted him or her as a pastor, a minister could not be admitted to a conference; once admitted, one could expect job tenure.

[6] Telephone conversation with Fumi Saito, February 22, 2001. The youth group in Eau Claire, Wisconsin, was led by the son of Melvin Laird, who, as head of the Defense Department, was overseeing the war.

[7] Lee C. Moorehead, eulogy for Perry H. Saito, Neenah, Wisconsin, February 10, 1985. From Mary Schroeder, Wisconsin Conference, United Methodist Church, Sun Prairie, Wisconsin.

[8] Kandace Hawkins, "When the Pastor Is under Pressure," *Milwaukee Journal*, October 15, 1983. From Mary Schroeder, Wisconsin Conference, United Methodist Church, Sun Prairie, Wisconsin.

[9] "Pastor Perry's Personal Paragraphs," *Tower*, publication of the Wauwatosa Avenue United Methodist Church, August 1982.

[10] Rita Wigg, "Churchman Moves On: Compassion and Commitment," *Wauwatosa News Times*, August 16, 1984. Collection of Fumi Saito.

[11] Axford, *Too Long Been Silent*, interview with Perry Saito, 74.

[12] Oral history interview with Frank Pace, Jr., February 25, 1972. Truman Library.

[13] Interview with Karl Bendetsen by Professor Jacobus tenBroek, July 8, 1952. JVAC collection, MSS 67/14c, Bancroft Library, University of California, Berkeley. TenBroek was conducting interviews for the book, *Prejudice, War and the Constitution*, a companion book to two sociological studies of the Japanese in America published as part of the University of California evacuation and resettlement study in 1946 and 1952.

[14] TenBroek, who was blind, dictated a three-page summary of the hour and a half conversation; it contains no quotes. Bendetsen reportedly complained to tenBroek that he had not been given his just credit for having initiated the idea of a Japanese-American combat team. Nothing in his papers at Hoover supports this claim. In the oral history, he claimed that DeWitt gave him command of a regimental combat team for four weeks (p. 82), but then that post was terminated so he could be executive officer for the first Joint Army-Navy Staff College, which lasted for eight weeks (p. 83). These statements are pure fiction—he listed none of these postings in his hand-edited brief of record, which accounts for all of his duties in 1943.

[15] B. Joseph Feigenbaum recounted this story in an oral history interview for the Earl Warren Oral History Project, Bancroft Library, Berkeley. Feigenbaum was a partner of Jesse Steinhart in the San Francisco law firm from which Bendetsen resigned in 1950. Feigenbaum had thought Bendetsen did make general. He began this episode: "Then comes, as it often does in life, kismet, fate."

[16] Champion International annual report, 1971. KRB papers, box 307.

[17] Brewer was from Montesano, Washington, the county seat, ten miles east of Aberdeen. One such quote came from Adam Bordon Polson, a former classmate of Brewer's, July 4, 1996.

[18] Champion International annual report. KRB papers, box 307. Interview with B. F. (Bim) Morrison in Aberdeen, December 6, 1995.

[19] Interview with Brookes M. Bendetsen in San Mateo, California, March 6, 1997.

[20] Interview with Ruth and Joel Wolff in Aberdeen, December 8, 1995.

[21] Beneditkkson's obituary information appeared in the *New York Times*, July 17, 1970; *Time*, July 20, 1970, and *Newsweek*, July 20, 1970.

[22] October 2, 1997, telephone conversation with Mrs. Goodie Fovargue of Aberdeen, who recalled that her sister attended a party with the Bendetsens in Texas at which he said he was Danish. Her sister was surprised.

[23] Recall that Albert M. Bendetson's parents were Samuel A. Bendetson, born in Germany, and Katherine Robbiner Bendetson, born in Germany or Lithuania. (See chap. 3 and, family tree in Appendix C). The only 'Beneditkkson' or similar name in U.S. immigration records are Icelanders, who migrated to French Canada. *National Cyclopedia of American Biography*, vol. L (1972): 481–83, plus full-page photograph.

[24] Charles (Chub) Middleton died in 1956, and his obituary noted that "during World War II [he] held the rank of lieutenant colonel, serving under Colonel Karl Bendetsen, former Aberdeen attorney." *Grays Harbor Post*, July 7, 1956.

[25] KRB was divorced from Maxine on June 10, 1972; he married Gladys on August 1, 1972. Dates obtained from KRB FBI file dated October 14, 1981.

[26] Rubin, *American Empress: The Life and Times of Marjorie Merriweather Post*, 341. Gladys appears in a photograph, and her engagement to Bendetsen is mentioned on p. 375. Gladys also appears on the Washington, D.C., Social Register.

[27] Bendetsen joined two prominent Palm Beach clubs: Everglades, and Bath and Tennis. According to Larissa MacFarquhar (in an article about Lilly Pulitzer), these clubs "began to allow Jews in as guests only a couple of years ago; Jews and blacks are still not admitted as members." *New Yorker*, September 4, 2000, p. 38.

[28] Interview with Brookes M. Bendetsen in San Mateo, California, March 6, 1997.

[29] KRB letter to Mr. Hiroshi Suzuki, who had addressed him as "Mr. Kerdetsen," June 11, 1976. KRB papers, box 324.

[30] Four exceptions: tenBroek in 1952; Truman Oral History, 1972; Memo to Christopher Cook of the BBC, 1978 (KRB papers, box 269); and Kai Bird for McCloy book, 1983.

[31] Oral history was conducted by Jerry N. Hess of the Harry S Truman Library in New York City, October 24, November 9, and November 21, 1972. Truman Library researchers did not challenge or verify any of Bendetsen's stories.

[32] Oral history-KRB, pp. 31–44. He told a version of the Pearl Harbor story in his interview with Kai Bird.

[33] Jack Herzig, who did considerable research during the redress era, tried hard to verify Bendetsen's claim of having gone to the Philippines in December 1941, and was unable to do so. (Personal communications with Jack Herzig, December 7–13, and December 16, 1995.) Bendetsen's archive contains proof that he was in Washington, D.C., in first week of December 1941.

[34] Oral history-KRB, p. 85.

[35] In the *Final Report*, voluntary migration is described on thirteen of the six

hundred pages. (After March 27, very few people were allowed to join family members who had left during the permitted voluntary migration.)

[36] No record of a visit by Bendetson to the Philippines exists in the set of orders or travel itineraries for the fall of 1941 found in his archive; however, since a travel order copy might not have been saved, this absence is inconclusive. Bendetson's personnel record in the army's records archive was apparently destroyed by fire. Mention of being a "spl. rep. sec. of war to Gen. MacArthur, 1941" first appeared in his *Who's Who* entry in the 1950–51 edition.

[37] Statement of military qualifications, March 20, 1943, edited in KRB's handwriting; this statement contains a record of prior qualifications, and makes no mention of being special representative of secretary of war to MacArthur. It mentions only "survey of the security situation along the West Coast." Hoover, boxes 349 and 350. Alumni article dated June 1942, in Hoover box 349.

[38] October 30, 1948, handwritten brief of record. KRB papers, box 350.

[39] Assistant Chief of Staff, Civil Affairs Division, to Assistant Chief of Staff, G–1, August 2, 1943. KRB papers, box 350, personal file. He enclosed orders "dated 21 August 1941 directing temporary duty beyond the continental limits of the United States (to go to Hawaii)."

[40] Interview with Brookes M. Bendetsen, March 6, 1997; Ruth and Joel Wolff encountered KRB and his son in a hotel in Hawaii when the latter were en route to the Philippines on that trip. Interview with Ruth and Joel Wolff, December 8, 1995.

[41] Bird, *The Chairman*. Bird conducted taped interviews with Bendetsen on November 9 and 10, 1983.

[42] Interview with Brookes M. Bendetsen in San Mateo, California, March 6, 1997.

[43] Interview with Professor Natsu Taylor Saito, law faculty, Georgia State University Law School, August 14, 1997 in Salt Lake City.

[44] Schwartz, *Super Chief: Earl Warren and His Supreme Court*, 14.

[45] Ibid., 15.

[46] Letter from Morse Saito, June 13, 2000.

[47] Telephone conversation with Morse Saito, July 9, 1997.

[48] Warren and his wife had six children. Warren, *The Memoirs of Earl Warren*, 147.

[49] Interview with Natsu Taylor Saito, August 14, 1997, in Salt Lake City.

[50] Hirabayashi defied the evacuation order and became the subject of a test case that went to the Supreme Court. In an August 14, 1997, interview, Morse's daughter, Natsu Taylor Saito, gave her sense of how the internment affected her father.

[51] Ibid.

CHAPTER 13: Legacy of History

[1] Maki, et al., *Achieving the Impossible Dream*, 65.

[2] All are Democrats, Inouye and Matsunaga from Hawaii, Mineta and Matsui from California. Mineta became secretary of transportation in the Bush administration in 2001.

[3] KRB letter to J. J. McCloy, August 19, 1981. KRB papers, box 324.

[4] Maki, et al., *Achieving the Impossible Dream*, 122, n. 25: William Hohri,

"Chicago Nisei Critical of Nat'l JACL Redress Drive," *Rafu Shimpo*, May 14, 1979.

[5] Hohri, *Repairing America*, 67.

[6] Ibid.

[7] Telephone conversation with Reverend Lloyd Wake of Glide Memorial Methodist Church, February 22, 2001. Wake recalled the event in detail. He had supported the NCJAR resolution.

[8] Report No. 81, Subject: Persons of Japanese Ancestry, pp. 582 and 862–63, *Journal of the 1980 General Conference*, The United Methodist Church. DePauw University Archives.

[9] Axford, *Too Long Been Silent*, Saito interview, pp. 67–69.

[10] Ibid, 67.

[11] Hohri, *Repairing America*, 69.

[12] United Methodist Web page biography of Marjorie Matthews. Also conversation with Dick Tuttle, August 2, 1996.

[13] KRB letter to McCloy, August 19, 1981. Hoover, box 324.

[14] To the annoyance of Bendetsen and McCloy, Tom Clark apologized when he retired from the Supreme Court:

"I have made a lot of mistakes in my life. . . . One is my part in the evacuation of the Japanese from California in 1942. . . . I don't think that served any purpose at all. . . . We picked them up and put them in concentration camps. That's the truth of the matter. And as I look back on it—although at the time I argued the case—I am amazed that the Supreme Court ever approved it." *San Diego Union*, California, July 10, 1966, reprinted by Weglyn, *Years of Infamy*, 114.

[15] Letter from KRB to Paul T. Bannai, August 5, 1981, and "Written Statement of Karl R. Bendetsen for the Commission on Wartime Relocation and Internment of Civilians. KRB papers, boxes 321 and 324. Statements on pp. 4, 17, and 18.

[16] Letter from KRB to Hon. John J. McCloy, July 22, 1981. KRB papers, box 321.

[17] Baker, *The Concentration Camp Conspiracy: A Second Pearl Harbor.*

[18] Published by Webb Research Group, Medford, Oregon, 1990.

[19] Edward J. Ennis, Calvert Dedrick, Philip Glick, and Laurence I. Hewes.

[20] Handwritten letter from Angus Macbeth to KRB, October 31, 1981. KRB papers, box 321.

[21] Letter from Jack Herzig, December 7–13, 1995.

[22] 1981 testimony, p. 6. KRB papers, box 324.

[23] Ibid.

[24] McCloy letter to KRB, August 11, 1981. KRB papers, box 321.

[25] Letter from Jack Herzig, Dec. 7–13, 1995.

[26] KRB's 1981 testimony from National Archives, College Park, Maryland, p. 92.

[27] Ibid., 95.

[28] Ibid., 97.

[29] Ibid., 99–100.

[30] KRB's version of the 1981 testimony. KRB papers, box 323.

[31] "Aberdeen Native Puzzles Relocation Panel," *Aberdeen Daily World*, November 3, 1981.

[32] William Hohri, *Repairing America*, 157.

[33] After this hearing, Bendetsen was essentially allowed to rewrite it as he thought he had stated it; he did not rewrite the questions from the panel; a copy of the original testimony with his extensive corrections and rewrites is in his archive. Milton Reporting, Inc. sent him a version with his corrections, but this does not appear to be the "official" transcript in the National Archives. KRB papers, box 323. Presumably the National Archives version was created from the taped hearing. I can get no clarification from the National Archives or Milton Reporting about the two versions.

[34] Wenig was a Stanford-educated lawyer, and a reserve officer who reported to the Presidio from the office of California Attorney General Earl Warren. See Irons, *Justice at War*, 121.

[35] Letter from Peter Irons to KRB, January 22, 1982. KRB papers, box 321. There is no reply to Irons's letter in the archive. When the author asked Irons about this letter, he did not recall it; May 2000, Seattle, Washington.

[36] Wes Peyton, *San Jose Mercury News*, October 9, 1983. KRB papers, box 323.

[37] KRB letters to Wes Peyton, October 31, and November 8 and 10, 1983. KRB papers, box 323.

[38] "The Japanese American Cases—a Disaster," by Eugene V. Rostow, *Yale Law Journal* 54, no. 3 (1945): 489–533.

[39] Eugene V. Rostow, "Shame on the Home Front," *Washington Post Book World*, October 23, 1983. KRB papers, box 322. Rostow declared the book flawed and skewed because Irons was himself involved in the legal defense research and was not objective about the "most spectacular conclusions of the book." (Irons, in *Justice at War*, presents a thorough account of events leading to the decision to promulgate Executive Order 9066, and of the alteration of the *Final Report* by Bendetsen and Colonel John Hall.)

[40] Letter to KRB from Rostow, February 20, 1984. KRB papers, box 322. Eugene V. Rostow, Yale University Law School.

[41] Letter from Morse Saito, October 2000.

[42] Axford, *Too Long Been Silent*, Saito interview, January 1985, pp. 74–75.

[43] Perry Saito sermon, May 13, 1984. Fumi Saito tape recording. "I have knelt in the silent forest, in the shade of ancient trees, but the dearest of all my altars was raised by my mother's knees."

[44] Resume and other information obtained from Mary Schroeder, Wisconsin Conference, UMC, Sun Prairie, Wisconsin.

[45] Lee. C. Moorehead, "The Celebration of the Grace of God in Perry Saito," February 1985. Obtained from Mary Schroeder, Wisconsin Conference UMC archive, May 2000.

[46] The name MAGIC attached to the translated cables because they were translated by cryptographers, with what seemed like magic. The cables discussed here were from diplomatic traffic. Translation of intercepts of military communications contributed substantially to America's defeat of the Japanese fleet at Midway in June 1942.

[47] Personal correspondence from Jack Herzig, December 7–13, 1995.

[48] KRB response to question by Mr. MacBeth, p. 42 of testimony in 1981.

[49] Tape 2, interview of KRB by Kai Bird, November 9 and 10, 1983.

[50] Ibid.

[51] Ibid. His father was a haberdasher in Aberdeen until he retired. His grandfather Samuel was a dry goods merchant. See family tree, Appendix C.

[52] Letter from McCloy to KRB, May 2, 1982. Hoover, box 321.

[53] The "MAGIC" Background of Pearl Harbor, Washington, D.C.: US Government Printing Office, 1977.

[54] Quoted by Peter Irons in *Illusion and Reality: The "MAGIC" cables and the Wartime Internment of Japanese Americans*, p. 924, Hearings before the Subcommittee on Administrative Law and Governmental Relations, Serial No. 90, June 20, 21, and 27, and September 12, 1984, pp. 430–41. (Hereafter, 1984 Hearings.)

[55] McCloy's statement, p. 130, 1984 Hearings. 98th Congress, Serial No. 90.

[56] CWRIC, *Personal Justice Denied*, 18.

[57] 1984 Hearings. Serial No. 90. Sept. 12, 1986, PAGE 802.

[58] Ibid., 670.

[59] Ibid., Ennis, 671.

[60] Ibid., 681.

[61] Ibid., 683.

[62] Ibid., 685.

[63] Ibid., 937.

[64] Ibid., 911–14.

[65] "Final Report to the President by the High Frontier Panel," January 8, 1982. KRB papers, box 353. The report recommended that the president issue an executive order to establish a council on assured survival.

[66] Interview with Brookes M. Bendetsen, March 6, 1997.

[67] Memorandum, Ennis to Solicitor General, April 30, 1943. Irons, *Justice Delayed*, 150–51.

[68] For a complete exposition of the *coram nobis* effort see Irons's book *Justice Delayed*.

[69] Peter Irons, "What did the Internment of Japanese Americans Mean?" ed. Murray, 67.

[70] Irons, *Justice Denied*, 225. Judge Marilyn Hall Patel, U.S. District Court for the Northern District of California, opinion on the Korematsu *coram nobis* petition. April 1984.

[71] Opinion of the US District Court Judge Patel, in Irons, *Justice Denied*, 243.

[72] Bendetsen is technically correct, the *coram nobis* does not overturn the Supreme Court's decision, but it weakens the value of the case as precedent. Irons, *Justice Delayed*, 243. Testimony, 1986 Hearings. 99th Congress, part I, serial no. 69, pp. 698–719.

[73] Ibid., April 28, 1986.

[74] The Bohemian Club of San Francisco has an annual summer encampment in rustic cabins near Monte Rio on the Russian River.

[75] Interview with Brookes Bendetsen, March 6, 1997.

[76] Letter from Geraldine Pugh, Bendetsen's secretary, to Mrs. Charlotte Elam, April 4, 1988.

[77] Arlington National Cemetery Web site, posted August 23, 2000.

[78] Introduction to Maki, et al., *Achieving the Impossible Dream*, xi.

[79] After giving each child $3,000, she used the rest to buy a Honda Civic, and regrets ever giving up that car. Conversations with Fumi Saito, February 6 and May 7, 1997.

[80] *Aberdeen Daily World*, week of November 21, 1989.

[81] Irons, *Justice Delayed*, 305. The post-hearing brief on behalf of Hirabayashi, 268–305 contains a point-by-point refutation of many of the assertions in the *Final Report*.

[82] Irons, *Justice Delayed*, 46.

[83] Axford, *Too Long Been Silent*, Saito interview, 76.

[84] Judge Donald S. Voorhees Memorandum Opinion of the U.S. District Court, *Hirabayashi v. United States*, April 28, 1986, taken from Irons, *Justice Delayed*, 377–85.

Epilogue

[1] The old "Post Office Building" was badly damaged by the earthquake of 2000; it has been condemned and fenced off.

[2] Kessler, *Stubborn Twig*, chap. 7.

[3] During incarceration he served as a staff member of the Japanese American Evacuation and Resettlement Study, and co-wrote *The Spoilage*, one of three official publications by that study. Some of Nishimoto's other writings are published in *Inside an American Concentration Camp*.

[4] Mentioned in chap. 13, Kai Bird interview.

[5] Among these are TV screenwriters Bob and Howard Bendetson (*Home Improvement*).

SELECTED BIBLIOGRAPHY

Manuscripts

Randich, Joe, and Dorothea Parker. *Polson Museum Chehalis County Nationality Survey, 1848–1915*. Polson Museum, Hoquiam, Wash. 1984.

Lamb, Frank. *Fifty Years in Hoquiam: Memoirs of Frank H. Lamb, 1948*. Hoquiam Public Library, Hoquiam, Wash.

Watanabe Clipping File. Collected by Yoriko Watanabe Sasaki during evacuation, 1942. Wing Luke Museum, Seattle, Wash.

National Archives, Washington, D.C.

National Archives at College Park, Maryland

Bancroft Library, University of California at Berkeley

FBI, Washington, D.C., and Seattle, Washington

Hoover Institution Archives, Stanford University

LDS Family History Library, Salt Lake City

Special Collections, Marriott Library, University of Utah, Salt Lake City

Truman Library Archive, The Harry S Truman Library, Independence, Missouri

Books

Anschel, Eugene. *Homer Lea, Sun Yat-sen, and the Chinese Revolution*. New York: Praeger, 1984.

Axford, Roger. *Too Long Been Silent: Japanese Americans Speak Out*. Lincoln: Media Publishing and Marketing, 1986.

Baker, Lillian. *The Concentration Camp Conspiracy: A Second Pearl Harbor*. Glendale: H & M Graphic Services, 1981.

Biddle, Francis. *In Brief Authority*. New York: Doubleday, 1962.

Binkin, Martin, and Mark J. Eitelberg, *Blacks and the Military*. Washington, D.C.: Brookings Institution, 1982.

Bird, Kai. *The Chairman: John J. McCloy: The Making of the American Establishment*. New York: Simon and Schuster, 1992.

Black, Allida M. *Casting Her Own Shadow: Eleanor Roosevelt and the Shaping of Postwar Liberalism*. New York: Columbia University Press, 1996.

Bosworth, Allan R. *America's Concentration Camps*. New York: W.W. Norton, 1967.

Cantwell, Robert. *The Land of Plenty*. c. 1934. Reprint, Carbondale: Southern Illinois University Press, 1971.

Chang, Gordon. *Morning Glory, Evening Shadow: Yamato Ichihashi and His Internment Writings, 1942–1945.* Stanford, Calif.: Stanford University Press, 1997.

The Columbia Encyclopedia. 3rd ed. New York: Columbia University Press, 1963.

Conn, Stetson. "Japanese Evacuation from the West Coast." In *The United States Army in World War II: The Western Hemisphere: Guarding the United States and Its Outposts,* Stetson Conn, Rose C. Engleman, and Byron Fairchild. Washington: Government Printing Office: 1964; reprinted 1990.

Corbett, P. Scott. *Quiet Passages: The Exchange of Civilians between the United States and Japan during the Second World War.* Kent and London: Kent State University Press, 1987.

Daniels, Roger. Albert Johnson biographical entry. In *American National Biography.* Vol. 12. New York: Oxford University Press, 1999.

———. *Asian America: Chinese and Japanese in the United States since 1850.* Seattle: University of Washington Press, 1988.

———. *Concentration Camps: North America; Japanese in the United States and Canada During World War II.* Malabar, Fla.: Krieger, 1981.

———. *The Decision to Relocate the Japanese Americans.* Philadelphia: J. B. Lippincott, 1975.

———. *Politics of Prejudice.* Berkeley and Los Angeles: University of California Press, 1962.

———. *Prisoners without Trial: Japanese Americans in World War II.* New York: Hill and Wang, 1993.

Daniels, Roger, ed. *American Concentration Camps,* 9 vols. New York: Garland, 1989.

———, Sandra Taylor, and Harry Kitano, eds. *Japanese Americans, from Relocation to Redress.* Salt Lake City: University of Utah Press, 1986.

Dinnerstein, Leonard. *Antisemitism in America.* New York: Oxford University Press, 1994.

Drinnon, Richard. *Keeper of Concentration Camps: Dillon S. Myer and American Racism.* Berkeley and Los Angeles: University of California Press, 1987.

Eisenhower, Milton. *The President Is Calling.* Garden City, N.Y.: Doubleday, 1974.

Final Report: Japanese Evacuation from the West Coast, 1942. Washington: United States Government Printing Office, 1943.

Fiset, Louis. *Imprisoned Apart: The World War II Correspondence of an Issei Couple.* Seattle: University of Washington Press, 1997.

FitzGerald, Frances. *Way Out There in the Blue: Reagan, Star Wars, and the End of the Cold War.* New York: Simon and Schuster, 2000.

Fugita, Stephen S., and David J. O'Brien. *Japanese American Ethnicity: The Persistence of Community.* Seattle: University of Washington Press, 1991.

Girdner, Audrie, and Anne Loftis. *The Great Betrayal: The Evacuation of the Japanese-Americans during World War II.* Toronto: MacMillan, 1969.

Goldberg, Robert A. *Enemies within: The Culture of Conspiracy in Modern America.* New Haven: Yale University Press, 2001.

Goodwin, Doris Kearns. *No Ordinary Time: Franklin and Eleanor Roosevelt: The Home Front in World War II.* New York: Simon and Schuster, 1994.

Grodzins, Morton. *Americans Betrayed: Politics and the Japanese Experience.* Chicago: University of Chicago Press, 1949.

Guterson, David. *Snow Falling on Cedars.* San Diego: Harcourt Brace, 1994.

Hodgson, Godfrey. *The Colonel: The Life and Wars of Henry Stimson, 1867–1950.* New York: Knopf, 1990.

Hohri, William Minoru. *Repairing America: An Account of the Movement for Japanese-American Redress.* Pullman: Washington State University Press, 1988.

Houston, Jeanne Wakatsuki. *Farewell to Manzanar; A True Story of Japanese American Experience during and after the World War II Internment.* 1974. Reprint, New York: Bantam, 1995.

Hughes, John. C., and Ryan Teague Beckwith. *On the Harbor: From Black Friday to Nirvana.* Aberdeen, Wash.: *The Daily World*, 2001.

Hewes, Lawrence. *Boxcar in the Sand.* New York: Knopf, 1957.

Ichihashi,Yamato. *Japanese in the United States.* c. 1932. Reprint, New York: Arno, 1969.

Ichioka,Yuji. *The Issei: the World of the First Generation of Japanese Immigrants, 1885–1924.* New York: The Free Press, Macmillan; 1988.

Inada, Lawson Fusao, ed. *Only What We Could Carry: The Japanese American Internment Experience.* Berkeley: Heyday, 2000.

Irons, Peter. *Justice at War.* New York: Oxford University Press, 1983.

———. *Justice Delayed: The Record of the Japanese American Internment Cases.* Middleton, Conn.: Wesleyan University Press, 1989.

Ito, Kazuo. *Issei: A History of Japanese Immigrants in North America.* Translated by Shinichiro Nakamura and Jean S. Gerard. Seattle: Japanese Community Service, 1973.

Jacoby, Harold Stanley. *Tule Lake: From Relocation to Segregation.* Grass Valley, Calif.: Comstock Bonanza, 1996.

Kessler, Lynn. *Stubborn Twig: Three Generations in the Life of a Japanese American Family.* New York: Plume, The Penguin Group; 1993.

Kitagawa, Daisuke. *Issei and Nisei: The Internment Years.* New York: Seabury, 1967.

Lea, Homer. *The Valor of Ignorance.* 1909. Reprint, New York: Harper and Brothers, 1942.

Lee, Josephine, Imogen I. Lim, and Yuko Matsukawa, eds. *Re/collecting Early Asian America: Essays in Cultural History.* Philadelphia: Temple University Press, 2002.

Maki, Mitchell T., Harry H. L. Kitano, and S. Megan Berthold. *Achieving the Impossible Dream: How Japanese Americans Obtained Redress.* Chicago: University of Illinois Press, 1999.

McWilliams, Carey. *A Mask for Privilege: Anti-Semitism in America.* New Brunswick: Transaction, 1948.

Minear, Richard H. *Dr. Seuss Goes to War: The World War II Editorial Cartoons of Theodor Seuss Geisel.* New York: The New Press, 1999.

Miyakawa, Edward. *Tule Lake, A Novel.* Waldport, Ore.: House by the Sea, 1979.

Morgan, Murray. *The Viewless Winds.* New York: Dutton, 1949. Reprint, Corvallis: Oregon State University Press, 1990.

Mori, Toshio. *Yokohama, California.* 1949. Reprint, Seattle: University of Washington Press, 1997.

Muller, Eric L. *Free to Die for Their Country: The Story of the Japanese American Draft Resisters in World War II.* Chicago: University of Chicago Press, 2001.

Murray, Alice Yang. *What Did the Internment of Japanese Americans Mean?* Boston: Bedford/St. Martin's, 2000.

Nakano, Jiro, and Kay Yokoyama, eds. *Poets behind Barbed Wire.* Honolulu: Bamboo Ridge, 1983.

National Cyclopedia of American Biography. Vol. L. Clifton, N.J.: James T. White, 1972.

Niiya, Brian, ed. *Japanese American History: An A-to-Z Reference from 1868 to the Present.* New York: Facts on File, 1993.

Nishimoto, Richard S. *Inside an American Concentration Camp: Japanese American Resistance at Poston, Arizona.* Tucson: University of Arizona Press, 1995.

O'Brien, Robert W. *The College Nisei.* Palo Alto, Calif.: Pacific, 1949.

Okada, John. *No-No Boy: A Novel.* Seattle: University of Washington Press, 1976.

Okihiro, Gary. *Cane Fires: The Anti-Japanese Movement in Hawaii, 1865–1945.* Philadelphia: Temple University Press, 1991.

———. *Storied Lives: Japanese American Students and World War II.* Seattle: University of Washington Press, 1999.

Pogue, Forrest. C. *George C. Marshall: Ordeal and Hope, 1939–1942.* New York: Viking, 1965.

Robinson, Greg. *By Order of the President: FDR and the Internment of Japanese Americans.* Cambridge: Harvard University Press, 2001.

Rubin, Nancy. *American Empress: The Life and Times of Marjorie Merriweather Post.* New York: Villard, 1995.

Schwartz, Bernard. *Super Chief: Earl Warren and His Supreme Court—A Judicial Biography.* New York: New York University Press, 1983.

Schoenburg, Nancy, and Stuart Schoenburg. *Lithuanian Jewish Communities.* New York: Garland, 1991.

Sone, Monica. *Nisei Daughter.* Reprint, Seattle: University of Washington Press, 1979.

Spicer, Edward H., et al. *Impounded People: Japanese-Americans in the Relocation Centers.* 1946. Reprint, Tucson: University of Arizona Press, 1969.

Spickard, Paul R. *Japanese Americans: The Formation and Transformations of an Ethnic Group.* New York: Twayne, 1996.

Steel, Ronald. *Walter Lippmann and the American Century.* Boston: Little, Brown, 1980.

Steinbeck, John. *The Grapes of Wrath.* New York: The Viking Press, 1939.

Suzuki, Lester E. *Ministry in the Assembly and Relocation Centers of World War II.* Berkeley, Calif.: Yardbird, 1979.

Takezawa, Yasuko I. *Breaking the Silence: Redress and Japanese American Ethnicity.* Ithaca: Cornell University Press, 1995.

Tamura, Linda. *The Hood River Issei: Oral History of Japanese Settlers in Oregon's Hood River Valley*. Chicago: University of Illinois Press, 1993.

Terkel, Studs. *"The Good War": An Oral History of World War Two*. New York: Pantheon, 1984.

Tateishi, John. *And Justice For All: An Oral History of the Japanese American Detention Camps*. New York: Random House, 1984.

Taylor, Sandra C. *Advocate of Understanding: Sidney Gulick and the Search for Peace with Japan*. Kent, Ohio: Kent State University Press, 1984.

———. *Jewel of the Desert: Japanese American Internment at Topaz*. Berkeley and Los Angeles: University of California Press, 1993.

tenBroek, Jacobus, Edward N. Barnhart, and Floyd W. Matson. *Prejudice, War and the Constitution*. Berkeley and Los Angeles: University of California Press, 1968.

Thomas, Dorothy S., and Richard Nishimoto. *The Spoilage: Japanese-American Evacuation and the Resettlement During World War II*. Berkeley and Los Angeles: University of California Press, 1946.

Thomas, Dorothy S. *The Salvage*. Berkeley and Los Angeles: University of California Press, 1952.

Uchida, Yoshiko. *Desert Exile: The Uprooting of a Japanese-American Family*. Seattle: University of Washington Press, 1995.

United States. Commission on Wartime Relocation and Internment of Civilians, *Personal Justice Denied: Report of the Commission on Wartime Relocation and Internment*. 1982 and 1983. Reprint, Seattle: University of Washington Press, 1997.

Van Syckle, Edwin. *The River Pioneers: Early Days on Grays Harbor*. Seattle: Pacific Search, 1982.

———. *They Tried to Cut It All: Grays Harbor—Turbulent Years of Greed and Greatness*. Seattle: Friends of the Aberdeen Public Library, Craftsman Press, 1980.

Warren, Earl. *The Memoirs of Earl Warren*. Garden City, N.Y.: Doubleday, 1977.

Weglyn, Michi. *Years of Infamy: The Untold Story of America's Concentration Camps*. New York: William Morrow, 1976.

Who's Who in America. Vols. 22–45. Chicago: Marquis, 1944–1988.

Articles

Daniels, Roger. "The Bureau of the Census and the Relocation of the Japanese Americans: A Note and a Document." *Amerasia Journal* (Spring 1982).

Seltzer, William, and Margo Anderson. "After Pearl Harbor: The Proper Role of Population Data Systems in Time of War." Paper presented at Population Association of America, March 2000, Los Angeles, Calif.

Linda Tamura, "High Hopes, Subtle Realities: The Issei Experience in Oregon." *Oregon Heritage*, Vol 1. No.1. (Spring 1994), pp. 10-17. Published by Southern Oregon Historical Society.

Taylor, Sandra C. "The Federal Reserve Bank and the Relocation of the Japanese in 1942." *The Public Historian* 5, No. 1 (Winter 1983).

INDEX

Klancy Clark de Nevers is a retired software engineer who lives in Salt Lake City, Utah. Born and raised in Aberdeen, Washington, she developed an abiding interest in World War II as her parents anxiously looked west and followed the progress of the war on a huge map. Four of her uncles served in that war, and two did not return. With Lucy Hart of Seattle, she edited *Cohassett Beach Chronicles: World War II in the Pacific Northwest* by Kathy Hogan, a book of Hogan's columns from the wartime pages of the *Grays Harbor Post,* a weekly published by de Nevers's family.